STEALING
JESUS

Also by Bruce Bawer

A Place at the Table: The Gay Individual in American Society
House and Home (with Steve Gunderson and Rob Morris)
Beyond Queer (editor)
Prophets and Professors: Essays on the Lives and Works of Modern Poets
The Aspect of Eternity
Coast to Coast
The Screenplay's the Thing: Movie Criticism, 1986–1990
Diminishing Fictions: Essays on the Modern American Novel and Its Critics
The Contemporary Stylist
The Middle Generation

STEALING JESUS

HOW
FUNDAMENTALISM
BETRAYS
CHRISTIANITY

BRUCE BAWER

CROWN PUBLISHERS, INC. • NEW YORK

Published by Crown Publishers, Inc., 201 East 50th Street,
New York, New York 10022.
Member of the Crown Publishing Group.

Random House, Inc. New York, Toronto, London, Sydney, Auckland

http://www.randomhouse.com/

CROWN and colophon are trademarks of Crown Publishers, Inc.

Printed in the United States of America

Design by Cynthia Dunne

LIBRARY OF CONGRESS CATALOGING-IN-PUBLICATION DATA

Bawer, Bruce, 1956–
Stealing Jesus : how fundamentalism betrays Christianity / Bruce Bawer. — 1st ed.
1. Fundamentalism—United States—Controversial literature.   2. Christianity—
Essence, genius, nature.   3. United States—Church history.   I. Title.
BT82.2.B39   1997
277.3'0829—dc21   97-20111   CIP

ISBN 0-517-70682-2

10   9   8   7   6   5   4   3   2

For Chris

Love never ends.

CONTENTS

Acknowledgments ix

1. "Are You a Christian?". 1

2. "Who Is My Neighbor?". 29

3. Love and Law 53

4. Darby's Kingdom 77

5. Rauschenbusch's Kingdom 91

6. "Shall the Fundamentalists Win?". 109

7. The Legalistic Boom 131

8. Takeover 155

9. God's Generalissimo 167

10. The Choirboy 187

11. "No More Gray". 201

12. "A Lie Straight from the Devil". 221

13. The Doctor and the Coach 247

14. "These Secular Times". 267

15. Did Lucy Convert? 285

16. Abiding Messages, Transient Settings 303

Bibliography 329

Index 334

ACKNOWLEDGMENTS

I must begin by thanking the Rev. Canon John Andrew, former rector of Saint Thomas Church in New York, whose sermons taught me how to think about Christianity.

For their formidable gifts, unwavering integrity, and loyal friendship, I thank my agent, Eric Simonoff, and my editors, Elaine Pfefferblit and Ann Patty, who are, respectively, the mother and stepmother of both this book and its predecessor, *A Place at the Table*. I am thankful as well to these people at Crown: Patrick Sheehan, Tina Constable, Amy Zevlin, David Tran, Cynthia Dunne, Robin Foster, John Sharp, and Jim Walsh. I give thanks also to Dr. James Dunn, the Rev. Charles Hefling, and the Rev. L. William Countryman for their meticulous reading and invaluable comments; to the *Beyond Queer* confraternity and my colleagues on the Sexuality Committee of the Diocese of New York for the stimulation of their ideas; to the officers of national Integrity (especially Kim Byham and Louie Crew) for affording me the opportunity to give a talk at their 1996 national convention in which I explored some of the questions dealt with in these pages; and to the Rev. Dan Ade of the Church of Saint Luke's in the Fields and everybody at Integrity/New York (especially Nick Dowen and Sandra Collins) for inviting me to deliver sermons which also anticipated parts of this book. I also thank my dear friends Frederick Morgan and Paula Deitz, editors of the *Hudson Review,* for encouraging my work in this direction. And I thank the editors of Trinity Church Wall Street's *Trinity News* for asking me to write an article for them about religion and film; its importance to this book will be readily apparent to them.

I am deeply grateful to my rector, the Rev. Herbert G. Draesel, and my fellow parishioners at the Church of the Holy Trinity for their fellowship; to my friend the Rev. Barbara Cawthorne Crafton for her inspiring writing and preaching; and to Barbara's flock at St. Clement's Church for welcoming me so warmly into their circle of communion on many Sunday mornings while I was writing this book.

For their moral support, I thank my parents and my friends Brendan McEntee, Chip Teply, Michael Joseph Gross, Kirk Read, Paul Jeromack, Stephanie Cowell and Russell Clay, Sally and Mel Whitehead and the whole McGaughey-Whitehead-Kettles clan, David Attoe, Tom DePietro, Judy White, the Rev. Richard T. Nolan, Randall Curb, Michael Smith and David Millspaugh, Michael Lind, Norah Vincent, Joanne Zyontz, Joshua Sherman and Jorge Martin, Terry and Liz Teachout, Robert E. Wright, Harriet Zinnes, Paul Lucre, Leo Carroll, and Rob Morris and Steve Gunderson. I also wish to thank Alex Wiscovitch for being there and for saying to me, at my lowest point, the most important words any human being can say to another: *"Dios te ama, y yo también."* Alongside those words, the next several hundred pages are mere commentary.

Finally, I wish to mention my grandfather Harry Everett Thomas, Sr., whom I never knew but whose presence I felt strongly while writing this book.

1

"ARE YOU
A CHRISTIAN?"

SPRING 1996, NEW YORK CITY. I'm standing on a moder-
ately crowded subway car reading a paperback when I look
up to see a man about my age—thirty-nine—who is standing a few feet away and staring at me with disconcerting
intensity. For an instant we gaze speechlessly into each
other's eyes. I expect him to say (as sometimes happens) that
he's read one of my books and recognizes me from my dust-
jacket photo. Instead he asks me a question.

"Are you a Christian?"

The question takes me aback, though I know why he has
asked it. I am reading *Rescuing the Bible from Fundamentalism,* whose author, the Episcopal bishop John Shelby
Spong, is notorious for his denial of many orthodox Christian doctrines and for his work on behalf of an inclusive

church. It occurs to me that my interlocutor, whose question marks him as a born-again Christian, has probably noticed the word *Bible,* which is in large type, and cannot make out the rest of the title.

"Yes," I reply.

"Are you born again?" His eyes meet mine in an unsettlingly intimate gaze.

I pause for a moment. We have entered difficult territory. Am I born again? Eight years ago, after a decade of feeling that one couldn't be both homosexual and Christian, and after a year or so of listening to sermons that had, for the first time, explained Christianity in a way that made sense to me, I was baptized at Saint Thomas Episcopal Church in New York.

Am I born again? I look into the man's eyes. "*I* think so."

"Do you accept Jesus Christ as your personal savior?"

Another pause. "Yes . . ."

"Then you're born again!" he declares conclusively. "Next time someone asks, answer with confidence that you are!"

"Well," I reply, falling into a tone that sounds to me rather stiff and academic in comparison with his unrestrained ardor, "if I sounded hesitant, it's because I consider myself 'born again,' but by some people's definition I'm not."

I don't explain that part of the problem for many people, himself probably included, would be that I'm gay. In the kinds of churches whose members are in the habit of describing themselves as born again, being gay is considered utterly incompatible with being Christian. Another part of the problem is that I'm an Episcopalian, a member of a church that fundamentalists and many conservative evangelicals don't consider a legitimate church at all because of what they see as its theological leniency. Nor do I add that the book I'm reading was written by someone who has helped to change the Episcopal Church in ways that would doubtless horrify my interlocutor.

"How long have you been a Christian?" the man asks, his eyes fixed on mine.

"Eight years," I tell him.

He seems delighted by my answer. Why? Because I've been a Christian that long? Or because I became one as an adult, which presumably suggests that, like him, I'm a "born-again Christian" who went through a "conversion experience," and am thus more serious and committed than many nominal Christians? Or because I remember how many years it's been—which suggests that my conversion continues to be an important event for me?

"I've been a Christian for nine years," he says. "I was going to commit suicide and then Jesus Christ saved me. I was filled with the power of the Holy Ghost."

I'm at a loss for words. What can I say in response to this testimony? After all, I'm an Episcopalian. Most of us don't talk that way, especially not to total strangers. "Good for you," I finally say.

When the man gets off the train a few moments later, we exchange a friendly good-bye. The doors close, and the train moves on. Yet the brief conversation haunts me for hours. I'm at once perturbed and impressed by the man's zealotry. Evangelical Christians, fundamentalist and otherwise, can walk up to strangers on the subway, tell them they're Christians, and testify about how they found Jesus. There's something wonderful about that. Mainline Protestants—members of such long-established, moderate-to-liberal denominations as the American Baptist Church, the Disciples of Christ, the Episcopal Church, the Evangelical Lutheran Church in America, the Presbyterian Church, the United Church of Christ, the United Methodist Church, and the Reformed Church of America—don't usually do that sort of thing. And we Episcopalians are probably the worst of all: Some of us are self-conscious about discussing God even in church. A century ago sex was seen as a private matter that simply shouldn't be discussed in public; today our secular society teaches us to view religion in the same way, and most of us unquestioningly oblige.

"Are you a Christian?" It's not as easy a question as it may sound. What *is* a Christian? How to decide who is or isn't one—and who does the deciding?

I probably wasn't more than seven or eight when I first noticed that the word could mean very different things, depending on who was using it. Many of my Protestant relatives in South Carolina routinely distinguished between "Christians"—meaning themselves—and "Catholics." In the middle-class neighborhood where I grew up in

Queens, New York, many of my Catholic neighbors made it clear that they regarded themselves and their coreligionists as the only true Christians, and that in their minds everyone else—Protestants, Jews, whatever—blended into a non-Catholic, non-Christian sameness. Among fundamentalist (and many evangelical) Protestants today, such an exclusionary posture toward outsiders is not only alive and well but is a matter of essential doctrine. Fundamentalists, by definition, view only themselves and other fundamentalists as true Christians; conservative evangelicals generally view only themselves, other conservative evangelicals, and fundamentalists as true Christians.

When we speak of American Christians, of course, we may divide them into Protestants and Catholics. (Eastern Orthodox Christians account for only 1 percent or so of the total.) But today there is a more meaningful way of dividing American Christians into two categories. The mainstream media often refer to one of these categories as the Religious Right or the Christian Right and call people in this category conservative Christians; people who fall into the other category are frequently dubbed liberal Christians. The terms *conservative Christian* and *liberal Christian* can be useful, but I will try to avoid using them here because they suggest political rather than theological orientation. Generally speaking, to be sure, the political implications are accurate: Conservative Christians tend to be politically conservative, and liberal Christians tend to be politically liberal. But there are exceptions; and, in any event, it needs to be underscored that what distinguishes the members of these two groups of Christians is not politics but their essential understanding of the nature of God, the role of the church, and the meaning of human life. It is not an overstatement, indeed, to say that these two groups, despite the fact that they both claim the name of Christianity, have fundamentally divergent conceptions of the universe.

What, then, to call these two categories? Most Americans employ *fundamentalist* as a general label for conservative Christians—which is why I've used *fundamentalism* in this book's subtitle—but in its strict sense the term is too narrow for my purposes. Phrases like *traditional Christian* and *modern Christian* are, to an extent, legitimate, for conservative Christians tend to champion tradition and to reject much of the modern science and biblical scholarship that liberal Christians embrace; yet, as shall become clear, it is extremely misleading to suggest that the kind of theology to which conservative Christians subscribe is truly more traditional, in the deepest sense, than that of liberal Christians. Likewise, labels like *biblical Christian* and *Bible-believing Christian,* which many conservative Christians attach to themselves, wrongly suggest that there is something unbiblical about the faith of liberal Christians. We might speak of "exclusionists" and "inclusionists," because conservative Christians, unlike liberal Christians, tend to define the word *Christian* in such a way as to exclude others—including, in most cases, a large number of their fellow conservative Christians.

But it seems to me that the difference between conservative and liberal Christianity may be most succinctly summed up by the difference between two key scriptural concepts: law and love. Simply stated, conservative Christianity focuses primarily on law, doctrine, and authority; liberal Christianity focuses on love, spiritual experience, and what Baptists call the priesthood of the believer. If conservative Christians emphasize the Great Commission—the resurrected Christ's injunction, at the end of the Gospel according to Matthew, to "go to all nations and make them my disciples"—liberal Christians place more emphasis on the Great Commandment, which in Luke's Gospel reads as follows: "Love the Lord your God with all your heart, and with all your soul, with all your strength, and with all your mind; and your neighbor as yourself."

Am I suggesting that conservative Christians are without love or that liberal Christians are lawless? No. I merely make this distinction: Conservative Christianity understands a Christian to be someone who subscribes to a specific set of theological propositions about God and the afterlife, and who professes to believe that by subscribing to those propositions, accepting Jesus Christ as savior, and (except in the case of the most extreme separatist fundamentalists) evangelizing, he or she evades God's wrath and wins salvation (for Roman Catholics, good works also count); liberal Christianity, meanwhile, tends to identify Christianity with the experience of God's abundant love and with the commandment to love God and one's neighbor. If, for conservative Christians, outreach generally means zealous proselytizing of the "unsaved," for liberal Christians it tends to mean social programs directed at those in need.

In these pages, accordingly, I'll refer to these two broad categories of Christianity as legalistic and nonlegalistic. Further, I'll use the terms *Church of Law* and *Church of Love* to describe the two different ecclesial ideals toward which the Christians in these respective categories strive—remembering always, of course, that every church and every human soul has within it a degree of legalism and a capacity for love.

This book will focus primarily on Protestant legalism and nonlegalism; some of the things I say will apply as well to the parallel split within Catholicism, while others do not. Though there are broad sympathies between legalistic Protestants and Catholics, and between nonlegalistic Protestants and Catholics, the strongly divergent doctrinal emphases of Protestantism and Catholicism make it difficult to generalize about "legalistic Christianity," say, as opposed to legalistic Protestantism or Catholicism.

Among the differences between legalistic and nonlegalistic Protestants are these:

- Legalistic Protestantism sees Jesus' death on the cross as a transaction by means of which Jesus paid for the sins of believers and won them eternal life; nonlegalistic Protestantism sees it as a powerful and mysterious symbol of God's infinite love for suffering mankind, and as the natural culmination of Jesus' ministry of love and selflessness.

- Legalistic Protestantism believes that Jesus' chief purpose was to carry out that act of atonement; nonlegalistic Protestantism believes Jesus' chief purpose was to teach that God loves all people as parents love their children and that all humankind is one.

- Legalistic Protestantism understands eternal life to mean a heavenly reward after death for the "true Christians"—the "Elect," the "saved"—who accept Jesus as their savior and subscribe to the correct doctrines; nonlegalistic Protestantism more often understands it to denote a unity with God that exists outside the dimension of time and that can also be experienced in this life.

- Legalistic Protestantism holds that God loves only the "saved" and that they alone are truly his children; nonlegalistic Protestantism holds that God loves all human beings and that all are his children.

- Legalistic Protestantism sees Satan as a real creature, a tempter and deceiver from whom true Christians are defended by their faith but by whom atheists, members of other religions, and "false Christians" are deceived, and whose instruments they can become; for non-legalistic Protestantism Satan is a metaphor for the potential for evil that exists in each person, Christian or otherwise, and that must be recognized and resisted.

- Legalistic Protestantism believes that individuals should be wary of trusting their own minds and emotions, for these can be manipulated by Satan, and that questions and doubts are to be resisted as the work of the Devil; nonlegalistic Protestantism believes that the mind is a gift of God and that God wants us to think for ourselves, to follow our consciences, to ask questions, and to listen for his still, small voice.

- Legalistic Protestantism sees "truth" as something established in the Bible and known for sure by true Christians; nonlegalistic Protestantism sees truth as something known wholly only by God toward which the belief statements of religions can only attempt to point the way.

- Legalistic Protestantism reads the Bible literally and considers it the ultimate source of truth; nonlegalistic Protestantism insists that the Bible must be read critically, intelligently, and with an understanding of its historical and cultural contexts.

- Legalistic Protestantism encourages a suspicion of aesthetic values and a literalistic mentality that tends to thwart spiritual experience; nonlegalistic Protestantism encourages a recognition of mystery and beauty as attributes of the holy.

Some legalistic Protestants are fundamentalists, whose emphasis is on keeping themselves apart from the evil mainstream culture and thus pure; others might more accurately be described as conservative evangelicals, whose emphasis is on bringing the word of Jesus to the "unsaved," or as charismatics, who seek to model their worship on early Christians' miraculous experiences with healing, prophecy, and "speaking in tongues"; some may consider themselves to be all three at once. Members of all these groups believe in a wrathful God who rewards "true believers" with an eternity in heaven and condemns all others to an eternity in hell.

More legalistic Protestants belong to the Southern Baptist Convention (the nation's largest Protestant group) than to any other denomination; many others belong to such Pentecostal bodies as the Assemblies of God and the Church of God, which place special emphasis on charismatic manifestations; still others belong to congregations, Baptist or otherwise, that are independent (often fiercely so) of any established denomination and that, in both worship and doctrine, may strike a unique balance among fundamentalist, evangelical, and charismatic features. Many mainline church members are also legalists, though the percentage varies widely: The United Church of Christ contains far fewer legalists, for example, than does the United Methodist Church. As noted, so-called traditionalist Catholics, who in earlier generations would never have been grouped (either by themselves or by others) with Protestant fundamentalists, fall into the legalistic category; so do most Mormons, Seventh-day Adventists, and Jehovah's Witnesses. Though many in this category would not consider many others in it to be genuine Christians at all, they share a propensity for narrow theological views and reactionary social and cultural values, and consequently they tend to function as practical allies in the so-called culture war against "secular humanism."

Fundamentalist, evangelical, and charismatic Christianity cannot easily be discussed and understood without reference to the distinctive characteristics of American culture. Yes, these forms of legalistic Christianity claim adherents on every continent; but it is in America that they have taken root most firmly and borne the most fruit. They barely exist in Western Europe; their success elsewhere owes everything to American missionary work among the poor and undereducated. In their suspicion of the intellect and their categorical assertion that the Bible contains all truth, these kinds of Christianity reflect the American distrust of mind described by Richard Hofstadter in his book *Anti-Intellectualism in American Life;* indeed, they can be understood as ways of avoiding the obligation to *think*—and, especially, to think for oneself. As William Ray puts it, "fundamentalism demands believers, not thinkers"; Ray's observation that "no evidence, no logic, no personal experience, *nothing* can change the fundamentalist's mind about 'revealed truth'"applies equally to conservative evangelicals and charismatics. "Questioning 'revealed truth' in any way, even hypothetically," notes Ray, "challenges the . . . belief system at its core. . . . The more successfully any 'revealed truth' is challenged, the more vehemently the challenge must be rejected."

Why did this kind of religion develop in America, of all places? Well, first of all, America is the place to which the Puritans came, and their fixation on stark antitheses (God and Satan, saints and sinners), their conviction that you're damned unless you believe exactly the right doctrine, and their tendency to equate immorality with sex all helped lay the foundations for today's legalistic Christianity. So did the pragmatism and materialism of the pioneers, whose respect for "honest work" and suspicion of professors, philosophers, and others who don't produce anything "real" spelled success for faiths that involved quantifiable sacrifice, little or no abstract reflection, and a concrete payoff in the form of a tangible heaven. Those pioneers' individualistic sentiments, moreover, made them distrust ecclesiastical elites and accept the right of every person to interpret the Bible according to his or her own lights; this emphasis on scripture was also fed by the notion of America as a new Eden, which, as the religious historian George M. Marsden has noted, "readily translated into Biblical primitivism," the idea that "the Bible alone should be one's guide." Yet given those pioneers' literal-mindedness and aversion to abstract interpretation, it was a short—and disastrous—step from the idea of the Bible as guide to a twisted insistence on biblical literalism.

Nonlegalistic Protestants figure far less often in the mainstream media than do legalists. Indeed, they sometimes seem virtually invisible. They worship a God of love, and they envision the church, at its best, as a Church of Love. They tend to belong to mainline Protestant churches or to relatively small bodies such as the Quakers and Unitarians. Some are Catholics; some are even Baptists or Seventh-day Adventists. If the public face of conservative Christians today is that of Pat Robertson and his Christian Coalition, liberal Christians as yet have no public face to speak of. Recently, liberal Christians have formed such national groups as the Interfaith Alliance and Call to Renewal, but so far they have failed to receive even a fraction of the media attention routinely accorded to the Christian Coalition. Few Americans even know they exist.

Nonlegalistic Christianity has its problems. Those who worship a God of love can sometimes appear to reduce the majesty and mystery of the divine to something pat and shallow. While legalists obsess over the presence of evil in the world, nonlegalists can seem naive, even blinkered, about it. How to explain the existence of evil, after all, if God is totally good? If God *does* love all his children unconditionally, then why do so many people live out their lives feeling worthless, lonely, and unloved? In a world full of heartless brutality, belief in a God of wrath is hardly inexplicable. Karen Armstrong, the distinguished author of *A History of God* and hardly a legalistic Christian, has written that we must "accept evil in the divine" in order to "accept the evil we encounter in our own hearts." This is certainly one solution to the age-old problem of evil, and it is consistent with much that we read about God in the Old Testament. But it is *not* the religion of Jesus.

In any event, the problem with legalistic Christianity is not simply that it affirms that God can be evil; it's that it imagines a manifestly evil God and calls that evil good. In effect, as we shall see, *it worships evil*. In America right now, millions of children are taught by their legalistic Christian parents and ministers to revere a God of wrath and to take a sanguine view of human suffering. They are taught to view their fellow Americans not as having been "created equal," as the Declaration of Independence would have it, but as being saved or unsaved, children of God or creatures of Satan; they are taught not to respect those most different from themselves but to regard them as the enemy, to resist their influence, and to seek to restrict their rights. This is not only morally offensive, it's socially dangerous—and it represents, for obvious reasons, a very real menace to democratic civil society. America's founding fathers, as I shall show, respected religion because they saw it as strengthening people's best selves and checking their worst selves; too often, legalistic Christianity—which has deceitfully portrayed the founding fathers as its philosophical allies—does precisely the opposite.

Now, what do I mean by the title *Stealing Jesus*?

In recent years, legalistic Christians have organized into a political

movement so successful that when many Americans today hear the
word *Christianity*, they think only of the legalistic variety. The mainstream media, in covering the so-called culture wars, generally imply
that there are only two sides to choose from: the God-of-wrath Christian Right and the godless secular Left. Many Americans scarcely realize that there is any third alternative. And many, unable to take the
Christian Right seriously as a cultural force, view it as a holdover of
"traditional Christianity" that has inexplicably lingered into these "secular times" and will gradually fade away.

This notion is dangerously misguided. To be sure, the kind of legalistic Christianity that flourishes in America today does have a long historical background of which Americans need to be more aware—and
which I will briefly trace in these pages. Legalism has, then, been a part
of the Christian picture from the beginning. Yet today's legalistic
Protestantism is very much (to borrow a favorite legalistic term) a
"new creation." As new species evolve from old because they are
specially equipped to endure a changed environment, so today's
legalism—an animal unlike any that had ever existed before—emerged
as an adaptation to modern secular democratic society. Far from being
a vestige of traditional Christian faith, in short, it is a distinctively modern phenomenon—one that, while making tradition its rallying cry, has
at the deepest level betrayed Christianity's most precious traditions. In
fact it has, as we shall see, carried out a tripartite betrayal:

- *Doctrine.* It has replaced the traditional emphases of Christian belief
  with bizarre doctrinal strictures that have no legitimate basis in
  scripture, reason, or tradition.

- *Authority.* It has replaced the foundational Protestant trust in the
  individual's "soul competency" with a dictatorial system of clerical
  absolutism.

- *Law.* It has replaced Christ's gospel message of love, which drew
  on the noblest parts of the Hebrew Scriptures, with the harshest
  edicts from the Pentateuch, the epistles of Paul, and the Book of
  Revelation.

Born out of anger, modern legalistic Christianity has, over the long
arc of the twentieth century, become steadily angrier in reaction to

spreading secularism. During that period it has also spread like a cancer, winning adherents by the million and posing an increasingly serious threat to other faiths and to democratic freedoms. It has, in the process, warped Christianity into something ugly and hateful that has little or nothing to do with love and everything to do with suspicion, superstition, and sadism. And, quite often, it denies the name of Christianity to followers of Jesus who reject its barbaric theology. In essence, then, it has stolen Jesus—yoked his name and his church to ideas, beliefs, and attitudes that would have appalled him.

Yet to an extraordinary extent, the American media—which are widely denounced as liberal and which tend to be controlled and staffed by secularists and by nonlegalistic Christians—have allowed their own way of using the word *Christian* to be strongly influenced by legalistic Christian activists. This is especially true, unsurprisingly, of the conservative press. In 1996, the right-wing policy magazine *American Enterprise* published a special issue on religion in which the word *Christian* was routinely used to mean only legalists. One article referred to the increasing "involvement of Christians in school boards"; another gauged the "Christian influence" on the media and adverted to "Christian media" and "Christian periodicals." Over and over, in short, the word *Christian* was used in a narrow way to include only legalistic Christians and to exclude pretty much everybody else. Certainly there aren't "more Christians" on school boards or on Capitol Hill than there used to be; there are simply more legalistic Christians in these places.

Such usage is probably to be expected in a periodical like *American Enterprise,* whose editors consider legalistic Christians their ideological allies. But it is rather more surprising in the case of the *New York Times,* which legalistic Christians almost universally despise for what they view as its liberal, anti-Christian slant. Given the fact that legalistic Christians tend to view the *Times* as their single greatest enemy in the media establishment, and given the *Times's* history of extremely careful usage, it was remarkable to find *Times* religion reporter Gustav Niebuhr, in a 1996 article, using the word *Christian* to mean a legalistic Protestant. Niebuhr refers to "Christian booksellers" whose "Christian bookstores" feature "Christian music videos" by "Christian musicians." That neither Niebuhr nor his editors considered it inappropriate to say "Christian" rather than, say, "conservative evangelical" indicates the extent of the Religious Right's success at getting even some of the most responsible and reflective elements of mainstream America to accept, however unconsciously, the notion that legalists are the only true Christians—or, at the very least, are in some way "more" Christian, or more urgently or authentically or fully Christian, than other Christians.

The increasing tendency to use the word *Christian* to mean only legalistic Protestants has given the word an unpleasant flavor for many Americans—Christians included. In a 1996 sermon, a friend of mine who is an Episcopal priest recalled that he cringed when, at a social event, he met a man "who rather quickly identified himself as a Christian." When the man said the word *Christian,* several other words immediately went through my friend's mind: "bigot, arrogant, mindless, intolerant, rigid, mean-spirited." Though the encounter proved pleasant, my friend was struck by his initial reaction to the man's self-identification as a Christian, and by the fact that the word had come to stand for so many bad things that even a devout clergyman could find himself recoiling at the sound of it.

A friend of mine who teaches theology at a Catholic university noted in a 1996 personal letter that at a recent meeting of his academic department, "one of my colleagues pointed out that the administration has found it unwise to use the word 'Christian' in its official statements. . . . Why unwise? Because in the public perception 'Christian' is hitched to 'Coalition.'" Indeed, as the Reverend Canon John L. Peterson, the secretary-general of the Anglican Consultative Council, observed in his opening remarks at an international evangelism meeting in 1995, "in certain parts of the world the word Christian has become an embarrassment because it has been aligned with movements which are contrary to the Loving Christ that is at the heart of our message. I hold my head in shame to hear Jesus' name being affiliated with political movements that isolate, inhibit and breed hate and discontentment between human beings."

Why haven't nonlegalistic Christians made more of an effort to rescue the word *Christian* from the negative connotations it has acquired in the minds of many Americans? Partly, I think, because nonlegalistic Christians are used to thinking of religion as a private matter; they

aren't in the habit of talking about what they believe, let alone organizing politically to do so. Partly because they feel cowed into silence
by the aggressive, unapologetic manner in which legalists draw boundaries between "true Christians" (themselves) and false ones. And partly,
perhaps, because they have a quite proper attitude of awe and humility about the fact that they are Christians—and an alertness to the danger of seeming smug, strident, and self-congratulatory in their
profession of faith.

Yet one unfortunate result of this reticence is that the nonlegalistic
Christian point of view has played an almost invisible role in the
discussions of religion and "values" issues that have roiled our society
in recent years. Instead, those discussions are almost invariably
represented in the mainstream media as a clear-cut contest between
"Christians" (that is, legalists), who supposedly uphold responsibility,
values, and family, and liberal secular humanists, who support rights,
tolerance, and separation of church and state. A major problem with
this vision of the conflict is that neither side of it, as presented by the
media, is speaking for Jesus Christ—for what he was and is really about.
Indeed, it often seems that the media, secular liberals, and legalistic
Christians alike take for granted that the most prominent legalistic
spokespeople—men and women like Pat Robertson, Ralph Reed,
Phyllis Schlafly, and James Dobson—*do* speak for Christianity. Even as
many secular media figures privately smirk at legalistic Christians and
tilt coverage in favor of secular humanism, they never publicly challenge the legalists' claim to speak on behalf of the Body of Christ—
because the Body of Christ is, to them, not something of value.

The time has come for this challenge to be made. For to be a serious nonlegalistic Christian in America today is to recognize that the
word *Christian*—and, more important, the real living Christ—are crying out to be unshackled from the prejudices and precepts to which
legalistic Christians have bound them. To be a serious nonlegalistic
Christian is to recognize that while legalists present themselves as "true
Christians," the narrow doctrines they profess, the authoritarianism
they practice, and the laws they uphold represent a damaging distortion and subversion of Jesus' message. And it is to recognize that in
recent years, even as serious biblical scholars have answered with
increasing clarity the question of who Jesus was and what he was

about, legalists have radically redefined Jesus, condemning the principles he really stood for and instead identifying him with their own ugliest tendencies. Meanwhile, secular Americans have looked on blindly or indifferently, for the most part either not realizing or not caring what was going on. And most nonlegalistic Christians have held their tongues.

Yet to examine the nearly two thousand years of tension between the Church of Law and the Church of Love—a tension that has mounted at an increasing rate around the world, and in America above all, over the course of this century—is to feel that the present millennial moment in America is a moment of truth for Christianity, a moment when there is an urgent need for the Church of Law to be challenged. This challenge will almost certainly have to come from within the mainline Protestant churches, and it will have to be issued by Christians whose unfamiliarity with the present conflict's historical background I hope to remedy here. I will seek to do this by showing how discontinuous much of today's Christianity is with the teachings of Jesus; by describing how extreme such Christianity has become in twentieth-century America; by demonstrating how fully it has succeeded in usurping the name of Christianity; by explaining why these developments endanger the stability, democracy, and pluralism not only of the United States but also of the world in which it is now the sole superpower; and by emphasizing how necessary it is—for the health of Christianity, of America, and of the world (which legalistic Protestants are at present aggressively evangelizing)—to reverse these developments *now.*

Why has mainstream society taken so long to realize fully what legalistic Christianity was doing to America—and to Jesus?

Part of the reason, I think, is that, for all the nation's cultural homogeneity—our thousands of identical fast-food outlets and mall stores, and our common popular culture of music and TV shows and movies—we are deeply fragmented in matters of religion. In no other Western country do so many denominations claim as their members such large proportions of the population. This lack of a shared religious culture, along with our overall indifference to history and our public schools' hands-off attitude toward religion, has made us a people who have a very fuzzy sense of what religion is and has been in America, of what things used to be like and how they have gotten to where they are.

For me, religion was always much more of a question mark than, say, music or math or geography. As someone who was raised in a conservative Republican household that was somewhere on the cusp between secularism and nonlegalistic Christianity, I was probably quite representative of many Americans who grew up in the second half of the twentieth century. During my childhood in the 1960s and my teenage years in the early 1970s, I was close to Catholics (both devout and lapsed), to Jews (both religious and secular), and to a wide variety of Protestants. I knew enough people of different faiths, indeed, to be struck over and over again by the extraordinary religious diversity of the society in which I lived, by how little most of the people in my life seemed to know about one another's faiths, and above all by the unreflective zeal with which some of those people could claim for themselves the label of Christian and deny it to others.

My family was itself pretty diverse: My father's parents, who had come to New York City from Poland during World War I, were Roman Catholics; my mother's father and mother in South Carolina were raised in Methodist and Baptist churches, respectively (though my grandmother later switched from Baptist to Methodist). Both of my grandfathers died in the 1950s, but my grandmothers lived on into the 1980s and continued to be regular churchgoers. In my Catholic grandmother's apartment a crucifix and a calendar painting of Jesus hung on the wall; my Protestant grandmother's house was piled high with Bibles, copies of Norman Vincent Peale's magazine, *Guideposts,* and small paperbound volumes of prayers and meditations.

My parents weren't churchgoers. My father had no apparent religion, while my mother, though disaffected from institutional religion by the racism and hypocrisy in the churches of her youth, considered herself a Christian. Though she sent me for several years to a Lutheran Sunday school, she did not have me baptized, for she was determined, in the Baptist fashion, to let me make that choice. She was not big on doctrinal statements but instead, like more than a few American parents, drove two points into my head over and over so that they would stick there forever (and they did). One point was that God was about love; he loved me and everybody else. The other point was this: "It doesn't matter to God what religion you are. What matters is whether you're a good person." Little did I know what a radical, unacceptable doctrine this was to millions of Americans who called themselves Christians.

As a child, I spent little time in church. Our family attended a few Lutheran Easter services, and every Christmas my sister and I accompanied Catholic friends to their church's midnight mass. I remember at one such mass being astonished by the priest's sermon, in which he ordered his flock not to watch the TV show *Maude* because a recent story line had concerned abortion. What business, I wondered, did this guy have giving such orders? And what kind of congregation tolerated such high-handedness? I knew so little about the authoritative role of the clergy in Roman Catholicism that I was astonished to hear such preaching, and appalled that it didn't raise an eyebrow among the folks in the pews. I wondered how many of those people actually obeyed the priest's command.

In those days my life was compartmentalized where religion was concerned. My Sunday-school classmates, of course, were all Protestants—in fact, they were pretty much the only Protestants I knew in New York. Most of my public-school classmates were Jewish, while almost all the kids on my block were Catholics who attended parochial school. On Jewish holidays, when I had the day off and the Catholic kids heading home from school saw me reading on our front steps, some of them would jeer at me, saying that I was a Jew and would therefore go to hell. "I'm not a Jew," I would protest. "If you're not Catholic, you're Jewish!" they would insist. "And you're going to hell!" I was amazed that these children, who attended a religion class every day of the school year, could think that everybody was either Catholic or Jewish. Hadn't they ever heard of Protestants—or Hindus, Buddhists, Moslems? What were those nuns teaching them? Even more amazing was the glee with which these supposed friends of mine declared that God would send me to hell—and would do so for no other reason, apparently, than that I had been born into the wrong faith. It was plain to me that the God of love that my mother had told me about would never run his universe that way. Why wasn't that plain to them? And why were they so eager to embrace such a brutal image of God, anyway?

If any of those young people ever inquired of their teachers why God had set up such a cruel, meaningless system of postmortem reward and punishment, I never heard about it. Few of them, indeed, seemed ever to reflect on the things they were told in religion class. Plainly, they had recognized from an early age that questions weren't welcome, that thinking wasn't acceptable, and that what was called for was unreflecting, unquestioning assent. I couldn't imagine how people my age could have taken all those religion classes and yet managed never to examine critically the things they were being told about the ultimate truths of the cosmos.

When I was thirteen, several of my Jewish classmates had bar mitzvah parties. I was confused when I was not invited to any, not even the one for my best friend. When my mother, sure that this was an oversight, called his mother, she was told that I hadn't been invited because I wasn't Jewish. She was miffed—and I was shocked. Suddenly I was aware that in the minds of my Jewish friends—or maybe just their parents?—there was a distance between me and them to which I had been blind. Their Jewishness had never made any difference to me; to discover that my non-Jewishness made such an immense difference to them was earthshaking.

Around that time, my Sunday-school classmates and I began to be prepared for our confirmations. Our teacher assumed that we had all been baptized, and when I told her I hadn't, she was sure I was mistaken. The people at the church checked with my mother, however, and when they learned to their horror that it was true, they made a series of insistent phone calls to her, demanding that I be baptized immediately. She refused. Finally an official church delegation called at our house and tried to scare her, solemnly declaring that if I wasn't baptized, I would go to hell. (Thus did I learn that it wasn't just Catholics who said such silly things.) Politely but firmly, my mother ordered the delegation out of the house and withdrew me from the Sunday school that I had attended for some seven or eight years. She was determined not to let anybody baptize me unless and until I decided that I *wanted* to be baptized.

What my mother did then was, I believe, inspired. On a succession of Sunday mornings, she took me to services at various Protestant churches in our neighborhood. One week it was the large stone Presbyterian edifice on Queens Boulevard, the next the small brick Congregationalist box on Eightieth Street. And so on. The idea was to acquaint me with my denominational options—to open my eyes to the variety of ways of worshipping the Almighty, at least within a Protestant context, and perhaps to find a church that I might want to belong to. Though I didn't end up joining any of those churches, the experience instilled in me a fascination with religion that has never abated. I noticed all the similarities and differences—in everything from music, liturgy, and preaching to the way the clergy dressed and the way the church interior looked—and I wanted very much to understand them.

That summer, in my uncle's house in South Carolina, I found a book that compared Methodism to Catholicism in elaborate detail, with the former coming out way ahead. (This outcome was not surprising, given that the book had been issued by a Methodist publishing house.) Among other things, the book cataloged the popes' villainous misdeeds. It was eye-opening. Imagine—popes who had murdered, stolen, kept mistresses, and fathered children! At about this time I also acquired a hand-me-down parochial-school history textbook whose biases were soon obvious even to me: By its account, the church was always right, the popes always virtuous. I was surprised that a schoolbook could misrepresent the truth so shamelessly. And I rejoiced that I attended a public school, where the schoolbooks weren't (I thought) slanted at all.

I was then only beginning to notice the gaping hole in my formal education. At school I learned about Western culture, but Christianity—which stood at its center—was almost entirely omitted. I studied American history, but the course materials included almost no details about the religions that had decisively shaped the nation from its beginnings. Where the subject could not be avoided, the textbooks and teachers handled it briefly and delicately, doing their best to skirt anything potentially controversial. I was taught, for example, that the Pilgrims and Puritans had come to America because they wanted to establish "freedom of religion"; I was also taught that Roger Williams, America's first Baptist preacher, had fled the Puritans' Massachusetts Bay Colony and founded Rhode Island because *he* wanted to establish "freedom of religion." Huh? If the Puritans had practiced freedom of religion, why had Williams been forced to flee Massachusetts? That question was never fully confronted. Nor did I learn much about what exactly the Puritans believed and how it compared to what most Englishmen believed—or, for that matter, to what other American colonists believed.

While I had a pretty good notion, moreover, of which national groups had migrated to which parts of America, I had only the vaguest understanding of the religions they had brought with them. Not until later in my teens, when I had begun to research my family tree, did I perceive how critical a role religion had played in my ancestors' coming to America—and, by extension, how important a dimension of the nation's history had been left out of my school lessons. One of my ancestors, for example, turned out to be a Quaker named Valentine Hollingsworth who had emigrated to the New World in 1682 with William Penn and settled in Delaware. Another, John Bristow, was an Anglican who came from England as an indentured servant and served as a church clerk in Virginia. One ancestor named Daugé, a member of France's embattled Protestant minority, the Huguenots, came to America around 1680 to escape Catholic persecution; another Huguenot ancestor fled France in the early 1700s and became an associate of a then-famous pioneer Baptist minister named Oliver Hart. If I was stunned to realize that my mother's family had preserved no living memory of these facts, and that I had had to discover them in dusty library records, I was even more stunned to learn what a vital motivating role religion had played in so many of my ancestors' lives—in the series of decisions that had led to, among much else, me.

In school I had learned about the Protestant Reformation, which had begun, we were taught, early in the sixteenth century when a German priest named Martin Luther got angry at the church for selling documents called indulgences that were supposed to guarantee purchasers a reduced sentence in purgatory. Beyond that, however, my teachers didn't teach much about the origins of Protestantism. They didn't go very deeply into Luther's profound theological rupture from Catholicism, at the center of which was his rejection of the church doctrine of salvation by works (you go to heaven as a reward for what you do on earth) in favor of a doctrine of salvation by grace (as sinners, we cannot merit heaven, but those who embrace Jesus as savior receive it as a gift). My teachers didn't examine the lives and beliefs of other Protestant reformers, and didn't help us to understand the ways in which these reformers' ideas, transported to the New World by their followers, had definitively shaped American society and culture.

By the time I started researching my family tree, to be sure, I knew a few scattered, superficial things about Christian history and theology—but I knew them only because I had picked up information on my own. I learned somewhere, for example, that the sixteenth-century Protestant reformer John Calvin had believed in predestination (the idea that every person is for all eternity designated unalterably either as damned or as a member of the heaven-destined "Elect") and that some of his followers had founded the Presbyterian Church. I knew about the Calvinist doctrine of "once saved, always saved," but I didn't know about the antithetical doctrine—known as Arminianism and preached by Methodism's founder, John Wesley—that it was possible to fall from grace. I knew something about Christian Science, mainly because my father's complete set of Mark Twain included Twain's book-length attack on its nineteenth-century founder, Mary Baker Eddy, which I read with fascination. I didn't know that the Quakers had been founded in the mid 1600s by an Englishman named George Fox, but I knew from the movie *Friendly Persuasion* that they believed in nonviolence and called one another "thee."

Then there were the Jehovah's Witnesses, founded in the nineteenth century by an American named Charles Taze Russell. I knew quite a bit about their beliefs because a nice old man came to our door two or three times selling Jehovah's Witness books for fifty cents. Each time he came, I bought one. And I read them—not because I found them theologically credible but because I found it incredible that other people did. One of the books, entitled *Then Is Finished the Mystery of God,* interpreted the mysterious, fantastic symbolism of the Book of Revelation in great detail. Among the twentieth-century events that the book cited as direct fulfillments of specific biblical prophecies were the dictatorship of Hitler, the Soviet invasion of Czechoslovakia, and the 1968 expansion of the Jehovah's Witnesses' Brooklyn printing plant. I read all this with open-mouthed astonishment. Could the nice old man who had sold me the book seriously believe such things?

I knew he did, because once when I was about sixteen and was hang-
ing out with friends on the block, he showed up and started telling us
about his religion. He said—to the jeers and gibes of my friends—that
the world would end soon and that, before it did, the most important
thing was for believers to evangelize and for nonbelievers to convert
or face hellfire.

I remember marveling at the man's unshakable calm in the face of
ridicule. I knew he was deadly serious about what he believed, and I
knew his beliefs—which included an expectation of a Judgment Day
that sounded like a cosmic-scale comic opera—were absurd. Why
would God set up a situation in which only those who embraced the
correct arcane scenario of the "End Times" would be saved? Why
would he turn salvation into an eenie-meenie-minie-mo guessing
game? Why would he bring the history of the universe to an end with
a grotesquely silly apocalyptic show? What would be the point, the
purpose, the meaning? Surely the universe had a greater ultimate significance than that; surely its God had more imagination. And what
about God's love? My experience with the old Jehovah's Witness, like
my experience with the Catholic kids who screamed at me that I was
going to hell, drove home to me the fact that certain people—not only
children, but grown-ups too—needed to believe that they were saved
and that somebody else wasn't. To be sure, it wasn't a need that necessarily manifested itself in an overtly nasty way: The old Jehovah's Witness man was unfailingly gracious and gentle, and certainly wanted to
save as many people as he could before the end. But deep down his
theology was still ugly, wasn't it?

By the end of my teens, then, I did have a smattering of knowledge
about religion in America—more, surely, than most young Americans.
But there was so much that I didn't know. In fact, I didn't even *know*
how much I didn't know. I had never heard of dispensationalism, the
baroque nineteenth-century theological system on which American
Protestant fundamentalism is founded. I had never heard of the Rapture and the Great Tribulation, both of which are bedrock concepts of
that theology. And I had never heard of the Scofield Reference Bible,
which had codified those concepts and which was a revered fixture in
countless American homes.

How little I knew was driven home to me every year when, after receiving the new edition of the *World Almanac* in my Christmas stocking, I perused once again the long list of U.S. religious denominations along with their membership figures. There I read, in bold print, the names of the large old religious groups—Baptist, Catholic, Jewish, and so forth—as well as other familiar names: Christian Science, the Society of Friends (Quakers), the Salvation Army. But there were also, in lighter print, dozens of other sizable groups with names that meant nothing to me—names like the Brethren, the Evangelical Free Church of America, the Bible Way Church of Our Lord Jesus Christ World Wide, and something called Triumph the Church and Kingdom of God in Christ. There were also numerous perplexing variations on the words *Church of God:* the Church of God; the Church of God (Anderson, Indiana); the Church of God (Cleveland, Tennessee); the Church of God, General Conference; the Original Church of God; the Church of God by Faith; the Church of God of Prophecy; the Church of God in Christ; the Church of the Living God; the Church of God, Seventh Day; the Church of God, Seventh Day (Denver); and, last but not least, something called the House of God, which is the Church of the Living God, the Pillar and Ground of the Truth. I didn't have a clue what most of these churches might profess, or what their history might be, or what kind of people you might find in their congregations. Nor could I imagine why there were so many of them. What difference could there be between a Church of God headquartered in Anderson, Indiana, and one headquartered in Cleveland, Tennessee? I knew that the difference must have something to do with theological particulars; for I had already begun to understand that while common spiritual experience could bring people together in love and worship, a tendency to insist on doctrinal specifics could cause enmity and division.

Why was I so ill-educated about these things? And why are most people in the United States, with its astonishingly high percentage of churchgoers, even more badly educated about them? The reasons aren't hard to fathom. Religion is a touchy subject, and America has a long tradition of church-state separation. In a diverse country where most children attend public schools, it's not easy to find an objective way to teach religion. Yet to omit it, for this reason, almost entirely from history education is to distort history beyond recognition. And it isn't just history. Pre-Romantic European literature, art, and music were to a

huge extent *about* Christianity. How can one fully appreciate Mozart's
Requiem Mass if one doesn't know how a mass is structured and why?
How can one fully appreciate a Madonna by Fra Angelico if one is
clueless about medieval faith? When I was in high school and college
and even graduate school (where I studied English literature), my
teachers assigned the work of Dante, Milton, Herbert, and Donne, religious poets all; yet, absurdly, most of us read, discussed, and even wrote
papers about them knowing only the most rudimentary facts about the
religious ideas that informed their works.

Indeed, though I had managed to acquaint myself, in a spotty way,
with American religious history, I came out of graduate school with
what I now recognize as a crude, essentially secular vision of Christianity and its place in history. And nothing was more crude—and
skewed—than my vision of Protestant fundamentalism. If I had been
asked about fundamentalism back then, I would have said that it was a
backward faith characterized by biblical literalism and horror of modern science, and that the 1925 trial of John T. Scopes for teaching evolution had marked the beginning of its end. That trial was depicted, of
course, in Jerome Lawrence and Robert E. Lee's 1955 play *Inherit the
Wind*. Virtually all of us nonlegalistic Christian and secular kids were
given that play to read in high school. Most of us came to it knowing
next to nothing about religion, fundamentalist or otherwise—and most
of us came away from it having absorbed its message that fundamentalism was on the wrong side of history. When we went on to college,
we were taught to speak and write as if nobody believed in religion
anymore, at least not educated Americans; many of us tried not to
notice how thoroughly this notion was contradicted by the reality
around us. We now lived, our professors explained, in a "post-
Christian" society; religion, if not yet completely dead, was unquestionably on its way out. Certainly fundamentalism was over, or very
close to it.

Was any proposition ever so misguided? Nowadays, if I want to
remind myself exactly how unsavvy I was then about the state of fundamentalism, I need only recall my response when in 1972, at fifteen,
I read "Trends," a science-fiction story by Isaac Asimov that was published in 1939 before the outbreak of World War II. In that story, a
futuristic work set in the 1970s, Asimov imagines a world where the

Second World War, beginning in 1940, has been followed by a politically reactionary era marked by a return to social conventions and "a swing toward religion." In 1973, a scientist named John Harmon plans to fly the first manned rocket ship. For this audacious aspiration, he is condemned by Otis Eldredge, a famed evangelist who sees advanced science and technology as things of the Devil.

"Gifted with a golden tongue and a sulphurous vocabulary," Eldredge forms an organization called the League of the Righteous that soon wins great power. Eldredge boasts that "after the next election Congress will be his." Sabotaged by an Eldredge follower, Harmon's rocket ship explodes before takeoff. While Harmon proceeds to build another rocket ship, American society grows even more conservative: In the 1974 elections, Eldredge wins control of Congress and outlaws scientific research. But Harmon is sanguine, explaining to his friends that "We're going through a momentary reaction following a period of too-rapid advance." In 1978, following Eldredge's death, Harmon flies to the moon and returns to be proclaimed a hero by an America now weary of right-wing evangelicalism. "The pendulum," Harmon observes with satisfaction, "swung back again."

Though I enjoyed Asimov's stories, "Trends" struck me as callow. Yes, I was impressed that a teenager in 1939 had foreseen a second world war within the year and space travel by the early 1970s. Yet I found ridiculous the idea that in the late twentieth century, reactionary evangelists could rise to political power. What could be more absurd?

To be sure, there were still people like that nice old Jehovah's Witness, and still Roman Catholic kids who gleefully damned their Protestant friends to hell. There were also evangelists like Rex Humbard and Kathryn Kuhlman whom I glimpsed now and then on low-budget, paid-access Sunday-morning TV shows. But these people, most of them old and tired-looking, were the very definition of fringe leaders. They were back numbers, the last relics of a movement that had long since seen its glory days. After all, the big-scale religious revivals led by flamboyant characters like Billy Sunday and Aimee Semple McPherson were ancient history. Weren't they? I had read with relish Sinclair Lewis's 1927 novel *Elmer Gantry,* about a crooked evangelist who soaked illiterate, superstitious rubes in the hinterlands, and I knew that that novel was a period piece, an artifact of a distant, more unsophisticated era. Wasn't it? And I had read the aforementioned *Inherit the Wind,* which made it perfectly clear what I and others of my generation were supposed to think of fundamentalism: It was a thing of the past, a thing that *belonged* in the past, and a thing that, to the extent that it still survived in remote rural pockets, was guaranteed to wither away and die.

Yes, guaranteed. After all, these were the early 1970s. America was growing more liberal and secular by the minute. In South Carolina, my older Protestant relatives still attended church, but none of my first cousins did; in New York, most of our adult Catholic neighbors hadn't been to mass in years, and most of their kids—the very ones who had damned me to hell a few years earlier—had transferred to public high schools.

For my part, though I hadn't been brought up as a regular church-goer, and still hadn't been baptized, I had been raised to say my prayers at bedtime, and I still did so. But I felt no need for church. Institutional religion seemed on its way out, and this didn't bother me. Not once had I attended a church service that had given me anything of spiritual value. I had never been a belonger, anyway. If anyone had told me that a few years later I would stop saying my prayers altogether, I probably wouldn't have been too surprised. If anyone had told me that, after another decade or so, I would undergo a baptism and become a regular churchgoer, a church committee member, and a deliverer of sermons, I don't think I would have believed it.

And what if I had been told that someday soon the most powerful figure in the Republican Party would be a preacher very much like Otis Eldredge who led a group very much like the League of the Righteous? I can't imagine how I would have reacted had I foreseen the Moral Majority (founded in 1979) and the Christian Coalition (1989). With shock? Terror? Of course I suffered from a malady that was nearly ubiquitous among secular people as well as nonlegalistic Christians: an almost utter ignorance of the real history of legalistic Christianity in America. For the fact is that in the mid-1920s, at the time of the Scopes trial, American fundamentalism, far from being on its deathbed, was barely in its infancy. Although fundamentalists called themselves traditional Christians, moreover, fundamentalist theology was not traditional at all, but was a relatively recent invention that had only begun to take shape in late nineteenth-century America as a fearful reaction to the human chaos of the Civil War and the spiritual chaos threatened by the theories of Darwin. The modern world wasn't killing fundamentalism off; on the contrary, the challenges, complexities, and pressures of modern American life were helping to drive more and more people out of mainline denominations and into the arms of fundamentalism.

It would be a long time before I learned these things. By the time I did, Pat Robertson's name would be a household word.

To look back over the last thirty years or so, and to compare my observations and experiences with what I now know to be the reality of America's religious past and present, is to recognize three things. One, that my understanding of American religion was astonishingly meager and misguided. Two, that I was not alone in this regard; on the contrary, I probably had a better grasp of religion in America when I was twelve than most adult Americans do today. Three, that for Americans to be ignorant of what is going on in their country's churches is dangerous. Had we been more knowledgeable about this subject, none of us would have been surprised by the rise of the Religious Right. Had we been more knowledgeable, we would have a better understanding of what made this rise possible, of how we should feel about this rise, and of what can and must be done about it. Had we been more knowledgeable, we would have been able to see the picture before us more clearly and to place it in its historical context. It is the purpose of this book both to clarify that picture and to provide that context—and to do so from the perspective of a concerned lay Christian who is equally discomfited by the notion of an America without Christianity and the notion of an American Christianity without love and logic.

It doesn't pretend to be comprehensive, or to be the work of a professional theologian, church historian, or cleric. In fact, that's part of the point here. This book may be understood, quite simply, as one layperson's map of the roads down which his own questions about ultimate reality have led him; my hope is that it will be of some use to others as they make their own journeys. I bring to this book my own experiences as a writer, a poet, a baby boomer, a middle-class gay white male American with mixed regional loyalties and with both Protestant and Catholic antecedents, and my conviction that the category of religion to which twentieth-century Americans have found their way in increasing numbers—a religion whose public faces today include those of Pat Robertson, Ralph Reed, James Dobson, and Jerry Falwell—is not a setting in which intelligent, serious people can expect to work out meaningful and responsible answers to ultimate questions. Nor is it something that the earliest followers of Jesus would have recognized as Christianity. I don't think it's an exaggeration, in fact, to suggest that if the first Christians were exposed to the rhetoric of Robertson, Reed, Dobson, Falwell, and company, they might well ask, in astonishment, "How did these vicious people manage to steal the name of Jesus?"

2

"WHO IS
MY NEIGHBOR?"

ANOTHER EVANGELIST ENCOUNTER. It's a warm, pleasant evening in early summer, 1996, and I've just given a reading at a Washington, D.C., bookstore with two writer friends. Joined by eight or nine others, friends of theirs and mine, we stroll down the balmy, tree-lined streets of the Dupont Circle neighborhood to a small Malayan restaurant where our group—all gay men—is shown to a sidewalk table.

The conversation is convivial. Aside from me, a New Yorker, everyone lives and works in Washington; all but one are white; most belong to the city's political establishment. Animatedly, they discuss the latest political news and gossip.

Flanking me at one end of the table are a friend who

now works as a senator's speechwriter and his companion, a photographer. Unlike the others, most of whom are libertarian Republicans and (I assume) atheists or agnostics, the speechwriter and his companion are both liberal Democrats and Southern Baptists. The three of us are chatting when all at once a middle-aged black man appears at the far end of the table.

"Hallelujah!" the man booms out in a voice as deep and mellifluous as James Earl Jones's. Our heads all jerk up. He's beaming. "Good evening, gentlemen!" he says. "Have you been saved?" As my Baptist friends and I exchange a look, the man begins to tell us about the love of Jesus, his eyes possessed by a visionary gleam. I notice that he holds a bunch of small tracts.

Sitting closest to the man are one of my writer friends and his companion, an Asian-American who is our only non-Caucasian. This companion now addresses the evangelist politely but firmly: "Excuse me, we're having a conversation here."

His expression unchanging, as if he doesn't even realize he's been spoken to, the evangelist preaches on. The writer's companion speaks to the evangelist more firmly. "Excuse me, sir, we're trying to have a conversation. Please leave."

The evangelist remains oblivious. "Jesus loves you!" he booms out, extending a tract. The companion places his hand on the evangelist's wrist and says sharply, *"No."* Their eyes meet; the evangelist's expression doesn't change. "Get out of here right now!" the companion demands. "If you don't leave immediately we'll call the police."

I glance at my speechwriter friend. I can tell from his expression that he's thinking what I'm thinking: that while the evangelist presumably lives in Washington, he plainly inhabits a different world than we do—namely, that of Washington's huge black underclass, which can sometimes seem invisible to Powertown's busy movers and shakers. I know further that the picture of a table full of relatively privileged men—none black and mostly Republicans—threatening police action against an African-American in downtown Washington, D.C., does not sit well with my Baptist friend.

Yet the situation is extremely complicated. Everyone at the table is gay. How many of us were told repeatedly in our childhoods that God hates homosexuals and condemns them to hell? How many of us thus view Christianity as a destructive force, a threat to our hard-won wholeness and self-respect? Some of my dinner companions are Jewish. Two generations after the Holocaust, how do they feel about Christianity, about being evangelized? I have only just met the Asian-American, so I am clueless as to what memories and emotions may have led him to speak to the evangelist so firmly. No easy judgment is possible here—no easy judgment of *anybody;* there is no simple answer to the question of what is and isn't a proper way to behave in these circumstances, which are, like the present religious situation in the United States, a tangled web of politics, race, class, sexual orientation, and radical metaphysical divergence.

As the evangelist moves away from the Asian-American and waves his tracts at the rest of us, my speechwriter friend reaches out a hand. "I'll take one," he says. So do his companion and I. "Jesus loves you," the evangelist says, still beaming, and moves along.

As he does, my Baptist friends and I look down at our tracts. Each consists of four three-by-five-inch pages. "THOUSANDS OF DEGREES HOT!" scream out bright red uppercase letters on the first page. "AND NOT A DROP OF WATER." Beneath these words is a crude drawing in red and black of a menacing figure—plainly Satan—with a pointed mustache and beard; behind him are the tortured, screaming faces of people whose bodies are immersed in what is apparently the lake of fire described in the Book of Revelation as the destination of all unsaved souls. The tract's title is printed in huge letters: "THE BURNING HELL: TORTURED LOST SOULS BURNING FOREVER!"

The inside pages are all text: "Jesus Christ believed in a BURNING HELL, that is why He left the Father's bosom and came to the world of sorrow. He left the streets of gold and the rejoicing of angels, to come to this earth to be crucified, so that you and I could escape THE BURNING HELL." The remainder of the text alternates between biblical quotations about hell and passages such as the following: "One day in HELL, you will not have to be bothered by some Christian trying to give you a gospel tract. . . . You will be crying, and begging for one drop of water to cool your scorching tongue. But it will be too late." The tract's last page gives the reader an opportunity to sign his or her name to the statement that he or she has now decided to accept Jesus Christ as savior and thus be spared the everlasting torments of hell.

After the evangelist's repeated declarations of Jesus' love, my Baptist friends and I are a bit jolted by the tract's hellfire message. Recalling the otherworldly gleam in the evangelist's eyes, I feel toward him a mixture of irritation and pity, and I wonder: Does he really believe in a God for whom a signature on a tract would make the difference between an eternity of torture and of bliss? I suppose he does. In his own view, certainly, the man was performing an act of love. Nonetheless I find the tract offensive. Addressing the entire table, I say, "Well, I wish he were still here, so I could tell him what I think of this tract, and tell him what evangelism is and isn't about. You don't get people to become Christians by scaring them to death."

Except for my Baptist friends, my dinner companions seem not to know how to reply to this comment. They're not believers in any religion, as far as I know, and they're not accustomed to sitting at dinner with people who are—or, at least, with people who talk about it. It occurs to me that if the evangelist had not appeared, the fact that anyone at the table *is* a believer would never have come up in conversation. In any event, as everyone else resumes talking about politics, my two Baptist friends and I continue to talk quietly about the evangelist and his tracts. "Maybe a Christianity that begins in fear," the photographer says hopefully, "can grow into a Christianity centered on love."

I shake my head. "No. Fear isn't a solid foundation for any healthy relationship, let alone one with God. To embrace Jesus because you fear God's wrath is to misunderstand God entirely. In fact it's to embrace something, or someone, that isn't Jesus at all."

That's what I believe. Yet it doesn't express the whole truth of the situation we've just experienced. For despite my discontent with the evangelist's methods, I'm keenly aware that he brought something to the table that it lacked. The twentieth-century American theologian Paul Tillich distinguished between two ways of relating to the world that he labeled horizontal and vertical. To be horizontally oriented is to be preoccupied with the transitory—day-to-day events, fads and fashions, temporal successes and failures. By contrast, to be vertically oriented—or, as Tillich puts it, to be "infinitely concerned," to live "in the dimension of depth"—is to be drawn to the infinite, the transcendent. As far back as 1958, Tillich lamented that "man in our time has lost such infinite concern." In a *Saturday*

Evening Post essay called "The Lost Dimension in Religion," Tillich
wrote that

> *Our daily life in office and home, in cars and airplanes, at parties and
> conferences, while reading magazines and watching television, while looking
> at advertisements and hearing radio, are in themselves continuous examples
> of a life which has lost the dimension of depth. It runs ahead, every moment
> is filled with something which must be done or seen or said or planned. But
> no one can experience depth without stopping and becoming aware of
> himself. Only if he has moments in which he does not care about what
> comes next can he experience the meaning of this moment here and now and
> ask himself about the meaning of his life. As long as the preliminary,
> transitory concerns are not silenced, no matter how interesting and valuable
> and important they may be, the voice of the ultimate concern cannot
> be heard.*

These things were true of American life when Tillich wrote his
essay in the 1950s, and they are even truer now. America is often called
deeply religious; in reality, however, it is a very horizontally preoccupied nation—one in which success is almost invariably defined in
coarsely materialistic terms, in which it is very difficult to step away
from the horizontal hubbub and experience the vertical, and in which
native-born theological concepts (of which there have been many
since the Pilgrims climbed off the *Mayflower*) tend to be extremely
earthbound. As I sit at the restaurant table thinking about the evangelist, I realize that, however misguided his message, he brought to our
table a reminder of the vertical orientation—the "dimension of depth"
from which most of the talented, busy, ambitious men at our table
have long been distracted by politics. The evangelist intruded into
our worldly talk with words that bespoke "ultimate concern": *Jesus
loves you!*

And yet I realize that the kind of Christianity that the evangelist
represents is not, in its essentials, a truly vertical phenomenon.

The vertical line is the line of spiritual experience; the horizontal line
is the line of doctrinal orthodoxy. Experience, doctrine. Love, law. Jesus

made it perfectly clear to his disciples which element in each of these pairings he was essentially about. In the Gospel according to Luke (10:25), a lawyer asks him, "What shall I do to inherit eternal life?"

"What is written in the law?" Jesus replies. "How do you read?"

In response, the lawyer brings together two separate directives—one from Deuteronomy, the other from Leviticus: "You shall love the Lord your God with all your heart, and with all your soul, and with all your strength, and with all your mind; and your neighbor as yourself."

Jesus tells him that he has answered correctly. But the lawyer has a further question: "Who *is* my neighbor?"

The question is a simple one, and the answer that Jesus gives, in the form of a parable, is also simple. Yet that parable takes us to the very heart of what it means—or is supposed to mean—to be a Christian.

What Jesus talks about in this parable is a road. He specifies which road it is—it's the one between Jerusalem and Jericho, two cities that lay in the heart of Judea. On that road, a man is beaten by robbers and left half-dead on the roadside. Since the temple was in Jerusalem and since many religious leaders lived in Jericho, it's not surprising that the first two passersby are Jewish religious leaders, a priest and a Levite. Both ignore the dying man. But a Samaritan—a native of Samaria, whose people were despised by the Jews of Jesus' day—comes along the road, sees the man dying, binds up his wounds, takes him to an inn, cares for him, and pays for his lodging.

Which of these passersby, Jesus asks, proved himself a neighbor to the man? And the lawyer gives the obvious answer: the Samaritan.

In a widely read 1994 book entitled *Crossing the Threshold of Hope,* each chapter, like the story of the good Samaritan, takes the form of a question posed and an answer given. In this case, the questions are asked not by a lawyer but by an Italian journalist named Vittorio Messori, and the answers are given not by Jesus but by Pope John Paul II. In one chapter, Messori asks the pope a question not very different from the lawyer's question about eternal life. The journalist's question is "Do heaven, purgatory, and hell still exist?"

The pope answers as follows: "Please open the Dogmatic Constitution on the Church, *Lumen Gentium,* to chapter seven, which discusses the eschatalogical character of the pilgrim Church on earth, as well as the union of the earthly Church with the Church in heaven."

Period.

The replies given by Jesus and John Paul II to their questioners could hardly be more different. The pope refers his questioner to dogma—indeed, to a work of doctrine written in theological jargon that would perplex all but the most educated Catholic readers; Jesus, by contrast, talks about an experience on a road, and does so in such a way that anyone within earshot can understand his message. The pope refers his questioner to an inflexible set of general propositions about spiritual reality—about the vertical plane—that exist apart from the particulars of any human situation and to which the faithful, whatever the nature of their own spiritual experiences, are obliged to declare their assent as they go about their lives in the horizontal plane. Jesus does exactly the opposite: He tells a story in which people (the priest, the Levite, the Samaritan) are confronted by a specific, unexpected, and challenging set of horizontal circumstances—as all of us are from time to time—and are required by those circumstances to make a choice that testifies to the degree of genuineness of their experiences of the vertical plane. The pope upholds law, which is the very essence of the horizontal plane; Jesus underscores the fact that no law is as important as the law of love, which is the very essence of the vertical plane.

It's important that Jesus' interlocutor here is a lawyer. Picture Johnnie Cochran, if you like, or F. Lee Bailey. The lawyer is not a student humbly asking Jesus for instruction. When he asks how to gain eternal life, he's baiting Jesus, testing him, asking a question to which he himself—as someone who is schooled in the law, and who knows that his question is essentially a question about the law—already knows the answer.

Jesus replies accordingly. "What is written in the law?" he asks. He knows the law, and he knows that the lawyer knows it too. Yet what Jesus' parable demonstrates is that for him, the commandment to love God and one's neighbor transcends all other laws. The lawyer, like the priests and Levites of Jesus' time, is horizontally fanatical, one might say, in his devotion to the letter of the law—to every last verse, that is, of Leviticus and Deuteronomy, some of which, as we know, were chillingly brutal toward those who violated the strictures regarding ritual purity.

That's why it is important that the traveler is left "half-dead." Looking at him, the priest and the Levite can't tell if he *is* dead; and because the letter of the law forbids them, as holy men, to touch the dead—an act which, like combining fabrics or having homosexual intercourse, was deemed a violation of the code of ritual purity, whose purpose was to keep the Jewish people distinct from other peoples in the region—they think it more important to cross to the other side of the road and avoid touching him, and thus avoid possible defilement, than to walk over to him and see if he needs care. By contrasting their actions with those of the Samaritan, Jesus compels the lawyer to recognize the Samaritan's love as superior to the rule-book mentality that the lawyer shares with the priest and the Levite.

It's important, then, that Jesus' questioner is a lawyer and that the victim is left half-dead. It's also important that the man of mercy is a Samaritan. No ancient people had a relationship to the Jews quite like that of the Samaritans, whose land lay sandwiched between Judea and Galilee. The Samaritans worshipped the Hebrew God and, like the Jews, regarded the Pentateuch (the first five books of the Hebrew Bible) as holy writ. Yet they were syncretists, which means that they combined Judaism with elements of other faiths; among other things, they believed that the expected Messiah would be a reincarnation of Moses. For centuries they'd had their own temple and lived in tension with the Jews, who considered them foreign, inferior, and semi-pagan. To the Jews, their religion was a mere cult.

The Samaritans were particularly despised in that era because of an incident that had taken place at Passover around the time of Jesus' birth. On that occasion, some Samaritans had defiled the court of the Jerusalem temple by strewing dead men's bones about the place. So for Jesus to suggest to a Judean lawyer that a Samaritan might attain eternal life, while a priest or Levite would not, was rather like telling a devout Roman Catholic in New York City, in the wake of the disruption of a mass at Saint Patrick's Cathedral a few years ago by the radical gay activist group ACT UP, that a member of ACT UP might be a better Christian than, say, New York's John Cardinal O'Connor.

The fact that the story of the good Samaritan has become a cliché makes it difficult for most of us to recognize how revolutionary a message it bears. Certainly for a Jewish lawyer in Jesus' day to accept this message would have required a radical leap of understanding. Any good Jew would have considered a Samaritan to be utterly outside of God's kingdom. For the lawyer—as for the rabbis—it went without saying that the word *neighbor* could refer only to fellow Jews. In the same way, if that Samaritan could be lifted up out of Jesus' story and set down among us today as an actual living person, practicing the same virtues that he does in the story and the same syncretist faith that an ancient Samaritan would have practiced, many Christians who purport to accept this story as a lesson in what Christianity means would insist that despite his virtues, this man's failure to confess Christ as his lord and savior condemns him to hell.

Yet the very point of this story is that in the only sense of the word that would have mattered to Jesus, *the Samaritan is a Christian.* He's a model of what it means to lead a Christlike life. He hasn't been baptized, he doesn't go to church. What he does is simply this: He loves his neighbor—and he recognizes that a neighbor is not just somebody who lives next door, or looks like him, or shares his beliefs and prejudices. A neighbor is simply another human being—any human being.

Those who belong to oppressed, despised, or disenfranchised groups may well read this story and recognize themselves in the figure of the Samaritan. They may feel affirmed by the fact that it is not the priest or the Levite, those symbols of the social and religious establishment, who prove to be good neighbors, but the Samaritan, the outcast. Jesus' message to his Judean audience—that a member of a group you despise may be a better neighbor to you and a better model of neighborliness *for* you than those whom you most respect—is one that many outcasts of our own time can hear with gratification.

But the story also offers those who are outcasts something more than mere affirmation. It presents them with a powerful challenge—a challenge to live in a world where many people despise them as fervently as first-century Jews despised Samaritans, and to love them anyway. It's a challenge not just to *say* that they love those who hate them; it's a lesson that tells them that to love is to *act* with love. It is to *do.* As the former Southern Baptist Convention president Jimmy Allen has written, "love in action is the only kind of love there is." To say this is not to abandon Protestantism's strong stand against what is called "works righteousness," the Roman Catholic doctrine that good works win us divine Brownie points; it's simply to say that real love—and real experience of the love of God on the vertical plane—always expresses itself in some kind of action on the horizontal plane. And that action— that acting out of love—is, as Jesus tells the lawyer, how you win eternal life. It's how you attain the kingdom of God, for the two terms are synonymous.

"Love the Lord . . . and your neighbor as yourself." What does it mean to be commanded to love? Can anyone love on command? It's a tall order, certainly; in some cases, a seemingly impossible one. In fact it is nothing less than a challenge to struggle constantly to overcome egotism, suspicion, and self-protectiveness, and to think in an entirely new way about one's relationship to others.

And it is a challenge that none of us meets perfectly. Is there, after all, a single person on earth who can act with love all the time, toward everyone? I doubt it. Nor do I think we're expected to. We *are* expected, however, to hold selfless love before us as the highest ideal— love, not the law.

The lawyer, of course, speaks of eternal life, of the kingdom, as if it were a payment in the afterlife for some specific deed or deeds in this life. Yet the story of the good Samaritan points to a radically different understanding. It cautions us not to disdain and disregard this present life when we seek the kingdom of God. The lawyer's question comes freighted with certain assumptions; Jesus turns those assumptions completely upside down. Loving your neighbor, he explains, is not an unpleasant burden that you take on in order to win some glorious prize beyond this life. The love, the shouldering of the burden, is itself the prize; in that love itself is the experience of the kingdom.

It's a great and a profoundly mystical truth, a truth conveyed by a simple story whose simplicity is its very point. It's a truth that many ordinary people have understood and embraced but that many highly sophisticated and theologically educated people—perhaps including a few popes—have failed to grasp. It's a truth that confounds those who think the whole point of Christianity is to win a happy afterlife for themselves by embracing this or that specific doctrine about God and his creation. Such self-centered, quid pro quo conceptions are the very essence of a horizontal mentality. Those of us who are Christians are expected to "die to self": What is this but another way of saying that in order to truly experience God and his love, we must let go of horizontal preoccupations and cease imagining eternity as a mere continuation of our own personal day-to-day existence?

The good Samaritan story is a classic example of the way Jesus taught. To be sure, the Gospel according to John presents Jesus as performing plenty of miracles, as speaking of himself continually in the first person ("I am the Way, the Truth, and the Light"), and as teaching by direct statement rather than by parable. Yet John's Gospel, which focuses less on the particulars of Jesus' earthly ministry than on abstract statements about the cosmic significance of Jesus' life, death, and resurrection, differs dramatically in these respects from the three other Gospels, which plainly are closer than John's to the actual story of Jesus' life and which are called synoptic because their accounts parallel one another in many respects. Of the Jesus that we encounter in those Gospels, we can say unequivocally that he rarely if ever taught by proffering theological statements of the kind in which organized churches have specialized for centuries. On the contrary, the synoptic Gospels depict a Jesus who taught through parables, who performed few miracles, and who never made public statements about himself. Jesus could have spent his ministry spelling out doctrines and telling his followers that they had to profess belief in these doctrines in order to attain eternal life; but the Jesus of the synoptic Gospels didn't do that at all. Instead, he served up parables, paradoxes, metaphors, and similes:

> The kingdom of heaven is like a grain of mustard seed which a man took and sowed in his field; it is the smallest of all seeds, but when it has grown it is the greatest of shrubs and becomes a tree, so that the birds of the air come and make nests in its branches.

> The kingdom of heaven is like leaven which a woman took and hid in three measures of meal, till it was all leavened.

Such similes drew on his listeners' experience of the real world—the horizontal plane—but they don't appeal at all to most people's horizontal values. Mustard seeds? Leaven? These are homely, mundane images. To be sure, they are both images that imply growth—the growth of a plant and of a loaf of bread, respectively. But they do not necessarily imply desirable growth. As the biblical scholar John Dominic Crossan has noted, the mustard plant, far from being welcome in most gardens, is a "pungent shrub" that "starts small and ends big," constantly threatening to "get out of control" and "take over where it is not wanted"; it is "something you would want only in small and carefully controlled doses—if you could control it." As for leaven, Crossan notes that it was in Jesus' time "a symbol of moral corruption"; in Jewish culture, where unleavened bread was part of sacred meals, leaven symbolized "the unholy everyday."

Why did Jesus employ these mundane images that bore connotations of bitter taste, rampant weedlike growth, and unholiness to convey the nature of what he called the kingdom of God or the kingdom of heaven or eternal life—terms which, by contrast with the mustard seed and the leaven, reach for the grandest concepts in space (kingdom) and time (eternity) that his listeners could grasp? He did so in order to challenge, to shock, to shake his listeners up and force them to look for the spiritual elsewhere than in the places where they had been accustomed to seek it out. Kingdom as mustard seed? Eternity as leaven? Though he drew his images from the ordinary daily life of his listeners, he sought in his teaching to convey, by reference to that ordinary experience, the nature of a mystery far beyond the quotidian—a mystery involving remarkable growth of a kind that was, in a sense, perfectly natural but that some might find repugnant, disturbing. Central to the effectiveness of these similes is that his listeners struggle in mind and heart and spirit to find their way to that experience.

What was Jesus' purpose? If John's Gospel is to be believed, Jesus answered this question himself: "I have come that they may have life, and may have it in all its fullness" (John 10:10). There is nothing here about heaven, hell, or substitutionary atonement—that is, the belief, first promulgated by Augustine early in the fifth century, that Christ's death on the cross took place because God the Father demanded that God the Son sacrifice his life in order to pay for the sins of humankind. When Jesus speaks of the purpose of his Incarnation, he refers to *life,* and does not draw a sharp distinction between this life and any other.

In reply to those who argued over the question of life after death, Jesus said, "God is not God of the dead but of the living; in his sight all are alive" (Luke 20:38). One can *feel* Jesus struggling to get his listeners to transcend their narrow, timebound way of understanding earthly existence and afterlife and to recognize human life instead as something that is always, inextricably, and mysteriously tied to God and that thus exists, in some ultimate sense, outside of time and space.

Today, legalistic Christians are taught to think about heaven in a very different way from that which Jesus intended. Many of them carry around in their minds an image of heaven that draws extensively on the visions described in the Book of Revelation. For more than a few of them, this image has been brought into focus by the depiction of heaven in Hal Lindsey's insipid—and disastrously influential—1970 book *The Late Great Planet Earth,* which presents heaven as a perfect vacation spot in the sky, where the saved will not only be eternally happy but will also have their appearances enhanced by the divine equivalent of plastic surgery. (I am not joking.) Legalistic theology of this sort, far from inviting Christians to enter into an intellectual and imaginative struggle toward a genuine vertical experience, demands instead that they assent blindly to an essentially horizontal set of propositions in order to gain entry to a heaven that is imagined in completely horizontal terms. Instead of embracing Lindsey's picture of heaven, it would be more spiritually edifying for legalistic Christians to look to Jesus' similes. This, however, calls for imagination and a capacity for mystical experience. It also fails to satisfy the desire for unequivocal answers to life's questions—and for concrete reward—that underlies many people's attraction to legalistic Christianity.

It is important to stress that Jesus didn't establish a doctrinal system or make theological demands. The relatively small number of verses attributed to him (mostly by John) in which he does say things that can be read as creedal statements, or in which he speaks of divine judgment and punishment, are philosophically and tonally at odds with everything else that he says and does, and have come to be recognized by many biblical scholars as later interpolations (though fundamentalists, of course, do not accept *anything* in the Bible as being inauthentic). In any event, most of the doctrines that are widely seen as essential to Christian belief were never mentioned by Jesus. At no point in the

Gospels, for instance, does he describe himself as having been born of a virgin. Saint Paul, at the beginning of his letter to the Romans, describes Jesus as being "on the human level . . . a descendant of David," which can mean only that Paul (whose letters predate the nativity stories in Matthew and Luke) regarded Joseph as Jesus' biological father. At no point, moreover, does Jesus even hint at the doctrine of substitutionary atonement. Yet these two doctrines—the virgin birth and substitutionary atonement—are key tenets for virtually all legalistic Christians; not to accept the veracity of both is, in their eyes, not to be a real Christian at all, and thus not to be truly saved.

As a boy, I was perplexed by a story in Luke's Gospel. Luke told how Jesus, at twelve, traveled with his parents to Jerusalem for Passover, and stayed behind when they returned to Nazareth with a large group of friends and relatives. Recognizing after a day's journey that Jesus was not in their party, Mary and Joseph went back to Jerusalem and, after three days, found him in the temple surrounded by the teachers, listening to them and asking questions. "And all who heard him," wrote Luke,

> were amazed at his intelligence and the answers he gave.
>
> His parents were astonished to see him there, and his mother said to him, "My son, why have you treated us like this? Your father and I have been anxiously searching for you."
>
> "Why did you search for me?" he said. "Did you not know that I was bound to be in my Father's house?"
>
> But they did not understand what he meant.

Didn't understand? This confused me. How could Mary and Joseph not understand? We had just finished reading Luke's nativity narrative, in which an angel tells Mary that her son had been conceived by the Holy Spirit and would be called the Son of God. Mary then delivers the prayer called the Magnificat, which begins, "My soul proclaims the greatness of the Lord, my spirit rejoices in God my Savior." When she gives birth, shepherds appear and tell her that they have just heard about her from an angel who described the child as "the messiah, the

Lord." And what of Matthew's Gospel, in which a star hovered over the manger, and wise men brought gifts, and Herod put a contract out on Jesus, forcing his parents to flee with him to Egypt? After all this, how could Mary be puzzled by Jesus' actions at age twelve? Had she forgotten everything? I was confused—but I didn't ask my Sunday-school teacher about any of this, for somehow I understood even then that one wasn't supposed to inquire about such things.

Years later, in my early twenties, I fell away from Christianity; I returned in my early thirties, still questioning my religion's truth claims. I didn't feel compelled to take the virgin birth literally; plainly this doctrine had been cooked up by ancient men who idealized female virginity. But the Resurrection was different. It was Christianity's central tenet, and for me it was a sticking point. I felt compelled to believe that Jesus had come back to life in exactly the way described in the Gospels. That wasn't easy. If honest with myself, I had to admit that a lie detector would register a lie if I said I believed in the Resurrection in that sense. I wondered if that was true of other people. Was it true of my rector? Of Billy Graham? Of the pope?

I struggled incessantly to believe that Jesus had walked out of his tomb and talked with his disciples. I felt I *had* to, because everything else about Christianity, as I understood it, made beautiful sense to me. Every Easter morning, my church would be so crowded, and the music and liturgy so glorious, and the congregation's shout that "The Lord is risen indeed!" so fervent—every aspect of the worship service, in short, would come together so sublimely to proclaim the all-transcending love of God and the profound significance and promise of human love—that for a precious instant it seemed impossible that such beauty and devotion could exist *unless* the stories of the Resurrection were literally true. In that moment (or so, at least, I told myself) I actually did believe. But during the rest of the year, the struggle to maintain that feeling was exhausting—and, usually, doomed. I knew that the Gospel according to Mark, which was probably the earliest Gospel, doesn't even contain any accounts of the post-Resurrection Jesus, and the accounts of the risen Christ in the other Gospels contradict one another in major ways. In a number of churches over the years, I heard sermons in which ministers defended the argument that Jesus had indeed returned to life after the Crucifixion. *Look at those details,* they would say. *Don't they seem authentic? Besides, why would Matthew lie? Why would Luke?* When I read in a book about the historical Jesus that his body had almost certainly ended up being devoured by birds, the image horrified me. I knew that deep down I believed this—and I didn't want to believe it.

Then I read works by Christian men and women who wrote about the Resurrection in ways that resonated with me very strongly. The important thing about the Resurrection, they pointed out, was that *something* extraordinary had happened after the Crucifixion to provide Jesus' demoralized followers with a profound illumination that turned their picture of things completely around and made them spend the rest of their lives preaching his Resurrection with all the fervor in the world. What form that illumination took ultimately doesn't matter. What matters is that it opened the disciples' eyes to the truths implicit in the way Jesus had lived and the things he had taught.

Jesus had been as deeply and remarkably human as anyone his disciples had ever known; and at the same time he had been touched by God in a way that seemed to them utterly without precedent. The two things—his profound humanity, and his intense closeness to God—were bound together inextricably, and at the heart of the mystery of that bond was love, a light that never went out. Jesus' execution horrified his disciples; yet in its wake they reflected on the man and his ministry. He had preached eternal life, which he had talked about in a mystical way and as a present reality; his teachings about God's kingdom were strange and new, and yet his words about that kingdom seemed to beckon them toward a truth that was powerfully affirmed in their hearts. As long as the eternal God existed, how could Jesus die? After the Crucifixion, something made them realize beyond a doubt and to the depths of their hearts that, in some mysterious sense, he *couldn't* die. And neither could they, in whose hearts he lived.

Understood simply as a miraculous physical reappearance, the Resurrection makes Jesus' life and teachings ultimately irrelevant; it is as if Jesus, during his ministry, had just been killing time until the Main Event. Understood as an illumination that grew directly out of everything Jesus had taught through his words and actions, however, the Resurrection became filled with meaning.

Certainly this was true for me: Clicking into this new understanding of the Resurrection, I felt as if a weight had fallen from me. Belief was no longer a struggle; now it all made sense. No longer did I worry about what this or that illustrious Christian really believed or didn't believe. I realized now that Christianity was not a matter of playing wearisome, dishonest, psychologically unhealthy mind games with oneself, or of leaning on the stronger beliefs of people in authority. It was a matter of truly having God within me. It was a matter of recognizing that faith is about dying to self—about totally, and joyfully, forsaking self-regard—and about striving toward a less earthbound and more God-bound mental posture in which one is freed from morbid, solipsistic preoccupation with one's own postmortem fate. It was a matter of recognizing in love a pointer to the fact that we all live in everlasting communion with a loving God who exists outside of our universe with its one temporal and three spatial dimensions, and that eternal life is accordingly not a matter of being transported after death to some other place but of sharing, in some mysterious way, in something external to space and time for which human language can have no words and toward which the human mind and heart can only reach in prayer, meditation, and love. It was a matter of realizing that salvation, paradoxically enough, is a matter of finding one's way to a psychological and spiritual place at which one can triumphantly and joyfully put one's own individual existence into the "Resurrection perspective."

This is, of course, not easy. Like believing in the literal Resurrection, it, too, is a struggle—but it is an honest struggle, a struggle to embrace something worthy and true. We might well fall to our knees and pray these words: "Lord, please take me out of my self; help me to be content that my love lives in others' love, my joy in others' joy, my thoughts in others' minds, as I know that the emotions that feel to me unique in their miraculousness have been felt and will be felt, as strongly and truly, by a billion others as worthy as I."

Tillich's concept of "God beyond God"—his recognition that there is something humanly unknowable beyond all theological doctrines— is a useful insight that made immediate sense to me when I first ran across it. Why can't we simply accept with humility, whatever our doctrinal differences, that we don't know all there is to know about God, and that we may actually be wrong about some things? Why must there be such powerful pressure from so many quarters to pretend that we know everything about God? Why can't we simply acknowledge that none of us is omniscient, and that above and beyond the various faith statements to which we subscribe is a single God who knows our hearts, understands our limitations, and loves us anyway?

Over the centuries, countless theologians and preachers have exhaustively discussed the things that Jesus said and did. Less attention has been paid to what he *didn't* say and do. His encounters with men and women in the Gospels are striking for the absence of any spelling out of theological specifics or any overt attempt at conversion. Except in John's Gospel, there is no mention of Jesus baptizing anybody; and John's implication that Jesus did baptize is unaccompanied by any suggestion that baptism was viewed by him or anyone as distinguishing insider from outsider. He presents the good Samaritan as a model, even though the Samaritan, at the end of the story, remains a Samaritan. The story of the good Samaritan, like other Gospel passages that cut to the heart of the Gospel message, makes it clear that for Jesus, evangelism was plainly not about bringing people into doctrinal conformity with himself or anyone else; it was about making people feel close to God and loved by God. It was about bringing people to a vertical *experience*—not about pressuring them, with threats of punishment or promises of reward, into accepting this or that horizontal *dogma*.

Huston Smith, the distinguished authority on religion, has written perceptively about this subject. "Instead of telling people what to do or what to believe," Smith writes in *The World's Religions,*

> he invited them to see things differently, confident that if they did so their behavior would change accordingly. This called for working with people's imaginations more than with their reason or their will. If listeners were to accept his invitation, the place to which they were being invited would have to seem real to them. So, because the reality his hearers were most familiar with consisted of concrete particulars, Jesus began with those particulars. He spoke of mustard seeds and rocky soil, of servants and masters, of weddings and of wine. These specifics gave his teachings an opening ring of reality; he was speaking of things that were very much a part of his hearers' worlds.

But having gotten them that far, having roused in them a momentum of assent, Jesus would then ride that momentum while giving its trajectory a startling, subversive twist. That phrase, "momentum of assent," is important, for its deepest meaning is that Jesus located the authority for his teachings not in himself or in God-as-removed but in his hearers' hearts. My teachings are true, he said in effect, not because they come from me, or even from God through me, but because (against all conventionality) your own hearts attest to their truth.

This passage offers a fair description of the way in which many non-legalistic Christians, down to the present day, understand Christianity. We turn to Jesus because something in us tells us to. We recognize, as did his disciples, that in Jesus, in some mysterious and sublime way, humanity encountered divinity. The seemingly paradoxical doctrine that Jesus was at once entirely God and entirely man—a doctrine that was defined at the Council of Chalcedon in A.D. 451—can be understood as an effort on the part of fifth-century Christians to express their powerful sense of Jesus as a unique bridge between Creator and Creation. This way of understanding Christianity could not be further removed from that of Pat Robertson, say, who encourages his followers to be suspicious of the testimony of their own minds and hearts. Today many legalistic Protestants are taught to see becoming a Christian as involving what Søren Kierkegaard called a leap of faith: One *decides* to believe, and, hurdling a chasm of doubt, establishes oneself in a fortress of faith, defending it ever after, without question or pause, from every violation of law, doctrine, and authority. Yet many nonlegalistic Christians balk at such an approach, which seems uncomfortably close to the ways in which Nazism and Stalinism operated; under these systems, as under every variety of totalitarian ideology, one was expected to defend the "faith" against any act or statement that contradicted it, however good that act or true that statement. To many nonlegalistic Christians, a Christianity that is understood in the same way seems a violation of what Jesus was really about.

"Jesus went about doing good," writes Smith. "He did so with such singlemindedness and effectiveness that those who were with him constantly found their estimate of him modulating to a new key. They found themselves thinking that if divine goodness were to manifest

itself in human form, this is how it would behave." As for the Crucifixion and Resurrection, these were not interpreted by early Christians
according to the theology of today's legalistic Christians—for whom
the cross is, quite prosaically and selfishly, about substitutionary atonement, and for whom the Resurrection (which is conceived in a totally
literal fashion) is about the promise of an afterlife. These events were,
rather, understood in a much more beautiful, meaningful, and selflessly
spiritual sense. As Smith puts it, the "claim" of the Resurrection
"extended ultimately to the status of goodness in the universe, con-
tending that it was all-powerful. . . . The resurrection reversed the cosmic position in which the cross had placed Jesus' goodness. Instead of
being fragile, the compassion the disciples had encountered in him was
powerful; victorious over everything, even the seeming end of everything, death itself."

Nothing could be more antithetical to the legalistic Christian
understanding of Christianity; for legalists, Christianity is about declaring one's acceptance of Jesus as savior (in much the way that a soldier
swears allegiance to his king) and in return being granted eternal life.
For legalists, suggesting that Christianity is ultimately about being good
is not only misguided—it is, quite literally, a teaching of the Devil. Yet
many people today become Christians (of the nonlegalistic variety) for
no other reason than that they respond to the Jesus that they find in
the Gospels—and in the sermons of a few special men and women—
in precisely the way that Huston Smith describes.

I know that I did. For many years I thought I had no need for any
kind of religion. Then something happened: I experienced an extraordinarily powerful love for another person. I experienced it as a mystery, a miracle, that was above and beyond all other human experiences.
It seemed to me to give meaning, shape, and dimension to my life, and
it seemed also to point toward the way in which my life connected to
the lives of other people and to some greater entity—a conscious, feeling entity—that subsumed all of us. That experience of love, in short,
challenged my whole understanding of the cosmos, for such love had
no place in the banal, mechanistic universe that I had imagined myself
to be living in.

I didn't immediately find my way back to Christianity. In fact I was
led to it, and resisted it. But I soon came to recognize that the religion

I was resisting made sense, as nothing else did, of everything I was feeling. For that religion told me that God is love; that the meaning of humankind's existence is tied up in some way with the reality of love; that our love for one another is a faint tracery of the love that God has for us; that Jesus, more than anyone who ever lived, at once modeled God's love for us and the way in which God wanted us to love him and one another. Jesus showed us that a life lived in love is an abundant life, and he came, as he told us, to bring us more abundant life. "In experiencing God as infinite love bent on people's salvation," writes Huston Smith, "Jesus was an authentic child of Judaism; he differed . . . only in not allowing the post-Exilic holiness code to impede God's compassion. Time after time, as in his story of the shepherd who risked ninety-nine sheep to go after the one that had strayed, Jesus tried to convey God's absolute love for every single human being. To perceive this love and to let it penetrate one's very marrow was to respond in the only way that was possible—in profound and total gratitude for the wonders of God's grace."

This passage (which I read for the first time only recently) provides a splendid summary of the way in which I came to understand Christianity: as a grateful and loving response to the love of God. And perceiving that love and allowing it to penetrate my marrow was not a matter of closing my eyes and taking a "leap of faith." It was a matter of opening my eyes and seeing something before me that I could not deny.

The experience of love, and the recognition of it as a reflection of God's own love, enabled me to believe that I, as well as everyone else, was indeed, as Christianity claimed, an infinitely precious child of God; yet at the same time it freed me from at least a degree of self-concern and made me recognize my obligation to struggle to grow as far as possible beyond that self-concern—to strive to reach a place at which I accepted the small place of my own life in the big picture of the universe, a place at which I cared about others—relatives, friends, strangers, even enemies—as much as I did about myself. Only by struggling to reach that place, I realized, could I be fully true to the love that I felt and that gave meaning to my life.

I read some theology, and I recognized in the best of it an attempt by people who had known this same experience to put its meaning into words. To read different theologians—good ones, anyway—was not like reading position papers by political parties that disagreed with one another; it was like reading love poems. No two of them were identical, but they pointed to the same category of experience, and the best of them resonated with readers who had firsthand knowledge of that category of experience. Because theology sought to convey a kind of knowledge and experience that transcended this life and this world, it could speak only in symbolic language, and was thus closer to art, music, or poetry than it was to biology or chemistry.

In the twelfth chapter of Mark, Jesus is described as walking in the court of the temple in Jerusalem with the chief priests, scribes, and elders of the Jewish people. They ask him questions, and he answers. Others join in. A group of Pharisees, who believe in the resurrection of the dead, and some "members of Herod's party" try to ensnare him with a question about the proper relationship of human beings to civil authorities; a group of Sadducees, who do not believe in the resurrection, try to trap him with a question about eternal life.

Finally one of the scribes asks an apparently sincere question: "Which is the first of all the commandments?"

Jesus replies by quoting from the fifth book of Moses in the Hebrew Scriptures. "The first is, 'Hear, O Israel: the Lord our God is the one lord, and you must love the Lord your God with all your heart, with all your soul, with all your mind, and with all your strength.' The second is this: 'You must love your neighbor as yourself.' No other commandment is greater than these."

"These are the most treasured verses of Judaism," note the editors of a standard biblical commentary. These verses are also at the heart of any true Christianity.

"Righteousness," the editors of the commentary point out, "is not to be understood as strict obedience to a complex code of laws and customs. The one commandment that is central is the principle of love." Jesus' unequivocal elevation of these verses above all other commandments demands that we test all scripture, all dogma, and even everything else that Jesus is reported to have said and done against this commandment, which many Christians call the Great Commandment, and which Anglicans call the Summary of the Law—for, mystery of mysteries, law itself is summed up in a law that not only allows but compels violation of lesser laws. "When there is wholehearted love for the All, for the universal good we might say," writes Huston Smith, "then the will wants that good and needs no rules."

This doesn't mean all law is null and void; it means laws that separate people from one another—that divide neighbor from neighbor and that compel unloving actions—are considered to be overridden. So it is, for example, that Christians have from the beginning set aside the strictures enumerated in the "Holiness Code" in Leviticus, which was intended to distinguish the Jews from other peoples (and which, incidentally, includes the verses most often cited against homosexuality) but which calls for brutal punishments for essentially innocuous acts. Jesus, writes Huston Smith, subscribed to much of the law but

> *found unacceptable . . . the lines that it drew between people. Beginning by categorizing acts and things as clean or unclean (foods and their preparation, for example), the holiness code went on to categorize people according to whether they respected those distinctions. The result was a social structure that was riven with barriers: between people who were clean and unclean, pure and defiled, sacred and profane, Jew and Gentile, righteous and sinner. Having concluded that Yahweh's central attribute was compassion, Jesus saw social barriers as an affront to that compassion. So he parlayed with tax collectors, dined with outcasts and sinners, socialized with prostitutes, and healed on the sabbath when compassion prompted doing so. This made him a social prophet, challenging the boundaries of the existing order and advocating an alternative vision of the human community.*

People (of whatever sexual orientation) often ask how one can be both gay and Christian. But as this passage from Smith makes clear, Christianity properly understood—understood, that is, in a way that is consistent with what Jesus and his earthly ministry were really about—does not reject outcasts but befriends them, welcomes them, loves them.

Love, not law; experience, not doctrine: This, at its heart, is what Christianity is about—or should be about, if it takes its Founder seriously.

3

LOVE AND LAW

THE CHRISTIAN COMMUNITY'S first belief statement was simple: "Jesus is Lord!" This was the extent of their theology, its alpha and omega. Since their religion was about loving community and closeness to God, they apparently felt no urgent need to elaborate upon this statement, to systematize their faith intellectually, to go into details. Their faith was not about giving intellectual assent to a certain set of propositions that had been formulated by someone else; it was about the powerful sense that they all shared of having been touched by God's love in the person of Jesus Christ, and of having sensed that in some mysterious way Jesus, more surely and more powerfully than anyone else who had ever lived, had been an expression of what God was like and had been a model of what men and women, who had been created in God's image, should strive to be like. The doctrine of the Trinity, which states that Jesus, with God the Father and God the Holy Spirit, is one of three "persons" that make up a single deity, had not yet been precisely formulated, and presumably the need for such a doctrine was not yet felt. The first Christians knew what they were experiencing, and they knew that since nothing like it had ever happened before, there were no words in any human language to express fully and properly the way in which Jesus had transformed and illuminated their relationship to God and to their fellow human beings. "See how they love one another!" exclaimed non-Christians in amazement when they observed these people in action. One might say that what set the early Christians apart from others was that they *didn't* set some people apart from others: Among them there was, as Saint Paul declared, no slave or free, no Greek or Jew, no male or female. Theirs was, by all indications, a true Church of Love.

Things didn't stay that way, however. It was Paul himself who laid the groundwork for the Church of Law. Originally a Pharisee named Saul of Tarsus who had viciously persecuted Christians, Paul became a member of the new sect after being vouchsafed (he believed) a vision of Christ, who (we are told) appeared in other visions to members of the fledgling Christian community and declared that Paul was his "chosen instrument" to spread his name to the world. So it was that Paul became the movement's first major theologian. Yet if Jesus had taught largely through parables, Paul set forth specific doctrinal statements. To be sure, some of the things he wrote about the new religion of Jesus Christ place him squarely within the Church of Love:

> What can separate us from the love of Christ? Can affliction or hardship? Can persecution, hunger, nakedness, danger, or sword? . . . I am convinced that there is nothing in death or life, in the realm of spirits or superhuman powers, in the world as it is or the world as it shall be, in the forces of the universe, in heights or depths—nothing in all creation that can separate us from the love of God in Christ Jesus our Lord. (Rom. 8:31–39)

> If I have no love, I am nothing. . . . Love is patient and kind. Love envies no one, is never boastful, never conceited, never

rude; love is never selfish, never quick to take offence. Love
keeps no score of wrongs, takes no pleasure in the sins of others,
but delights in the truth. There is nothing love cannot face. . . .
Love will never come to an end. . . . There are three things that
last forever: faith, hope, and love; and the greatest of the three
is love.

Make love your aim. (1 COR. 13:4–8,13,14:1)

Other propositions from the books traditionally ascribed to Paul, however, foreshadow the Church of Law. Indeed, some of the following
passages are among those most quoted and preached upon by legalistic Christian ministers:

Should anyone, even I myself or an angel from heaven, preach a
gospel other than the gospel I preached to you, let him be
banned! (GAL. 1:8–9)

What you say must be in keeping with sound doctrine. . . .
[Women must] be temperate, chaste, busy at home, and kind,
respecting the authority of their husbands. . . . Slaves are to
respect their masters' authority in everything and to give them
satisfaction. . . . Remind everyone to be submissive to the government and the authorities. . . . If someone is contentious, he
should be allowed a second warning; after that, have nothing
more to do with him, recognizing that anyone like that has a distorted mind and stands self-condemned in his sin. (TITUS 2:1, 2:5,
2:9, 3:1, 3:10–11)

Every person must submit to the authorities in power, for all
authority comes from God, and the existing authorities are instituted by him. It follows that anyone who rebels against authority is resisting a divine institution, and those who resist have
themselves to thank for the punishment they will receive. Gov-
ernments hold no terrors for the law-abiding but only for the
criminal. You wish to have no fear of the authorities? Then continue to do right and you will have their approval, for they are
God's agents working for your good. But if you are doing wrong,

then you will have cause to fear them; it is not for nothing that
they hold the power of the sword, for they are God's agents of
punishment bringing retribution on the offender. (ROM. 13:1–4)

In this passage from his letter to the Romans, Paul seems to have forgotten for the moment that Jesus himself had resisted authority and
been viewed as an offender by government officials, at whose hands he
suffered the ultimate punishment. Jesus had said, "Render under Caesar that which is Caesar's," but he had never suggested that his Roman
oppressors were the agents of God.

In the King James Bible, the word *law* appears in the synoptic
Gospels only thirteen times altogether, and crops up a dozen or so
times in John. In the Acts of the Apostles and the letters of Paul, by
contrast, the word appears scores of times. Given Paul's background as
a Pharisee—a lawyer who believed strongly in the letter of the law—
this is not surprising: Indeed, Paul's writings shift frequently back and
forth between an understanding of God that derives clearly from the
teachings of Jesus about love and an understanding of God that reveals
the continuing influence on Paul of pharisaical patterns of thought. In
the contradictions within Paul's heart and mind—the contradictions,
one might say, between Saul the Pharisee and Paul the Apostle—one
can see some of the first inklings of what would be a two-millennium-
long struggle between the Church of Law and the Church of Love.

Of course, it hardly took Paul to bring this struggle into being.
Human beings are what they are. The first Christians expected Jesus to
return imminently and usher in the end of the world; as that expectation gradually faded, and as each new generation of early Christians
succeeded the last, human frailties predictably reasserted themselves.
Some people crave power over others; some people ache just as desperately for other people to be in charge and to tell them what's true
and what isn't and what they should and shouldn't do. A sense of spiritual fullness can dissipate over time; unconditional love for one's
neighbors can give way to an irritation at them and a perceived need
to set and enforce rules and boundaries, to define rights and responsibilities, to found institutions and invest them with authority. With
time, the desire to separate people into categories also reasserted itself.

As time went by, then, fewer and fewer Christians had a constant and transforming sense of being filled with Jesus' love. Once, it had been clear who was and wasn't a Christian: Christians were people who lived in community with other Christians and were charged with the undiscriminating love and presence of Jesus; now, as the number of Christians rose and as the passionate devotion of the early Christian community abated, many Christians felt a need for something other than their intense experience of Jesus by which they could define themselves. Once, the statement "Jesus is Lord" had been all they needed by way of a declaration of faith; now that many Christians' souls were less powerfully charged with that mystical truth, the Christian community felt a need for more elaborate statements of belief.

At first, such statements posed no problem. "The original confessions of faith," notes the distinguished Swiss theologian Hans Küng, "were in no way concerned with dogmas in the present-day sense. They were not doctrinal laws." Far from representing "a legal foundation," the early confessions were "a free expression of the faith of the community." But that soon changed as the concept of orthodoxy began to take hold. And when some doctrines were made orthodox at four councils in the fourth and fifth centuries, it was usually not because the community of the faithful all shared the same understanding of things, but because someone with power was forcing his understanding of things on others.

"The theology which became manifest at the councils," writes Küng, "led to a considerable alienation fron the New Testament. In four centuries the simple and easily understandable baptismal formula in Matthew ["I baptize you in the name of Jesus"] had become a highly complex trinitarian speculation." The concept of orthodoxy ("this unbiblical word") was now all-important; and along with orthodoxy came the concept of heresy. The fourth-century Roman emperor Theodosius the Great "made Christianity a state religion, the Catholic church a state church and heresy a state crime"; thus "it took less than a century for the persecuted church to become a persecuting church. . . . For the first time Christians killed other Christians over a difference in faith." (They also began to kill Jews—for the same impulse that gave birth to institutional creeds and hierarchies also gave new life to anti-Semitism.) As the community of Christian believers developed into an institutional and dogmatic church, and as the faithful became divided hierarchically into a clergy that established laws and creeds and a laity that was expected to be perfectly pliant, Christianity came to be understood, writes Küng, "less and less as existential discipleship of Jesus Christ and more—in an intellectual narrowing—as the acceptance of a revealed doctrine about God and Jesus Christ, the world and human beings."

Christianity's most influential doctrine-maker by far was Augustine of Hippo (354–430), who put such concepts as original sin, election, and predestination at the center of Christian theology in the west. Part of the reason why he and other so-called church fathers began to work out a theological understanding of the faith, of course, was an admirable intellectual curiosity. What *did* it mean to say that Jesus was Lord, and that he was still alive? Was Jesus man or God or both? If both, how? What was the relationship between God and Jesus, and between Jesus' humanity and divinity, and what was the relationship of both of these to the Holy Spirit that Jesus had spoken of? What was the meaning of his death?

An exhaustive study entitled *The Faith of the Early Fathers,* which enjoys the official approval of the Roman Catholic Church, identifies no fewer than 1,046 distinct doctrines that were propounded by one or more of the early church fathers. These doctrines concern such matters as the authority of scripture, tradition, and the church, the nature of God and Jesus, the soul, faith, hope, sin, grace, justification, the sacraments, worship, death, judgment, and heaven. Of these 1,046 doctrines, only nine concern love. Love figures far less frequently in the works of most of the church fathers, in fact, than almost every other subject treated by them. In the centuries that followed, the church continued to add doctrines to which members were compelled to declare their assent. Some of these involved concepts that early Christians had certainly never conceived of. In 1950, for instance, Pope Pius XII declared that the Virgin Mary, at her death, had been taken up bodily into heaven, and that Catholics were required to believe this. Now, it is hard to know what this doctrine can mean, since in order to believe it one has to conceptualize heaven as a place in the sky to which a physical body can travel. Moreover, since this idea had not occurred to anybody until late in the fourth century, and had never been a part of standard church teaching, virtually all Christians who lived before the twentieth century would be heretics in the eyes of the church if they were somehow transported to the present and asked for an accounting of their beliefs.

By later Roman Catholic standards, then, the early Christians would all have been considered apostates destined for hell. The Roman Catholic Church has tried to skirt this problem by proclaiming that new doctrines are examples of "progressive revelation." "It is possible," wrote the nineteenth-century Catholic historian Philip Schaff, "for the church to be in possession of a truth and to live upon it, before it has come to be discerned in her consciousness." In other words, the early Christians all really believed in doctrines that weren't developed till centuries later; they just didn't *know* they believed in them.

This bizarre dodge notwithstanding, the fact remains that the Roman Catholic Church's leadership has exhibited for centuries a ferocious need to systematize the faith in ever-greater detail and to demand total allegiance to it. This kind of faith, of course, is utterly different in kind from that of the early Christians; for it is a faith primarily defined not by vertical experience but by an assent in the horizontal plane to a set of propositions. I was amazed as a teenager when I discovered that Roman Catholic friends who regularly attended mass didn't make any attempt to get into the experience of it; the very idea was alien to them. They had been taught that they had to show up every week and take Communion; it didn't matter if, while they did so, their minds were on yesterday's TV show or tomorrow's ball game. As long as you performed the act, you had carried out your side of the deal, and God would carry out his. A deal: That's what it was, not an experience; a horizontal event, not a vertical one. In this kind of religion, the basic idea is that the average believer is expected to follow rules laid down for behavior on the horizontal plane, while the church takes care of the vertical.

That's not a good thing. Which is not to dismiss theology. Theology is valuable to the extent that it represents the effort of an individual to capture his or her experience of God. Honest, intelligent attempts of this kind can be of value to all believers as they, too, seek to understand and articulate their own experience of God. Theology is bad to the extent that it is prescriptive and official; theology that forces Christians to deny their own experience of God and to declare their allegiance to a set of propositions that may run contrary to that experience is destructive of true spirituality. At its worst, indeed, such theology can deprive Christians of access to the vertical dimension and keep them yoked to the horizontal. Further, such theology can encourage them to think that some of their horizontal experiences are in fact experiences of God. (It is people with this kind of horizontal faith, for example, who rush to see weeping Madonna paintings and the like, thinking that this is how one encounters God.)

The Roman Catholic Church has always represented itself as being in sole possession of the truths of the soul. Yet during John Paul II's papacy, the church has punished some of its most brilliant members for seeking the truth when that search has taken them, as it was bound to do if they were being honest with themselves, afield in any way from official doctrine. A notable case is that of Hans Küng, who helped shape the theological agenda of Vatican II but who in later years, on orders from John Paul II, was dismissed from a theology professorship at a Catholic university. It is sometimes said that churches that insist on theological rigidity are devoted to truth; but in fact such a posture reflects not a genuine concern with truth but a desire for control, order, discipline, and a false show of unanimity. A church that really cares about truth gives its most intelligent communicants free rein—as responsible scientific institutions do—to explore, to examine, to share their insights, and to challenge, correct, and learn from the insights of others.

There have, of course, always been Christians who took on the institutional church, placing love above law. Supreme among these, in pre-Reformation history, was Francis of Assisi. As Jesus had challenged the Pharisees to resist institutional, legalistic thinking and to give priority to God's commandment to love, so Francis challenged the pope and his bishops to do the same. In this regard, Francis was a forerunner of the great Protestant reformers, who, seeing the Roman Catholic Church as irredeemably committed to legalism, broke away from it in hopes of establishing less legalistic bodies of worship; the difference is that Francis remained a loyal member of the church and never rejected its authority to speak for God, to set laws, and to establish doctrines.

Born late in 1181 or early in 1182, Francis was a worldly youth who dressed stylishly and spent his father's money on amusements. At twenty-five, soon after setting out for the Crusades, he heard a voice telling him to return home. He did, and began to dress plainly and to give his good clothes—and money—to beggars. At first mocked and stoned in Assisi, he came to be tolerated, then respected. Like Christ, he began to draw disciples to his side, a development that wasn't part of his original intent. The Franciscan order just *happened*. Why? Part of the reason lies in his simplicity of life, thought, and expression. His "Canticle of the Sun" (now considered the first great poem in Italian), his letters, and the rules he wrote for his order reflect a firm and uncomplicated conviction that human beings were put on earth to praise, serve, and rejoice. As Küng has noted, Francis is of all medieval figures the one with whose view of Christ today's Christians can most readily identify. No intellectual giant, no maker of systematic doctrine, he appeals to many Christians' antipathy for abstruse formulations. His warning that knowledge could be self-destructive—a warning motivated by his belief that theological discourse had severed the clergy from God's pure message of love and from the laypeople they were called to serve—speaks loudly to the anti-intellectualism of the average man or woman in the average pew.

For scholars, this aspect of Francis can be troubling. Yet it was the farthest Francis could go in challenging the idea of institutional orthodoxy. In the time and place in which he lived, the notion that theology didn't necessarily have to be laid down by the church hierarchy, and that every individual with a mind should use it to be his or her own theologian, as it were, wasn't even on the table. In practice, of course, Francis *was* his own theologian—but he was not a systematizer, and was certainly not an imposer of theology on others. "In whatever way you think you will best please our Lord God and follow in His footprints and in His poverty," he wrote one of his companions, "take that way with the Lord God's blessing." In saying this, the most popular of Christian saints was anticipating the most radical of Protestant theological tenets: the idea that in matters of faith, individual conscience is paramount. Francis even saw the heathen as his brothers—a novel idea in thirteenth-century Europe, where Crusaders were promised heavenly rewards for slaughtering infidels. Traveling in 1219 to Egypt, he bravely crossed the Crusaders' battle lines to meet the Egyptian sultan, Malek El-Kamil, whom he sought to convert and whose nephew he accompanied to a mosque, where he prayed, saying, "God is everywhere."

Francis exercised what is nowadays called prophetic obedience. Though he disobeyed ecclesiastical authority from time to time, he never did so without the firm conviction that he was obeying a higher authority—namely, God's law of love. (It seems reasonable, incidentally, to suggest that Francis's reluctance to produce a rule for his order grew out of an admirable disinclination to impose on his followers any theological or behavioral test.) For all his rebelliousness, however, Francis remained a loyal Roman Catholic who accepted the right of his church's hierarchy to formulate and enforce doctrine. It took Luther, Calvin, Zwingli, and the other leaders of the Protestant Reformation to deny this right. To be sure, they did not abandon the idea of institutional orthodoxy. Luther's followers were obliged to accept the doctrines outlined in a document called the Augsburg Confession; Calvin's were equally compelled to embrace the Westminster Confession.

A third important Protestant tradition was somewhat different in this regard. Anglicanism grew out of the unique historical circumstances of late sixteenth- and early seventeenth-century England, which was marked by a powerful sense of national identity and whose populace was split between Catholics and Protestants. Long before the Protestant Reformation, the English church was notorious for its sense of independence. Finally severed from Rome under Henry VIII—whose principal opposition was not to Catholic doctrine but to papal authority (and whose principal motive for the break with Rome, as everyone knows, was his wish to divorce the first of his six wives)—the Anglican Church took shape theologically under Henry's three children: Edward VI, a firm Protestant who reigned for six years, long enough to institute the first Book of Common Prayer, a decidedly Protestant document; Mary I, a devout Catholic who reigned for five years, long enough to reinstate certain Catholic practices that Edward had proscribed; and finally the pragmatic Elizabeth, who in her forty-four-year reign labored brilliantly to forge not only a society but an established church that was broad enough to include all but the most extreme Catholics and Protestants.

The result was—and is—a church of astonishing theological

breadth. But it is not breadth in a lax, lazy, anything-goes sense. The Anglican Church, when truest to its own theological traditions, views the mind not as a potential instrument of the Devil but as a gift of God. And it takes seriously the idea of the community of faith as a context within which people from different backgrounds and with varying perspectives can openly share their experiences of God, can attend to one another in a spirit of love, and can thereby gain insights that may help every member of the community to move somewhat closer to God's truth. Defenders of strict church orthodoxy argue that any organization has the right to make its own rules and to say who is qualified to be a member and who isn't; part of the genius of Anglicanism is the recognition that the church, if it takes itself seriously as the body of Christ, is *not* just another organization.

This understanding of the nature of the church can be traced back to the theologian Richard Hooker (1554–1600), who maintained that corporate spiritual truths could best be arrived at as a consequence of institutional openness and tolerance for breadth of belief. He also stressed the importance of distinguishing between essential core doctrines that everyone shared and inessential, peripheral doctrines on which people could respectfully differ.

The Anglican theologian John E. Booty notes several key ingredients of Anglicanism that derive from Hooker. In all these aspects, Anglicanism contrasts sharply with today's Protestant fundamentalism. If Anglicanism has, in Booty's words, a "positive attitude toward God," who is seen as a merciful deity desiring "the salvation of all people and of all creation," fundamentalism focuses not on a God of love but on a God of wrath and judgment who will grant salvation to the few; if Anglicanism emphasizes "the holy, the beautiful, the good and the true," fundamentalism is indifferent to beauty, places less value on goodness than on doctrinal correctness, and upholds the "true" not as something to be sought through honest inquiry but as something that, having already been definitively laid out by preachers and "reference Bibles," is to be mindlessly and uncritically embraced; if Anglicanism believes in "every Christian's responsibility for the welfare of every other living being," fundamentalism encourages believers to attend to their own souls (and those of their nearest and dearest) and not to care overmuch for the welfare of others (especially nonfundamentalists).

Anglicanism is not utterly without dogma. For centuries its doctrine

was spelled out in the thirty-nine (originally forty-two) "Articles of
Religion." Yet these Articles were worded in such a way as to strike an
acceptable balance among Lutheran, Calvinistic, and Zwinglian beliefs
and to be acceptable to all but the most die-hard Roman Catholics, at
one extreme, and, at the other, the radical Anabaptists (who, like their
Baptist posterity today, rejected infant baptism and affirmed the
"believer's baptism"). Confessional orthodoxy has never been an Anglican priority.

Nor do I mean to deny that like every other major religious institution, the Anglican Church and its American counterpart, the Episcopal Church, have terrible blots on their histories; among other
things, both churches have, to an extraordinary degree, always been
fruitful breeding grounds for snobbism and hypocrisy. Yet one must
distinguish the church at its worst from the theological system at its
best. And the fact is that, of all the major institutional approaches to
doctrine that grew out of the Protestant revolt, the Anglican theological method most surely commends itself to those who seek an intellectually solid, broadly inclusive foundation for a true Church of Love.

The Anglican Church, of course, had been the established national
church of most of the colonists who first settled North America. Yet
if the history of English-speaking Canada has been marked by
Anglican-style religious amity, the United States has, since its inception, been a country of powerful sectarian tensions and is today far
more torn between legalistic Christianity and secularism than any
nation in western Europe. These tensions can be traced to the conflict
between the two very different worldviews that predominated in colonial America and in the young Republic. One of these worldviews was
the Puritanism brought to America by the early Massachusetts settlers.
Despite their rejection of Catholicism, the Puritans mirrored the
Roman emphasis on orthodoxy and authority; and that emphasis has
been retained by their twentieth-century spiritual heirs. The first Puritans came to America in 1630 less because they sought religious freedom than because they considered themselves to be God's Elect and
saw the virgin continent as a second Eden where they could be American Adams who, this time, would not succumb to Satan's temptations.

Many of them also identified the New World with the postapocalyptic New Jerusalem of the Book of Revelation. Their apocalyptic emphasis and their conviction that America is somehow special in God's sight live on today in the hearts of their legalistic heirs.

The Puritans were Calvinists, which means, among much else, that they considered some people to be Elect—destined from birth for heaven—and some not. As Karen Armstrong observes, God "did not seem to imbue them [Puritans] with either happiness or compassion. Their journals and autobiographies show that they were obsessed with predestination and a terror that they would not be saved. Conversion became a central preoccupation, a violent, tortured drama. . . . Often the conversion represented a psychological abreaction, an unhealthy swing from extreme desolation to elation." The Puritans placed a "heavy emphasis on hell and damnation"; Satan "seemed as powerful a presence in their lives as God. . . . at its worst, the Puritan god inspired anxiety and a harsh intolerance of those who were not among the elect." All these attributes of Puritanism—the agonized preoccupation with the threat of hellfire and the drama of conversion, the overwhelming sense of the reality of Satan and of a wrathful God, and the profound sense of distance and opposition between the saved and the unsaved—remain, to this day, identifying characteristics of legalistic Christianity in America.

If Anglicanism stressed the love of God for all humankind, the Puritans, rebelling not only against the Roman papacy but against Anglicanism's generally congenial image of God (as well as what they saw as its worldliness, insufficient attention to sin, and high-toned worship), introduced into Christianity an extreme focus on divine wrath. Fearing God's retribution against wicked man, they saw European culture as being too tolerant of evil and sought to establish a despotic theocracy. The Puritans' censorious attitude toward the London theater is replicated in the attitude of legalists today toward Hollywood movies and network TV. In many ways, indeed, the present American "culture war" between secular humanists and legalists replays the seventeenth-century English conflict between Anglican breadth and Puritan narrowness. Like many of today's American legalists, the English Puritans warned that cultural depravity would bring down God's punishment on the nation and sought political power so that they might prohibit certain behaviors. In 1642, after the Puritans won control of Parliament, it was decreed that in order to "appease and avert the wrath of God, . . . public stage plays shall cease and be forborne." Laws were also passed against swearing, which included saying such things as "God is my witness."

The second seminal influence on American culture was that of the Enlightenment philosophy of the French Revolution, with its emphasis on individual experience, reason, reflection, and the possibility of positive change. This philosophy strongly influenced America's founding fathers and helped shape the scientific method, the twentieth-century democratic sensibility, and the category of religious belief (popular among eighteenth-century intellectuals) known as deism, which dismissed revealed religion and divine intervention while affirming the existence of a loving Creator. (The deists' denial of Jesus' divinity became the distinguishing characteristic of the Unitarian Church, to which many educated nineteenth-century New Englanders belonged.)

Central to the Religious Right's political program is the claim—made repeatedly by Pat Robertson and other leaders—that the United States was founded as a "Christian nation." Consider the following:

- The right-wing American Family Association sponsors a nationwide student group whose members subscribe to a covenant declaring, "I deserve to know what our founders taught, how they lived and the Christian principles upon which America was founded."

- At the second presidential debate in 1996, which followed a "town hall" format, a minister asked Bob Dole the following question: "This great nation has been established by the founding fathers who possessed a very strong Christian beliefs [sic] and godly principles. If elected president of the United States, what could you do to return this nation to these basic principles?"

- Pat Robertson, in his book *The New Millennium,* contrasts the American Revolution, which "produced a constitution and a government based on biblical principles of Christianity," with the

French Revolution, which "was, at its core, anti-Christian." Among those that Robertson quotes approvingly is Gary Amos, a faculty member at Regent University (founded by Robertson), whose book *Defending the Declaration* argues that the Declaration's framers were indeed Christians according to Protestant legalists' narrow conception of the term.

- Addressing the Christian Coalition's 1996 convention, Senator Jesse Helms claimed that Benjamin Franklin told the Constitutional Convention that "we are forgetting the Providence from whom we receive all our blessings" and that America was "born in His [God's] name." According to Helms, Franklin then suggested that the delegates all "get down on our knees and pray." Helms admitted that historians deny the incident ever happened, but he offered no evidence that it *did* happen; indeed, he seemed to be implying either that historians were conspiring to misrepresent the incident or that the truth should not stand in the way of a story that serves the Religious Right's purposes. Helms drew from his anecdote the conclusion that "this nation was created in God's name and with His grace, and we have made the mistake of forgetting it." America, he said, "was intended to be" a Christian nation, "and I will argue with anybody who says that's wrong."

Another version of Helms's Franklin quotation appeared in a special 1995 religion issue of the conservative journal *American Enterprise* that also cited passages from Madison, Adams, Washington, Webster, and Lincoln. The quotations were meant to show that "America was founded as a religious sanctuary," that the founding fathers were actively interested in promoting religion, and that they didn't think the federal government "should be strictly neutral in the contest between agnosticism, atheism, and religious faith." (Why Webster and Lincoln were included in a list of founding fathers was not clear.) Typical of the quoted passages are the following:

> FRANKLIN: *Have we forgotten that powerful Friend? Or do we imagine we no longer need His assistance? . . . God governs the affairs of men. . . . I therefore beg that henceforth prayers imploring the assistance of Heaven . . . be held in this assembly every morning, before we proceed to business.*

ADAMS: The highest glory of the American revolution was this: that it connected in one indissoluble bond the principles of Christianity with the principles of civil government.

WASHINGTON: Let us with caution indulge the supposition that morality can be maintained without religion. . . . It is impossible to govern rightly without God and the Bible.

For *American Enterprise* to serve these quotations up as evidence that the founding fathers were devout Christians by today's legalistic standard is ludicrous. What they reflect is less profound piety or Christian boosterism than a pragmatic recognition of religion as a force for social stability and a spur to moral action.

Ralph Reed, who until recently served as the executive director of the Christian Coalition, vociferously denies in his 1996 book, *Active Faith,* that the organization views America as a Christian nation. Yet in March 1997, Reed's then boss, Robertson, gave over an entire hour of *The 700 Club* to hawk a new videotape claiming that America is indeed a Christian nation. Entitled *Victory in Spite of All Terror* and produced by Robertson's Christian Broadcasting Network, the videotape asserted that Americans were God's special people, created for the sole purpose of spreading the gospel. Yet, beginning in the 1920s, they had turned their backs on this purpose, "trad[ing] God's mission for worldly pursuits." The videotape recounts the ensuing "battle for America": In the twenties, people like Margaret Sanger and Clarence Darrow "attempted to humiliate God"; in the thirties, under FDR, "America shifted its trust from God to government"; in later decades, the Supreme Court, which in 1878 had affirmed that "this is a Christian nation," betrayed America's Christian heritage by removing prayer, religion classes, and Bibles from public schools. An ad for the videotape on CBN's official Web site proclaimed: "America stands at the crossroads of history! . . . Will we honor our centuries-old covenant, or turn our back on destiny?" The videotape made it clear that for Robertson and his constituents, the conviction that America is a Christian nation is fundamental. It is what "the battle for America" is all about.

Again and again, legalistic Christians go back to the beginning—the founding fathers—to make their case. Robertson, in one of his books, contends that the founding fathers were indeed Christians by his definition, and quotes from their writings to support this claim. Yet his citations are from official documents containing formulaic references to the deity that anyone then would have been in the habit of employing. Robertson notes, for example, that Washington dated his signature to the Constitution "In the year of our Lord, 1787." Robertson's ludicrous comment: "There was only one Lord whose birthday dated back 1787 years: Jesus Christ. The founding document of the United States of America acknowledged the Lordship of Jesus Christ, because we were a Christian nation." Robertson cites the founding fathers in the same dishonest, proof-texting way that he cites biblical passages, taking them out of context and insisting that they mean something that, when read in context, they plainly do not.

Even as he distorts the founding fathers' record on religion, Robertson accuses his opponents of doing so. On July 2, 1996, he complained on *The 700 Club* that "There has been a revision of history reminiscent of the book *1984*" on the part of people who want to deny that the founding fathers were Christians. The United States, Robertson insisted, was founded by "devout Christians." Jefferson, he said, "was claimed to be a deist but he was much more of a Christian than many that claim to be Christian today." Robertson admitted that Thomas Paine—who, unlike the other founding fathers, wrote extensively about his religious views—was a deist, but maintained that most of the founders "were deeply committed to the historic Christian religion." Routine passing references to the founding fathers are common on Robertson's program. For example, on December 5, 1996, the day after a Hawaii court ruled in favor of same-sex marriage, Robertson told his *700 Club* audience that "Jefferson said . . . our liberties are a gift of God," but that "we are trampling on God's law" and risking his wrath through such actions as the Hawaii ruling.

Were the founding fathers Christians by today's legalistic standards? The record shows unequivocally that they were not. To examine writings by the principal framers of the Declaration (Jefferson, Franklin, and Adams), by the chief author of the Constitution (Madison), and by the "father of our country" (Washington) is to note the striking degree to which they all shared attitudes toward religion that Robertson would definitely *not* consider Christian.

First, all these men emphasized the supreme importance of individual reason and conscience—*not* ecclesiastical authority and dogma—in the shaping of personal faith. Jefferson said that he was "not generally disposed to seek my religion out [i.e., outside] of the dictates of my own reason and feelings of my own heart." Our first president agreed; his biographer James Thomas Flexner wrote that "Washington could not accept conclusions on the basis of authority or long-standing belief; he was no mystic, he felt he did not know and could never know." Virtually all the founding fathers would have agreed with Madison's statement that there is a natural "finiteness of human understanding" when it comes to matters of the spirit.

For the founding fathers, what followed from this recognition of man's limited understanding of God and his universe was that reasonable people should not be dogmatic and should respect others' rights to believe as they wished. Madison asserted that "the Religion then of every man must be left to the conviction and conscience of every man." Washington wrote to General Lafayette that he was "no bigot myself to any mode of worship" and was "disposed to indulge the professors of Christianity in the church, that road to heaven which to them shall seem the most direct, plainest, easiest, and least liable to exceptions." Washington added that he didn't care which religion immigrants to the United States might profess: "If they are good workmen, . . . they may be Mohammedans, Jews, or Christian of any sect, or they may be atheists." A shocking sentiment in these days of Pat Robertson, who laments the influx into America of people who don't share his beliefs.

The founding fathers, to be sure, recognized religion's valuable social role. Flexner writes of Washington that "organized religion appealed to him primarily . . . as a civilizing force within secular society." And Madison declared that "belief in a God All Powerful wise and good is so essential to the moral order of the World and to the happiness of man, that arguments which enforce it cannot be drawn from too many sources." Yet all the founding fathers cherished the separation of church and state. "There is not a shadow of right in the general government to intermeddle with religion," Madison affirmed. "Its least interference with it would be a most flagrant usurpation." Madison inserted a "freedom of conscience" article in the Virginia Declaration of Rights, and as a member of the Virginia House of Delegates he vigorously opposed a 1784 resolution to tax citizens "for the support of the Christian religion." Shortly thereafter both he and Jefferson fought a Virginia bill that would make Anglicanism an established church; Madison's petition against church establishment won such solid public backing that it spelled the beginning of the end for state support of churches or of religious education in the United States until the ascent of the Religious Right almost two hundred years later. That petition stated that "in matters of religion, no man's right is abridged by the institution of civil society, and that religion is wholly exempt from its cognizance." Comparing established churches to the Spanish Inquisition, Madison wrote that "they have been seen to erect a spiritual tyranny" that in turn upholds "the thrones of political tyranny; in no instance have they been seen the guardians of the liberties of the people."

The founding fathers' open-mindedness characteristically transcended mere tolerance to embrace the possibility that Christians could—horrors!—learn things about God from other religions. Franklin's willingness to learn was so pronounced, in fact, that his biographer Esmond Wright speaks of him as exhibiting "a touch of polytheism." Page Smith writes that Adams "wished for a 'more liberal communication of sentiments' between all the nations of the world on the subject of religious beliefs. Each nation doubtless had something to contribute, since each might be assumed to have gained at least a partial apprehension of the divine." Adams himself wrote that he hoped "translations of the Bible into all languages and sent among all people . . . will produce translations into English and French, Spanish and German and Italian of sacred books of Persians, the Chinese, the Hindoos, etc., etc., etc. Then our grandchildren and my great-grandchildren may compare notes and hold fast all that is good." There is nothing here of the animus toward ecumenism and toward familiarity with other faiths that today's legalistic Christians display.

Unlike Pat Robertson and company, the founding fathers placed far less emphasis on any theological doctrine than they did on Jesus' gospel message of love. Wright notes that Franklin, though he belonged to an Episcopal church in Philadelphia, "came to honor virtue far more than orthodoxy; his ethic was social." "The most acceptable Service we render to him [God]," wrote the author of *Poor*

Richard's Almanack, "is doing good to his other Children." Wright says that "from this reasonable man's creed, theology and dogma were noticeably absent." Flexner likewise notes our first president's "lack of doctrine and dogmatism." (He also points out that Washington preferred to speak of "Providence" rather than of "God" and was more likely to spend a Sunday writing letters than attending church.) Adams valued Christianity for bringing "the great principle of the law of nature and nations—Love your neighbor as yourself, and do to others as you would have that others should do to you—to the knowledge, belief and veneration of the whole people," and said that "if mankind should come someday to live in universal brotherhood it would be because it came finally to accept the great Christian ideals as its own."

Even as they extolled Christian moral principles, the founding fathers expressed skepticism about the chief Christian doctrines, including Jesus' divinity. "I have . . . some Doubts as to his Divinity," wrote Franklin, "tho' it is a question I do not dogmatize upon, having never studied it, and think it needless to busy myself with it now, when I expect soon an Opportunity of knowing the Truth with less Trouble." Adams, says Page Smith, became "more and more plainly Unitarian" as he aged. Though a regular churchgoer, Adams "rejected the notion of the Trinity as superstition and with it the idea of the divinity of Christ." And Jefferson, who according to his biographer Fawn M. Brodie "despised clergymen all his adult life" and evinced a "hatred of the established faith" that was well-nigh unparalleled in his time, made it one of his chief aims during the Revolution to quell the power of the Anglican Church. A year before his death, he described himself as a Unitarian; several years earlier, he declined to serve as a baptismal sponsor because he did not accept the Trinity. Jefferson dissented so strongly from many conventional Christian tenets, indeed, that during the 1800 presidential election campaign he was, as Dumas Malone points out, "denounced . . . in press and pulpit as an atheist"; when, years later, the House of Representatives considered purchasing his library, it was objected that his books were "irreligious." Brodie notes that when Jefferson first ran for president, "clergymen told their parishioners that a vote for Jefferson was a vote against Christianity, and warned that if he won they would have to hide their Bibles in their wells."

In fact none of the founding fathers was truly irreligious. All were essentially deists. Wright sums up Franklin's belief system as "a rational but pragmatic deism." Flexner states bluntly that "George Washington was, like Benjamin Franklin and Thomas Jefferson, a deist." (A footnote points out that despite Washington's deism, "the forgers and mythmakers have been endlessly active in their efforts to attribute to Washington their own religious acts and beliefs." This footnote was written some years before Pat Robertson and company began seeking to enlist the founding fathers retrospectively in their cause.)

Like many of their deist contemporaries, the founding fathers tended to invoke "Nature" as an authority. In their view, human beings had a "natural right" to religious freedom, and the greatest evidence for God's existence lay in Nature's order and beauty. Franklin's "Articles of Belief" begins with a quatrain from Cato:

> Here will I hold—If there is a Pow'r above us
> (And that there is, all Nature cries aloud,
> Thro' all her works), He must delight in virtue
> And that which he delights in must be happy.

Page Smith writes that Adams drew "his conviction of God's existence . . . primarily from the extraordinary variety and beauty of the observable world—'the amazing harmony of our solar system . . . the stupendous plan of operation' designed by God to act as a particular role 'in this great and complicated drama.'"

Despite their deism, most of the founding fathers described themselves as Christians—a label that Pat Robertson would deny to anyone nowadays who held similar views. Jefferson wrote a friend: "I am a Christian, in the only sense he [Jesus] wished any one to be; sincerely attached to his doctrines, in preference to all others; ascribing to himself every human excellence; and believing he never claimed any other." And Adams said that Christianity "will last as long as the world. Neither savage nor civilized man without a revelation could ever have discovered or invented it. Ask me not then whether I am a Catholic or Protestant, Calvinist or Arminian. As far as they are Christians, I wish to be a fellow disciple with them all." One could hardly imagine a clearer statement of membership in the Church of Love, not of Law;

and one could hardly imagine a notion of Christianity less congenial to the likes of Pat Robertson.

The founding fathers' religious beliefs, then, fell far beyond the narrow orthodoxy insisted upon nowadays by Pat Robertson and other legalistic Christians. And yet Robertson pretends otherwise. Though he accuses his opponents of rewriting history in Orwellian fashion, it is clear who is really doing so. But one should hardly be surprised, for what Robertson has done to the founding fathers is, as we shall see, nothing compared to the way he has distorted the meaning of the life of a certain carpenter from Galilee.

Robertson has made a point of the fact that new members of Congress are routinely presented with a Bible. This indicates plainly, he argues, that America is a Christian nation. Ralph Reed, too, manages to work a mention of the Congressional Bible, "an edition of the Scriptures commissioned by the U.S. Congress shortly after the founding of the nation," into *Active Faith*. What both Robertson and Reed fail to mention is that the Bible in question is in fact Jefferson's redaction of the four Gospels, which he entitled *The Life and Morals of Jesus of Nazareth*. Jefferson's Bible consists of a single account of Jesus' ministry made up of passages from all four Gospels; it omits the entire Old Testament, the Acts of the Apostles, the Epistles, and the Book of Revelation. It also omits duplications, omits gospel passages that seemed to Jefferson to be at odds with the spirit of Jesus, and omits the Resurrection. It ends with Jesus being laid in his tomb.

Jefferson explained that his Bible was "a document in proof that I am a *real Christian,* that is to say, a disciple of the doctrines of Jesus," and that he had compiled it because he felt that Jesus' teachings had suffered as a consequence of having been written down not by Jesus himself but by "the most unlettered of men, long after they had heard them from him, when much was forgotten, much misunderstood, and presented in every paradoxical shape." Jefferson's aim was to remove from the gospel things that, in his view, had obviously been added on by the gospel writers themselves, and thus to give readers a purer picture of an individual who was "the most innocent, the most benevolent, and the most eloquent and sublime character that ever has been exhibited to man."

"Like other Enlightenment rationalists," writes the theological historian Jaroslav Pelikan, "Jefferson was convinced that the real villain in the Christian story was the apostle Paul, who had corrupted the religion *of* Jesus into a religion *about* Jesus." This corruption had resulted in "the monstrosities of dogma, superstition, and priestcraft, which were the essence of Christian orthodoxy. The essence of authentic religion, and therefore of the only kind of Christianity in which Jefferson was interested, needed to be rescued from these distortions, so that the true person and teachings of Jesus of Nazareth might rise from the dead page." Pelikan notes the opposition drawn by Jefferson and others "between the universal religion of Jesus and the Christian particularity of the religion of Paul": Though Paul insisted that in Christ there was no slave or free, no Greek or Jew, no male or female, he erected barriers between Christian and non-Christian that Jesus himself, in Jefferson's view, would have found repugnant.

Robertson would never consider Jefferson's Bible an authentic Bible; indeed, if this edition of the Gospels were the work of a committee of contemporary scholars and were introduced today by the United States Government, it would draw howls of outrage from the Religious Right. One can only imagine the fury with which legalistic Christians would react to a cut-and-paste job on what they consider the Word of God—especially a cut-and-paste job that unequivocally affirms the Church of Love and rejects the Church of Law.

4

DARBY'S KINGDOM

"THERE IS NOT a young man now living in the United States who will not die an Unitarian." Such was the prediction of Thomas Jefferson, who had confidence that Unitarianism—with its emphasis on reason and conscience and its denial of Jesus' divinity—would appeal more than any other church to the younger generation of his day. It was not a foolish supposition: Jefferson spoke at a time when the kind of irrational Christianity he deprecated appeared to be on the wane. Yet in fact it was on the upswing. As it turned out, nineteenth-century American religion would be dominated by evangelical Protestantism, with its tent-meeting revivals, extreme moralism, and bizarre apocalyptic theology. If educated urbanites were largely immune to this kind of religion—which grew out of the most legalistic, anti-intellectual strains of colonial Puritanism—the rural, semiliterate poor packed tents by the thousands and responded powerfully to the messages preached there, because those messages were tailored precisely to them. The evangelists, with their dramatic rhetoric about the threat of hellfire and the promise of heaven, played expertly on the miseries, anxieties, and resentments of the provincial poor, on their fears of the unknown in this world and the next, on their desperate desire for a paternal, authoritarian figure to give their lives a sense of order and direction, and on their eagerness to believe in the promise of a postmortem existence more worry-free than this one. Evangelists have always appealed to the isolated and desperate, to people living on the edge—and such people are generally not inclined to subject to penetrating critical analysis the rules, doctrines, and faith statements that are presented to them as the keys to the Kingdom. So it was with the tent-meeting crowds, who eagerly and unreflectingly affirmed the things they were told to affirm.

Throughout the nineteenth century, religion was a growth industry in America. Though Pat Robertson and others on the Religious Right today routinely insist that the early American republic was overwhelmingly Christian, this widespread notion has been put to rest by the sociologists Roger Finke and Rodney Stark, who conclude from a careful study of census figures and other documents that "on the eve of the Revolution only about 17 percent of Americans were churched" and that even "in the puritan Commonwealth of Massachusetts religious adherence probably never exceeded 22 percent." By the time of the Civil War the nationwide churchgoing figure had climbed to 37 percent; from then on, the national rate of churchgoing rose steadily to about 62 percent in 1980. In the face of such statistics, to claim that eighteenth-century America was a "Christian nation" is absurd. Indeed, Finke and Stark describe America as having "shifted from a nation in which most people took no part in organized religion to a nation in which nearly two thirds of American adults do."

While Unitarianism failed to achieve a position of dominance in the nineteenth century, the mainline churches of Jefferson's day—Congregational, Episcopal, and Presbyterian—retained some degree of ascendancy, forming part of the American Protestant establishment and coming to be seen, toward the century's end, largely as props for Victorian respectability, middle-class conformism, and the socioeconomic status quo of unrestricted robber-baron capitalism. Yet the ascendancy of these churches was threatened to some degree by a wide range of new religious developments, above all the Baptist and Methodist movements. In theology as well as in manner of worship, these new groups, with their emphasis on Jesus as one's personal savior and on profound spiritual feeling, could hardly have differed more strikingly from Jefferson's Unitarians, who rejected Jesus' divinity and cultivated a sedate rationalism. Yet the Baptists and Methodists shared with the Unitarians an antagonism both to the strict mainline orthodoxies and to the clerical hierarchy and prescribed liturgy of the Episcopalians. They also shared an urgent devotion to Jesus' message of love. As Protestantism itself had been a revolt against papal authority and orthodoxy, so the Methodist, Baptist, and Unitarian movements all represented a further step away from the authority and orthodoxy of institutional Protestantism and toward an affirmation of individual mind and conscience and of the individual's authentic relationship to God. Or, as Tillich might say, away from the horizontal and toward the vertical.

Founded in eighteenth-century England by the Anglican cleric John Wesley, Methodism began as a movement to spiritually revitalize Anglicanism. Separating from the Anglican Church in 1784, Methodism developed in the nineteenth century into a major mainline church and the largest single component of the Protestant establishment. In the late nineteenth century, this process repeated itself when many Methodists who first sought to reinvigorate *their* church as part of the so-called Holiness movement eventually broke away to form such denominations as the Church of the Nazarene and the Salvation Army. It was in some of these Holiness sects, in the first decades of the twentieth century, that there first developed the movement known as Pentecostalism, whose adherents' intense experiences of the Holy Spirit (or so they claimed) were manifested in such phenomena as faith healing, prophecies, and speaking in tongues. Eventually many Pentecostals, in turn, broke off into their own denominations, the largest of them being the Assemblies of God.

The Baptist movement, which proved even more successful than Methodism, began in 1609 as a small fringe group in England and grew enormously in America during the 1800s. Today Baptists of various denominations form the single largest group of American Protestants, and the Southern Baptist Convention is the single largest Protestant denomination. Yet for anyone whose knowledge of Baptist belief is based only on familiarity with today's self-identified "traditional" Southern Baptists, the actual nature of historic Baptist doctrine can come as a shock. In an early twentieth-century high-school textbook about Baptist belief, W. R. White noted that for Baptists, "the individual is primary. . . . No building, work of art, human or religious institution is to be valued above him." In a 1909 book, Philip L. Jones agreed: "The doctrine of the individual relationship of the soul to God has always and everywhere been insisted upon by Baptists. Indeed, no doctrine has been, nor is, more Baptistic than this."

Flowing from this emphasis on the individual is an insistence on total freedom of conscience: "The individual has a right to express his religious or antireligious convictions," writes Jones. This doctrine— known as soul competency—is strikingly antithetical to the theology of many so-called "traditional" Baptists today, who have been taught to distrust their consciences, which may be manipulated by Satan.

Historic Baptist faith is indeed biblically based, but White emphasizes that for Baptists, the New Testament—*not* the harsh edicts of Leviticus and Deuteronomy—is their "law and only law." Nor, White says, is it appropriate for Baptists to pluck verses out of context: "The method of throwing proof texts together, as we would the contents of a scrapbook, is very unsound. We must look to the whole revelation of God, reaching its completeness in Christ, for the truth on any major subject." Again, this recognition of the need to read the Bible as a whole is not greatly in evidence in today's Southern Baptist Convention. Nowadays most "traditional" Southern Baptists not only engage in vigorous proof-texting but reject any contextual reading of Bible verses as heresy and routinely privilege the harshest Old Testament pronouncements over verses from the Gospels.

Love is the most important element in traditional Baptist belief. "To the true Baptist," writes Jones, love "is the supreme controlling, governing force. . . . It is love and not law that is supreme. . . . God is love and love is God." For this reason, Baptists don't believe in doing anything that might be seen as an attempt to legislate belief. The Baptist, Jones says,

> does not much believe in legislation in order to advance the interests of the
> kingdom. . . . He would not write the name of God in the constitution of

either the nation or the State. . . . He does not even contest very
strenuously for the reading of the Bible in our public schools.

For Baptists, Jones adds, "it is the inner spirit and not the external letter that should control. . . . Everywhere and always they discount righteousness by edict, and seek to implant righteousness by love." In a time
when the public rhetoric of "traditional" Southern Baptists emphasizes
God's wrath far more than his love, and when Southern Baptists agi-
tate for laws and constitutional amendments permitting organized
school prayer, Jones's characterization of classical Baptist attitudes could
hardly seem more at odds with contemporary reality.

Finally, Jones envisions God's kingdom coming about through a
gradual increase of love in the hearts of men and women:

> *The kingdom of our Lord . . . cannot come by legal enactment; it cannot*
> *come by any coercion, whether applied to the individual or to men in the*
> *mass; it cannot come by the influence of any external act or rite or service. It*
> *can come only by the enthronement of this supreme love of God and Jesus*
> *Christ in the heart of the individual man. . . . Where abounds the love of*
> *God and the love of man, there his kingdom will be set up, and it is this*
> *kingdom in the supremacy of its dominating emotion, love, for which the*
> *true Baptist stands.*

As we shall see, this conception of God's kingdom is dramatically at
odds with the "End Times" theology subscribed to by most "traditional" Southern Baptists today.

To be sure, the Baptist churches were in practice never quite the
Church of Love that White and Jones depict. (Which church ever
was?) Yet Christine Leigh Heyrman's 1997 book, *Southern Cross,* a
study of the diaries of eighteenth- and nineteenth-century Baptist and
Methodist clergy, shows that the teachings of pre-Revolutionary
preachers in both of these churches were utterly at odds with that of
today's self-styled "traditional" Baptists and Methodists. Far from making an idol of the family, upholding paternal authority, and reinforcing
the Southern cult of masculinity and male honor, eighteenth-century
Southern evangelicals prized "religious fellowship over family,"
affirmed female equality, and questioned the idea that youth should
always defer to age. In contradistinction to the pro-slavery and then

pro-segregation stance of their successors, moreover, white Baptist and
Methodist clergy in the early South preached a radical message of racial
equality. *This* is the true Baptist tradition—and it was betrayed in the
early nineteenth century by preachers who, upholding "the superiority of white over black and of men over women," exchanged God's
truth for the values of the secular society of their day.

So it was that Baptist churches in the antebellum South soon
became identified with the defense of slavery. For American Baptists,
the pivotal nineteenth-century event was the 1845 withdrawal of the
Baptist churches in the South from the national Baptist body, then
called the General Missionary Convention, whose Boston-based leaders had voted not to allow slaveholders to participate in foreign mission work. The Southern churches, which supported their members'
right to own slaves, proceeded to form the Southern Baptist Convention. What followed in the decades after the Civil War was ironic:
While the North's Baptist churches became, with the mainline
churches, a part of the Protestant establishment—and also declined,
along with the mainline churches, in membership and influence—the
Southern Baptist Convention thrived as a bulwark of racism, an oppo-
nent of Reconstruction and evolution, and, in the mid-twentieth century, as a foe of integration, civil rights, and secular culture. Formerly
devoted above all to the gospel, Southern Baptist preachers (with some
honorable exceptions) came to be known for their devotion to harsh
Old Testament law. In recent years, an ex-president of the Southern
Baptist Convention declared that God does not hear the prayers of
Jews, and the Convention itself issued a report that purported to indicate what proportion of the membership of various Christian communions would be saved. (Unsurprisingly, Southern Baptists came out
in the number one position, bringing to mind Jesus' statement that the
last shall be first.) So it was that a movement originally founded to
establish a Church of Love devolved into America's most powerful
Church of Law.

This shift in the orientation of the Baptist churches was only part of
a broader development in American Protestantism that began in the
early nineteenth century and that has continued to the present day.

I am referring to the remarkable reversal of the Protestant movement's progress toward a Church of Love and the almost total replacement of the gospel message with an emphasis on bizarre moralistic and apocalyptic doctrines.

The first major figure in this revolution was John Nelson Darby, an Englishman who was born in 1800, the year Thomas Jefferson was elected president of the United States. In 1824, after studying law at Trinity College, Dublin—a fact that seems not totally irrelevant to his role as the godfather of today's American Protestant legalism—Darby was ordained to the clergy of the Church of Ireland (the Anglican Communion's Irish branch). Yet he soon came to feel uncomfortable with the idea of ordination, later explaining that Saint Paul would not have been permitted to preach in his church because he hadn't been ordained. Accordingly, Darby resigned his curacy in 1827 and joined a denomination called the Brethren which rejected formal ordination. In the 1840s he founded a breakaway faction, the Plymouth Brethren (also known as Darbyites), the theology of which centered on a remarkable set of beliefs propounded by Darby and known as dispensational premillennialism.

Premillennialism—the origins of which are shrouded in the mists of time and which did not rise out of obscurity until the nineteenth century—is a belief that the cryptic apocalyptic visions found in the Book of Revelation and elsewhere signify that Christ will someday return personally to earth, will establish an earthly kingdom with its capital in Jerusalem, and will reign over the earth from that city for exactly one thousand years. Dispensational premillennialism—without which Protestant fundamentalism as we know it today would not exist—adds to this belief the notion that human history has broken down into several periods, known as dispensations, during each of which human beings lived under a different set of divine laws and criteria for salvation. According to this scheme, the present period is the "church age," or sixth dispensation, which Darby described as an era marked by apostasy and the erosion of Christian morality. This period will be followed by an event called the Rapture, or Secret Rapture, when all saved Christians will ascend into the sky to meet Christ and to be safeguarded from the Great Tribulation, a time of violence and death that will eventually be succeeded by Christ's triumphant thousand-year reign on earth and his Last Judgment of humankind.

The utterly untraditional nature of dispensationalism can hardly be overstated. The religious historian Sydney E. Ahlstrom notes that although adherents of dispensationalism claim to be biblical literalists, "its extensive use of typology, its commitment to numerology, and its dependence on highly debatable (not to say fanciful) interpretations of some obscure apocalyptic passages have led many to insist that its interpretation is anything but literal." Indeed. Yet dispensationalism has thrived. Though the Plymouth Brethren remain a tiny sect, with a total membership in the United States of about forty thousand, the theology of Darby—who spent much of his later years spreading dispensationalism to North American clergy—has taken root far beyond the denomination he helped found.

This success owes much to a near contemporary of Darby's—namely Charles Darwin, whose theory of evolution, set forth in *Origin of Species* (1859), was viewed by some Christians with alarm. The Bible said that God had made the world in six days and had finished the job by creating Adam and Eve; Darwin deduced from fossil evidence that human beings had evolved from other life forms over millions of years. While some Christians perceived readily enough that certain Bible stories need not be taken literally and thus didn't contradict Darwin's discoveries, others—for whom Christianity was essentially a matter of fixed, unyielding law and doctrine—saw Darwinism as striking at the very core of their religion.

Also perceived as a threat was the so-called Higher Criticism. In 1835, a German biblical scholar named David Friedrich Strauss published *The Life of Jesus Critically Examined*. In this meticulous study, Strauss sought to separate out the Bible's historical elements from the merely legendary. Strauss (whose work had been anticipated not only by Jefferson but also by an eighteenth-century German linguist, Hermann Samuel Reimarus) was the first of many nineteenth-century scholars to bring the objective methods of historical research and textual analysis to bear upon scripture. Along with various successors, who like him made use of archeological discoveries in the Holy Land, Strauss sought to determine the circumstances under which the scriptures had been written and to obtain as accurate as possible a picture of the historical context of the Bible and, especially, of the man called Jesus. What these scholars sought, quite simply, was the truth: What had

Jesus really been like? What had he really preached, expected, stood for? In what ways had the Church, over the centuries, distorted his message? While many Christians welcomed this scholarly approach to the Bible, which they hoped would bring a clearer understanding of the truth of God, others felt that the Higher Criticism—which drew attention to biblical errors in science and history as well as to scores of internal contradictions that for centuries had been quietly ignored by preachers and seminaries—represented a potentially deadly threat to the Christian faith.

The profound effect of evolution and of the Higher Criticism on many American Protestants can be summarized in one word: panic. Literal-minded believers were terrified by an intimidatingly recondite set of scientific and scholarly propositions that implicitly denied the literal truth of much of scripture and seemed to threaten to topple the old-time religion. These believers sought a refuge, a bulwark against the dangerous new learning—and they found the perfect one in dispensationalism. Why perfect? Because dispensationalist theology consisted of a set of theological assertions as complex and recondite as those advanced by Darwin or the Higher Critics; the difference was that dispensationalism proffered blessed assurance of the Bible's literal truth.

Indeed, though dispensationalism is utterly unscientific, in that it was formulated without the slightest regard for scientific method, Darby's theology exhibits a rigor, complexity, and internal consistency that can make it look quite scientific to people who don't know any better. Marsden notes that C. I. Scofield, whose 1909 Scofield Reference Bible codified and advanced the cause of dispensationalism, "contrasted his work to previous 'unscientific systems'" and that the dispensationalist Reuben Torrey saw himself as a kind of scientist whose job it was, in Torrey's words, to apply "the methods of modern science . . . to Bible study." These men and others like them helped shape an American fundamentalist mentality that, to this day, as Marsden notes, reads "the Bible virtually as though it were a scientific treatise" and views Christianity as a system of knowledge that has "no loose ends, ambiguities, or historical developments."

Dispensationalism never had many adherents in the British Isles. But in nineteenth-century America, which seems never to have seen an apocalyptic creed it didn't like, Darby's teachings spread widely among

modestly educated rural Americans, thanks largely to panic over evolution and the Higher Criticism. So widely did dispensationalism
spread that by the year 1882, which saw the deaths of both Darby and
Darwin, it had virtually supplanted traditional Christian belief in many
nonmainline Protestant churches. The extraordinary extent of this dis-
placement would be hard to exaggerate. Thanks to Darby, as the soci-
ologist Nancy Tatom Ammerman has noted, millions of American
Protestants had begun "to read the scripture as if it were a puzzle containing clues to God's historical timetable." They also began to look at
Christianity in an aggressively horizontal way, seeing it as centered not
on the individual's spiritual experience but on total assent to a highly
specific and ahistorical set of theological propositions. For dispensationalists, salvation is dependent not only on one's acceptance of Jesus
Christ as savior but on one's acceptance of the truth of the entire dispensational historical schema. Those who declare their belief in the
dispensations, the Rapture, and so forth will be saved; those who don't
will endure the pains of hell. Period.

Where does love fit into this picture? Nowhere. In dispensational
theology, the kingdom that Jesus described in the Gospels as something
that exists already in our midst and that can be attained through love
for God and one's neighbor was thoroughly banished from the picture
and replaced by an exclusively future kingdom to which one can gain
entry in only one way: by subscribing to dispensationalist theology.
What's love got to do with it? Absolutely nothing.

More than any other nineteenth-century figure, Darby laid the
foundations of legalistic Protestant belief in America today. Few men
or women of his century exerted more influence on twentieth-century
American culture. Yet the only thing as staggering as the breadth of his
influence is the fact that he remains virtually unknown among mainstream Americans—including mainline Protestant clergy. Indeed, many
standard works of religious and historical reference that treat far less
influential persons at length do not even mention Darby's name.

Darby was not alone in effecting radical changes in American religion
during the nineteenth century—or, for that matter, in promoting
apocalyptic theology, which had figured importantly in American reli-

gion since about 1820. Though many people today think of previous centuries as eras when American Christianity remained firmly moored in tradition, Christianity in America has in fact always been exceedingly volatile. Among the new theologies to appear on the nineteenth-century American landscape were those of William Miller, whose disciple Ellen White founded the Seventh-day Adventists in 1863, and Charles Taze Russell, a sometime Adventist who organized the Jehovah's Witnesses in 1878. Like Darby's followers, the members of these movements were premillennialists—but not dispensationalists—who expected the imminent personal return of Christ. (Adventists still commemorate "The Great Disappointment" of October 22, 1844, when the Millerites, heeding a prediction by their leader, packed their bags and waited for Jesus to raise them to heaven.) Also founded in the nineteenth century were Mary Baker Eddy's Christian Science (1879) and Joseph Smith's Church of Jesus Christ of Latter-day Saints, or Mormons (1830), now one of the world's fastest-growing religious groups.

These new sects varied widely in doctrine, but most of them had something significant in common: If the original Protestant Reformation and the later Baptist and Methodist movements had been born out of longings for a Church of Love and not of Law, these nineteenth-century sects tended to be founded by legalists who, offended by the decrease in legalism among the mainline Protestant churches and terrified by evolution, the Higher Criticism, and other manifestations of modern life and modern science, sought to establish newer, stricter Churches of Law—churches whose walls, so to speak, were high and strong enough to protect them, in their doctrinal certitude, from a world full of ambiguity and doubt.

Yet Darby would have a greater impact on religion in twentieth-century America than did any of his contemporaries. One aspect of that impact was a sharp division that continues in America to this day. By the end of the nineteenth century the findings of Darwin and the Higher Critics had been embraced by many educated Christians (especially in the cities and in New England) and by influential figures in the media, universities, and seminaries; these people who accepted the "new learning" came to be called modernists or liberals. Meanwhile, millions of Americans (especially in the South and rural areas) rejected modernism vehemently and affirmed the literal truth of the Bible; these people would come to be known as fundamentalists.

By century's end, most major Protestant denominations had become divided into modernist and antimodernist wings (the staunchly antimodernist Southern Baptists were an exception), while the major seminaries and theological reviews came to be identified with one or the other side of the controversy. During the last twenty-five years of the nineteenth century, antimodernist ministers (mostly Baptists and Presbyterians) met annually at the Niagara Bible Conference, where in 1895 they issued a statement insisting that there was no true Christianity where there was not total acceptance of Christ's divinity, virgin birth, physical resurrection, and future physical return to earth. Also insisted upon was the doctrine of the substitutionary atonement—the belief (still central to Protestant fundamentalism today) that Jesus, in some kind of cosmic transaction with God the Father, paid the price of his earthly life to redeem human beings, who through their own sinfulness had forfeited salvation.

The antimodernists also demanded belief in biblical inerrancy. That every word of the Bible was literally true had been a popular sentimental notion—and had been vaguely affirmed by some church figures—for at least two centuries, but had never been considered a key theological doctrine or developed in any systematic way. There was a good reason for this—namely, the fact that the Bible is chock-full of internal contradictions as well as errors in history, botany, medicine, physics, and other fields of knowledge. These errors ranged from the obvious (Joshua's command that the sun stop in its course was plainly based on a pre-Copernican understanding of astronomy) to the not-so-obvious (for example, Jesus' statement that the mustard seed is the smallest of all seeds).

Among the many contradictions were these: The lists of Jesus' disciples differ from Gospel to Gospel; in the synoptic Gospels Jesus' ministry lasts one year, while in John's Gospel it lasts two or three; the synoptics place Jesus' cleansing of the temple at the end of his ministry while John puts it at the beginning; in the synoptics, but not in John, Jesus has a formal trial before the Sanhedrin; the synoptics and John give different dates for the Crucifixion; Matthew, Luke, Acts, John, and I Corinthians give contradictory accounts of Jesus' Resurrection appearances; and Luke and Acts provide conflicting reports of his Ascension. The genealogies of Jesus in Matthew and Luke, moreover, are totally irreconcilable; since both trace his descent through Joseph, moreover, neither genealogy is consistent with the claim of his virgin birth, which Paul in turn directly contradicts when he says that Jesus "was made of the seed of David according to the flesh" (Rom. 1:3).

In addition to these factual contradictions, the Bible contains large-scale incongruities that, for a legalistic Christian, cut to the heart of the faith. How does an inerrantist explain, for example, the often chillingly wrathful actions attributed in the Old Testament to the God whom Jesus describes in the New Testament as a perfectly loving Father? How does an inerrantist square the Pauline doctrine of justification by faith with the Epistle of James, which says that "it is by action and not by faith alone that a man is justified" (James 2:24)?

Such errors and inconsistencies abound in the Bible. Yet with the advent of modernist thinking, the doctrine of biblical inerrancy nonetheless became a major rallying point for antimodernists at every level of the American Protestant Church. Over the years, moreover, this doctrine—which was defined and disseminated by the antimodernists who dominated the Princeton Theological Seminary—would harden into a transcendently irrational article of faith that allowed for no exceptions whatsoever. Marsden notes that in the 1870s the theologian Charles Hodge, while stating that the Bible was divinely inspired, "could easily allow for errors in biblical texts"; a generation later, however, "his son, A. A. Hodge, and colleague, Benjamin Warfield, pushed his ideas to new heights of certainty. . . . literalism became dogma." In their view, God had not merely inspired the Bible; he had dictated it word for word. When forced to acknowledge blatant contradictions in scripture, the younger Hodge and Warfield came up with the bizarre notion that the Bible had been inerrant in its original manuscripts (which of course no longer existed) but that errors had been introduced later by copyists. This version of the inerrancy doctrine is still ardently affirmed by many legalistic Protestant churches, whose faith statements contain affirmations to the effect that "the Bible is without error in its original autographs."

It was at the annual Niagara conferences, and at a few other contemporaneous events, that Darby's dispensational premillennialism established itself as *the* orthodox theology among fundamentalist leaders. Among the more important of these leaders was the popular evangelist Dwight L. Moody, who spread Darby's teachings far and wide through his sermons as well as through his Moody Bible Institute. Founded in 1886, Moody's school—and others modeled on it—would serve as a reactionary alternative to the increasingly modernist mainline seminaries. Yet for all his devotion to dispensationalism, Moody was far less legalistic than are his present-day heirs. "The one feature that almost everyone noticed" about his preaching, writes Marsden, "was that Moody emphasized the love of God" and "did not preach Hellfire and God's wrath," a subject with which Moody was uneasy. "Terror," Moody insisted, "never brought a man in yet." Yet by embracing dispensational theology and rejecting modernism, Moody inadvertently helped set his segment of American Christianity on the road to being a Church of Law.

So it was that the turn-of-the-century middle-American reaction against modernism took shape around a fixation on strict dogma and biblical literalism. Never before had the professed faith of so many Christians been so utterly at odds with the accepted scientific knowledge of their own day. Faced with the chance to embrace new knowledge and reason, American fundamentalists—unlike virtually all other Christians around the world—chose instead to ally themselves with ignorance and irrationality.

5

RAUSCHENBUSCH'S
KINGDOM

IF JOHN NELSON DARBY helped lay the nineteenth-century foundations for the contemporary American Church of Law, the career of a northern Baptist named Walter Rauschenbusch likewise helped shape the ideas with which many members of America's more liberal and mainline churches have since attempted to build a Church of Love. How many Christians today, however, would even recognize the name of Rauschenbusch, whose work influenced (among others) Mahatma Gandhi, Martin Luther King, and Desmond Tutu? The son of a German preacher who was considered "the father of the German Baptists," Rauschenbusch was born in 1861 in upstate New York, to which his parents had immigrated and where his father taught at Rochester Seminary. The young Rauschenbusch was raised on the orthodox Protestant doctrines of the day, including biblical literalism and the substitutionary atonement; yet when he entered Rochester Seminary, he found these teachings radically challenged. For one thing, he encountered the Higher Criticism, as a result of which, he later explained, "my inherited ideas about the inerrancy of the Bible became untenable." He also came to doubt the substitutionary atonement because, as he wrote, "it was not taught by Jesus; it makes salvation dependent upon a trinitarian transaction that is remote from human experience; and it implies a concept of divine justice that is repugnant to human sensitivity." What kind of a cosmic justice system, in other words, would require a loving God to take his son's life in exchange for humankind's salvation? The idea made no sense to him, moral or otherwise.

Rauschenbusch's changed views did not shake his faith; they refocused it. He found kindred spirits in the early-nineteenth-century Congregationalist Horace Bushnell, who had written that Jesus had sought to reveal God's love for all humanity and "to win them to new life," and in the Anglican Frederick W. Robertson, who had written that "the attempt to rest Christianity upon miracles and fulfillments of prophecy is essentially the vilest rationalism; as if the trained intellect of a lawyer which can investigate evidence were that to which is trusted the soul's salvation." (Or, as Tillich might put it, the preoccupation of much Protestant theology with miracles and prophecies was exemplary not of genuine vertical orientation, but rather of a fixation on supposed horizontal manifestations of Godhead.) Rauschenbusch copied out the following line from Robertson: "To the question, Who is my neighbor? I reply as my Master did by the example that He gave: 'the alien and the heretic.'"

This became Rauschenbusch's answer as well. "The hallmark of his new position," notes Rauschenbusch's biographer, Paul M. Minus, "was the importance of living like Christ, not of believing a prescribed doctrine about Christ." It is no coincidence that Rauschenbusch, like Robertson, referred to Jesus more often as "Master" than as "Savior" or "Lord"—a usage that reflects an emphasis on Jesus as a teacher and life model, rather than on such doctrinal matters as his divinity or substitutionary atonement. (This usage would later be taken up by Harry Emerson Fosdick.) Nor is it a coincidence that these developments of

Rauschenbusch's early adulthood took place in America during the second half of the nineteenth century, when the mainline Protestant churches had become instruments and allies of the American social and political establishment, in effect supporting the economy's domination by robber barons, the extreme income disparity in the cities, and the practice of child labor. Most church leaders saw these socioeconomic facts as having little or nothing to do with their ministries. Today, when many people take social outreach programs for granted as an essential part of church mission, it can be hard to realize how strongly these assumptions differ from those of many mid-nineteenth-century ministers and theologians. Scandalized by his colleagues' apparent indifference to suffering, Rauschenbusch considered it his obligation as a minister of the gospel to seek to ameliorate social conditions. To love one's neighbor, in his view, was to *act* with love. To spread the gospel was a matter not of shrill proselytizing but of living out Jesus' message.

While more and more Americans were preaching Darby's despicable theology of the kingdom, then, Rauschenbusch was developing an utterly different kingdom theology. At an 1886 political rally, a Catholic priest struck at Rauschenbusch's imagination and conscience—and captured the spirit of what would eventually be called the Social Gospel—when he began a speech by saying, "Thy Kingdom come! Thy will be done on earth." That was what Rauschenbusch came to be about: spreading the kingdom. For him the gospel was central to Christianity, and central to the gospel, in turn, was the concept of the kingdom of God. For him, spreading the kingdom did not mean hellfire evangelism; it meant seeking to lead a Christlike life. Jesus had come, Rauschenbusch proclaimed, not to die in an act of substitutionary atonement but rather "to substitute love for selfishness as the basis of human society." Yet Christians had forgotten that purpose. They had forgotten, as Rauschenbusch wrote, that "Christianity is in its nature revolutionary." Rauschenbusch's job, as he saw it, was to remind them of that fact.

To this end, Rauschenbusch and some friends formed a group in 1892 called the Brotherhood of the Kingdom. Writing in their charter that "the Spirit of God is moving men in our generation toward a better understanding of the idea of the Kingdom of God on earth," they declared their intention "to reestablish this idea in the thought of the church, and to assist in its practical realization in the world." In a pamphlet, Rauschenbusch developed this point:

> *Because the Kingdom of God has been dropped as the primary and comprehensive aim of Christianity, and personal salvation has been substituted for it, therefore men seek to save their own souls and are selfishly indifferent to the evangelization of the world.*

> *Because the individualistic conception of personal salvation has pushed out of sight the collective idea of a Kingdom of God on earth, Christian men seek for the salvation of individuals and are comparatively indifferent to the spread of the spirit of Christ in the political, industrial, social, scientific and artistic life of humanity, and have left these as the undisturbed possession of the spirit of the world.*

> *Because the Kingdom of God has been understood as a state to be inherited in a future life rather than as something to be realized here and now, therefore Christians have been contented with a low plane of life here and have postponed holiness to the future.*

From the Social Gospel's very beginning, legalistic Christians have accused its proponents of abandoning the rigor of "traditional Christianity." The truth is absolutely the other way around: The Social Gospel sought to return Christianity beyond its "traditions" to its beginnings, to the real message of the real Jesus, which was and is too radical and challenging for many Christians to embrace:

> As he was starting out on a journey, a stranger ran up, and, kneeling before him, asked, "Good Teacher, what must I do to win eternal life?"
>
> Jesus said to him, "Why do you call me good? No one is good except God alone. You know the commandments. . . ."
>
> "But Teacher," he replied, "I have kept all these since I was a boy."
>
> As Jesus looked at him, his heart warmed to him. "One thing you lack," he said. "Go, sell everything you have, and give to the poor, and you will have treasure in heaven; then come and follow me." (Mark 10:17–21)

For seeking to put this injunction into practice (however incompletely), Rauschenbusch was widely condemned as heretical, Romish, socialist. Leading the attacks was Dr. James Willmarth, a Philadelphia Baptist preacher and premillennialist, who claimed that Rauschenbusch's views had no scriptural warrant. This was an outrageous charge, given that Rauschenbusch had found his theology in the gospel, whereas Willmarth's theology represented a perverse interpretation of a few cryptic and obviously symbolic biblical passages.

During the generation after the founding of the Brotherhood, the Social Gospel gained a broad influence and Rauschenbusch published several books. Most important was *Christianity and the Social Crisis* (1907), in which he wrote that "no man shares his life with God whose religion does not flow out, naturally and without effort, into all relations of his life and reconstructs everything that it touches. Whoever uncouples the religious and the social life has not understood Jesus. Whoever sets any bounds for the reconstructive power of the religious life over the social relations and institutions of men, to that extent denies the faith of the Master."

Christianity and the Social Crisis represented a total repudiation of the Church of Law. Yet it did something more, which many nonlegalistic Christians today may find problematic: It emphasized society's responsibility rather than the individual's. Rauschenbusch traced this emphasis through the entire Bible. The Old Testament prophets, he argued, were "less about the pure heart for the individual than of just institutions for the nation"; for them, "personal religion was chiefly a means" to a social end. Rauschenbusch argued in a later book, *Theology for the Social Gospel,* that baptism was, for John the Baptist, "not a ritual act of individual salvation but an act of dedication to a religious and social movement." Jesus, in a similar way, was less concerned with transforming individuals than with reforming Jewish society as a whole. "The better we know Jesus," Rauschenbusch wrote, "the more social do his thoughts and aims become." As for the kingdom of God, it "is not a matter of getting individuals to heaven, but of transforming the life on earth into the harmony of heaven." If "the fundamental virtue in the ethics of Jesus was love," it is because "love is the society-making quality. . . . Love creates fellowship."

Well, yes, it does—but many Christians today may recoil at this almost coldly pragmatic characterization of the value of love. Many, indeed, may dismiss Rauschenbusch's concept of the sinfulness of society as meaningless: What, they may ask, does it mean for a society to be sinful? Many may also consider Rauschenbusch's societal approach to Christianity inapplicable to a pluralistic culture of the sort we live in today. But his most problematic trait of all, for Christians today, may be one he shares with Jefferson: namely, his insufficient attention to the cultivation of individual spiritual experience. Almost invariably, his references to spiritual experience feel grudging, obligatory, *pro forma*. Though his heart was indubitably in the right place, he seems to have drastically underestimated the human need for a church that emphasizes action in the horizontal dimension without slighting the vertical dimension—for a church that brings the two dimensions together in a truly Christian way, making people feel to the core of their souls the profound truth that a love for one's neighbor is implicit in, is demanded by, and flows directly from, one's love for God. (It comes as no surprise to learn that Rauschenbusch was impatient with religious ceremony, which is, after all, an attempt to lift the minds and hearts of worshippers beyond the horizontal plane and into communion with their Maker.)

But then individuality itself gets short shrift from Rauschenbusch, who in his enthusiasm to reform society often seemed to neglect the individual's integrity as a moral and spiritual being and even to forget that loving others means loving them not as members of society but as individuals, each of whom is precious in God's sight. Especially in the wake of twentieth-century mass movements such as Nazism and Communism, Rauschenbusch's enthusiasm for a religion that views people less as individuals than as parts of a social organism can make one very uncomfortable. Nonetheless, Rauschenbusch's legalistic contemporaries were unfair to accuse the Social Gospelers of exchanging religion for social work. Not so: For them, working to improve socioeconomic conditions was literally the building up of the kingdom of God. They were drawn to that work by a love of Jesus, and the work itself brought them closer to Jesus—and they recognized that it was that love and intimacy, and not adherence to any law or doctrine, that was the essence of Christianity. "True Christianity," wrote Rauschenbusch, "puts a man face to face with Christ and bids him see what he can find there." Rejecting the kind of scriptural literalism that demanded obedience to even the most uncompassionate laws in Leviticus and Deuteronomy, Rauschenbusch proclaimed that "Jesus Christ is the standard of judgment about the Bible, as about all things," meaning that every doctrine and law must be interpreted through the prism of Jesus' life and teachings. This is, as we have seen, classic Baptist theology; but by Rauschenbusch's time this view had been so widely abandoned in practice that his insistence upon it seemed, to many, heretical.

The Social Gospel had its moment in the sun—actually, several years. But by the time of World War I, legalistic Christianity had begun to reassert itself, this time heavily dominated by dispensational premillennialism, and the Social Gospel was on the wane. Increasingly, American Christianity had become an open battleground between modernism, mostly in the form of the Social Gospel, and antimodernism, mostly in the form of dispensational premillennialism. A key reason for dispensationalism's rise was an amazing 1909 document called the Scofield Reference Bible, the work of a Texas preacher named C. I. Scofield (1843–1921).

One mark of the continuing distance between fundamentalist culture and that of mainstream America is how difficult it can be to get your hands on a copy of this seminal work in a place like midtown Manhattan. There are major metropolitan library systems that don't own a single copy; there are huge general bookstores that don't keep it in stock. Another mark of that distance is the fact that most histories of America and many religious reference books don't even mention it. Yet go into almost any small Southern town and you'll find a "Christian bookstore" that carries not only the Scofield Reference Bible but the New Scofield Reference Bible, a revision that appeared in 1967.

The Scofield Reference Bible looks like a lot of Bibles: Each page contains two columns of scripture separated by a narrower column of cross-references. What distinguishes it from most Bibles is that it also contains extensive footnotes. These footnotes add up to a highly tendentious dispensationalist interpretation of the Bible. There are whole books of Scofield's Bible in which the annotation is minimal, almost

absent; but in other books there are pages on which the annotation
takes up far more space than the text. Like Jefferson's Bible, then,
Scofield's Bible is an extraordinary act of audacity. But the two men
came at Scripture from utterly opposite directions. Jefferson sought to
preserve Jesus' moral teachings and to remove materials (including
accounts of miracles and prophecies) that seemed to him ahistorical
and thus, as Jaroslav Pelikan has written, to "find the essence of true
religion in the Gospels." Scofield also sought "the essence of true religion," but he located this essence not in the moral teachings of the
Gospels but in the miracles and prophecies, most of them located outside the Gospels. Jefferson's chaff, in short, was Scofield's wheat.

The Scofield Reference Bible was a brilliant idea. Over the centuries, countless theologians had written learned books in which they
grappled with the complex, ambiguous, often contradictory meanings
of scripture. But Scofield plainly knew two important things about the
people he wanted to reach. One: They didn't read books of theology,
but they did look at their Bibles (if only occasionally). Two: They
didn't want to grapple with complexities and ambiguities and contradictions; they wanted certitude, orthodoxy.

This Scofield gave them in spades. His footnotes never offer up different possible interpretations of a given text; instead, they set forth,
with an air of total authority, a detailed, elaborate, and consistent set
of interpretations that add up to a theological system that few Christians before Darby could have conceived of—and that, indeed, marked
a radical departure from the ways in which most Christians had always
believed. Yet Scofield brazenly proffered his theology as if it were
beyond question. And he presented it as if *it* were traditional, and as if
every other way of understanding the nature of Christian belief
marked a radical departure from the true faith. His notes refer only
implicitly to opposing theological views: In a footnote to a passage in
the Book of Acts, for example, Scofield tacitly alludes to symbolic
interpretations of the Second Coming (such as Fosdick's) by declaring
that Christ's promised return "is an event, not a process, and is personal
and corporeal." The *chutzpah* here is mind-boggling.

At the center of Scofield's theology is his version of Darby's
schematic vision of human history, which is broken down into seven
successive dispensations—into periods, that is, during each of which

man's life on earth is governed by a different set of laws—and eight successive covenants between God and humankind. The dispensations are as follows: the Dispensation of Innocency, which obtained in the Garden of Eden; the Dispensation of Conscience, which began with the expulsion from the garden; the Dispensation of Human Government, which was established after the flood; the Dispensation of Promise, which was instituted by God's promise to Abraham to "make of thee a great nation"; the Dispensation of Law, which was founded on Mosaic law; the Dispensation of Grace, which Christ made possible through his Incarnation and sacrifice; and the Dispensation of the Kingdom, which will begin after the Second Coming with the founding of Christ's millennial kingdom.

One way to begin to form a picture of the mental landscape of Scofield's followers is to peruse a 1972 book entitled *A Companion to the Scofield Reference Bible.* The very fact that such a book was published sixty-three years after the first appearance of the Scofield Reference Bible testifies to that volume's enduring significance. In the early pages of the *Companion,* its author, a dispensationalist named E. Schuyler English, denies that there are contradictions in the Bible and insists that dispensational theology is unequivocally true and must be embraced by believers in order for them to earn salvation. English then proceeds to outline that theology as presented in Scofield's footnotes. First he covers such doctrines as the virgin birth and baptism, and the nature of temptation, sin, and death. Then he discusses Christ's various "messages": his "Kingdom Message," his "Redemptive Message," and his "Many Other Words." Ignoring Jesus' own assurance that the kingdom is among us, English maintains that Christ's "Kingdom Message" concerns a totally future event, the "Kingdom Age" that will follow the present "Church Age." The category entitled "Christ's Many Other Words" is a grab bag that divides those words into "comforting words," "stern words," "prophetic words," and "words of wisdom."

English makes it clear, by the way he apportions his attention among these various matters, that for him and other dispensationalists, Christ's words are nowhere near as important as the End Times theology that can be gleaned from the Bible if one reads it according to their prescriptions. For the bulk of this book consists of the closing chapters on Christ's transfiguration, Crucifixion, Resurrection, and Ascension (all of which are given extensive treatment) and, especially, on the matters considered under the general heading of "Last Things": "The Rapture," "The Judgment Seat of Christ," "The Marriage of the Lamb," "The 'Tribulation,'" "The Second Coming of Christ," "The Four Judicial Acts," "The Millennium," "The Final Judgment: The Great White Throne," and "Eternity." Several of these chapters are in turn divided into subchapters.

The End Times theology as presented by English in these pages is, in its essentials, identical to that subscribed to by most Protestant fundamentalists in America today, and represents, for the most part, a free interpretation of the extremely obscure symbolic account of the Apocalypse in the Book of Revelation. "At a time not known precisely," English writes, "the Lord Jesus Christ will descend from heaven and meet His Church in the air." (This prophecy derives from Rev. 1:7: "Look, he is coming with the clouds; everyone shall see him, including those who pierced him.") It is important to recognize that English does not mean this metaphorically: He wants it to be understood that Jesus will descend bodily from heaven, and that saved Christians will rise into the air bodily to meet him. "When this occurs," English writes, "all who have died in Christ will be raised and, together with a living generation of believers, will be translated into His presence, to be with Him forever." This event is referred to as the Rapture. (Many fundamentalists today have conducted sober theological inquiries into the question of what will happen, say, to passengers on an airplane whose pilot has been "raptured.")

The Rapture, English explains, will be followed by the seven-year Tribulation, an "era of divine wrath upon the earth" in which "judgments will fall upon people everywhere." English writes that "sometimes God will employ wicked instruments to accomplish His judgments. He will, for example, allow the dragon (i.e., the devil) to persecute Israel. . . . One of the divine purposes of these judgments is to recognize the Lord Jesus Christ as their Messiah, so that they will turn to Him. Another reason for God's wrath is to judge the nations for their lawlessness and rebellion against Him." English outlines several specific events of the Tribulation, during which, he says, Jesus "will destroy His enemies." For one thing, he says that two people called witnesses will "bear testimony to the Lord Jesus until they are slain by the beast. Their dead bodies will lie in Jerusalem's streets for three and a half days. Then God will raise and translate them to heaven while their enemies view their ascension." Also, a woman "clothed with the sun" (presumably English reads this, at least, symbolically) who "represents Israel" will be targeted by Satan "but God will guard her among the nations for 1260 days, the latter half of the 'tribulation.'"

The climactic events of the Tribulation, English explains, will be triggered when a "political messiah" who heads a "ten-kingdom federation" makes "a seven-year covenant with the Jews" and "exalt[s] himself above God." This messiah, or "beast," will then break his covenant and persecute the Jews. "It is at this time," writes English, "that the ascended Christ arises from His Father's right hand and comes to earth in power to destroy His enemies and put them under His feet. . . . What begins with a false messiah riding a white horse on earth ends with Christ the Lord descending on a white horse from heaven to earth as the Faithful and True, the Word of God, King of kings and Lord of lords."

Christ's return "will be a spectacular event. Nature will announce it—the sun and moon will be darkened, stars will fall from heaven, and the powers of the heavens will be shaken." He will descend to earth to the Mount of Olives in Israel, accompanied by "all the holy angels" as well as "the armies of heaven," and "every eye will see Him." He will then proceed to "destroy the armies of the beast" and "consign the beast and the false prophet [another villain in this drama] to the lake of fire." Also, "the devil will be bound with a chain, cast into the abyss, and sealed there for 1000 years." Jesus will then assume "His glorious throne on earth" and will separate the saved from the unsaved: "He will place the sheep, composed of those Gentiles who have been saved during the 'tribulation,' on His right hand. On His left hand He will assemble the goats, composed of all the Gentiles who have rejected Him during the same period." The goats will be tossed into everlasting fire, while the sheep will remain on earth to enjoy Christ's thousand-year reign over the earth, which is known as the Millennium or the Kingdom Age. Indeed, the sheep "will rule with Him."

This will, make no mistake, be a literal reign, a "theocratic rule" marked by righteousness and peace. During this period, people will journey to "a temple on a high mountain in Jerusalem . . . to offer praise to God." Yet "sin and rebellion" will also occur, and at the end of the thousand years Satan will emerge from his bonds and make war against Jerusalem. "But fire and heaven will devour his hosts," writes English. "It is then that the execution of God's long-standing judgment of the devil will be consummated. He will be cast into the lake of fire to 'be tormented day and night forever and ever.'" (This last scriptural quotation, like most of those cited to support the dispensationalist vision of the End Times, is from the Book of Revelation.) After the Devil has been thus dealt with, "the wicked and unregenerate dead . . . will be raised and brought before the great white throne for judgment" by Christ. One by one, they will face Christ and offer up to him the record of their good works. Yet because they refused in life to accept Christ as their savior, "every one of them will be cast into the lake of fire" where they, like the Devil, will burn forever. This sentence having been pronounced, saved Christians will dwell with God for eternity in Jerusalem. The only matter in the whole book on which English admits some degree of uncertainty is the question of whether this Jerusalem will be the actual city of Jerusalem on earth or whether it will be located somewhere else. For English, this doesn't really matter, for "wherever He is, is heaven." In this heaven,

> there will be nothing but blessedness. God will dwell with His people. He will wipe away all the tears of the ages past, and all things will be new. There will be no more death, or sorrow, or pain, or poverty. No sin will be there, no curse. The throne of God and the Lamb will be there. His saints will serve Him, beholding His face forever and ever.

If I have described the dispensationalist scenario of the End Times in exhaustive detail, it is because no real understanding of Protestant fundamentalism in twentieth-century America is possible without an awareness of the particulars of these beliefs. "The Scofield Bible," writes Charles Strozier, "*is* the inerrant text of God in the minds of many unsophisticated fundamentalist believers." For such people, he adds, Scofield's notes are "canonical." Indeed, "most popular fundamentalist books are either slightly revised versions of the Scofield notes, or adapt his theory to contemporary events. It may well be that the Scofield Bible has touched the lives of more people than any other single book published in this century."

Yet nearly a century after the book's first appearance, most Catholics, Jews, Moslems, mainline Protestants, and secular people in the United States continue to know virtually nothing about the Scofield Bible, or about dispensational theology generally. When I mentioned Darby and Scofield to several Episcopal priests, they said they had never heard of either. Ditto dispensationalism. In the minds of most mainstream Christians and secular Americans, Protestant fundamentalism is just like nonfundamentalism, only more so. Yet English's book underlines the fact that Protestant fundamentalism is not a more "extreme" version of mainstream Christianity—it is a different creature entirely. Though many individual fundamentalists may be loving people, the theology to which they subscribe delights in a God who casts his children by the millions into eternal hellfire, and who has ordained a sequence of End Times events that amounts to a grotesque pageant of slaughter and bloodshed without any visible moral significance or spiritual dimension. English never explains, let alone asks, what the meaning of this End Times drama is, and why it should happen this way and not some other way. Nor does he ever show any hesitation in worshipping a God who in his savagery seems barely distinguishable from Hitler, Stalin, or Mao.

Nowhere does English cite the Great Commandment. Nowhere does he cite Paul's insistence that love is greater than faith and hope. Yet if English omits all words about love from his book, he emphasizes what he calls Jesus' "stern words." "Jesus did not hesitate to speak severely against hypocrisy and sin of every kind," English claims. "Furthermore, He declared unequivocally that eternal judgment will fall on those who reject Him. It would be difficult to find anywhere in literature stronger denunciation than Christ pronounced over the scribes and Pharisees . . . shortly before His trial and death. 'Woe unto you, scribes and Pharisees, hypocrites! For ye compass sea and land to make one proselyte, and when he is made, ye make him twofold more a child of hell than yourselves.'" (English omits to acknowledge that what Jesus criticized the scribes and Pharisees for, as we shall see, is their fundamentalism—their subordination of love to law, dogma, and institutional hierarchy.) English also cites with enthusiasm another ambiguous line that John attributes to Jesus—"If you believe not that I am he, ye shall die in your sins"—which English interprets to mean, "If you believe not that I am the Son of God . . ." English's distortion of the gospel's real emphases is outrageous—yet it reflects very faithfully the horrible monster that twentieth-century legalistic Christians have made out of their God and Savior and the hateful institution that they have made out of his church.

It was in the midst of the tension between premillennialism and modernism that a series of pamphlets appeared that would give a name to the antimodern faction. Issued largely in response to the Social Gospel, *The Fundamentals: A Testimony to the Truth* consisted of twelve volumes, each containing several essays by ministers, theology professors, and church historians. Appearing between 1910 and 1915, the pamphlets attacked evolution and the Higher Criticism and defended biblical inerrancy with well-nigh unprecedented stridency.

A foreword to *The Fundamentals* described the series as having been published through the generosity of "two Christian laymen" (a pair of rich brothers named Lyman and Milton Stewart) who "believe that the time has come when a new statement of the fundamentals of Christianity should be made." The foreword explained that the series would be "sent to every pastor, evangelist, missionary, theological professor, theological student, Sunday school superintendent, YMCA and YWCA secretary in the English speaking world, so far as the addresses of all these can be obtained." (This was a time when the Young Men's and Young Women's Christian Associations really *were* associations of young Christian men and women.) Printed in millions of copies, *The Fundamentals* sought to awaken people to the danger that "modernist" thinking posed to "traditional" religion, and to give them ammunition with which to fight back.

The thematic thrust and tone of the material collected in *The Fundamentals* are fairly represented by an essay in the third volume, "My Personal Experience with the Higher Criticism" by Professor J. J. Reeve of Southwestern Baptist Theological Seminary. Characterizing modern science as a threat to religion, Reeve argues that in a world where all experience was subject to scientific analysis,

> *there would be all science and no religion. In the array of scientific facts all religion would be evaporated. God, Christ, the Bible, and all else would be*

reduced to a mathematical or chemical formula. This is the ideal and goal of
the evolutionary hypothesis. The rationalist would rejoice at it, but the
Christian mind shrinks in horror from it. The Christian consciousness
perceives that an hypothesis which leads to such results is one of its
deadliest foes.

What is extraordinary here is the palpable fear, insecurity, and defensiveness—the horror, to use his own word—that Reeve feels at the thought of his religion's confrontation with science. It is as if Christianity were a fragile, defenseless creature and science a strapping new bully on the block. Reeve admits quite frankly that he is essentially closing his eyes to expanding knowledge out of fear that it will rob him of his faith. In a more sardonic tone, Reeve claims that in churches presided over by modernist Christians, "Jesus Christ is politely thanked for his services in the past, gallantly conducted to the confines of His world and bowed out as He is no longer needed and His presence might be very troublesome to some people. . . . Such a religion is the very negation of Christianity . . . a distinct reversion to heathenism." This representation of modernist Christians is absolutely unfair: Far from dismissing Jesus, modernist ministers of those times come off in their writings as being far more surely in touch with Christ than do their fundamentalist detractors. Yet Reeve denies that such people's religious experiences are genuine. To them, he claims, "the Bible itself becomes a plaything for the intellect, a merry-go-round for the mind partially intoxicated with its theory." This characterization of thinking as a childish, potentially dangerous pastime has continued to be common among fundamentalist Christians such as Pat Robertson, who has complained that in a secular world, "the mind becomes a playground of ideas."

Apropos of the "core doctrines" of "traditional" Christianity, Reeve says, "If all these things are not true to fact or to life, then God has been an arch-deceiver." This peculiar theme—that if some of the miracles reported in the Bible are not literally true, then God is a liar and Jesus a madman—has run through legalistic Christian writings ever since. For example:

• A 1996 issue of *In Touch,* a legalistic Southern Baptist magazine, maintains that "To say Jesus did not rise again is to call Him a liar."

- "If He did not in fact rise," writes the theologian J. B. Phillips, "His claim was false, and He was a very dangerous personality indeed."

- In a 1996 book, *The Empty Church,* Thomas C. Reeves writes: "Christianity without miracles is dead, and its Founder and the Apostles madmen."

- A legalistic Christian Web site says of Jesus that "He was either telling the truth, He was crazy, or He was a liar. But since everyone agrees that Jesus was a good man, how then could He be both good and crazy, or good and a liar? He had to be telling the truth. He *is* the only way."

There's a powerful emotion at the heart of such statements as these—an emotion that presumably lay latent in the minds of many legalistic Christians until they found their understanding of the faith challenged by science and scholarship. What kind of emotion? Well, such statements would certainly seem to affirm that beneath many legalists' insistence on their total belief in a totally inerrant Bible there lies a profound uncertainty, and with it a terror, either conscious or unconscious, that if they abandon what is essentially a self-deceiving pretense to belief, they will be left spiritually unmoored, emotionally helpless, intellectually spun off into chaos, without any psychological bearings whatsoever. Deep down, they know that the doctrines in which they claim to believe are indeed untrue, and for this reason, despite their vigorous protestations of faith, they *do* resent God and see him as an arch-deceiver—though they might never admit this resentment even to themselves.

J. J. Reeve acknowledges that Christianity "must and will be somewhat modified by the conception of a developing revelation and the application of the historical method." Yet he insists that Christianity "must prevail in all its essential features" because "it has a noble ancestry and a glorious history." It is surprising to see Reeve admitting the need for theological modification—but it is also rather odd to see him placing supreme value on Christianity's "noble ancestry" and "glorious history." Does Reeve even begin to understand the real value of Christianity? It's as if he's discussing some family with aristocratic pretensions rather than a faith that claims to offer the ultimate truth about the universe. Reeve's modernist contemporaries appear to have been much more certain about the genuine universality of Christ than does Reeve, whose concern seems less with preserving the essence of truth, goodness, and beauty for future generations than with not doing anything to upset adherents of "old-time religion."

The Fundamentals wasn't as rousing a success as the Stewart brothers had hoped. Yet it had a lasting impact in at least one respect. In 1920, Curtis Lee Laws, editor of a Baptist publication called *The Watchman Examiner*, was writing about a new antimodernist group in the Northern Baptist Convention when, seeking a catchy label for them, he recalled the title of the series of pamphlets the Stewart brothers had bankrolled some years before. Thus was born the term *fundamentalist*. Now both sides of the controversy had names: There were modernists and there were fundamentalists. And then there was the large mass of Protestants in between, not quite sure what to make of it all. Such was the state of American Christianity as the nation approached the 1920s—a decade that would prove to be crucial for the future of the struggle between the Church of Love and the Church of Law.

6

"SHALL THE FUNDAMENTALISTS WIN?"

EVERY YEAR FROM my infancy to my mid-teens, I spent my summers at the house of my maternal grandmother in Florence, South Carolina. The most neglected room of that house was a small den whose walls were covered with shelves full of books that had belonged to my late grandfather. In addition to running his own small business, my grandfather had been a Methodist evangelical singer, traveling from church to church to warble hymns in his fine tenor voice. What scandalized many in that small conservative town was that he performed not only in white but in "colored" churches, and counted black people among his friends. He was also an intellectual, and a maverick one at that; he read not only the Bible and traditional theological works but also books about new scientific discoveries and political ideas. To examine the titles on his books was to see the library of an earnest, wide-ranging seeker.

Among those books were several by a man whose unusual name stuck in my mind long after: Harry Emerson Fosdick. My mother told me that Fosdick had been one of my grandfather's heroes; she recalled the familiar sight of Granddaddy sitting in his chair and leaning in toward the radio to hear Fosdick preaching far away in New York. I later discovered that Fosdick had, in fact, been a hero to many. Virtually forgotten today—like Rauschenbusch—Fosdick, a Baptist preacher who was born in 1878 and who occupied the pulpit successively at New York's First Presbyterian Church, Park Avenue Baptist Church, and Riverside Church, was in his own day, for both his allies and his enemies, the very personification of the modernist point of view. He was at the white-hot center of the modernist-fundamentalist clash; more than anybody else, it was he who explained to Americans how Christianity might be meaningfully reconciled with what he called "the new knowledge" provided by science, archaeology, and the Higher Criticism.

Fosdick is not alone in being virtually forgotten. Also essentially absent from American popular consciousness today is the fact that in the 1920s the growing tensions between modernism and fundamentalism came to a head in a dramatic way. To be sure, the conflict was not as fierce in some denominations as in others. As Sydney Ahlstrom notes, the controversy "was minor where liberalism was weak or nonexistent (Southern Baptist) or predominant (Congregational), or where doctrinal concerns had always been secondary (Methodist)." Yet for a few years, several Protestant denominations underwent an unprecedented culture war that for a time seemed destined to tear them apart. This conflict was, in many ways, strikingly similar to the current face-off between "traditional Christians" and "secular humanists"; the difference is that in the 1920s, the people on both sides of the struggle were Christians.

To follow that struggle in the pages of the *New York Times* is to get the impression that it began almost overnight. The *Times* index for October–December 1923 is the first to contain a subentry for "Religion: Fundamentalism vs. Modernism"; the list of articles under this heading is more than two columns long, by far the longest subentry under "Religion" in that index volume. In the indexes covering the next four years, the "Fundamentalism vs. Modernism" subentry fluctuates in length from one-fifth of a column long to two columns long, and includes many substantial front-page stories. By 1927 the category is reduced to a handful of minor entries, and in late 1928 it disappears altogether for the first time. Included in those several years' worth of coverage are news articles concerning developments all over the country and in a wide range of denominations. The headlines alone paint a vivid picture of cultural conflict: "Seventh-Day Adventists Plan National Campaign for Fundamentalism"; "Presbyterian Ministers at Stony Brook Assembly Plead for the Old Faith."

The name that appears most often in the "Fundamentalism vs. Modernism" category is Fosdick's. Though he had been ordained as a Baptist, and had spent eleven years as a preacher in a New Jersey Baptist church, in 1922 he was teaching practical theology at Union Theological Seminary and serving as a "special preacher" at New York's First Presbyterian Church, where he regularly delivered the sermon at the main Sunday service. Fosdick had been an influential figure for years; yet it was not until May 21, 1922, that he gave the sermon that placed him at the center of the fundamentalist-modernist controversy.

Entitled "Shall the Fundamentalists Win?" this sermon came to be seen by his supporters as a seminal outline of the antifundamentalist case and by his opponents as (in the words of one of them) "an authoritative statement of the present opposition to the evangelical faith." In clear, vigorous prose, Fosdick noted that fundamentalists "insist that we must all believe in the historicity of certain special miracles, preeminently the virgin birth of our Lord; that we must believe in a special theory of inspiration—that the original documents of the Scripture, which of course we no longer possess, were inerrantly dictated to men a good deal as a man might dictate to a stenographer; that we must believe in a special theory of the atonement—that the blood of our Lord, shed in a substitutionary death, placates an alienated Deity and makes possible welcoming for the returning sinner; and that we must believe in the second coming of our Lord upon the clouds of heaven to set up a millennium here, as the only way in which God can bring history to a worthy denouement."

Fosdick examines three of these doctrines—the virgin birth, biblical inerrancy, and the Second Coming—and sets forth the fundamentalist and modernist perspectives on each. In the case of the virgin birth, he notes that it is common, indeed almost routine, for the founders of religions to be described by their followers as having been born of virgins; so Buddhists do with Buddha, Zoroastrians with Zoroaster, and Confucians with Lao-Tse. "When a personality arose so high that men adored him," Fosdick writes, "the ancient world attributed his superiority to some special divine influence in his generation, and they commonly phrased their faith in terms of miraculous birth." So it was with Jesus. Like us, he says, early Christians saw Jesus as having come "specially from God" and carrying with him "God's special influence and intention"; yet they expressed this specialness "in terms of a biological miracle that our modern minds cannot use."

In regard to the inerrancy of scripture, Fosdick notes that fundamentalists believe that "everything there [in the Bible]—scientific opinions, medical theories, historical judgments, as well as spiritual insight—is infallible." But he notes that when you actually read the Bible front to back, you find the idea of God constantly changing, so that statements in two different parts of scripture often contradict each other. Consequently modernist Christians view scripture not as an infallible historical account but as "the record of the progressive unfolding of the character of God to his people from early primitive days until the great unveiling in Christ."

Finally, Fosdick examines the Second Coming. The fundamentalist notion "is that Christ is literally coming, externally on the clouds of heaven, to set up his kingdom here." Believing this, "they sit still and do nothing and expect the world to grow worse and worse until he comes." To a liberal (a word Fosdick uses in this sermon in place of *modernist*), the idea that "Christ is coming!" means that "his will and principles will be worked out by God's grace in human life and institutions until '*he shall see of the travail of his soul and shall be satisfied.*'"

Fosdick asks, "Has anybody a right to deny the Christian name to those who differ with him on such points and to shut against them the doors of the Christian fellowship?" He answers this in the negative, and concludes by making several observations:

- There is a need for tolerance—on both sides. Though "just now the Fundamentalists are giving us one of the worst exhibitions of bitter intolerance that the churches of this country have ever seen," young modernists need to respond "not by controversial intolerance, but by producing, with our new opinions, something of the depth and strength, nobility and beauty of character that in other times were associated with other thoughts."

- Love is more important than doctrine. "There are many opinions in the field of modern controversy concerning which I am not sure whether they are right or wrong, but there is one thing I am sure of: courtesy and kindliness and tolerance and humility and fairness are right. Opinions may be mistaken; love never is."

- The mind is a terrible thing to waste. "Science treats a young man's mind as though it were really important." (Alas, Fosdick, in the manner of his time, tended to speak as if ideas, religious or otherwise, were the exclusive province of men.) The churches, by contrast, say, "Come, and we will feed you opinions from a spoon. No thinking is allowed here except such as brings you to certain specified, predetermined conclusions." The mind, Fosdick underscores, is not a threat to faith but an instrument by which we can better understand God and our relationship with him.

- The main business of Christianity should be not to discuss details of theology but to minister to human misery. At the time that Fosdick gave his sermon, the Armenian holocaust was under way. Such "colossal problems," he insisted, "must be solved in Christ's name and for Christ's sake"; to devote one's energies instead to theological controversy is "immeasurable folly."

Fosdick's reference in his sermon to young people reflects his special concern with reaching intelligent Christians of tender years who rejected fundamentalist dogma but hungered for spiritual experience. Unless the church made an effort to communicate its message to them in terms that did not outrage their intelligence, Fosdick insisted, they would be lost to the church—and the church would be lost to them. Fosdick, throughout his career, would make a special effort to reach young audiences. In addition to his sermons, which at the height of his fame routinely drew overflow crowds, he gave addresses at major universities and lectures to YMCA groups. In reading through old newspaper accounts of Fosdick's exploits, I realized that my maternal grandfather was only one of countless young people of the 1920s who responded enthusiastically to the Baptist preacher's message that you didn't have to close your mind to embrace Jesus as your savior.

Published later in 1922 as a pamphlet (under the title *The New Knowledge and the Christian Faith*), "Shall the Fundamentalists Win?" occasioned widespread attacks and made Fosdick, in the eyes of both friend and foe, the standard-bearer of Christian modernism—and its principal lightning rod. On September 24 John Roach Straton of New York's Calvary Baptist Church delivered a sermon attacking Fosdick and challenging him to a debate. (Fosdick declined the invitation.) Clarence Edward Macartney of Philadelphia's Arch Street Presbyterian Church responded to Fosdick's sermon both by publishing his own tract, entitled "Shall Unbelief Win?" and by taking institutional action, which resulted in the first of dozens of front-page *New York Times* articles about Fosdick. On October 18, 1922, the newspaper reported that the Presbytery of Philadelphia, at Macartney's instigation, had submitted to the Presbyterian Church's General Assembly a document of protest that took issue with "the kind of preaching done in the First Presbyterian Church of New York." Fosdick was not mentioned by name, but it was clear to everyone that the protest had been occasioned by "Shall the Fundamentalists Win?"

To read Fosdick's once-famous sermon today is to be astonished by its continuing power and by the enduring relevance of its salient points, among them:

- The continuity of modernist Christians' faith with historic Christian faith.

- The fact that letting go of fundamentalism does not imperil faith but in fact makes the Bible "more inspired and inspiring" and renders spiritual experience more vital. The fundamentalists' "static and mechanical theory of inspiration," he writes, is "a positive peril to the spiritual life."

- The alienness of the fundamentalists' mean-spiritedness and intolerance from the character of Jesus. "If he [Jesus] should walk through the ranks of the congregation this morning, can we imagine him claiming as his own those who hold one idea of inspiration and sending from him into outer darkness those who hold another?"

- The fact that if the fundamentalists continue to prevail in the established church, they will drive members away and destroy the institution. Because of fundamentalism, Fosdick warns, "educated people are looking for their religion outside the churches." Young people of faith who don't think "in ancient terms" are considered anathema by fundamentalists. This cannot go on, he says. "A religion that is afraid of the facts is doomed."

Near the end of "Shall the Fundamentalists Win?" Fosdick stated, "There is not a single thing at stake in the [fundamentalist-modernist] controversy on which depends the salvation of human souls." His fundamentalist opponents—among them James M. Gray, dean of the Moody Bible Institute—could not have disagreed more vehemently. Gray's response to Fosdick, an essay entitled "The Deadline of Doctrine Around the Church," amounts to a précis of the fundamentalists' antimodernist arguments. For me it brought to mind a passage in Fosdick's book *As I See Religion* (1932) that distinguishes between religious and scientific truths. Implicitly separating himself from fundamentalists who render putative religious truths with pseudoscientific precision (the ultimate example thereof, naturally, being Darby's seven dispensations), Fosdick noted that

> though religion is interested in truth, . . . often with a fierceness that science cannot surpass, it is interested rather as art is; and in a scientific age this leads to all sorts of misunderstanding. . . . We are convinced beyond peradventure that he who travels merely the path of electrons, atoms, molecules toward a vision of the Ultimate misses it, and that he who travels the road of spiritual values—goodness, truth, beauty—finds it. . . . Many who use the symbols of religion do not know what they are doing. They read poetry as prose, take similes with deadly literalness, make a dogma from a metaphor. They call God a person, and to hear them do it one would think that our psychological processes could naïvely be attributed to the Eternal. It is another matter altogether, understanding symbolic language, to call God personal when one means that up the roadway of goodness, truth, and beauty, which outside personal experience have no significance, one must travel toward the truth about the Ultimate—"beyond the comprehension of the human mind." Of course, that is vague; no idea of the Eternal which is not vague can possibly approximate the truth.

To read "The Deadline of Doctrine" on the heels of Fosdick's sermon is to recognize that Gray's essay perfectly illustrates Fosdick's distinction between reading the Bible as poetry and reading it as prose. Gray, of course, does the latter.

He opens by rejecting Fosdick's terminology. The word *fundamentalist,* he says, "is unnecessary . . . because the body of truth for which it stands has always had a name which requires neither explanation nor defense." In other words, the present struggle is not between two kinds of Christians; it is between true Christians and pretenders. Gray asks, "Is liberalism Christianity?" His answer: a firm and angry no. What Fosdick calls fundamentalism, Gray says, introducing a quotation from a familiar hymn, is quite simply the "Faith of our fathers, living still, / In spite of dungeon, fire, and sword"; what Fosdick calls liberal Christianity is anathema. Gray refers to Fosdick's identification of the virgin birth, scriptural inerrancy, substitutionary atonement, and the Second Coming as the "four stakes which the fundamentalists are driving *'to mark out the deadline of doctrine around the church,'*" and to Fosdick's assertion "that no one has a right to deny the Christian name to those who do not hold these doctrines, or to shut against them the doors of Christian fellowship." Gray disagrees, arguing that Saint Paul himself demands such a denial and a shutting of doors: "Though we, or an angel from heaven, preach any gospel unto you than that which we preached unto you, let him be accursed" (Gal. 1:8–9). This quotation from Saint Paul has continued, down to the present time, to be a favorite of legalistic Protestants.

Gray blames Fosdick's "new movements in Christian thought" for Bolshevism and World War I. The latter connection is particularly odd, as Fosdick's sermon exudes a peaceable spirit while Gray's essay is chockablock with violent images. For example, Gray quotes the letter to Timothy enjoining him to "war a good warfare" (1 Tim. 1:18–19); he cites Peter's statement that "false teachers" will *"bring upon themselves swift destruction"* with their "damnable heresies" (2 Pet. 2:1); and he takes note of John's command that "if any one cometh unto you and bringeth not this teaching, receive him not into your house, and give him no greeting" (2 John 7:11). Gray concludes from these passages that it is incumbent upon Christians of good conscience "to withhold the Christian name from, and shut the door of Christian fellowship against the deniers of such doctrines." While Fosdick's account of Christianity draws on the most beautiful passages in scripture, principally from the Gospels, Gray's response to that account draws on some of the Bible's ugliest and most violent passages, few of them from the Gospels.

Having denied Fosdick and his followers the name of Christian, Gray proceeds through the four matters of doctrine on which Fosdick focuses in "Shall the Fundamentalists Win?" His method is essentially one of assertion: The Bible says these things are so; case closed. Does extra-scriptural evidence suggest otherwise? Then perhaps Satan is at work. "Would it occur to him [Fosdick], that possibly the prince of darkness might wish to forestall the effect of the biological miracle of Jesus' birth by counterfeiting it in the annals of paganism?" In other words, were the references to virgin births in other faiths planted by Satan, perhaps, in order to challenge Christians' faith in the *real* virgin birth? To read Fosdick's sermon and then Gray's response is to feel that they inhabit entirely different mental worlds. In Fosdick's world, other faiths are to be respected, for all have something in them of God; in Gray's world, elements of other faith traditions may well have been designed by Satan to weaken Christians' faith. Fosdick's religion centers on the person and the teachings of Jesus, which for him can be separated easily from such "tiddledywinks and peccadillos" as the virgin birth, angelic annunciations, and sundry miraculous happenings; Gray's faith is constructed of that very tissue of miracles, and to challenge any part of it is to threaten to destroy the whole. For Fosdick, Satan and angels and so forth are metaphors, and the gospel is to be read as a poetic attempt to convey the essence of Jesus; for Gray, Satan and angels are quite literal realities, and the gospel narratives are to be read as pure history. For Fosdick, all of Christianity flows out of the commandments to love God and one's neighbor, and the validity of other parts of scripture is to be measured by the degree to which they are consistent with those commandments; for Gray, every line of scripture is equally valid, and indeed he is inclined to quote verses that directly contradict the commandment to love one's neighbor. For Fosdick, fundamentalism arrests spiritual growth; for Gray, modernism destroys belief and thwarts salvation. Fosdick holds out hope for entente between the two parties, envisioning a church in which fundamentalists and liberals live together in harmony; Gray insists that it is the obligation of "true Christians" not to compromise in any way with apostasy.

In Gray's essay as well as in other fundamentalist responses to Fosdick, one may note certain recurring elements that remain hallmarks of fundamentalist rhetoric:

- An insistence that modernist Christians are *not* Christians. Samuel Craig, in a 1923 essay in the *Princeton Theological Review* entitled "Genuine and Counterfeit Christianity," distinguishes between "those who are Christians and those who merely call themselves Christians. . . . Those to whom Jesus is not a present object of worship, and who have no consciousness of themselves as sinners redeemed by His blood, are of a totally different religion from those to whom He is an object of faith and whose hope for time and eternity is grounded in the conviction that He bore their sins in His own body on the tree." And Reeve in *The Fundamentals* argues that people who buy into Fosdick's views thereby "forsake the Christian standpoint" and that "a preacher who has thoroughly imbibed these beliefs has no proper place in an evangelical Christian pulpit." (This is the ultimate reactionary posture: seeing a preacher's function as being to affirm believers' attitudes, not to challenge their assumptions and values, to make them think, to beckon them to a higher spiritual plane.)

  From Fosdick's time until our own, fundamentalists have talked about nonlegalistic Christians as if Jesus is not a present fact to them. They are wrong. For nonlegalistic Christians Jesus *is* a present fact. What fundamentalists are uncomfortable with is the degree to which nonlegalistic Christians assume that present Jesus to be continuous and consistent with the Jesus of history, whom they take as a life model. The hostility of fundamentalists to the historical Jesus can reach astonishing proportions; many fall just short of saying "The hell with the Jesus of history!" The Baptist theologian Calvin Miller goes so far as to say that Christians "are not interested in talking about the Jesus who *was*. They are interested only in the

Christ who *is*. The academic, historical Jesus is not to be compared with the Christ of the *right now*. This is not the Christ of theology or of history, but the Christ of faith." If, for contemporary legalists like Miller, the Jesus of history threatens the institutions and ideologies they have constructed around the concept of the saving Christ, it is plainly because the Jesus of history had values that differed dramatically from their own.

• Martial metaphors. As Gray quotes Saint Paul's injunction to Timothy to "war a good warfare," so George Whitfield Ridout opens a reply to Fosdick with a two-page poem that likens the conflict between fundamentalists and modernists to all-out war. The poem, "Valiant for the Truth" by Frances Ridley Havergal, begins with the line "Unfurl the Christian Standard! Lift it manfully on high," and goes on to identify Christian values with soldierly virtues: "No faint-hearted flag of truce with mischief and with wrong, / Should lead the soldiers of the Cross, the faithful and the strong." To Ridout, clearly, love and peace are not virtues in the fundamentalist-modernist controversy but marks of faintheartedness; the true virtue is a steadfast willingness to fight. Saying that "it is high time that the Protestant Church should awake to the perils that beset us," Ridout quotes twelve lines of another poem filled with images of warfare, including the following: "Dread not the din and smoke, / The stifling poison of the fiery air; / Courage! It is the battle of thy God!" In similar spirit, Samuel Craig refers antagonistically to those who cry "Peace, peace; when there is no peace," and asks, "If the trumpet give an uncertain voice, who shall prepare himself for war?"

It is instructive to compare such rhetoric to that of Fosdick, who complains in his 1925 book *The Modern Use of the Bible* that "Our Western civilization is built on war. . . . We have bred men for war, trained men for war; we have gloried in war; we have made warriors our heroes and even in our churches we have put the battle flags beside the Cross. . . . With one corner of our mouth we have praised the Prince of Peace and with the other we have glorified war."

• A preoccupation with Christianity as the "faith of our fathers," in the words of Frederick William Faber's nineteenth-century hymn.

Gray, as noted, quotes the first two lines of Faber's hymn in his essay, saying that what Fosdick calls fundamentalism is quite simply the "Faith of our fathers, living still, / In spite of dungeon, fire, and sword." Ridout, in his aforementioned essay, quotes the hymn's last two lines: "Faith of our fathers, Holy Faith, / We will be true to thee till death." None of Fosdick's opponents seems to have quoted the hymn's third stanza, which was more up Fosdick's theological street than their own:

> *Faith of our fathers! we will love*
> *Both friend and foe in all our strife,*
> *And preach thee, too, as love knows how,*
> *By kindly words and virtuous life.*

The tone of these "faith of our fathers" arguments tends to be self-consciously desperate and pathetic. To read some of Fosdick's fundamentalist opponents is to get the impression that they have determined that they are on the *Titanic,* as it were, and have decided to go down with it, singing hymns and brandishing swords. But God doesn't need this kind of fierce protection: We're not his saviors and protectors; he's ours. If these fundamentalists were defensive, it was because something precious to them was indeed threatened— namely the American Protestant establishment. If Christianity, for Fosdick, was about rejecting that establishment's narrow social ideas and prejudices in the name of Jesus, for many of his opponents lifting high the cross became essentially equivalent to hoisting the Confederate flag. When one reads Ridout's charge that Christian modernism is "robbing Protestants of their Bible" and "striking at the foundation of our Republic," one cannot help thinking that Jesus' earliest followers were criticized in similar terms for overthrowing the Old Faith and threatening the Roman Empire's stability. It should be remembered, too, that the Republic whose foundation Ridout was defending was one in which white fundamentalists forbade blacks to worship in their churches and turned a blind eye to lynchings.

The "faith of our fathers" position is the very antithesis of a living faith. An attachment to a faith that is based on sentiment, nostalgia, or filial loyalty may be many things, but it is not Christianity. On the contrary, what it amounts to is an equation of faith with social order, stability, and continuity. It is these conservative values, and not faith itself, that fundamentalism has always been fundamentally about. Modernist views, charges Reeve, will "undermine many of the most cherished beliefs of the churches." *Cherished* is a striking choice of words; it enshrines sentimental attachment, habitual affection, as a key criterion of faith statements. Not recognized at all here is the value—indeed the Christian obligation—of being ready to challenge the familiar (or at least to entertain challenges to the familiar) and the need to confront the comfortable.

- A tendency to connect modernism with elitism and secularism. Ridout notes a recent speech by Fosdick to a packed audience at Harvard University. How, Ridout asks, did that audience "stand from the viewpoint of the evangelical Christian?" He quotes the *Christian Century* to the effect that at "a recent religious meeting at Harvard," only four of the several hundred present had read the Bible through or had prayed the day before, and "only about one-fourth believed in a personal God." Instead of recognizing that these students had real spiritual longings and sought an understanding of Christianity that made sense to them, Ridout—presaging today's "cultural elite" rhetoric—is cruelly dismissive: "This, then, is the class that Dr. Fosdick wants us to modernize Christianity for. He wants us to reverse the faith of the ages to meet this class of young people!"

Often accompanying the charge of elitism, then as now, is the claim that those who are willing to reconsider entrenched theological propositions are arrogantly setting themselves up as God. As Reeve writes in *The Fundamentals,* "When one makes his philosophy his authority, it is not a long step until he makes himself his own god. His own reason becomes supreme in his thinking and this reason becomes his lord." Such, Reeve says, is the case with the Higher Critics, who "recognize no authority but their own moral instincts and philosophical reason. Now, as the evolution theory makes all things exist only in a state of change, of flux, or of becoming, God is therefore changing and developing, the Bible and Christ will be outgrown, Christianity itself will be left behind. Hence, there is no *absolute* truth, nothing in the moral religious world is fixed or certain." Translation: Unless you slavishly accept total biblical literalism, you're "your own God." This has become a standard legalist line. What is expressed here is, of course, a terror of change, a desperate need for propositions that are absolute, fixed, certain.

Fundamentalists covet absolutes: For them, true religion is a matter of giving oneself over to a set of inflexible doctrines and of keeping one's own mind and spirit in check to the extent that they threaten to rebel. The doctrines cannot be questioned, even if they are plainly inconsistent with the testimony of reason and experience and even if they contain blatant internal contradictions. To Fosdick, by contrast, true Christian faith is a matter of attaining an internal harmony of precept, reason, and experience, spiritual and otherwise. Ridout's reading of this is that "Dr. Fosdick is a law unto himself." But of course if Fosdick was being a law unto himself, then so was Darby when he invented dispensationalism.

The Fosdick controversy stepped up in 1923. In January, a group of New York Baptists formed the Baptist Fundamental Association of the Metropolitan Area in order to combat "the increasing boldness of radicals and religious rationalists in the Baptist denomination." The *New York Times* weighed in on April 14, lauding Fosdick in an editorial as "a preacher whom any pulpit in the world should be eager to welcome" and chiding those who sought to silence him. In June, Fosdick was severely censured by the Presbyterian General Assembly for "Shall the Fundamentalists Win?" He submitted his resignation, but his church refused to accept it. That month, 198 New York City ministers attended a luncheon in Fosdick's honor, described by one participant as "a love feast." One of those ministers, Henry Sloane Coffin, praised Fosdick as "an outstanding conservative. He conserves to the Church the many thinking men and women who would otherwise be lost to it. He conserves the central doctrines of the faith by interpreting them in forms which appeal convincingly to the mind of today. He conserves the Church as an institution, building it up and rendering it far more powerful in our city and land."

Fosdick's attack on fundamentalists, and their efforts to oust him, created a sense of crisis on both sides. On June 3, in a sermon entitled "The Present Crisis in Presbyterianism," a Staten Island minister called Fosdick "the most dangerous of all liberals" and a tool of Satan. On the same day the president of the conservative National Bible Institute attacked Fosdick in an address entitled "Christianity's Foundations Impregnable." Meanwhile, at the Brick Presbyterian Church, the modernist minister Henry Van Dyke defended Fosdick in a sermon on "The Perpetual Crisis in the Church." A few days later the *Times* reported that groups of students from Columbia, Cornell, and Mount Holyoke had written letters in support of Fosdick. When, on June 10, Fosdick mounted the steps of his pulpit, First Presbyterian was packed with an overflow crowd that heard him place individual spiritual experience above institutional dogma: "There are some things that no man can specialize in for anybody else. All vital experiences are individual. There are no proxies for the soul. You must know God for yourself."

The year 1924 began with a bang. On January 1, the *Times* reported that Lee W. Heaton, an Episcopal clergyman in Fort Worth, Texas, had given a sermon denying the virgin birth and been brought up on a heresy charge. Heaton's bishop refused to proceed with a trial, but in the next few weeks, developments in the fundamentalist–modernist controversy came fast and furious. On January 4, Henry Van Dyke gave up his pew in Princeton's First Presbyterian Church because of a sermon given there by J. Gresham Machen, a professor at Princeton Theological Seminary, who was widely considered the leading figure in the fundamentalist camp. Complaining that Gresham "practically accuses the liberals of denying their Lord" and "said they were both disloyal and pagan," Van Dyke commented: "That is the kind of preaching I can't stand." Later that week the *Times* reported that the faculty of the Episcopal Theological Seminary in Cambridge, Massachusetts, had suggested that the Episcopal Church "make the use of its creeds . . . permissive instead of obligatory." Wrote the faculty: "The Church is greater than the creeds. The central faith in God as He is found in Christ, upon which the Church is built, is not destroyed or diminished by doubts concerning the method of Christ's birth, of His return to God or of His future judgment."

That Monday, January 7, the *Times* reported that "the controversy between Fundamentalists and Modernists was renewed yesterday in many pulpits in this city." At the Church of the Ascension, Percy Stickney Grant preached on the question "Can Religion Stand New Truth?"; at Community Church, Dr. Charles H. Parkhurst spoke on "The Real Fundamentals of Religion," insisting that Christianity be viewed as a matter of personal experience and not as a philosophical or intellectual system. Two days later, the *Times* reported that "leading Modernists in the Protestant Episcopal Church made plans to carry on the Church war at a three-hour meeting yesterday morning at the Union League Club." One of the participants stated that the meeting represented "the launching of a serious movement to modernize the Episcopal Church." That same day, the special Presbyterian committee charged with investigating Fosdick's sermons exonerated him of heresy charges. On January 18, the fundamentalist group of the Presbytery of New York held a mass meeting at Harlem–New York Presbyterian Church to defend "historical Presbyterianism." Calling Fosdick "a foreigner within our gates," A. Gordon MacLennan, pastor of Bethany Presbyterian Church, demanded that he "leave the Presbyterian fold."

Recognizing that denominational pressure would not abate, Fosdick submitted his resignation again later in 1924 and this time it was accepted. He left First Presbyterian in March 1925 and agreed to take up the pulpit at Park Avenue Baptist Church. Every major stage of this job switch—Fosdick's resignation, its acceptance, his farewell sermon at First Presbyterian, the invitation from First Baptist, and his acceptance of it—made the front page of the *Times*.

Yet the defining story of the fundamentalist-modernist controversy would take place that summer not in New York City but in Dayton, Tennessee. It was there, in July 1925, that William Jennings Bryan, the former secretary of state, three-time presidential candidate, and living symbol of Protestant fundamentalism, prosecuted a case against John T. Scopes, a twenty-four-year-old science instructor at Rhea County High School who had been accused of violating a Tennessee law against teaching evolution. Clarence Darrow, America's most famous lawyer, a notorious agnostic, and a leading defender of underdogs and of progressive learning, served as the defense attorney. It didn't take long for both sides of the fundamentalist-modernist controversy to recognize the case's symbolic importance. To read the *New York Times* reports on the trial—which appeared on the paper's front page every day for nearly three weeks—is to be reminded again and again of today's legalistic Christians:

- Bryan, upon arriving in Dayton for the trial, told the *Times* that "the contest between evolution and Christianity is a duel to the death.... If evolution wins in Dayton Christianity goes—not suddenly, of course, but gradually—for the two cannot stand together." This flat-out insistence on the utter incompatibility of Christianity and evolution continues to be a standard element of legalistic Christian rhetoric.

- The *Times* noted that "nobody paid any attention to the anti-evolution law or the fact that evolution was being taught until Scopes was arrested. Now that the flood has descended upon them, Dayton folk feel that something momentous is in the air, and that Mr. Bryan is the champion of God, but that about ends their mental reaction." Today's legalistic multitudes often seem to operate in the same way, finding little or no problem with certain social developments until their leaders tell them to.

- In an emotional jeremiad delivered on the eve of the trial, Bryan's fellow prosecutor, Attorney General A. T. Stewart, asked, "Would they have me believe that I was once a worm and writhed in the dust? Will they take from me my hope of a hereafter? I want to go beyond this world to where there is eternal happiness for me and others." What is at once manifest about this plaint is that it implicitly sets aside any question of truth or falsity: Evolution is opposed not because it is wrong but because, in Stewart's view, it quashes his hope of heaven. This is an essential aspect of legalistic Christian thinking: It evinces, as does the thought of devotees of other totalitarian systems, a fanatical desire to suppress propositions that contradict those by which they have chosen to live, and that are feared precisely to the extent that they do indeed appear to be true.

- Stewart's speech was countered eloquently by Darrow's defense-team partner Dudley Field Malone, who, in response to those who

would say "destroy science, but keep our Bible," commented, "Keep
your Bible, keep it as your consolation, keep it as your guide, but
keep it where it belongs—in the world of your own conscience, in
the world of your individual judgment, in the world of the Protestant conscience that I heard so much about when I was a boy." That
Malone's comment was well received by his fundamentalist audience
shows that legalistic American Christians are not necessarily incapable of being reached by modernist thinking. Though complex
intellectual arguments by nonlegalists often backfire because legalists tend to respond by bristling at perceived condescension and by
retreating defensively from confusing ambiguities into simplistic
putative certainties, appeals that address them with an implicit
assumption of their basic fairness, good humor, and good sense, and
that frame the issues at hand in clear language that doesn't seem to
pose a threat to their highest values and hopes, are not automatically doomed to fall on deaf ears.

The Scopes trial lasted over two weeks, but the high drama didn't
come till the last day of testimony, July 20. "At last it has happened,"
began the article on page 1 of the *Times* the next morning. "After days
of ineffective argument and legal quibbling, with speeches that merely
skirted the matter which everyone wanted discussed in this Scopes
anti-evolution trial, William Jennings Bryan, Fundamentalist, and
Clarence Darrow, agnostic and pleader of unpopular causes, locked
horns today under the most remarkable circumstances ever known to
American court procedure." What was most remarkable was that
Bryan, who agreed to be put on the stand by Darrow as an expert on
the Bible, ended up making a fool of himself and being jeered at by
his own supporters. In order to accommodate more spectators, the trial
had been moved from the courtroom onto the courthouse lawn, and
it was there, wrote the *Times* reporter, that a huge crowd of locals "saw
Darrow and Bryan in actual conflict—Mr. Darrow's rationalism in
combat with Mr. Bryan's faith—and forgot for the moment that
Bryan's faith was its own."

In a scene that was, years later, pretty faithfully reproduced in the
play and movie *Inherit the Wind,* Darrow posed a series of questions
that revealed Bryan's almost total ignorance of ancient history and

modern science and that also devastatingly exposed the conflicts between, on the one hand, common sense and universally accepted scientific fact and, on the other, biblical literalism. For example, in a time when people accept that the earth goes around the sun, what does it mean to say that Joshua made the sun stand still? And what of the passage in the Bible about Cain, one of Adam and Eve's two sons, taking a wife: Where did she come from? "He was entangled," pronounced a *Times* editorial about Bryan's disastrous performance, "and made to turn himself inside out; and there was little or nothing inside. It has long been known to many that he was only a voice calling from a poorly furnished brain-room. But how almost absolutely unfurnished it was the public didn't know till he was forced to make an inventory." Though the judge found for the plaintiffs, the trial dealt Bryan a terrible blow. A week later, still in Dayton, he died suddenly of an aneurysm complicated by a cerebral hemorrhage.

Yet the trial's repercussions reached far beyond Bryan. It also caused a dramatic change in the status of the fundamentalist cause. For the mainstream media—which were controlled by urbanites who were either modernist Christians or members of the nascent secular culture—the trial established Protestant fundamentalism as a crude, rustic, marginal phenomenon that was not to be taken seriously. Certainly the utter humiliation of Bryan's testimony made fundamentalists realize that they could not confront the Darrows of the world in fair public debate and come out ahead. For many on both sides, Bryan's death seemed to foreshadow the imminent passing of fundamentalism. As a consequence of Bryan's humiliation in Dayton, then, fundamentalists proceeded to withdraw from the public square and remained essentially withdrawn from it for nearly half a century. Ralph Reed has described this period as "two generations of self-imposed retreat from political involvement." During these two generations, Reed writes, "fundamentalists and their evangelical brethren built a picket fence against the encroachments of what they came to call 'secular humanism,' a faith in the capacity of man to solve his problems without the help of God."

Though the fundamentalist-modernist controversy did not die out after the Scopes trial, it did disappear, to an amazing extent, from the front pages and from most Americans' consciousness. For a time, fun-

damentalist preachers had believed that if they mounted a vigorous
defense of "tradition," modernist thinking might be driven out of the
church; for a time, modernists had believed that if they could only get
people to listen and *think,* they could bring church doctrine into line
with "the new learning." What each side discovered, however, was that
its opposition would not be easily conquered or driven out. Over the
years, fundamentalists introduced resolutions in national church bodies that would forbid modernist teachings in seminaries, ban modernist
preaching from pulpits, and deny ordination to candidates who failed
strict tests of doctrinal orthodoxy; though such resolutions won passage in the Southern Baptist Convention, fundamentalists generally
proved unable to muster enough votes to pass similar measures in the
other major denominations. Marsden, in writing about what appeared,
in the 1920s, to be the triumph of modernist Christianity over fundamentalism, emphasizes the importance of the fact that the modernists
"took their stand on the question of tolerance"; since "most American Protestants were neither modernists nor militant fundamentalists,"
he writes, "overtures for peace and tolerance often could command
substantial support." By 1926, then, "it became clear that policies of
inclusiveness and tolerance would prevail."

The conflict between modernism and fundamentalism did not evap-
orate overnight; yet by 1927 the subcategory of "fundamentalism vs.
modernism" in the *New York Times* index had shrunk to a handful of
minor entries. Preachers on both sides began declaring the issue dead.
Most major denominations began to steer around controversial questions. So firmly did modernism establish itself as a part of the mainstream culture that, just as the word *talkies* became unnecessary when
silent movies disappeared, so the word *modernist* gradually ceased being
used to mean "nonfundamentalist Christian." Eventually Americans
would forget that it had ever meant such a thing.

In the years after the Scopes trial, Fosdick's career flourished. With fundamentalists out of the mainstream picture, he came to be seen less as
a controversial figure than as an ornament of mainstream American
religious culture. In 1931 he began preaching at New York's interde-
nominational Riverside Church, which John D. Rockefeller (a mod-

ernist Baptist) had built for him. Fosdick went on to be the country's most celebrated minister, preaching on social justice and on his vision of Christianity. Yet he largely left the fundamentalist–modernist controversy behind him, generally choosing not to attack fundamentalists directly. It was as if everyone on both sides had begun to feel that there was no point in further attacks: The fundamentalists were about one thing, and the modernists were about another, and the situation seemed destined to stay that way. In any event, most modernists believed that as rural education improved, as the South advanced, and as younger generations of Americans grew to adulthood, fundamentalism would die out of its own accord.

7

THE
LEGALISTIC BOOM

YET LEGALISTIC RELIGION in America did not die out. Far from it. In the early nineteenth century, Jefferson had looked ahead and foreseen an America dominated by Unitarianism—and had been dead wrong. In the same way, as modernist Christians looked ahead after the Scopes trial, many foresaw a twentieth-century America dominated by mainline churches whose congregations and ministers had theological views much like Fosdick's. Yet what happened was something quite different. Yes, mainstream American culture did progress in a generally liberal direction during the century's middle decades, and the mainline churches went along for the ride. But that mainstream culture also became increasingly secularized, and as it did so, the mainline churches, especially the more liberal ones, declined steadily in both membership and influence.

Meanwhile, far from the consciousness of most Americans, legalistic Christianity underwent a quiet boom. On the margins of society, out of the media spotlight, dispensationalism advanced apace, winning away from the mainline churches men and women who, intimidated by the modern world, wanted certitude, fixity, and strict guidance. If you perused major newspapers and newsmagazines during World War II, you might come away with the idea that Fosdick was the most popular minister in the United States; but if you actually went out into the country, you would soon discover that Fosdick's celebrity was minuscule compared to that of the fundamentalist preacher Charles E. Fuller, whose *Old Fashioned Revival Hour* was the nation's most popular radio program. That program's high ratings were especially remarkable owing to the fact that the national radio networks, under the influence of the mainline denominations that made up the Federal Council of Churches, denied fundamentalist preachers access to their airwaves, forcing Fuller to invent the idea of syndicating his programs to local stations. His example was followed by many other legalistic ministers.

While fundamentalism flourished, so too did another form of religion that was then perceived as differing dramatically from it. Pentecostalism traces its modern history to New Year's Eve, 1900, when Charles F. Parham, a young Methodist minister in Topeka who had been seeking to recover the enthusiasm of the early church, placed his hands on a young woman's head and she began emitting sounds that neither of them understood. Parham spread the word. Soon many American ministers were claiming that they had recovered the miraculous gifts of the Holy Spirit described in the New Testament, including prophecy, faith healing, and "speaking in tongues," or glossolalia. The Book of Acts described how on the day of Pentecost, fifty days after the Resurrection, the disciples "were all filled with the Holy Spirit and began to talk in other tongues, as the Spirit gave them power of utterance." Accordingly this new kind of faith was called Pentecostalism; its distinguishing gifts were called charismatic, from the Greek word for gifts, *charismata*. At first Pentecostalism found its way into established congregations, mostly in Baptist, Methodist, and

Holiness churches; soon, however, independent Pentecostal denominations—such as the Assemblies of God and the Church of God
(Cleveland, Tennessee)—came to be formed. Before long America
had a huge subculture of Holy Rollers (as they were jocularly called)
that was largely rural, underclass, and African-American, and thus
virtually invisible to the white overclass and the mainstream media.
So it remained until the 1960s, when an immense "charismatic
renewal" saw Pentecostal practices spread to churches in virtually every
denomination—Roman Catholics included—and to middle-class
Americans of every race.

Early in the century, Protestant fundamentalists looked upon Pen-
tecostalists with suspicion as practitioners of a very different form of
religion. Fundamentalism centered on fixed institutional doctrine, Pentecostalism on intense individual experience. Charismatic Christianity
even has its own distinguishing rite, the Baptism of the Holy Spirit,
which is often accompanied by glossolalia. Yet over the decades the
line between fundamentalism and Pentecostalism blurred. Today, as a
result of the charismatic renewal, many fundamentalist and evangelical
congregations incorporate charismatic gifts in their worship to some
degree; meanwhile, the biblical literalism, clerical authoritarianism, and
strict sexual morality of most Pentecostal churches make them, in
many ways, indistinguishable from non-Pentecostal fundamentalist
churches. Pentecostalism has, in short, become an integral part of the
spectrum of American legalistic Christianity. Indeed, the man whose
name is, in most American minds, a veritable synonym for Protestant
fundamentalism—Pat Robertson—is a Pentecostalist; more than anyone else, Robertson is responsible for bringing fundamentalism, Pentecostalism, and conservative evangelicalism together into a single
coherent movement.

Why, in the twentieth century, did mainline churches dwindle and
legalistic churches prosper? One reason: the advent of mass communi-
cations. Tent-meeting revivals had been a fact of rural life well into the
first quarter of the century, and made national celebrities of people like
Billy Sunday and Aimee Semple McPherson; as late as 1927, two years
after the Scopes trial, Sinclair Lewis's novel *Elmer Gantry* took on the
vulgarity, hypocrisy, and emotional manipulation practiced by tent-
meeting evangelists. But radio rendered tent meetings obsolete; the

mass audience that traveling evangelists had reached could now be addressed en masse by radio ministers like Charles E. Fuller. Fuller knew how to speak to that audience. He knew that the radio audience, like the tent-meeting crowds, didn't want to be helped to reflect intelligently on God and to attain a profound personal experience of the numinous; they wanted a preacher who set forth clearly what they had to do and say in order to be saved from hellfire. They also wanted to feel part of a group of people who believed the same things, shared the same values, and followed the same orders. (So it was that Pat Robertson, decades later, called his flagship TV program *The 700 Club*, the implication being that his viewers were not just sitting home alone but belonged to a club.) Fuller spoke to these people's needs, and he taught millions of them to think as he did about life, death, and the Almighty; they flocked, in turn, to local churches where ministers preached the gospel as he did, and when their sons expressed an interest in the ministry, they sent them to Fuller's own seminary. In later decades, televangelists like Jimmy Swaggart and Oral Roberts shaped American religious life in similar ways, feeding the growth of legalistic churches.

Several observers have sought to explain why those churches grew while mainline churches shrank. Books like Dean M. Kelley's *Why Conservative Churches Are Growing* and Roger Finke and Rodney Stark's *The Churching of America 1776–1990: Winners and Losers in Our Religious Economy* are crowded with graphs showing the dramatic changes in membership numbers and charts detailing the connection between these numbers and other factors. Their conclusions are almost identical: As Kelley sums it up, strong churches tend to demand doctrinal absolutism ("we have the Truth and all others are in error"), behavioral conformity, unquestioning obedience, group solidarity and commitment, and a zeal to convert (but remain separate from) an evil and error-ridden world. Weak churches, meanwhile, respect diversity and individuality, encourage critical inquiry and dialogue with outsiders, and are characterized by indecision, laxity, indifference to evangelism, and a tendency to keep one's spiritual experience and insight to oneself. In short, to borrow the terminology of Finke and Stark's subtitle, legalistic churches are inclined to be "winners," and mainline churches are apt to be "losers." *"Religious organizations,"* write Finke and Stark (the italics are theirs), *"are stronger to the degree that they impose significant costs in terms of sacrifice and even stigma upon their members."* What makes for a strong church, then, is a strong framework—one that makes people feel safe and special, that provides unambiguous answers to all their questions, and that gives direction to them in every aspect of their lives, thoughts, and feelings. The flip side of this is that "to the degree that denominations rejected traditional doctrines and ceased to make serious demands on their followers, they ceased to prosper."

By "prosper," of course, Finke and Stark mean "grew in numbers." They discuss the "winners and losers" in breathtakingly businesslike terms; their book is as fixated on the number of bodies in the pews as it is indifferent to the spiritual health of the souls inhabiting those bodies. They wax sarcastic about those in the mainline churches who suggest that "religion is not meaningfully reduced to membership counts" and that "what matters is what is in people's hearts (and presumably that is beyond measure)." You can almost hear the sneer in that parenthetical remark. Yet for serious Christians, there *is* something in the human heart that is beyond measure; that Finke and Stark can mock this idea reveals a great deal about the shallow materialist values that inform their study.

What of the argument, advanced not only by Finke and Stark but by Kelley as well, that churches grow because they impose a stigma? This is absurd. Perhaps in the academic world that Finke and Stark inhabit (they teach sociology at Purdue and the University of Washington, respectively), being a Pentecostalist or a Southern Baptist fundamentalist, say, would carry some stigma. But among the underclass white southerners who make up the bulk of these churches' members, belonging to them doesn't impose a stigma at all. On the contrary, fundamentalist and Pentecostalist churches draw in members who feel that their own cultural values and prejudices have been stigmatized by a national culture that is too liberal and well-educated for their comfort. These churches offer such people the comfort of membership in a community that reflects their own discomfort with mainstream society. To the extent that they do feel a stigma for belonging to a certain church, the stigma is generally experienced positively, as a reminder that they are "saved" and that those who stigmatize them are "unsaved," and as a means of reinforcing their sense of solidarity with other members of their church. As we have seen, Protestant legalists routinely discuss their relations with the outside world in military terms, and indeed one of the psychological benefits of membership in a legalistic church is that one enjoys the positive aspects of being on the "right" side of a full-scale war (among them self-righteousness, unit cohesion, and black-and-white moral clarity) without most of the negative aspects.

What about the suggestion that legalistic churches demand more sacrifice? That depends on what you mean by sacrifice. Legalistic Christians are generally willing to give their churches money and time. They are also willing to sacrifice their right—some of us would say their Christian obligation—to use their minds to figure out what is good and right and true. Many of them are willing to turn their lives upside down to evangelize in distant lands (but then, one of the reasons why people join such churches in the first place is that they are incapable of finding or creating meaning for themselves and desperately want another person or institution to change their lives and infuse them with meaning); but such people are not willing—and they are rarely asked—to sacrifice their prejudices and their "I'm saved and you're not" mentality. They're not willing to sacrifice their America Firstism, their support of segregation, their desire and admiration for material success, their enthusiasm for the military-industrial complex, their self-righteousness. What all the "successful" legalistic churches have in common, indeed, is that they cater to these attitudes and prejudices; if they asked people to give them up, they would be far less "successful."

As noted, Finke and Stark flaunt their hard-nosed, practical worldliness—their horizontal orientation—and jeer at those who measure church success in more "vertical" ways. Yet they then turn around and equate the Southern Baptists' phenomenal growth in numbers with a supposed achievement on the vertical plane, equating the Baptist emphasis on doctrine with a "vivid otherworldliness" and connecting the mainline underemphasis on doctrine with this-worldliness. In fact, the connection works quite the other way: As Fosdick pointed out decades ago, the more elaborate and compulsory an official church doctrine, the more the individual's capacity for spiritual reflection and for true experience of the Absolute is stifled. Finke and Stark also contradict their argument that the strength of conservative churches lies in their spiritual emphasis when they cite, as a major reason for the decline of American Catholicism, the fact that priests and nuns no longer enjoy the "status and power" they once did. What could be less spiritual and more "horizontal" than this?

Finke and Stark claim that as mainline churches became more liberal, their clergy grew more sophisticated and well-educated and worship was "shorn of mystery, miracle, and mysticism." The "active supernatural realm," they claim, was "replaced by abstractions concerning virtue"; "a message of conversion" gave way to "a message of erudition." At the same time, they say, church rules grew less demanding. As a result, these churches lost members to groups like the Baptists, who were more supernaturally oriented and who "made serious emotional, material, and social demands"; to be a Baptist or Methodist or (for that matter) a Catholic "was a far more serious undertaking than to be a Congregationalist or an Episcopalian." One of the outrageous implications here is that theological education and Christian faith are conflicting values—that the more theologically sophisticated one becomes, the more one's faith declines. Finke and Stark point out, for example, that the so-called traditionalism of Southern Baptist clergy is inversely proportional to their level of education. Of course, to examine these statistics and then attack education and defend "traditionalism," as Finke and Stark do, is deeply cynical; it amounts essentially to embracing the atheistic view that religion is not really true and that in order to stay religious, one has to remain ignorant and try not to think too hard.

Finke and Stark speak up for hellfire sermons. For Baptists and Methodists, they argue, "the power of God was experienced as well as taught, and their message seldom excluded the topics of sin and salvation, or hellfire and redemption. . . . By contrast, the denominations of the colonial mainline offered a message that was literate and intellectual, but one that increasingly said less about salvation, hellfire, or the other principal themes of the Baptist and Methodist sermons." What Finke and Stark are suggesting here is remarkable: In their view, apparently, intellectually engaging sermons about a God of love don't lead to spiritual experience, while scare rhetoric about hellfire does. Can someone who thinks in this way ever have had a spiritual experience? Or do Finke and Stark share the view of many secular intellectuals that there is no such thing as a spiritual experience, that it is by definition something that happens only to the ignorant and gullible? Finke and Stark speak approvingly of the "high octane faith" of members of sects that preach hellfire; this, they say, is what brings in the faithful and creates zealots. But does it create true disciples of Christ? This is a question in which Finke and Stark apparently have no interest whatsoever. They refer with what seems complete approval to the late-nineteenth-century Landmarkian movement among Southern Baptists, which drew sharp lines between saved "authentic Christians" (Baptists) and unsaved false Christians (everyone else), and they speak disapprovingly of Methodists and Northern Baptists who during this same period were becoming more inclusive in their theology, shifting emphasis from a God of wrath to a God of love.

Finke and Stark automatically assume that because people are flocking to legalistic churches, those churches are doing something right and the mainline churches are doing something wrong. When they speak of "the essential good health of rural churches" in the 1920s, they mean simply that those churches had a lot of members. That most such churches were, among other things, fiercely racist goes unmentioned. And the question of what Jesus would make of those churches goes unasked. Finke and Stark do not acknowledge that many people are drawn to legalistic churches for reasons that have nothing to do with an experience of God and with the love of Jesus; they do not acknowledge that in an aggressively horizontal, unreflective mass culture, churches that encourage individual spiritual exploration and reflection, that challenge people's self-centeredness by promoting outreach to the poor, and that preach a gospel of unselfish love will often lose out to churches that offer easy and purportedly certain answers to life's difficult questions, that cater to people's solipsism, and that offer members the opportunity to say to their neighbors, "I'm going to heaven and you're going to hell." Finke and Stark quote with enthusiasm the Jewish scholar Will Herberg's argument that the Roman Catholic Church "must take its stand against the world, against the age, against the spirit of the age—because the world and the age are always, to a degree, to an important degree, in rebellion against God." This is an oft-heard argument from conservative Protestants and traditional Catholics. But the question is: In which ways is the age (that is, the secular culture) rebelling against God? In which ways is the church rebelling against God while the secular culture does his work? Too often in recent generations, the secular culture has effected changes that institutional churches have at first resisted and then, much too late, recognized as positive developments.

The point here, apropos of Kelley's and Finke and Stark's arguments, is simple. The question should not be, "How can we fill our churches?" It should be, "How can we make churches, society, and people more truly Christian?" If a novel by a hack writer sells more copies than a novel by a great literary artist, that doesn't mean that the artist should try to write more like the hack; it means that the mass audience needs to have its taste improved. Similarly, if millions of Americans flock to legalistic churches, it doesn't mean that the mainline churches should imitate those churches; it means that American culture is in desperate spiritual straits and that we need to do something about this if we want our children to live in a spiritually healthy culture.

Arguing that the Social Gospel lost out to legalism because "people went to church in search of salvation, not social service," Finke and Stark add that the Social Gospelers "seemed to have nearly forgotten about religion altogether." That depends, of course, on what one means by religion. What the Social Gospelers meant by religion was what Jesus had meant by it when he told the parable of the good Samaritan. He did not intend to found an institution to which people could go selfishly, week after week, in order to have their ticket to the afterlife stamped and to dwell fondly on the thought that outsiders would be consigned to hellfire; rather, he sought to inspire in the hearts of people a love for those outsiders that would express itself not in Bible-thumping evangelism but in selfless action. That's a momentous challenge. The mainline churches, to the extent that they issued that challenge in the decades surrounding the turn of the century, lost members to the churches that welcomed, and indeed encouraged, ignorance and self-concern. Legalistic Christianity triumphed, in short, not because it demanded more of believers but because, at the profoundest level, it demanded far less.

For American Protestant fundamentalism, then, the decades after the Scopes trial were a period not of stagnation but of revivals, youth rallies, and rampant church growth, virtually all of which took place below the radar of the mainstream media. Yet this was also a period of serious internal tensions in the fundamentalist camp. In the early 1940s fundamentalism began to separate into two distinct movements, one of which, by the late 1950s, had retained the label of fundamentalism and the other of which had come to be known as the New Evangelicalism. The fundamentalists, most of them dispensational premillennialists, and most belonging to the Southern Baptist Convention, believed in the total inerrancy of the Bible and also believed in keeping apart from the mainstream culture and the mainline denominations. The New Evangelicals, having been influenced to some extent by modernist theology, allowed for some degree of interaction with the mainstream culture and even for membership in mainline denominations; some but not all of them rejected biblical inerrancy. Each party had its own institutions: The fundamentalists had the American Council of Churches, founded in 1941, which encouraged separation from the mainline denominations; the New Evangelicals had the less-separatist National Association of Evangelicals, founded a year later. Perhaps even more important, the New Evangelicals had a young man named Billy Graham, a minister in the evangelical Youth for Christ movement whose 1949 Los Angeles rally made him the nation's most famous evangelist. Marsden observes that during the 1950s and 1960s it was easy to tell whether someone was a fundamentalist or a New Evangelical: All you had to do was ask what he or she thought of Billy Graham. To this day, fundamentalists despise Graham as a sellout because he affirms the value of Catholic and Jewish faith; to a true Protestant fundamentalist, of course, Catholics and Jews are destined for hell.

In his definitive history of Fuller Theological Seminary, which was founded in 1947 in Pasadena by the fundamentalist Charles E. Fuller but which eventually became the flagship seminary of the New Evangelicalism, Marsden vividly depicts an institution whose self-contradictions and outright absurdities reflect those of the movement it represented (though this is not a point that Marsden seeks to underscore). Consider the case of Harold Ockenga, the institution's first president and a founder of the National Association of Evangelicals, who refused to abandon biblical inerrancy. His explanation for this refusal: not that the Bible is inerrant, but that once you abandon inerrancy, you're on a slippery slope to utter apostasy. For Ockenga, in other words, holding fast to inerrancy was a matter not of embracing truth over falsity but of choosing to remain moored to a rigid doctrine rather than risking the open sea. Ockenga's position is astonishing for the questions it raises about the nature of the New Evangelicals' faith and fears, not to mention about the nature of what it means to be an educator in a subculture where certain orthodoxies cannot be questioned and certain thoughts cannot be uttered.

This paradox haunted the New Evangelicalism. On the one hand, the leading lights at Fuller longed for respectability and prestige— which, to them, meant being taken seriously by the most distinguished mainline seminaries and theologians in America and Europe. Yet to be taken seriously by those institutions and individuals—which Fuller, in good evangelical fashion, claimed to regard as secularist and apostate, and which in return tended to look down on evangelicalism as primitive and anti-intellectual—meant having something fresh to say about the nature of God and faith, and this almost inevitably entailed violating the narrow bounds of acceptable evangelical doctrine.

Virtually every crisis that plagued Fuller during its early decades seems to have flowed out of this paradox. In 1949, seeking to enhance the school's reputation, Fuller's administration hired a distinguished Hungarian theologian named Béla Vassady. Yet when Vassady published an article that year calling for "one church" in "one world," his Fuller colleagues panicked, because, as Marsden writes, these concepts were "linked in the fundamentalist mind . . . as signs of the approach of the empire of Antichrist and his allies." Vassady soon left Fuller. Likewise, when Fuller professor Carl Henry published a book, *The Uneasy Conscience of Fundamentalism,* accusing the fundamentalist movement of having a "harsh temperament" and a "spirit of lovelessness and strife," and when Fuller's second president, Edward J. Carnell, issued a pamphlet that placed the love of God and one's neighbor above all other laws, firestorms resulted. "To ears attuned to the rhetoric of fundamentalism," writes Marsden, "such talk of love and tolerance smacked of modernism." Carnell's fundamentalist colleague Charles J. Woodbridge responded to his pamphlet by angrily accusing him of "sweet, forgiving *appeasement* toward heretics"—that is, mainline Protestants.

At the heart of the New Evangelicalism, plainly, was a tension between the Church of Love and the Church of Law. Woodbridge charged that the New Evangelicalism emphasized "love, not doctrine" and thundered that this emphasis made it "the worst menace that has confronted the church since the time of Luther." To many mainline Protestants who viewed the New Evangelicalism from the other direction, by contrast, the fact that a place like Fuller compelled its faculty to sign rigidly formulated declarations of belief, and fired those who refused, suggested that the movement was far more about doctrine than about love. Indeed, to many mainline Protestants, there seemed little difference between the fundamentalists and New Evangelicals (who eventually came to be called simply evangelicals).

In Marsden's account, the administrators and teachers at Fuller during its first several decades were eager to make mainline Protestants see the difference between themselves and fundamentalists. They wanted Fuller to be recognized as a serious educational institution that pursued the truth and rejected fundamentalism. In reality, however, education at Fuller took a backseat to orthodoxy, for the school's faculty were allowed to pursue the truth only so far. In theory, teachers and students were encouraged to study the Bible honestly and freely; yet when they did so, they saw things there that they weren't free to admit honestly to seeing. To that extent, their religion was not a truth but a lie. The ways in which professors of integrity dealt with this morally and spiritually challenging situation recall the stories about Soviet writers and professors who sought to placate institutional ideology while continuing to write and teach as much as possible of the truth as they saw it.

Ironically, the hero of Marsden's history of Fuller turns out to be Charles E. Fuller's son Daniel, who had studied theology at Princeton and whose insistence that the school acknowledge scriptural error eventually won the day. Ockenga's indignant response to young Fuller—"Well, what are we going to do then? Dan Fuller thinks the Bible is just full of errors"—is almost touching in its display of insecurity in the face of truth. For too many legalistic Christians, this kind of insecure, embattled clinging to a set of tenets that one knows on some level to be untrue *is* the substance of faith, and any departure from it is a plunge into the abyss. Ockenga and many of his colleagues were haunted by a situation that Marsden sums up tidily: "Beginning with the gradual slippage of Harvard into Unitarianism, the past two hundred years had seen an endless repetition of the same story. Most of America's greatest academic institutions had been founded by conservative Bible-believing evangelicals. But nearly every one of these schools had eventually fallen to the onslaughts of theological liberalism, and then to outright secularism. Except in a few cases, such as Wheaton College or Moody Bible Institute, where conservatives had kept the tightest control on innovation, their efforts at institution building had proved futile." Marsden might instead have spoken of control on *thinking*—for it is thinking that poses the greatest danger to legalistic "institution building."

While evangelicalism, fundamentalism, and Pentecostalism expanded rapidly and clashed with one another during the century's middle decades, the mainline American religious establishment either ignored these developments or viewed them with condescension. The Episcopal and Presbyterian leaders in their New York offices and glorious downtown churches simply couldn't take seriously the ragtag little independent houses of worship that were springing up in places like Kentucky and Arkansas. In the same way, the distinguished theologians who taught Ivy League graduates at the eminent mainline seminaries couldn't take very seriously the fundamentalist Bible institutes like Moody, or even the evangelical seminaries like Fuller, most of whose professors had little or no reputation as scholars and most of whose students were ill-educated rural youngsters. What would those mainline church leaders have said if someone had told them that in a few decades their own churches would be challenged for cultural dominance—if not utterly dwarfed—by churches led by those sometime youngsters?

When I was a boy in the early 1970s, spending summers in my mother's South Carolina hometown, I met some white kids who had recently withdrawn from public school and begun attending a new private academy. They explained the switch: Their public schools had been integrated by Supreme Court order, and their parents were sending them to this new institution in order to protect them from attending school with "niggers." Thus did I witness the birth of the Religious Right.

In recent years, Religious Right leaders have suggested that their

movement grew out of discontent with the 1963 Supreme Court decision against compulsory prayers in public schools. Yet Ralph Reed
himself admits that "the greatest spark of the [Religious Right] movement was not abortion but an attempt by the Carter-appointed head
of the Internal Revenue Service to require Christian and parochial
schools and academies to prove that they were not established to preserve segregation or they would risk losing their tax-exempt status. . . .
For conservative evangelicals it was nothing less than a declaration of
war on their schools, their churches, and their children." Reed is being
disingenuous here, for anyone who spent any amount of time in the
South then knows that a whole network of private schools sprang up
after the Supreme Court ordered public-school integration; the only
reason for these private schools' existence was to serve white parents
who didn't want their children going to school with blacks. Jimmy
Carter, as a southerner, knew very well that this was the case. That his
action was the main impetus for today's Religious Right political
movement says a great deal about where that movement's head and
heart really are. Not to mince words, the Religious Right didn't grow
out of a love for God and one's neighbor—it grew out of racism, pure
and simple.

Even as government actions on education were propelling legalistic
Protestants into political involvement, a bizarre book by a man named
Hal Lindsey was reshaping many of the same people's religion around
the notion of biblical prophecy.

In the summer of 1996, I went to several New York City libraries
in search of a copy of that book, *The Late Great Planet Earth*. This
immensely influential work, which has been a touchstone for legalistic Protestants since its publication in 1970, always turned out to be
missing from the collection. Later that summer I was staying with
friends at a rented Georgia beach house when I looked up to see a
battered copy of Lindsey's book staring out at me from the shelves.

I should not have been surprised: *The Late Great Planet Earth* is a
book you should go looking for not in New York City libraries but
in Southern homes. This isn't a volume that has gathered dust in
libraries; it's something that's been *read*—widely, religiously, and with
fanatical credulity. Marsden records that although the book was never
on the *New York Times* best-seller list, it was in fact the number one

best-selling book in the United States during the 1970s. The fact that
it never appeared on the *Times* list—which is based on sales in "general" bookstores, not "Christian" bookstores—only underlines the
width of the gulf between the mainstream culture reflected in the
Times and the huge nonmainstream culture for whom Lindsey's book
was, quite literally, a revelation. (Though none of the large bookstores
that I canvassed in New York City carried Lindsey's book, I eventually
bought my own copy at a small "Christian" bookstore in Cumming,
Georgia, which had several copies in stock.)

I was thrilled to find Lindsey's book on the shelves of that beach
house. Dusting it off, I took it down from the shelf, carried it out to
the beach, and sat down to read it next to one of the friends I was
staying with, who had once been a fundamentalist. When she saw the
book, she let out a shriek. "Where did you find *that?*"

I told her. "Have you read it?" I asked.

"Of course I read it, we *all* did! Yuck! Just don't set it down anywhere near me."

It didn't take long for me to understand her reaction. If Scofield, in
his Reference Bible, had interpreted a number of supposedly prophetic
biblical passages to suggest a certain outline of the End Times, Hal
Lindsey brought further specifics to this outline and showed a new
generation of fundamentalists how various current events represented
(according to him) a fulfillment of some of the biblical prophecies
Scofield had identified and how, in the next few years, world history
would play itself out in such a way as to complete the fulfillment of
Scofield's End Times scenario. *The Late Great Planet Earth* became a
veritable second Bible in many fundamentalist homes.

Why was it so popular? After one has begun reading Lindsey's introduction, the answer doesn't take long to form itself. The introduction
begins with a lament about the chaos of contemporary American society. What can we do about this chaos? "On one side," Lindsey says, "we
hear that the answer to our dilemma is education. Build bigger and
better schools, hire more teachers, develop a smarter generation. Has
the academic community found the answers? There are many students
who are dissatisfied with being told that the sole purpose of education
is to develop inquiring minds. They want to find some of the answers
to their questions—solid answers, a certain direction." Those "solid

answers," he says, can be found in the Bible, which he describes as a work of prophecy containing "clear and unmistakable prophetic signs."

Already, in these opening sentences, several of the book's key attributes—and the secrets of its popularity—are in plain view. One is its extreme anti-intellectualism. Consistently, Lindsey pounds home the message that the important truths of life cannot be discovered through education, scientific experimentation, and objective critical analysis, but rather through predictions by seers who have demonstrated their premonitory prowess. Over and over again, Lindsey makes the point that people with fancy educations don't know the things that really matter and that they are dangerous because they lead others astray.

Another striking attribute here is Lindsey's emphasis on certitude. Lindsey knows his audience: They don't want ambiguous information and ideas that they are obliged to think about; they want clear-cut answers. Lindsey provides them, and with breathtaking audacity. Words such as *certain, sure, solid, clear,* and *unmistakable* abound.

Something else that is obvious early on in Lindsey's book is its narrow understanding of the word *prophecy.* Christians have long understood prophecy to be a special quality of spirituality and courage; theologians speak of the prophetic obedience of Saint Francis, who knew that the institutional church was misguided in some ways, and who on occasion respectfully defied its authority out of a desire to lead it closer to the truth. The vulgar notion of a prophet as merely a fortune-teller or seer of the kind featured nowadays in supermarket tabloids has nothing to do with the traditional Christian concept of prophecy and everything to do with the contemporary American infatuation with astrology, magic tricks, psychic readings, and the like. Yes, the Old Testament prophets occasionally predicted that certain events—whether messianic or cataclysmic—would occur at some time in the future, and the Gospel writers adjusted elements of the story of Jesus so that they would seem to be fulfillments of some of those predictions. Yet this kind of prognostication was always only a minor element of the prophetic role, and no one ever interpreted those prophecies in the extremely specific way that Lindsey does. Being a prophet in biblical times was not about forecasting future events but about being close to God and helping God's people to feel closer to him. In the true biblical sense, the prophets of the twentieth-century

Christian world are not people like Jeane Dixon of *National Enquirer* fame but people like Catholic Worker founder Dorothy Day and South African archbishop Desmond Tutu—people who, often in tension with established church authority, have spoken bravely and inspiringly of what it means and doesn't mean to be a Christian and have shown by their example what posture Christians should take toward the established order.

Lindsey, by contrast, depicts biblical prophecy in an outrageously crude manner. Dipping into the scriptures, he cites examples of prognostications that turned out to be true, congratulating one Old Testament prophet for his "Accurate Short-Range Prophecy" and saying that the prophet Micaiah earned "a straight 'A' in prophetic marksmanship." By making forecasts that turned out to be true, Lindsey says, these and other prophets "passed the test—summa cum laude." Chief among these forecasts, he emphasizes, were those concerning the Messiah. If the Jews had attended properly to their prophets' messianic predictions, they would easily have recognized Jesus as their savior. Yet they paid insufficient attention to those predictions and consequently rejected their Messiah. As a result, "for almost 2000 years the sons of Abraham, Isaac, and Jacob have wandered around the earth with no country of their own, in constant fear of persecution and death."

Lindsey now warns his readers, "Will we repeat history? Will we fail to take the prophets literally and seriously?" The key word here is *literally.* Lindsey is speaking to an audience of people who do not understand the concept of symbolic truth or metaphoric language. Raised in an aggressively "horizontal" culture, they lead lives in which only the tangible is real and in which there is little or no "vertical line." Such people, if confronted with actual spiritual truths, might well be irked, put off, perplexed. They prefer, and perhaps can only understand, a religion that presents itself in literal form—and the more literal, the better. Lindsey, recognizing this, encourages his readers' tendency to read the Bible and its prophecies literally—and to think that this is equivalent to taking them seriously.

Having established the vital importance of biblical prophecy today, Lindsey proceeds to set forth the supposed literal truths to which he says that prophecy points. "Current events," he claims, "are fitting together simultaneously into the precise pattern of predicted events.

Israel has returned to Palestine and revived the nation. Jerusalem is under Israeli control. Russia has emerged as a great northern power and is the avowed enemy of revived Israel. The Arabs are joining in a concerted effort to liberate Palestine under Egyptian leadership." Saying that all these events fulfill biblical prophecies, Lindsey proceeds to extrapolate from the current events of circa 1970 on the basis of those prophecies. Of course the prophecies he quotes are ambiguous enough that a writer at any point in the last two thousand years could have made a similar case that the current events of his own time were likewise "fitting together simultaneously into the precise pattern of predicted events."

"Some time in the future," Lindsey writes, "there will be a seven-year period climaxed by the visible return of Jesus Christ." He proceeds to describe the Rapture and the Great Tribulation in terms consonant with those of Darby and Scofield. Yet to Scofield's more general picture of the Tribulation, Lindsey has added up-to-date specifics. "Egypt will attack the revived state of Israel, which will then be under the control of a false Messiah. This man will probably be a Jew who works closely with the world dictator who will come to power in Rome." The Jews will suffer greatly "until many cry out to the true Savior, Jesus," at which point God will deliver 144,000 of them. (Lindsey's comment: "What a great demonstration of God's loving heart!") These Jews will be "144,000 Jewish Billy Grahams turned loose on this earth" and will "have the greatest number of converts in all history." Also, a ten-nation united Europe will emerge under "the greatest dictator the world has ever known," a "completely godless, diabolically evil" figure who "will proclaim himself to be God" and "will establish himself in the Temple of God" on Mount Moriah in Jerusalem. Aiding this "Antichrist" will be the "False Prophet," whose "mark" will be the number 666. Not to worry, however: In the end, God will destroy "all ungodly kingdoms" with "a thermonuclear blast."

Like Scofield, Lindsey does not mean for any of this to be read in symbolic terms. The End Times picture that he paints is meant to be understood literally, down to every detail. And so it was, and is, by millions.

It is only after painting this picture of the Great Tribulation that Lindsey jumps back and depicts the Rapture, "the 'blessed hope' for all true believers," when Jesus returns "to meet all true believers in the air." This event, Lindsey promises, "will be the living end. The ultimate trip." He then shifts from his sixties slang into the argot of TV commercials: "Will you be here during this seven-year countdown?" he asks. "Will you be here during the time of the Tribulation when the Antichrist and the False Prophet are in charge for a time? Will you be here when the world is plagued by mankind's darkest days?" Because Jesus Christ has paid for our sins, Lindsey writes, "God can offer a totally free gift of forgiveness." Protestant fundamentalists think that they're rejecting the modern world and its values, but those who respond to such rhetoric as this are in fact succumbing to the psychology and jargon of Madison Avenue. Lindsey is selling salvation as if it were a lottery ticket: You can't win it if you don't get in it! Act *now* and win the "free gift" of eternal life! (The redundant term *free gift* is used with amazing frequency, in legalistic Christian publications and websites, to refer to the hope of heaven.)

Lindsey's vision of heaven is of a thoroughly literal, tangible future place that is part peaceable kingdom, part election-campaign promises, and part *Lifestyles of the Rich and Famous* dream vacation. "Even the animals and reptiles," Lindsey writes, "will lose their ferocity and no longer be carnivorous. All men will have plenty and be secure. There will be a chicken in every pot and nobody will steal it. . . . If you can think of the most beautiful place you have ever been, then amplify its beauty beyond your comprehension and imagine what it would be like without death, disease, or any curse upon it, you may have an inkling of heaven." Lindsey interprets the biblical line "And we shall be changed" to mean that after the Rapture, saved Christians will be changed by God "in essence, but not completely changed in appearance. If you're not too satisfied with the face or body you now have, you will have a glorious new body." God, in short, is a celestial plastic surgeon, offering deliverance in the form of a face-lift and tummy tuck. Lindsey's comment: "Just think how excited a woman can get about a new wardrobe. How much more excited we should be about acquiring a new body!"

Lindsey envisions the Rapture by depicting various imaginary people's reactions to the sudden, mysterious disappearance of others. He imagines, for example, a motorist recalling that he was on the freeway when suddenly he saw driverless "cars going in all directions" around him. Someone recalls how a quarterback disappeared from a football game—"completely gone, just like that!" A professor says, "It was puzzling—very puzzling. I was teaching my course in the philosophy of religion when all of a sudden three of my students vanished. . . . They were quite argumentative—always trying to prove their point from the Bible. No great loss to the class." And a preacher tells his congregation, "Many of you have lost loved ones in this unusual disappearance of so many people. However, I believe that God's judgment has come upon them for their continued dissension and quarreling with the great advances of the Church in our century. Now that the reactionaries are removed, we can progress toward our great and glorious goal of uniting all mankind into a brotherhood of reconciliation and understanding." Among all these folk who scratch their heads over the Rapture, Lindsey includes one wise soul whose wife was raptured and who has seen the light. "I think all that talk about the Rapture and going to meet Jesus Christ in the air wasn't crazy after all," the husband tells a friend. "I don't know about you, brother, but I'm going to find myself a Bible and read all those verses my wife underlined. I wouldn't listen to her while she was here."

So it goes. That people will be raptured away in their cars underscores that salvation will come to ordinary people in the course of their daily lives; that the Rapture will take up a quarterback illustrates that there's no contradiction between being a macho, rough-and-tumble athlete and being a saved Christian. That those who are left behind include a know-it-all theology professor who rejects biblical literalism (and who uses non-macho words like "quite") and a clergyman who believes in "brotherhood" and "reconciliation" and "understanding" among "all mankind" makes the point that all this liberal intellectualism and love-thy-neighbor stuff isn't what will save you. You'll only be saved if you take your Bible, underline the right passages, and accept Lindsey's interpretations of them without exception. Note that the man whose wife was raptured doesn't plan to read the whole Bible and try to make sense out of it; he just plans to read the parts his wife underlined, obviously in accordance with Darby, Scofield, and Lindsey.

To be sure, Lindsey says, not "all believers" will be taken off by

Christ. Those who deny the truth of the Rapture will be denied eternal life. "We may have to go over to some of them," Lindsey avers, "and say, 'I told you so, friend.'" His book speaks to an utterly unchristian impulse, feeding people a sadistic scenario of themselves saying "I told you so" to supposed "friends" who are damned for eternity. If this is religion, it is religion that encourages attitudes about oneself and other people that are precisely the opposite of those that Jesus preached. It is religion for people who think that joining a religion is like betting on a horse; it is religion for people who are so utterly lacking in any sense of a vertical orientation that they can be interested in the idea of heaven only if it includes a new body that is prettier than the one they're inhabiting now; it is religion for people who can only read the mystical language of scripture about being "changed" in the most literal way. To read Lindsey's book is to be struck by how overwhelmed people can be by the world's complexities, how terrified of their own mortality, how incapable of finding strength, solace, and sense in the realm of the spiritual, and how ready to accept notions of God and heaven that have nothing at all to do with a vertical dimension.

God's plan for humankind, as presented by Darby, Scofield, Lindsey, and others, exists on the intellectual, moral, and spiritual level of card tricks or jigsaw puzzles. Lines and images are plucked out of context from every part of scripture, the idea being that God put all these lines in these various places so that men like Lindsey could come along and weave them together into a scenario of the End Times—a scenario whose believers will be saved and whose detractors will be damned. To read the Bible in this way is precisely like reading Shakespeare in search of secret anagrammatical messages, while missing entirely the beauty of the writing and the author's insights into human emotions and relationships. At no point in *The Late Great Planet Earth* does Lindsey ever answer (or even ask) the question, What exactly is the reason for, and the higher meaning of, the Rapture and Great Tribulation and so forth? If God wanted us to know about and believe in this comic-book scenario of the End Times, and for this reason placed all the details of it in scripture, why did he scatter those details around in various books of the Bible like pieces of a puzzle? What kind of a God plays such games, makes up such puzzles? More important, what kind of a God saves people because they embrace a particular scenario of the End Times and damns others because they don't? Where is the morality in that? Why on earth should the meaning of life come down to such silliness?

There would not be a huge audience for works of "prophecy" like Lindsey's, to be sure, if there were not also a huge number of adult Americans with very low levels of education. For in order to even begin to accept Lindsey's interpretation of history and current events, a reader of *The Late Great Planet Earth* has to have virtually no knowledge of history and no understanding of other modern civilizations. Readers must also either be utterly ignorant of contemporary scientific knowledge or be able to hold in their minds two thoroughly incompatible sets of ideas at the same time. Legalistic Christians speak of themselves as being traditional, true to the faith of their fathers; but in fact their faith could not be more radically different, not only in its tenets but also in its essential nature, from that of Christians who lived as recently as two centuries ago. The belief systems of earlier generations of Christians were grounded in an understanding of the universe that was thoroughly consistent with the most advanced scientific knowledge of their time; premillennialism, as set forth in Darby, Scofield, and Lindsey, requires one either to dismiss today's science or to ignore the flat-out contradictions between what one claims to believe and what one knows to be true.

Another key point: The world situation has changed dramatically. Since the appearance of Lindsey's book in 1970, the Soviet Union, a key factor in his prophecy, has ceased to exist, and the Egyptian government no longer spearheads a pan-Arabic anti-Israel movement. Recognizing this, Lindsey came out in 1994 with a new book, *Planet Earth—2000 A.D.*, which replaces the supposedly prophecy-fulfilling events of a generation earlier with more recent happenings and replaces Communism with another great international evil, "religious zealotry." Lindsey doesn't mean premillennialism—he means Islam: "The greatest threat to freedom and world peace today," he writes, "is Islamic fundamentalism." Why? Because the goal of Islam, whose adherents he describes repeatedly as "fanatics," "zealots," and "radicals," is to wage "holy war" against non-Moslems. Lindsey's generalizations about Islamic fundamentalism, which are every bit as applicable to his own Protestant fundamentalist readers, remind us that people often find their enemies among those who are most like themselves.

Planet Earth—2000 A.D. was reissued in a revised edition only two years after its first appearance. In a new preface, Lindsey explains that prophetic events are coming along faster and faster as we near "the final, climactic stages of world history" and that he and other "students of prophecy" are thus kept busier than ever interpreting them. When he first wrote *2000 A.D.*, he states, "the enduring image of ethnic unrest and the media attacks on the justice system in the U.S. was Rodney King—but that was before O. J. Simpson. The World Trade Center gave way to the Oklahoma City Bombing." What Lindsey is saying here is surprising. In *The Late Great Planet Earth,* he pretended to be interpreting biblical prophecies definitively; this or that biblical passage indubitably pointed to this or that current event. Now, he all but admits that every year brings a new set of developments that can be plugged into biblical prophecy just as easily as last year's headlines. If his reinterpretation of biblical prophecies, and with it his pushing back of Armageddon, has caused any misgiving or perplexity on the part of his followers, there has been no sign of it.

With *The Late Great Planet Earth* and its successors, Lindsey has taught a generation of American legalistic Christians to look at current events not with an eye to understanding them for what they are, but rather as clues to Armageddon. He has taught them to look at other people's religions and political systems not as possible sources of enlightenment about the human condition but as creatures of Satan and potential enemies in the Ultimate Battle. In these and other ways, Lindsey has been instrumental in shaping the combative, paranoid, and aggressively ignorant temperament of the people who, after two generations of obscurity, would step out of the shadows to form the Religious Right.

8

TAKEOVER

In the 1970s, notes Sydney Ahlstrom in his 1974 *Religious History of the American People,* "an inchoate conservative tendency could be noted, though no one could say what this frightened and perplexed multitude portended as a political force." If we wish to observe the way in which that multitude of legalistic Christians stepped out of the shadows, made its presence known, and proceeded to establish itself as a powerful social, cultural, and political force, we can do worse than to examine the recent history of the Southern Baptist Convention. Indeed, some observers would say that the return of legalistic Christianity from its decades of obscurity began with what Walter Shurden describes, in the title of a collection of essays by Baptist moderates, as "the struggle for the soul of the SBC."

As we have seen, the Southern Baptist Convention, America's largest Protestant denomination, has its roots in such founding Baptist concepts as soul competency and the priesthood of the believer. According to Baptist tradition, no individual believer can be forced against his or her conscience to accept any church law or doctrine or to obey any minister. Every Baptist has the right to read and interpret the Bible according to the way in which he or she feels directed by the Holy Spirit. As recently as 1986, Gordon James wrote in *Inerrancy and the Southern Baptist Convention* that

> *Southern Baptists were founded on the premise that there would always be*
> *room for everybody, including people who asserted differing views but were*
> *still within the general realm of what Baptists believed. . . . Baptists*
> *irrevocably believe that every individual has the right to construct his own*
> *statement of belief, likewise do churches, associations, and conventions,*
> *groups of individuals or any combination hereof. This being an absolute of*
> *Baptist belief, it is also an absolute that an individual is only bound by*
> *personal beliefs. No church can be bound except by its own beliefs. . . . It is*
> *the foundational position Southern Baptists have called soul competency,*
> *and the related doctrine called the priesthood of the believer and liberty.*

Shurden, in a 1993 book entitled *The Baptist Identity: Four Fragile Freedoms,* argued that what it means to be Baptist comes down to four kinds of freedom: Bible Freedom (meaning a freedom of access to scripture, freedom from creedal restrictions on scripture, and freedom of the individual to interpret scripture); Soul Freedom (meaning the freedom to "deal with God without the imposition of creed, the interference of clergy, or the intervention of civil government"); Church Freedom (meaning the freedom of individual churches from any denominational authority); and Religious Freedom (meaning an insistence on the absolute separation of church and state).

For a number of years now, however, these core elements of the Baptist tradition have been under steady and ruthless attack by members of the Southern Baptist Convention who call themselves traditionalists and who seek to impose dogmas on the Convention that have never been a part of Baptist doctrine. Like the Episcopal Church, Baptist churches are not and never have been "confessional": Baptists do not derive their unity from doctrinal statements that are carved in stone. To be sure, just as the Episcopal Church has its traditional "Articles of Religion," the Southern Baptist Convention has its "Baptist Faith and Message," a statement of beliefs that has undergone revisions over the years. Yet like the Episcopal Articles of Religion, the Baptist Faith and Message is a general statement of Christian beliefs that has less specificity, and less of a binding character, than the confessions that are central to such denominations as the Methodists and Presbyterians. In both the Baptist and the Anglican traditions, the right of individual conscience is sacrosanct, and no statement of belief has the power to abrogate that right.

In the hands of slaveowners and, later, segregationists, the traditional Baptist emphasis on individual conscience became a cynical tool for the defense of racial prejudice and exploitation. Yet in the mid-twentieth century, moderate Southern Baptists made some successful efforts to turn the SBC into an instrument for love and enlightenment. Many reactionary members of the Southern Baptist Convention, angered by these efforts as well as by the movements for racial and gender equality, began to take action to turn the SBC against its heritage of freedom and to impose harsh legalistic dogma upon its traditionally independent churches and members. In 1979 began what is known in the SBC as the takeover—the gradual wresting of denominational power from the moderates by the fundamentalists, whose intense political strategizing and hardball tactics were carried out under the direction of two influential Baptists named Paul Pressler and Paige Patterson. (Though the umbrella term *legalist* would probably be more accurate here than *fundamentalist,* since some of these people are conservative evangelicals as opposed to strict separatist fundamentalists, I will follow Southern Baptist usage and call them fundamentalists.)

In many ways the fundamentalist takeover of the Southern Baptist Convention was a warmup for the Christian Coalition's later seizure of the Republican Party in the South. A friend who is active both in the SBC and in the Democratic Party recalls how members of the Christian Coalition took over local Republican parties. "They used to be run by country-club types," he says of the local Republican parties. "Then suddenly you'd have two buses full of people show up from a church in Selma or someplace." They would all vote as a bloc for their own candidate, "and you'd realize your candidate had lost, and it wasn't even close. It was five to one. Who were these people who had shown up out of nowhere? Economically, they were traditional Democrats. But suddenly they'd taken over the local Republican Party."

That, my friend notes, is "exactly how they took over the Southern Baptist Convention. They bused people in by the thousands. The moderates did a poor job of resisting it." One problem, he said, was that the SBC's Training Union, which used to educate Baptists in the fundamentals of Baptist freedom, had been dissolved by the time my friend, born in the sixties, was in high school. As a result, he recalls, he "never heard of the separation of church and state till I went to college." Between the 1950s and the 1980s, the SBC doubled in size. The new members, who had never learned why the separation of church and state is important, were suddenly in the majority—and moderate SBC leaders "realized that this was no longer their Convention."

Since 1979, fundamentalist candidates have won every election for SBC president; as their hold on this top job has lengthened, they have steadily gained power at all levels and used it to remove moderates from posts in the denominational hierarchy and at Baptist seminaries. (In 1996, for instance, Richard R. Melick, Jr., was forced to resign as president of Criswell College in Dallas because he didn't believe in the pre-Tribulation Rapture.) Several Baptist seminaries are now nothing more than fundamentalist indoctrination centers; at many of them, every non-inerrantist professor has been fired and every entering student is compelled to declare his belief that the Bible contains no error of any kind. In response, moderate Baptists have established new seminaries in Richmond, and at Baylor, Hardin Simmons, and Mercer Universities, and Baptist Studies programs at various non–Baptist seminaries. Another thing the fundamentalists have done is to pass resolutions at the denomination's annual conventions. One after another, these resolutions have, in the name of tradition, laid waste to the Baptist heritage of freedom.

The 1980 convention, for instance, passed a resolution declaring that it was important "to carefully preserve the doctrinal integrity of our institutions" and proclaiming the infallibility of the Bible. This resolution was a direct result of the biblical inerrancy movement of the late 1970s, which in the wake of Harold Lindsell's 1976 book *The Battle for the Bible* reversed a gradual drift among New Evangelicals away from insistence on inerrancy. Heading up the inerrancy movement in the SBC was its ex-president (and notorious former segregationist) W. A. Criswell, pastor of First Baptist Church in Dallas and author of the book *Why I Preach That the Bible Is Literally True*. Though inerrancy had never been a Baptist doctrine, Criswell and other Baptist fundamentalists acted as if it had *always* been one.

It was also in 1980 that Bailey Smith, then SBC president, created a stir by saying that "God Almighty does not hear the prayer of a Jew." Smith never retracted or apologized for this comment, and far from damaging his reputation among his constituency, it affirmed him as a hero. Indeed, Smith's comment might well be a good one-line test by which to divide the SBC into moderates and fundamentalists.

Further SBC resolutions tell the story:

- At the 1982 Southern Baptist Convention, a resolution was passed endorsing the unscientific doctrine of "creation science" that fundamentalists proffer as a substitute for evolution.

- Also passed in 1982 were resolutions supporting constitutional amendments to outlaw abortion and to permit voluntary prayer in public schools. Both resolutions reversed the historic Baptist opposition to government involvement in religion.

- In 1984, a resolution was passed endorsing female submission to men, "because man was first in creation and the woman was first in the Edenic fall." This represented a direct repudiation of traditional Baptist doctrine, which makes no gender distinctions.

- In 1988, two years after Criswell proclaimed that every pastor was the "ruler" of his church, a resolution was passed affirming that "the doctrine of the priesthood of the believer in no way contradicts the biblical understanding of the role, responsibility, and authority of the pastor." The resolution cited Hebrews 13: "Obey your leaders, and submit to them."

By 1989, the fundamentalists enjoyed solid control of the Convention. In 1996, still firmly in charge, they passed several resolutions that made headlines across America:

- One of those resolutions censured the Disney Company for releas-
  ing the movie *Priest* (about a gay clergyman), for providing health-
  care coverage to its employees' same-sex companions, and for other
  actions that were seen as placing "promotion of homosexuality"
  ahead of "commitment to traditional family values."

- Another resolution—by far the longest passed that year—fulminated
  over the Hawaii Supreme Court's ruling that the state may be con-
  stitutionally obligated to recognize same-sex unions. "Promotion of
  homosexual conduct and relationships by any society," the resolution declared, "is an abominable sin calling for God's swift judgment
  upon any such society."

- A third resolution said that Jews "need to come to their Messiah,
  Jesus, to be saved" and that Southern Baptists should step up efforts
  at converting Jews.

Only two of the fourteen resolutions passed in 1996 seemed to take
the Great Commandment into account. One was an obligatory, *pro
forma* condemnation of the burning of black churches. (This resolution's flat language formed a stark contrast with the passion of the antigay resolutions.) The other, which acknowledged "the need to support
hunger and relief ministries," suggested that Southern Baptist churches
"set aside one Sunday each year as a time for considering the role that
Baptists can and must play in meeting" the needs of the hungry and
homeless. One Sunday each year, out of fifty-two! Even this resolution, though, defended concern for the poor not as an obligation under
the Great Commandment but as a way of carrying out the Great Commission: "Southern Baptists recognize the vital role that meeting
human needs plays in their effort to demonstrate Christ-like compassion in bringing the lost to saving faith in Jesus Christ." It is as if SBC
fundamentalists wanted to be sure that no one mistook their evangelical Church of Law for a Church of Love.

And so it goes. In June 1997, citing Disney's continued "promotion
of homosexuality" and in particular the coming-out episode of *Ellen*
(a sitcom on Disney's ABC network), the SBC overwhelmingly passed
a resolution calling on Southern Baptists to boycott the theme parks,
TV networks, film and recording companies, and sports teams owned

by Disney. "Disney," said Richard Land, president of the SBC's Christian Life Commission, "is going to find out just how many regiments and how many divisions of godly people Southern Baptists have."

Such is the current status of what Finke and Stark glowingly call "The Baptist Triumph." Their book came out in 1992, at which time they noted that "it was not until about 1986 that the traditionalists [their erroneous term for the fundamentalists] began to be a majority on most of the SBC boards, and thus there has not been much time for the Patterson-Pressler plan to produce results." Well, by 1997 the plan's results were clear: It had turned the SBC, against all its finest traditions, into America's standard-bearer of hate. Finke and Stark claim that the SBC, which has grown by leaps and bounds in recent years, has done so because it has challenged its members; on the contrary, it was the SBC's pre-takeover moderate leadership that represented a challenge to the denomination's fundamentalist majority. "When successful sects are transformed into churches," write Finke and Stark, "that is, when their tension with the surrounding culture is greatly reduced, they soon cease to grow and eventually begin to decline." But a big part of the reason why the SBC has been so "successful" in recent years is that it has been in *no* tension at all with its culture—that is, the white southern underclass.

"As recently as 1990," write Finke and Stark, "nearly two thirds of self-identified Southern Baptists . . . expressed firm agreement with the statement 'The Bible is the actual word of God and is to be taken literally, word for word' and rejected the alternative 'The Bible is the inspired word of God but not everything in it should be taken literally, word for word.'" Finke and Stark approve of this vote. Yet it is utterly irrational, ignoring the plain fact that scores of biblical passages directly contradict one another. Pat Robertson has equated supposed modernist revisionism about the founding fathers' religious views with *1984,* George Orwell's novel about a totalitarian dystopia in which today's newspaper is dropped "down the memory hole" so that history may be altered tomorrow. Yet to declare belief in a totally inerrant Bible is in fact the equivalent of what that novel's hero is ultimately forced to do: affirm that two plus two equal five. One is reminded of the all-powerful Party's slogan in *1984:* "IGNORANCE IS STRENGTH." To Finke and Stark, and to others who defend legalistic Christianity on the sheer pragmatic grounds of its worldly "success," this is apparently what authentic religion is about: zealously embracing the "truth" of a statement about the universe that educated people recognize as false. Finke and Stark approve of this zealous embrace, and are far from alone in doing so.

Legalists aver that whole areas of learning must be avoided because they threaten faith. To believe this, of course, is to belie the notion that one's religion is in any sense "God's truth." For truth is never a threat to truth. A believer confident of the truth of his faith does not fear truth from any source, but welcomes it as a means to enhance his understanding of God's truth. Nonlegalistic Christianity, at its best, is based on the belief that there *is* a truth at the heart of Christianity— a truth that we have yet to fully discover, that at its deepest level can be reconciled with the truth claims of most other faiths, and that growing scientific knowledge can help bring us closer to. The best kind of nonlegalistic Christianity views knowledge as something to be embraced, not feared; reflected on, not rejected out of hand. By contrast, the faith of legalistic Christians often seems to have as its foundation an unspoken belief that religion *is* all really fake, and that one must consequently run from truth in fear.

For many Protestants, amazingly, the fundamentalist-run SBC is not nearly legalistic enough. In a 1994 attack on the SBC, an independent Baptist complains that the SBC is "radically ecumenical" (because it has, among other things, "conducted formal dialogue with the Roman Catholic church"); that SBC fundamentalists refuse to "separate" from moderates, as true fundamentalists would do; that SBC churches "set up deacons over God-ordained pastors"; that "women are allowed to hold leadership roles in the SBC"; that "the SBC has refused to discipline Billy Graham," a Southern Baptist, who has done "more than any other man in this generation to break down the wall between truth and error and to muddy the waters of the Gospel"; and that "the charismatic movement is working unhindered in many SBC churches." The critic's chief complaint, however, is that the SBC is permeated by "false teaching," which he defines as follows: "Any denial or questioning of the Bible is false teaching. I don't care if you call it Modernism, or Liberalism, or Neo-orthodoxy, or Neo-evangelicalism. . . . If a man questions the authenticity of any portion of the Bible, that man is a heretic, and he should be marked as such and rejected from the congregation and avoided." Thus speaks the Church of Law in our time.

The year 1979, which saw the beginning of the fundamentalist takeover of the Southern Baptist Convention, also saw the founding by Jerry Falwell of the Moral Majority. In that year, Ralph Reed has written, Falwell and other preachers "awakened the slumbering giant of the American evangelical church." Ten years later, the Moral Majority having come and gone, Reed's boss Pat Robertson founded the Christian Coalition. In the intervening years, a conflict that had come to be known as the culture wars had taken center stage in American society.

James Davison Hunter's 1991 book *Culture Wars* has been widely regarded as an objective depiction of that conflict. Yet Hunter's picture is seriously skewed. Central to that picture is a division of America into two ideological camps, the "orthodox" and the "progressive." His "orthodox" label would seem to correspond roughly to the same phenomenon that I designate with the word *legalistic;* but his characterization of that group could hardly be more different from mine. Whether Catholic or Protestant or Jewish, Hunter says, orthodoxy *"is the commitment on the part of adherents to an external, definable, and transcendent authority"* (his italics) which "defines, at least in the abstract, a consistent, unchangeable measure of value, purpose, goodness, and identity, both personal and collective. It tells us what is good, what is true, how we should live, and who we are."

By contrast, in progressivism "moral authority tends to be defined by the spirit of the modern age, a spirit of rationalism and subjectivism. Progressivist moral ideas tend, that is, to derive from and embody (though rarely exhaust) that spirit. From this standpoint, truth tends to be viewed as a process, as a reality that is ever unfolding." Those progressivists who continue to "identify with a particular religious heritage," he writes, tend "to translate the moral ideals of a religious tradition so that they conform to and legitimate the contemporary *zeitgeist.* In other words, what all *progressivist* worldviews share in common *is the tendency to resymbolize historic faiths according to the prevailing assumptions of contemporary life."* Hunter argues that such progressivism is seen in the "rejection of Biblical literalism" and the notion that "people have to interpret the Scripture for themselves."

Hunter's representation of this dichotomy is worth examining closely because it reflects a widely accepted (yet incorrect) view of religion in America. That view derives almost entirely from Religious Right propaganda, according to which the orthodox are driven by "faith" and by disciplined subordination to eternal values and unchanging truths, while the progressivists are driven by moral relativism and subjective self-indulgence. But Hunter, the author of a book on evangelical Christianity, certainly must know that most legalistic sects in this country didn't even exist a few generations ago, and, contrary to what he suggests about their devotion to eternal truths, have adjusted their theology frequently in response to "the spirit of the times"—as they did, for example, in embracing dispensational premillennialism in a reactionary backlash against modern thought. And legalists have done their share of accommodating with the *zeitgeist*: Many legalistic Protestant groups that once opposed racial integration and interracial marriage on supposed religious grounds changed those views (at least publicly) when they became socially and politically untenable; many such groups have also, in practice, repudiated the biblical passages affirming slavery and enjoining women to be silent in the churches; Mormons' belief in the legitimacy of polygamy, once central to their faith, was reversed by a timely "divine revelation" when the federal government threatened to stop the practice by force.

The Roman Catholic Church, too, has repeatedly adjusted its theology in response to "the spirit of the times." During the nineteenth century, members of the educated upper classes, and men of all classes, ceased attending services in droves, leaving behind a church composed mostly of women and the undereducated. To appease those members' sentimental superstitions, the Vatican added new doctrines about the Virgin Mary, first declaring that she had been conceived without sin, and later (in 1950) professing that she had been assumed bodily into heaven; both doctrines—which, to a thinking believer, were meaningless—had their basis not in scripture but in folk piety.

Of course, Hunter's argument that a rejection of biblical literalism is a facet of "progressivism" ignores the fact that the doctrine of scriptural inerrancy is itself a relatively recent development. And even those who claim to read the Bible literally and to lead their lives according to its precepts are, in actual practice, highly selective about which parts of the Bible they live by and which they don't. Jesus' condemnations of wealth and war are generally ignored; so are Levitical prohibitions on eating pork, wearing mixed fabrics, and so forth. Though legalistic Christians accuse nonlegalistic Christians of selective interpretation and relativistic morality (of adjusting the Bible, in short, to suit their own lifestyles and prejudices), what is usually happening is that nonlegalists are, as the Baptist tradition puts it, reading the Bible with Jesus as their criterion, while the legalists are, without any philosophical consistency whatsoever, embracing those laws and doctrines that affirm their own predilections and prejudices and ignoring the rest.

Which brings us, at long last, to Pat Robertson.

9

GOD'S
GENERALISSIMO

THE HISTORY OF the Church of Law is populated by lawyers.
Saint Paul was a lawyer. John Nelson Darby went to law
school (but never practiced law). And so did a certain senator's son who, after attending Yale Law and failing the bar,
didn't really know what to do with his life.

This may be hard to believe nowadays, for Pat Robertson seems almost to have been *born* to be a TV preacher.
Yet there were several stops along the way. A former Golden
Gloves boxer and Marine Corps officer, Robertson worked
for a time as an overseas "troubleshooter" for W. R. Grace
and as an electronics entrepreneur before ministry beck-
oned. And in fact his TV manner today reflects something
of all these elements of his background: The pugilist's
punch-happy pugnacity combines with the marine's steady,

steely glint; the company man's polish blends with the small businessman's go-getter zeal. And of course in Robertson, the politician is
fused inextricably with the clergyman: Leaning forward in his chair,
the white-haired, square-faced Robertson relates his political views
with the twinkly-eyed smile of a family preacher on a pastoral visit;
standing on the *700 Club* stage in suit and tie, he spins out his appalling
End Times theology with the slickness of a politician delivering a
stump speech. Like Ronald Reagan, he's a man with a worldly, privileged past who has acquired an aw-shucks, folksy persona that appeals
to middle Americans; like many legalistic preachers, he's a man with a
thin coating of warm-and-fuzzy gentleness and a hard core of ruthless, rigid authoritarianism. His constituents take comfort from his
refusal to compromise with the mainstream culture; opponents find his
manner bullying and threatening, and find much of his rhetoric anything but godly.

Raised as a Baptist, Robertson wasn't particularly religious until
1956, when he met a dynamic Dutch mystic named Cornelius
Vanderbreggen. Years later, when Robertson described their first
encounter in his autobiography, the part that seemed to have impressed
itself most strongly on his memory was Vanderbreggen's lesson that a
man of God can live well. "God is generous, not stingy," Vanderbreggen
told him as they dined at an elegant hotel. "He wants you to have
the best." In a 1995 *Sojourners* article, Michael Smith notes that
Robertson's "theology of capitalism" is founded on the parable
(Matt. 25:14–30) in which a servant who puts his master's money into
a business and makes a profit is praised, while a servant who buries the
master's gold in the ground is rebuked. Robertson has never appeared
to find any conflict in a theology that preaches a God who wants him
to live in luxury yet who will condemn most human beings to everlasting torment.

But then, Robertson's autobiography consistently portrays him as
God's chosen instrument and routinely implies that people who have
gotten in his way, or who have seen things differently than he does, are
agents of Satan. Exposed to the charismatic revival at its start, he
responded immediately to the movement's powerful sense of the
world as a battleground between God and Satan and did not take
long to begin seeing himself as God's generalissimo. Soon after his
conversion, spending several weeks at a "religious camp" where he

sought to discern God's will for his life, Robertson received a letter from his wife, Dede, summoning him home. "Was this God telling me to go home," he writes, "or was it Satan?" (That it may have been just Dede is apparently not a possibility.) Ever since then, Robertson has been convinced that God was sending personal messages to him through the Bible:

> "God, give me a word," I prayed. I let my Bible fall open. There on the page before me was his answer.

> I picked up my Bible and put it in my lap. "God, what do you want me to do?" I prayed.
>   I opened the Bible and reached out and put my finger in the middle of one of the pages. I read the verse I was pointing at.

When Dede too became a charismatic Christian, Robertson rejoiced in "her willingness to submit herself to my spiritual headship." Robertson recalls: "I reached over and pulled her to me, thanking God for this surrender." Presently God led him to Tidewater, Virginia, where Robertson bought a dilapidated TV station. "In 1959," Robertson writes,

> the Tidewater area of Virginia was literally a spiritual wasteland. For years it had been in the grip of demon power. Virginia Beach was advertised as the psychic capital of the world. It was the headquarters of Edgar Cayce and the Association for Research and Enlightenment (ARE). Mediums, clairvoyants, and necromancers flocked to Virginia Beach saying the vibrations in the air made their work easier. These Satanic vibrations, which traverse space and time, are the communications channels to which sensitives or mediums must attune themselves, and Virginia Beach was renowned as the prime receiving station of the Universal Transmitter (Satan).

Robertson changed all that in 1960 when he founded the Christian Broadcasting Network directly under this "umbrella of Satanic oppression." The empire that Robertson built on the foundation of CBN would play a huge role in elevating the Church of Law to a position of ascendancy in America. "As much as anybody," observes Tim Stafford in a 1996 issue of *Christianity Today,* the flagship publication of New Evangelicalism, Robertson "has put his stamp on American Christianity as it approaches the third millennium." He has, Stafford notes, "shaped three major religious developments: the charismatic renewal, Christian TV, and evangelical politics." Indeed, Robertson was instrumental in mainstreaming all three of these developments and tying them together. Identifying with both the charismatic and evangelical movements (he calls himself a "Spirit-filled evangelical"), he helped "shape the charismatic movement as a wide, ecumenical, and comfortable phenomenon" that brought "Pentecostalism closer to the mainstream of American life" even as he did much to "transform evangelicalism from a small, defended backwater to the leading force in American Christianity."

The 1976 election to the presidency of a born-again Southern Baptist, Jimmy Carter, drew Robertson into serious political involvement. Yet when Carter's administration proved too liberal for him—and for other legalistic Protestants as well—Robertson began organizing religious conservatives in hopes of forming a counterforce to Washington liberalism. This political involvement eventually led to the 1989 founding of the Christian Coalition, which by 1997 had a national network consisting of thousands of local chapters, tens of thousands of precinct and neighborhood coordinators, and a total membership of 1.5 million. In the 1994 elections, Christian Coalition workers made over half a million phone calls to get out the vote; in 1996 they distributed 46 million voter guides through more than 126,000 churches. Meanwhile CBN prospered, as did other Robertson properties (some of which he sold to Rupert Murdoch in 1997 for over $100 million) ranging from the Family Channel, MTM Entertainment, and the Ice Capades to the Founders Inn hotel chain and Regent University.

Since the Christian Coalition's founding in 1989, the average American's sense of who legalistic Christians are and what their lives are about has been increasingly shaped by Robertson—and even more, perhaps, by Ralph Reed, who served as the Christian Coalition's executive director from the outset. (Reed announced in April 1997 that he would step down from that position in September to head up a new political consulting firm that would work for right-wing candidates at both the national and local levels.) There has been a clear division of labor between these two men: While Robertson speaks to his constituents (mainly on *The 700 Club*), Reed addresses mainstream America on behalf of that constituency. The difference between the two men's messages is dramatic—and instructive.

Those messages are summed up in two recent volumes. One of them is Robertson's *Collected Works,* a thick 1994 volume that includes his books *The New Millennium* (1990), *The New World Order* (1991), and *The Secret Kingdom* (1982, 1992). Taken together, the three books (which I will refer to for convenience's sake as a trilogy) amount to a summary of Robertson's theology and politics, which are inextricably connected with each other. The other book is Reed's *Active Faith: How Christians Are Changing the Soul of American Politics* (1996).

It doesn't take long to notice the general differences between Robertson's and Reed's books. Robertson's trilogy centers on theology, though he is constantly connecting his religious views to political propositions; Reed's focus is on politics, though he tries not to let religion get too far out of the picture for too long. Robertson is writing for his constituents—for "conservative Christians" who look to him for instruction in scripture, history, and prophecy; Reed's book, by contrast, is aimed chiefly at the mainstream reader—at mainline Christians, Jews, and secular Americans whose unease about his movement he is at pains to quell. Both men clearly aim to help strengthen the Christian Coalition's power: While Robertson seeks to solidify his constituents' loyalty to him and to bring their religious beliefs and political objectives more into line with his own, Reed labors to pacify the coalition's opponents and perhaps even win their political alliance, if only on pragmatic grounds.

These differences are understandable, given the difference between the audiences for which the two men's books are intended. But there are more striking variances—indeed, outright contradictions— between Robertson's trilogy and Reed's book. An examination of these volumes, of the ideas that they present, and of the ways in which they contradict each other can go a long way toward illuminating the reality of the legalistic Christian worldview—and the outrageous distinction between that reality and the thoroughly phony image that the Christian Coalition seeks to project to outsiders.

Robertson's trilogy offers a bizarre account of biblical prophecy that is in the direct line of Darby, Scofield, and Lindsey. Like Lindsey,

Robertson offers a twisted account of history and current events by way of supporting his biblical prophecy. The principal difference is that Robertson places more emphasis on the political lessons and prescriptions that he draws from that prophecy. Like Lindsey, Robertson relies on the fact that his readers know little about the history he is manipulating. One illustration of that ignorance is a glaring error that appeared in *The New Millennium* in 1990 and, astonishingly, remained uncorrected when that book was reprinted as part of *The Collected Pat Robertson* four years later. I am referring to Robertson's condescending reference to "Henri Beyle (pronounced baal), who wrote under the name of Voltaire" and who "was essentially an atheist." In fact Marie-Henri Beyle—whom Robertson here tries shamelessly to link with Baal, the Canaanite deity whom the Israelites identified with Satan—was the birth name not of Voltaire (whose birth name was Arouet) but of the French novelist Stendhal. What is to the point here is not the error itself—which I have never seen pointed out anywhere—but the fact that it went unnoticed and uncorrected in the four-year period between the book's initial publication and its appearance in the *Collected* volume. The perpetuation of this error only indicates how little Robertson's readers know about most of the things he writes about—and how manipulable they therefore are. Robertson can distort history to an outrageous extent, yet his readers will accept the conclusions he draws from the historical record because they don't realize how much he is distorting it.

The perpetuation of this error also underscores the fact that Robertson's readership is almost entirely confined to the Religious Right. Members of the mainstream media, intelligentsia, and political establishment—people, that is, who might notice slipups like the one about Voltaire and call them to the attention of his publishers—don't read Robertson's books. Few of them even look in on *The 700 Club* occasionally to see what America's most politically powerful Republican is up to these days. Consequently these mainstream opinion makers have only the most rudimentary acquaintance with the theological ideas of the man at the Christian Coalition's helm. If you asked many of these opinion makers, some of whom cover the Christian Coalition on a regular basis, they would probably say that the coalition members' theology is not their affair and that they are interested only in the movement's political manifestations. Yet because they take this attitude, Reed has been able to go on TV and routinely soften the coalition's image without the other participants recognizing the extent to which he has been doing so. Robertson and Reed, then, have made a highly efficient team: One of them distorts history and the Bible by way of fashioning a theology for his followers, and the other misrepresents that theology by way of fashioning a viable national political movement.

As I have noted, one way in which Reed has softened the Christian Coalition's image has been by insisting that the Christian Coalition stands for tolerance and pluralism—that it doesn't view America as a Christian nation and isn't trying to make it one. Robertson's books make it clear that this is absolutely not the case. America, he writes, is undergoing a war between "Christians" (that is, legalistic Christians) and "secularists" (which, in Robertson's lexicon, includes nonlegalistic Christians as well as people of other faiths). Robertson declares, for instance, that the Anglican Church is full of "liberals" who are "fighting to secularize the Anglican creed." The people to whom he refers are, of course, Christians, but because they believe differently from Robertson, he calls them secular.

"From its inception," Robertson writes, "secularism has focused intently on the overt de-Christianizing of America. It starts with dialogue about 'pluralism' and 'tolerance' and 'relative values,' as it did in France 200 years ago, but it always ends with an outright assault on Christianity and the Church." By contrast, Reed, in *Active Faith,* denies "that our movement is . . . morally intolerant" and claims that "the religious conservative community has greatly matured in recent years by broadening its message and narrowing its aspirations to those that are appropriate for any other group in a pluralistic society." Reed's affirmation here of tolerance and pluralism is precisely the sort of thing that Robertson criticizes as secular "de-Christianizing." Reed's tendency to dish out "pluralistic" rhetoric to mainstream readers explains his shaky position in the hearts of hard-core Christian Coalition activists, who have had it drilled into them by Robertson, Hal Lindsey, and their local preachers that "pluralism" and "tolerance" are euphemisms for compromise with the Devil.

Reed writes about "people of faith" in such a way as to suggest that he feels a sense of kinship with anyone who belongs to some religion.

("We want to give people of all faiths—Jewish, Christian, or any other faith—a voice in government," he said in a January 1997 interview on MSNBC.) Robertson, by contrast, virulently condemns religious traditions other than his own. He describes Hinduism, for example, as offering "a chilling and joyless vision of life" and maintains that it "has, as its origin, demonic power." He charges that Jehovah's Witnesses and Christian Scientists belong to "cults which claim to be Christian" but whose doctrines contain falsehoods that will "bring down the wrath of God upon their own heads." He characterizes meditation as "at best . . . absurd" and "at worst . . . demonic" in that it opens people up "to evil powers and spirits." And he calls Islam "a Christian heresy."

Many secular Americans read such things and shrug. "Well," they sigh, "that's what it means to be religious, isn't it? You're obliged to feel that what you believe is right and what other people believe is wrong." No. Even the Roman Catholic Church, that most dogmatic of institutions, has stated that there is some degree of truth in all faiths, that people are entitled to follow their consciences, and that adherents of different religions should respect one another. Traditional Baptist doctrine, as we have seen, stresses freedom of conscience. More liberal Christian bodies have asserted that nobody can pretend to know the whole truth of God, that what different faiths offer is not so much competing truths as different ways of understanding a single overarching truth, that Jesus taught us to be less concerned with theological particulars than with our love for God and humanity, and that people from diverse traditions can learn much from one another about the nature of God. This is not a specifically modern or liberal or "secular" way of thinking; as we know, our founding fathers took much the same view, and five centuries before them Francis of Assisi prayed with a Moslem in a mosque, saying, "God is everywhere." He did not say, "My faith is correct and yours isn't." He recognized the Moslem's faith as genuine, meaningful, and good; he saw that they both were praying to the same God and were brothers in God's sight.

Though Robertson says little in his books about God's love or about Christians' obligation to love people of different faiths, he has much to say about God's wrath, a subject about which he is extremely enthusiastic. "Bible history tells us," he reports, "that because of their hardness of heart, God scattered the Jews time and time again. The

Egyptians and the Babylonians and the Assyrians were allowed to make slaves of them. However, God eventually brought down His wrath upon those nations and eradicated their empires." Robertson loves the parts of the Bible that depict God as avenging, punishing, destroying; he loves the scriptures' *Sturm und Drang*. Yet the gospel passages about love seem lost on him. He rarely quotes from them. Indeed he avoids them almost entirely, choosing instead to focus on Old Testament law and prophecy and New Testament evangelism and prophecy, giving special attention to everything lurid, vicious, and ugly.

When Robertson is not focusing on these parts of scripture, he is often busy setting forth lurid, vicious visions of his own. He enthusiastically imagines, for example, the death of those whom he considers enemies of "true Christianity," writing that "if homosexuals continue in their homosexuality, they will commit genocide." AIDS aside, he argues, "homosexuality is nothing short of self-extinction and suicide," for if gays "continue their self-destructive lifestyle, sooner or later their share of the population will die out." Robertson repeats this comment twenty pages later: "Certainly homosexuality should die out since the homosexuals are unable to reproduce themselves." He says much the same thing about those who commit abortion: If they keep aborting their fetuses, they will disappear, too. The fact that homosexuality has always existed, and that people have been aborting fetuses from the dawn of time, seems not to enter into his calculations. (It is ironic, by the way, that though Robertson continually reminds us how evil homosexuals are, he also approvingly cites works by gay writers with great frequency, presumably without knowing that they are gay. One of these writers is Allan Bloom, whose book *The Closing of the American Mind* Robertson admiringly represents as an argument for Christian education, even though Bloom—in addition to being homosexual—was a secular Jew.)

In connection with his condemnation of homosexuality and abortion, Robertson cites Leviticus, saying that it contains "a catalog of offenses so heinous that they will not only cause a society to fall but will cause the land itself to 'vomit out' its inhabitants. The list includes homosexuality, adultery, bestiality, and the sacrifice of children. Every one of these offenses, with the exception of bestiality, is now rampant in America." Robertson purports to take that "catalog" seriously. Yet also included in it, though Robertson omits it from his version of the list, is having intercourse with a woman during menstruation. If he means to be consistent in his devotion to Levitical law, presumably Robertson considers this act as heinous—and as deserving of the death penalty—as he does the others in the catalog.

What Robertson is doing here is making selective use of an ancient tribal code that has no application to life in America today. To read the Levitical laws in context is to be struck by how specific they are to their own time and place. Consider the first several chapters of Leviticus, which set forth in detail how the Israelites should present animal offerings to the Lord. It is directed therein that if a priest inadvertently sins, he must bring a bull to the entrance of the Tent of Meeting, put his hand on its head, slaughter it, bring its blood into the tent, dip his finger in the blood, sprinkle it seven times before the sanctuary curtain, smear some of it on the horns of the altar, pour out the remainder at the base of the altar, and do various other things with the bull's fat and its hide. What does Robertson have to say about the contemporary relevance of this passage? Nothing, of course. Further Levitical laws prescribe at length, among other things, the brutal ways in which the community should treat people with skin disorders. These prescriptions would nowadays be considered utterly cruel, and one cannot imagine a modern church endorsing them. Leviticus also contains elaborate rules about cleanness, rules that nobody now would take seriously. Among the rules are these:

> When a man has emitted semen, he must bathe his whole body in water and be unclean till evening. (LEV. 15:16)

> When a woman has her discharge of blood, her impurity will last for several days; anyone who touches her will be unclean till evening. (LEV. 15:19)

Leviticus prescribes extreme punishments for a variety of acts. "When a priest's daughter makes herself profane by becoming a prostitute, she profanes her father" and "must be burnt" (Lev. 21:9). The high priest "must not enter the place where any dead body lies. . . . He is to marry a woman who is still a virgin" (Lev. 21:11ff). The blind and lame are not permitted to make offerings at God's altar (Lev. 21:18). All these statutes carry the same penalty: "if you . . . fail to obey all my commandments," Leviticus 26 quotes God as saying, "I shall bring upon you sudden terror, wasting disease, recurrent fever, and plagues that dim the sight and cause the appetite to fail. . . . Instead of meat you will eat your sons and daughters. . . . I shall pile your corpses on your lifeless idols . . . I shall make your cities desolate." The point is clear: This punishment holds for violation of *any* Levitical rule. Yet Robertson quotes these rules very selectively (and the only one that any modern church really takes seriously is the one about men lying with men).

Consistent with Robertson's preoccupation with the more barbaric scriptural passages is his routine use of brutal turns of phrase in situations where such language seems inappropriate. He speaks, for example, of the Christian Broadcasting Network's ability to "blitz an entire nation for Christ." *Blitz* is, of course, the German word for lightning, and for most people it recalls, above all, the Nazi term *blitzkrieg:* "lightning warfare." This is, to say the least, a disturbing way to refer to the act of spreading the gospel—and it underscores dramatically the extreme divergence between the gospel of Jesus Christ and that of Pat Robertson. Indeed, Robertson is a man with a repulsive vision, a picture of the End Times in which only fundamentalists survive and triumph. He may claim to be horrified by Nazi and Stalinist atrocities, but in his own division of the world into a holy "us" and an unholy "them," and in his bloody vision of "their" fate, he differs little from the most chilling totalitarian dictator.

Unsurprisingly, Robertson's worldview is a deeply disturbing one. He sees the present day as suffering from vast social evils because "Christian America" has been undermined by "humanism and socialism." These evils are "family disintegration, unrestrained sex, a holocaust of abortion, an epidemic of drugs and alcohol, deteriorating educational standards, growing poverty amidst unrestrained opulence, business greed and fraud, and a runaway federal budget." Reed's book features a similar list: American society, he writes, has been "torn asunder by explicit sex and violence on television, rampant divorce, skyrocketing

illegitimacy, epidemics of crime and drugs, and a million teen preg-
nancies every year." But "the most important issue . . . is the culture,
the family, a loss of values, a decline in civility, and the destruction of
our children." The implicit assumption in both men's books is that life
in America a hundred years ago, say, was much more "Christian" and
better for children. Yet those good old days to which Robertson and
Reed would presumably have us return were a time of institutionalized racism, segregation, and lynching, of robber barons, sweatshops,
and child labor, of urban blight and rural tar-paper shacks without
plumbing or electricity; it was a time when the federal government
imposed no income tax on the fortunes made by the Fords, Rocke-
fellers, and Vanderbilts and did nothing to help poor children or ailing
senior citizens, nothing to regulate the quality of food and medicines,
nothing to protect people from being fired or evicted for being (say)
Irish or Jewish or black. The only reason why Robertson can get away
with the argument that social conditions are incomparably worse now
than they were in the past is that most of his readers, having little or
no knowledge of American social history, have formed an image of
"the good old days" that has everything to do with nostalgia and little or nothing to do with reality. (Reed's strong rhetoric about "the
destruction of our children" is especially striking given the Christian
Coalition's exceedingly unchristian efforts to eliminate federal programs to aid poor children; clearly, he makes a distinction between
"our children" and *their* children.)

Among today's social evils, according to Robertson, is what he
describes as the low quality of contemporary American education. He
attributes this problem to the secularism of American schools. Yet he
is vigorously anti-intellectual, writing that in a secular world, "the
mind becomes a playground of ideas." This phrase might well have
been plucked right out of *The Fundamentals,* in which, as we have seen,
the early-twentieth-century "modernists" were accused of turning the
Bible into "a plaything for the intellect." In Robertson's view, this presumably infantile thirst for ideas "is the hunger for the apple all over
again; the lust for the knowledge of good and evil; the desire to attain
what Satan promised, 'you shall be as gods.' " In short, to want to *know,*
to want to understand as much as possible about how the universe
works, is evil. To be open to ideas, to refuse to reject them out of hand

before weighing them against one's reason and experience, is to turn the mind into a "playground." Yet this is precisely what education is about; it is what the human mind was made for; it is what distinguishes humans from animals (a crucial distinction to legalistic Christians, who rebel at the idea that they are mere primates). What Robertson is lamenting here, in reality, is not the low quality of American education but the fact that what is indeed taking place in America's public schools, by and large, *is* education and not indoctrination into Robertson's brand of religion.

Over and over again, those who respond most positively to Robertson's rhetoric about education have made clear that they do so not out of a real concern for educational excellence but out of a worry that teachers are filling their children's heads with ideas that might challenge their own "values" and "beliefs." Especially guilty of a pernicious interest in knowledge, Robertson charges, are "the Liberal Jews" who "have actually forsaken Biblical faith in God, and make a religion of political liberalism." Accusing these Jews of seeking "to undermine the public strength of Christianity," he warns darkly that "one day a vote against Israel will come in the United Nations when the United States neither abstains or [*sic*] uses its veto in the Security Council to protect Israel." As a result, "that tiny little nation will find itself all alone in the world. Then, according to the Bible, the Jews will cry out to the one they have so long rejected." (This brutal, retributionalist vision of the conversion of the Jews, of course, comes straight out of premillennialist theology.) In a footnote in *Active Faith,* Ralph Reed quotes a claim by the political writer Michael Lind that Robertson, describing Jews as "spiritually deaf" and "spiritually blind," stated that many of them would be converted to Christianity in the End Times. Reed's comment: "Robertson never made such a statement." What he fails to acknowledge is that Lind's characterization of Robertson's theology is perfectly accurate.

A standard element of legalistic Christian rhetoric is the claim that scientists whose discoveries contradict legalistic theology are not just objectively pursuing truth but actively seek to destroy Christianity. About Marx, Darwin, and Freud, for instance, Robertson says that "each of these men—in company with a cadre of German theologians who emerged on the heels of the Revolution—were [*sic*] committed to debunking the Bible, turning against the supernatural, and teaching their own rationalistic theory that man and all the creatures of the animal world are mere products of blind evolution." This is true enough of Karl Marx, who attacked religion as the opiate of the masses, but not of Darwin or Freud. Charles Darwin was a Christian whose insistence that his discoveries did not challenge any key tenet of his belief was basically ignored by fundamentalist churchmen. Sigmund Freud, for his part, was a scientist whose desire to understand how the mind works led him to make discoveries and posit theories that some Christians saw as a threat to their faith; unlike his colleague Carl Jung, he disdained religion, which he considered a neurotic manifestation, but it is misleading to suggest that his driving motivation was a desire to destroy faith and debunk scripture. In reply to Robertson's charge against scientists, one can only quote the *New York Times* editorialist who noted that

> *The real plot against him, if he only knew it, is the existence of the spirit of scientific inquiry. . . . This motive he interprets as a secret but cooperative endeavor to break down revealed religion. To him the idea of rejoicing in scientific investigation for its own sake and of delighting in free inquiry, carefully tested, as a means of arriving at the truth, is utterly incomprehensible.*

The above comments appeared in the *Times* on July 21, 1925, and were written about William Jennings Bryan. Yet they apply equally well to Robertson today, whose comments on science and learning reflect a profound discomfort with any kind of intellectual curiosity that is not tightly yoked to his own narrow, absolute version of Christianity.

If he is suspicious of free intellectual inquiry and artistic creativity, and is a committed enemy of anything remotely socialistic, Robertson adores capitalism, which he sees as not only consistent with the gospel but also implicit in it. "There is only one system of economics in the history of mankind that truly makes sense and leads to the prosperity and well-being of the people," Robertson writes (in bold print), "and that is the free-market profit-oriented economic system we know as

Capitalism." He quotes Jesus: "Do unto others as you would have them do unto you." This is, of course, a call to selflessness—but not for Robertson, whose gloss is staggering: "In that statement," he writes, Jesus "recognized individual self-interest as being a very real part of the human makeup, and something not necessarily bad or sinful." Robertson says of God, indeed, that "enlightened self-interest was . . . obviously His plan. So the profit motive, *per se,* the desire for economic betterment, is not at all contrary to scripture." This claim is utterly at odds with the gospel. There is no hint here of the selfless love that Jesus preached—and certainly no hint of Rauschenbusch's concern about the excesses of capitalism. Indeed, in the hands of Robertson (who elsewhere refers to Tom Peters's *Thriving on Chaos* as "the best management book that I have read, other than the Bible"), Jesus sounds uncomfortably like the writer Ayn Rand, who argued that selfishness is a virtue.

If Robertson (himself a wealthy man) celebrates the accumulation of wealth with the same zeal that Jesus devoted to preaching against it, he can sound heartless when referring to poor individuals and nations. "The poorest countries," Robertson complains, "contribute less than one-hundredth of 1 percent of the United Nations budget" yet enjoy the same voting power in the General Assembly as the United States. Robertson, who seems to view poverty as something not to be ameliorated but punished, explains Christianity to his followers in such a way as to encourage their financial self-interest, and to reinforce in their minds the idea that if they sign on with Jesus, they will reap monetary rewards for doing so. Given Robertson's ardor for "enlightened self-interest," it was hardly surprising when, in late April 1997, the Associated Press reported that planes flown to Zaire as part of Operation Blessing—a CBN project publicized often on Robertson's *700 Club* as exemplary of Religious Right humanitarianism—had in fact been "used almost exclusively for his diamond mining business." Nor is it a surprise that he considers liberation theology, by contrast, to be "nothing short of communist repression dressed up as social reform." Speaking of the clergymen and women who, inspired by that theology, have sought at great personal peril to help improve the lives of oppressed people in Latin America and elsewhere, Robertson expresses the hope that people in the church will "either reform the reformers" who practice liberation theology "or cast them from the temple." So much for Reed's pretense that the Christian Coalition believes in tolerance and pluralism, and so much also for Reed's attempt to represent the Religious Right as "the social and political heir of the Social Gospel, with its focus on the least among us."

To read Pat Robertson, as I happened to do, with the 1996 Republican National Convention on television in the background is to get a crystal-clear picture of where much of that party's recent rhetoric has been coming from. I had noted, in preceding weeks, the Republicans' constant deprecatory references to the Democratic "bureaucracy" and their equally frequent celebratory references to "family." The ideology was hardly unprecedented, but what did seem rather new was the incessant pairing of these two words and the concomitant implication that the coming election would be a contest between bureaucracy, a Democratic evil, and family, a Republican virtue. Where, I wondered, did this odd oppositional linking of bureaucracy and family come from? Then I read these two sentences (also in boldface) by Robertson: "Bureaucracy is unnatural and ineffective. The institution created by God for development and nurturing is the family."

The family? Yes, the family *is* about development and nurturing. But this is hardly an exclusively Christian concept. All civilizations and religions have recognized the role of the family and have honored family ties. The Gospels, by contrast, powerfully challenge the primacy of those ties. Our earliest post-Nativity picture of Jesus is of him leaving his parents at age twelve to go to the temple and rebuking his mother when she questioned him. Years later, Jesus did something else that no good Jewish son would have done: He left his parents to travel with a group of men and women who, though not his biological relatives, were, in a very real sense, his family—though one could hardly imagine Robertson and most Christian Coalition members acknowledging such a group as a family.

"If anyone comes to me and does not hate his father and mother, wife and children, brothers and sisters, even his own life," Jesus said, "he cannot be a disciple of mine" (Luke 14:26). It was a typically hyperbolic statement: One does not feel that Jesus really wanted anybody to hate, but one recognizes that he considered such strong words necessary to get the point across that one's ties to other human beings transcended the traditional boundaries of family and tribe. "Mother, behold your son," Jesus said to Mary from the cross, speaking not of himself but of his beloved disciple. "Son, behold your mother" (John 19:26,27). The message is clear: Love, not blood, makes a family.

The rhetoric that comes out of today's major Religious Right institutions—not only the Christian Coalition but Focus on the Family and Promise Keepers, among others—centers to a huge extent on the value of family love and devotion. Over and over these organizations tell America that family, above all, is what Christianity is about. Devotion to one's family is, indeed, a wonderful thing. Yet it is hardly something to brag about. For all except the most pathologically self-absorbed, love for one's parents, spouse, and children comes naturally. Jesus did not make it his business to affirm these ties; he didn't have to. Jews feel them, Buddhists feel them, Confucians and Zoroastrians and atheists feel them. Christianity is not about reinforcing such natural bonds and instinctive sentiments. Rather, Christianity is about challenging them and helping us to see all of humankind as our family. It seems clear that if Jesus had wanted to affirm the "traditional family" in the way that Pat Robertson claims, he would not have lived the way he did.

Yet to read Robertson, you would think that Jesus' main cause was the "traditional family." Jesus, according to Robertson, taught us that "instead of always looking out for number one, we must care for others, particularly those who look to us for affirmation and support." But the purpose of Jesus' ministry was not to tell us that mothers need to care for their children. The whole point of his words on the cross to Mary and his beloved disciple is that mothers should try to see *all* children as their children, and people should try to see *all* mothers as their mothers. Jesus strove constantly to persuade his disciples to look with love upon those most different from themselves, and to see them not as threatening foreigners but as fellow children of God. This position could hardly be more different from that of Robertson, who is fixated on the danger supposedly posed to America by cultures that differ from our own, and who encourages his followers to see themselves as being engaged in a culture war with people who do not live in "traditional American families."

For Robertson, indeed, the single great enemy is "globalism"—the notion (characterized by him as liberal wickedness) that Americans should care not only about their fellow countrymen but also about people beyond their borders. He says that many universities seek "to indoctrinate a new generation of Americans into the globalist and nonstatist mode of thinking. That means creating educational structures for thought modification (read that, 'thought control') and accepting idealistic theories that will lead inevitably to revolutionary activism." (The parenthetic reference to "thought control," by the way, is Robertson's, not mine.) Yet what is Jesus' parable of the good Samaritan if not a brief for what Robertson calls globalism? Jesus' message is that we should not regard borders—whether between individuals or families or nations—as limits on our love for our fellow human beings. Plainly, a large part of what makes "globalist" thinking dangerous in Robertson's eyes is that in most foreign nations nowadays, fundamentalist Christians wield far less power than they do here. Western Europe, he laments, has essentially abandoned Christianity, while Japan is a non–Christian country that does not share "our values." For these reasons, he sees an increasingly united Europe and an increasingly powerful Japan as menaces to America. For the same reasons, he inveighs against one-world government, which, he says, would only be a utopian "counterfeit of the millennial government that Christ will establish."

Jesus taught his listeners not to attend overmuch to the sins of others but to love other people and to look rather into the sins of their own hearts. Robertson turns this teaching completely around. When we become Christians, he says, we see our own sins and recognize them as forgiven, and then (that little matter having been taken care of) turn to "see the sins of others—our relatives and friends who are not saved, indeed, the whole world." This is typical of legalistic Christian thinking: The moment you join the club, you're "saved," and thus permitted—indeed, encouraged—to turn your attention from the condition of your own soul to whatever you may choose to perceive as the sins of those around you.

For Robertson, of course, Protestant fundamentalists are the only true Christians. In *The New Millennium,* he defines Protestant fundamentalists as "those who actually believe the Bible is the Word of God and that it contains truth which must be believed and followed." Eventually, he says, "the believers will stand firmly astride the fallen and crumbling ruins of the secular colossus." In Robertson's view, plainly, a major part of the reward for "believers" is that one day they will joyfully and triumphantly walk over the battered and bloodied remains of fallen nonbelievers. We are a long way here from the parable of the good Samaritan.

As the liberal lobbying group People for the American Way noted in a 1996 press release, Ralph Reed has said that "We believe in a separation between church and state that is complete and inviolable," while Robertson has described separation of church and state as "a lie of the left" that "we're not going to take . . . anymore." Reed has consistently maintained that the Christian Coalition does not seek to force its members' beliefs upon others; Robertson, by contrast, complains that "our government has officially insulted Almighty God and has effectively taken away from all public school children any opportunity for even the slightest acknowledgment of God's existence"—his point plainly being that it is part of the American government's job to introduce schoolchildren to religion. Which of our founding fathers would ever have agreed that public schools should indoctrinate children in this or that faith tradition? Robertson actually claims that the Supreme Court's decisions on compulsory school prayer and other such issues called down upon the United States "the wrath of God." As evidence for this, he cites a series of national tragedies: the assassination of John F. Kennedy, the 1969 stock market plunge, the rise in oil prices and U.S. trade deficit of the early 1970s, President Nixon's resignation, the Iranian hostage crisis, and so forth. Of course, American history before 1963 was at least equally crowded with unfortunate events; but Robertson counts on the fact that his readers, by and large, will not realize that. He also counts on his followers' image of the Almighty being close enough to his own that they will believe God induced Lee Harvey Oswald to kill Kennedy in order to punish the nation—and with the expectation, of course, that in the fullness of time Pat Robertson would come along and explain to America exactly what it had done to anger its Creator.

10

THE CHOIRBOY

IT'S CLEAR WHY Robertson chose Ralph Reed to serve as the Christian Coalition's public face in the mainstream media. The slight, boyish Reed, with his wide-eyed choirboy countenance, would seem to have been born to disarm mainstream Americans and to remind Christian Coalition members of their favorite young preacher or youth leader. Indeed, at first glance Reed—who grew up in Miami and at a tender age became, in his own words, a "political junkie"—looks very much like a high-school student council president, his earnest, wholesome appearance, perfect posture, and ubiquitous blue business suit only reinforcing the image of an eager boy playing grown-up; he would appear to embody a bright-eyed, squeaky-clean type of American youth that was once portrayed in movies by the likes of Mickey Rooney and Jimmy Lydon.

Yet Reed's innocuous, unworldly appearance is utterly deceptive—for when he opens his mouth, he proves to be as adept as anyone on Capitol Hill at political "spin." Addressing the Christian Coalition, he can make the right pious noises about uncompromisable ideals; speaking with politicians, he can compromise with the best of them; appearing on network TV, he can make the Religious Right agenda sound decent, modest, reasonable. He is as slick as they come. Yet his effectiveness is blunted by the fact that he ultimately stands for nothing. Though Christian Coalition members tolerated his leadership for eight years, many have been at best lukewarm about him, sensing—and distrusting—the very pragmatism and inside-the-Beltway savvy that helped win the Coalition clout in official Washington.

One mark of Reed's pragmatism is the dramatic contrast between many of his public statements and many of Robertson's. There have always, of course, been shades of difference between the rhetoric that pressure-group leaders direct at nonmembers and the rhetoric they direct at members. But Reed and Robertson took these differences to schizophrenic lengths. Reading their statements on the same subjects, one might never have known that one of them worked at the time for the other. If Robertson reflects the extreme social, political, and theological views of many legalistic Christians, Reed presents an equally clear picture of the moderate image of legalistic Christianity that its political leaders seek to cultivate among mainstream readers.

The subtitle of Reed's book—*How Christians Are Changing the Soul of American Politics*—is typical of his "spin." We may pass over the implication here that the only *real* Christians are those who seek to change America under Reed's and Robertson's direction and may simply observe that if these Christians have indeed changed the soul of American politics, they have done so by introducing into it not a long-needed spirit of Christian fellowship but unchristian rancor, disinformation, and scare tactics. They have done so on such an immense scale, moreover, that they have managed to make American politics even uglier than it was before. Indeed, though Reed makes conspicuous use of such words as *Christian* and *soul,* and though he strains to convince non–Religious Right readers that his movement's agenda derives from universal and enduring Christian values, *Active Faith* makes it clear that Reed has the soul of a consummate political strategist for whom Christian principle always takes a backseat to strategic considerations.

One slippery thing that Reed does is to shift continually between employing terms like *religious, Christian,* "people of faith," and "faith community" in their broadest sense—using *Christian,* that is, to describe members of all Christian groups, and using the other terms to describe people of all faiths—and employing these terms in the usual legalistic Christian way, to refer only to fundamentalists and conservative evangelical Christians. Reed moves back and forth between these two ways of speaking as it suits his purposes. When he wants to make a point about how devout Americans are, he says that the overwhelming majority are churchgoing Christians (in saying this, of course, he is including people whom most legalistic Protestants would not consider true Christians). Likewise, when he wants to show that "people of faith" have always played a role in American politics, he focuses on liberals like Rauschenbusch and Fosdick (and even FDR!), whose beliefs would most certainly not qualify them as Christians in the eyes of legalistic Protestants. In the same way, when Reed wishes to suggest that Religious Right members are more affluent and educated than some people think, he cites poll results craftily: "Surveys show that religious conservatives are not the boobs some think they are. The average committed Christian who attends church regularly is a forty-year-old woman who has attended college, is married with children, and whose household income of $40,000 is one-third above the national average." Of course Reed is here equating "committed Christian" with "religious conservative."

Reed lumps nonlegalistic Christians in with legalists, in short, when he wants to make the statistics on his constituency more impressive to a general readership. Yet when he wishes to validate his movement's political views, he uses *Christian* and other terms in a narrow sense, implying a connection between essential Christian belief and his movement's politics. For example, he speaks of "the Christian view of homosexual practices" as if all Christians held the same view about those "practices." Similarly, Reed writes that when he attended a 1988 Republican Party precinct caucus in Atlanta, "the party establishment had reacted to this influx of religious folk with all the horror of a country club invaded by yahoos." The implication here is that the country-club types were not "religious folk"; yet surely most members of the Republican Party establishment in Atlanta in 1988 were Christians of one kind or another.

The political writer Michael Lind has commented shrewdly on Reed's use of terms like "Christian conservatives," "pro-family voters," and "people of faith" as labels for his constituency. "The purpose of the term 'Christian conservative,'" notes Lind, "is to pass off the narrow, and often bizarre, political-moral agenda of the tiny minority of Americans who are far-right Protestant evangelicals as the agenda of the substantial number of Americans who are both Christian (in one or another tradition) and conservative (usually in a rather vague and moderate way)." Indeed, the groups whom Reed labels pro-family, people of faith, and Christian conservatives constitute a far smaller subset than all people who are pro-family (who, after all, is *against* the family?), all people who subscribe to some faith (does Reed's "faith community" include Hindus, whose religion Robertson considers satanic?), and all who identify themselves as both Christian and conservative.

According to Reed, the Christian Coalition accepts that one can be both Christian and liberal. Yet Reed also suggests that because they are liberal on certain issues, Jimmy Carter and Bill Clinton can't possibly be real Christians. Reed protects himself by making these charges indirectly; he cites a remark by Dinesh D'Souza to the effect that, by 1980, President Carter "was viewed as a dangerous apostate" and adds that "for some evangelicals and Roman Catholics, Bill Clinton is another Jimmy Carter, someone who accedes to a pro-abortion and liberal social agenda and promotes it beneath the veneer of Scripture." Reed's point is clear: If you're a liberal, your Christianity can't be real but is only a "veneer." Routinely, Reed uses views on abortion and homosexuality as a litmus test for true spirituality. Liberals, Reed maintains, "have learned to mask their retreat [from Christian morality] with the rhetoric of values and spirituality. While embracing the counterculture and the radicalism of feminists and gay rights activists, the Democrats maintain the facade of the traditional morality that was their hallmark from Jefferson to Bryan." This closing

flourish is absurd, for Thomas Jefferson—who was far less of a traditional moralist by the standards of his time than any prominent
Democrat is today by the standards of *our* time—would unquestionably have been appalled by Bryan's attempt at Dayton to squelch public education in the name of religion. In suggesting that both Carter
and Clinton are phonies—people who say they're Baptists but really
aren't—Reed is echoing a sentiment common in legalistic churches:
namely, that liberal Baptists aren't real Baptists, nontraditional
Catholics aren't real Catholics, and so on. Yet Reed perversely
attempts to take the sting off this charge by referring to Jimmy Carter
and John Anderson as "two of the most devout Christians in the history of recent politics."

Reed's rhetorical shell game with words like *Christian* is not an isolated tactic. For though the Christian Coalition presents itself as being
devoted to Christian values, it has engaged in some of the most sweep-
ingly dishonest political practices on display in America today. For
instance, the Christian Coalition gained much of its power through the
use of "stealth tactics": telling candidates for local elections not to
advertise their Christian Coalition connection. So strongly identified
are stealth tactics with the Christian Coalition that Reed spends an
entire chapter trying to deny (in the face of mountains of proof to the
contrary) that the organization has used such tactics. With equal bra-
zenness, he describes the Christian Coalition's notorious voter guides
as examples of "voter education literature" that are "studiously nonpartisan" in that they merely outline candidates' positions. Yet every
politician in the United States knows that those voter guides, which are
distributed in churches by the million on the Sunday before Election
Day, are designed to shift votes to the Christian Coalition's preferred
candidates, and that, to this end, they calculatedly omit some issues and
routinely misrepresent candidates' positions on others. (For instance, the
Christian Coalition asked many 1996 candidates for their views on
a ban on "semi-automatic firearms," but represented those views
on voter guides as positions on "firearms"—which can be understood,
of course, to mean hunting rifles.) In August 1996 the Federal Election Commission condemned these guides as political propaganda, not
educational tools, and declared that the Christian Coalition, by issuing
them, endangers its status as a tax-exempt nonpolitical organization.

Reed responded by repeating the outrageous claim that the guides are nonpartisan and objective.

꧁

Reed's basic thesis in *Active Faith* is simple. He claims that liberals object to Religious Right political activities on the grounds that religious Americans have no business working for laws that reflect their beliefs. Reed argues that religion does have a place in American politics and always has. The difference, he says, is that earlier American political movements by "people of faith" were liberal—he goes on at length about abolitionism and the Social Gospel—whereas the current influx of religion into politics is overwhelmingly a conservative phenomenon.

This thesis is disingenuous: Few people of any political stripe would dispute that religion has always motivated some people to be involved in politics, and few would deny such people's right to vote their convictions. The principal concern that many Americans have about people on the Religious Right is not that they are motivated by religion but that they seek, in the name of religion, to pass laws that restrict other people's civil rights and preserve social and economic injustice; by contrast, members of such religion-inspired political movements as abolitionism and the Social Gospel always strove to *secure* other people's civil rights and to improve their social or economic status.

In defending his argument that the Religious Right should be involved in politics, Reed quotes the abolitionist preacher Theodore Parker to the effect that "the curve of the moral universe is long, but it leads toward justice." It is astonishing for Reed to quote Parker, not only because Parker was a Unitarian (a fact that Reed calculatedly omits) but also because Parker's words reflect the widespread nineteenth-century American confidence in social and moral progress, which is utterly at odds with the dispensationalist belief that the world is in a steady moral decline toward the Great Tribulation. For Reed to quote from Parker, then, is both to risk angering his constituents and to make mainline Protestant readers think that those constituents are much closer to them theologically than is the case. Indeed, Reed's use of Parker to defend the Religious Right is a historical outrage—for today's Christian Coalition loyalists are as hostile to the struggles for social justice by Parker's spiritual heirs as their spiritual (and, in many cases, biological) ancestors were to Parker's own efforts in the same direction.

Reed even has the audacity to measure the Social Gospel against his own movement's notions of Christian orthodoxy. "The Social Gospel," he writes, "was a radical movement even as it retained many traditional Christian tenets, such as a belief in a sovereign, all-powerful God; the imminent millennial return of Christ; and the power of prayer." It is outrageous for Reed to oppose the Social Gospel's "radicalism" to "traditional Christian tenets": The Social Gospel was radical precisely *because* it flowed out of the Gospels. Reed is careful to distort Rauschenbusch's theology—to omit it, in effect—and he plainly does so because if he didn't, he would have to deal with the thorny question of whether Rauschenbusch's religion is a legitimate form of Christianity or not. Nonlegalistic Christians would say that it is; most legalistic Christians would say that it isn't. Reed also devotes several pages to an attempt to suggest that some continuity exists between his movement and Martin Luther King's. But it's ultimately clear that he regards King and others as strategic and tactical models, not as moral teachers, and that Reed himself is a purely political creature for whom morality is a concept to be manipulated to strategic ends.

"If America has a national political tradition," Reed insists, "it is that of religious activism firmly rooted in millennialism." He cites Rauschenbusch and King as examples. But they were postmillennialists, not premillennialists; in their view, the millennium would come about through growing Christian love and service. In any case, their focus was not on the millennium but on their calling to live out the gospel message. It should be remembered that while Rauschenbusch was working to help the poor, his premillennialist contemporaries were condemning people to hell in God's name. They showed little concern about the living conditions of the poor, and they enthusiastically envisioned the lake of fire into which God would cast those whose beliefs differed from their own. It was these premillennialists, not Rauschenbusch, who were the spiritual ancestors of today's Religious Right.

To be sure, Reed acknowledges that his "faith community" was "on the wrong side of the most central cause of social justice in this century"—that is, racism—and he claims to be grieved by this. "The white evangelical community," he writes, "allowed our black brothers and sisters to be held in bondage and treated as second-class citizens for four centuries, and we quoted scripture to justify it." Yet while admitting that "the sad record of religious conservatives on race gives liberals reason to hurl charges of bigotry and intolerance at us," he adds that "they are wrong in making those attacks today," because "the white evangelical . . . legacy of racism" is "now being wiped clean." Wiped clean? White legalistic Protestant churches are still segregated; white legalistic Protestant parents still send their children to private schools, or home-school them, so that they won't have to mix with black children. White legalistic Protestants applaud black Republican Alan Keyes because he says what they want to hear and because it makes them feel unprejudiced to cheer a black man; yet how many of them would welcome an African-American as their pastor or son-in-law? In 1996 a white legalistic church in Georgia voted to dig up the body of a dead girl from its graveyard because she was black. That remains the prevailing mentality of many such churches today.

The burning of several black southern churches in 1996 only raised the question, If racism is really a thing of the past in the American South, then why are there still such things as black churches and white churches? Reed complains that "commentators have by and large completely missed" the white evangelical community's efforts at "bridge-building" with blacks; yet how can anyone take such gestures seriously, given that community's ardor for Pat Buchanan? Reed, far from repudiating Buchanan, defends him. "I never attacked Pat Buchanan as some did," Reed brags. "When Buchanan was denounced by some as an 'extremist,' I rejected that label and called such charges the 'trappings of demagoguery.'" Yet Reed never answers the question, How can "love ye one another" be reconciled with Buchanan's combative slogan "lock and load"?

To Reed, of course, love is essentially a rhetorical device. "Among conservative evangelists," Reed insists, "love for the Jewish people and the state of Israel is a defining characteristic." In fact, legalistic Christians love Jews so much that they want them to become Christians. In the same way, they love gays so much that they want them to become straight. This is a very special kind of love, obviously. Apropos of gays, Reed uses the favorite legalistic Christian line about loving the sinner and hating the sin—which posits a judgmental dynamic in which it is always the *other* person who is the sinner, never oneself. In *Active Faith,* Reed lists sins that violate the Ten Commandments, and manages to slip into the list exactly one item not mentioned in the command-ments—homosexuality. But then the Christian Coalition has done an excellent job of making its constituents think that homosexuality *is* in the Ten Commandments. (In 1996, when the SBC voted to censure the Disney Company for providing health-insurance benefits to employees' same-sex partners, the *New York Times* quoted a thirty-five-year-old Southern Baptist mother who said she approved of the reso-lution because homosexuality "falls under the Ten Commandments as adultery.")

Reed contradicts himself in *Active Faith* on the question of whether the Christian Coalition wishes to change laws. On the one hand he seeks to squelch the image of the Religious Right as a group of extremists attempting to impose their worldview on American society; on the other hand, he argues for the importance of laws that do just that. "There are some in the evangelical community today," he writes, "who counsel retreat from constitutional or legal restrictions on abor-tion. 'We must first change hearts and minds,' they say. But [Frances] Willard [the first president of the Women's Christian Temperance Union] understood that politics is culture—that the law is a teacher, and that ballots can achieve much in shifting social attitudes." Thirty pages later, however, Reed says exactly the opposite: "We must seek to change hearts and save souls first, believing that the laws will change only as the culture does." He claims that "unlike fundamentalist polit-ical movements in the Middle East, religious conservatives in the United States are properly understood as an interest group within a democratic order. If they gained power, they would not repeal the Constitution or attempt to impose their religion on others through the state." Yet in its so-called Contract with the American Family, a set of ten proposals for legislative action issued on May 17, 1995, the Chris-tian Coalition called for "a constitutional amendment to protect the religious liberties of Americans in public places," the idea being to cir-cumvent Supreme Court directives safeguarding the separation of church and state. The Christian Coalition also placed immense (and ultimately successful) pressure on the Republican Party to secure sup-

port in its 1996 platform for several additional Constitutional amendments, one of which would indeed impose religion on others by permitting organized prayer in public schools. Reed also contradicts
himself—not only in his book, but in recent public statements—on the
question of which matters most to the Christian Coalition, the so-
called moral issues, such as abortion and gay rights, or economic issues;
these contradictions plainly emerge from his attempt both to please his
constituency and to calm the fears of mainstream readers.

"The proper perspective of faith in politics," writes Reed, is "a fiery
conviction of right and wrong tempered by a humility before God and
a respect for one's foes." If this is the test, the Christian Coalition fails
it. Reed lists "a decline in civility" as one of the organization's main
concerns. Yet the Coalition is composed overwhelmingly of white het-
erosexuals many of whom are anything but civil to blacks and gays,
and who at their 1996 convention displayed an astonishing incivility.
One elderly rank-and-file member was seen on TV ranting to a journalist about how she was "sick of" various things; her list consisted
mainly of categories of people different from herself. Reed himself
notes that at the 1992 Republican Convention, a CNN commentator
was "jostled" and his fiancée "heckled" by "some of the more unruly"
evangelicals. He says he regrets this. But why were these activists
unruly? When had delegates at national conventions ever behaved in
this way? That evening, Reed recalls, he was being interviewed on the
convention floor by Nina Totenberg of National Public Radio when
nearby delegates (who, he says, were not Christian Coalition members)
called her a whore and "other unprintable epithets." Reed wants mainstream America to think that he genuinely regrets this kind of hooli-
ganism; yet he refuses to acknowledge that such behavior is in fact
common among legalistic activists and that the Christian Coalition
encourages it.

Like fundamentalists early in the century, Reed and other Christian
Coalition leaders have made extensive use of military images. When
Pat Robertson opened the organization's annual convention in Sep-
tember 1994, he called the Christian Coalition "a mighty army"; in
Active Faith, Reed cites a conversation in which Robertson told him

how to "energize the troops." Elsewhere in the book, Reed betrays an
awareness of the strategic unwisdom of using such language: "Early in
the 1990s, I occasionally used military metaphors for effect. When they
were quoted out of context by the left, they sounded frightening and
were a liability. After the 1992 elections I realized that such language
had allowed the media and the organized left to caricature our movement as intolerant and uncaring. Moreover, I felt such rhetoric was
inappropriate for a Christian organization because it lacked the
redemptive grace that should always characterize our words and deeds.
I sent out a memorandum to our grassroots leaders urging them to
avoid military rhetoric and to use sports metaphors instead."

Here, without realizing it, Reed points up the problem at the heart
of his relationship with his constituency. As we have seen, the fundamentalist movement has always used military metaphors—violent,
angry ones—and it has done so because it viewed the struggle in
which it was engaged as a battle to the death in which God was on
its side and the Devil on the other. The movement did not and does
not believe in pluralism; it did not and does not believe that its "foe"
means well. It believes, on the contrary, that its opponents are the
instruments of Satan. If rhetoric to this effect frightens mainstream
Americans, it is with good reason, for the rhetoric fairly represents the
way these people think and suggests how far they would be willing to
go if they gained political power. For Reed to call off such rhetoric
is a purely strategic move designed to disguise his constituents' real
feelings. Reed's comment about the need for "redemptive grace" in
"our words and deeds" sounds exactly like something that Harry
Emerson Fosdick would have said—and that the fundamentalists who
opposed Fosdick would have rejected angrily. To such people, the idea
of addressing modernists with respect and charity—indeed, of treating
them as anything other than the tools of Satan—was and is anathema.
In any event, Reed forgets to follow his own directive: He writes that
during Colin Powell's book tour, the Christian Coalition "chose to
keep our powder dry," and speaks of the organization's members as an
"army." Along similar lines is a slip made by William Bennett in a September 1996 speech at the Christian Coalition convention: Intending
to refer to "the cross on Calvary," Bennett spoke instead of "the cross
on cavalry." A month later, in an address at the National Press Club,

Reed, meaning to say that Christian Coalition voter guides help people "to cast an intelligent ballot," instead said "intelligent battle." These slips betray a dangerous warrior mentality that should not be taken lightly.

What do the agenda and rhetoric of the Christian Coalition have to do with Christianity? Nothing. Reed admits as much when he states that "religious conservatives still lack a theology of direct political action" and "will need to develop one to achieve their full potential over time." Translation: There *is* no real connection between his constituents' professed Christianity and their politics. It is an extraordinary admission. Reed notes that in a 1993 survey, "we found that evangelical voters listed the economy and jobs as their top issue, followed by taxes and the deficit, crime, and education. Abortion was one of these voters' lowest priorities. This came as a startling revelation to those who assumed that evangelical voters were driven into politics exclusively by the cluster of social issues that included gay rights, abortion, and school prayer." Indeed, the Christian Coalition's "Contract with the American Family" was far less concerned with so-called moral issues than with traditionally conservative economic measures. Citing "welfare reform, tax relief, and a balanced budget amendment" as key concerns, Reed writes in *Active Faith* that "these are issues that resonate strongly with people of faith." This statement is nothing short of hilarious: To use the word *faith* in such a way is to drain it of all meaning.

These and other statements by Reed have made clear his desire to "mainstream" the Christian Coalition. So does the wide detour he makes in his book around Robertson's esoteric theology: Clearly, Reed recognizes that the more mainstream Americans know about what Robertson really believes, the more they will realize that his faith is anything but traditional or moderate. A recent manifestation of Reed's mainstreaming efforts is the Christian Coalition's "Samaritan Project," unveiled in early 1997. Touted as "a bold and compassionate plan to combat poverty and restore hope," the program in fact takes familiar right-wing proposals that are hostile to the interests of poor urban blacks and puts a kinder, gentler spin on them. "It is time," Reed said in announcing the plan, "for religious conservatives and their estranged liberal brethren to unite to strengthen the essential building blocks of the family and the church for urban—and American—renewal."

Though the proposals themselves were far from liberal, Reed's rhetoric about uniting with "estranged liberal brethren" may well prove too much for many legalistic Christians at the grassroots; indeed, it may well be that Reed's efforts in this direction had more than a little to do with his departure from the Christian Coalition's executive directorship.

11

"NO MORE GRAY"

To GET A look at the reality of the legalistic Christian grass-roots, one need only turn off any one of ten thousand roads around the United States. Set fifty or so yards back from one of those roads, a winding two-lane blacktop an hour northeast of Atlanta, is a plain, one-story brick structure that might easily be taken for a Rotary meeting hall or a local labor-union headquarters. Only the low roadside sign—which features the place's name, its slick modern logo (which might well be taken for a corporation's), and an invitation to "come in and meet our pastor"—identifies it as a house of worship.

On a mild Sunday morning in October, I park in the unpaved lot and enter the building. The auditorium is aus-tere, undecorated. About a hundred people—all of them white, most of them couples in their thirties and forties, some with children—sit in folding chairs facing a slightly raised stage. Most of the men are in casual shirts and jeans; the women are all in dresses or skirts and blouses. At stage right are three young male guitarists, three singers, a keyboardist, and an elderly woman with a tambourine; at stage left is a large projection screen; at center stage is a lectern and, a few feet behind it, a cross-shaped opening in the wall. Behind that opening stand a slim man of about sixty in a blue suit and tie, obviously the pastor, and a schoolgirl in white, whom he is holding by the shoulders and whose hands are clinging to his wrist. Suddenly and swiftly he lowers her backward out of sight; there is a sound of splashing, and he says, "I baptize you in the name of the Father, and the Son, and the Holy Spirit." When she rises again, the band strikes up a "praise song" (a musical genre with which most mainline Protestants are entirely unfamiliar). During the song, the pastor steps around the baptism tank and approaches the lectern.

"Baptism. It's important, isn't it?" he asks his congregation when the song is over. His voice is firm, loud, authoritative, with a mild regional twang. Around me, heads nod affirmatively. "And what's important," he adds, "is to have a *believer's* baptism. It's not enough to be baptized as an infant. You've got to be baptized as a believer. Right?"

"Amen!" the congregation replies in unison.

"And the preferred biblical method," he goes on, "is by full immersion. How many of you are glad to be Christians?" He spits out the question like a drill sergeant issuing an order; I'm the only one who doesn't raise a hand. (Yes, I'm glad to be a Christian, but I'm wary of this raise-your-hands business.) "How many of you are glad to be in the Lord's house?" Again, everyone but me shoots up a hand.

That settled, we move on to the announcements. The pastor tells us about this week's scheduled meetings. A man rises and reports on his efforts to win local prison inmates to Christ. Then the pastor plugs the forthcoming "men's meeting," which, he says, is "dedicated to the maturing of men in the service of Christ." He tells us that the meeting is scheduled for November 22, and then, just to make sure the congregation has gotten the information, he asks, "What day is it?" In one voice, the congregation shouts back, "November twenty-second!"

Five minutes into the service it's already clear that this man speaks to his congregation as if they're elementary-school children, and that they're happy to respond in kind.

Now, the pastor tells us, it's "worship time." All around me, the Bibles come out: In this church, the people bring their own, one per couple. I watch as, with an awkward reverence, they remove the books from bags and open them, as directed, to Psalm 145. I don't know whether the Bibles are all the same translation, but they certainly aren't all the same edition: They're different shapes and sizes, the bindings variously brown, black, green, maroon. All are larger, thicker, more expensive-looking than those usually found in the pews of mainline churches. Some come in custom-made cases, padded and zippered. The ones around me all look pristine, as if they're not actually read very much, though one man near me has plenty of very neat underlining in his. Together the congregation reads aloud from the psalm: "I will exalt thee, my God and King; I will bless Thy name for ever and ever. Every day will I bless Thee, and praise Thy name for ever and ever."

The psalm over, the Bibles are put away. A member of the congregation stands to announce that it's "Pastor Appreciation Time." A dozen people step up onstage and present the pastor with two gifts. He opens the first: It's a big picture of our first president, framed above a quotation from Washington that the pastor reads aloud: "It is the duty of the Nation to acknowledge the Providence of Almighty God." The congregation murmurs its approval. The pastor comments, "May we find *that* spirit in the White House today!" His flock replies, "Amen!" The other gift turns out to be a framed picture of Andrew Jackson, with a quotation from Old Hickory about the need to thank God for American freedom. "Did you know," the pastor says, "Andrew Jackson was a Sunday-school teacher? He'd arrange his schedule to come back from campaigning in the war to teach his classes." (In other words, he exterminated Indians on Saturday and taught the gospel on Sunday.) "Was he *your* Sunday-school teacher?" someone near the front asks. There is general laughter. The pastor responds with the obligatory smile.

After the presentation of the gifts, the pastor raises his hands and says loudly, "Praise God!" It is time to exchange the peace. Everybody rises; there are hugs all around. Several men clamber up onstage and stand in line to hug the pastor. That done, they return to their seats and the pastor resumes his lectern. "You know, church," he says, "if we don't operate on the dynamic of God's love for us and our love for each other, we cease to be a church." He thanks the people for their enthusiasm and explains that *enthusiasm* means "God in you." Then the musicians begin to play and the words of a praise song appear on the projection screen. The congregation sings:

> *Mighty is our God*
> *Mighty is our King*
> *Mighty is our Lord*
> *Ruler of everything*
>
> *Glory to our God*
> *Glory to our King*
> *Glory to our Lord*
> *Ruler of everything.*

The music, simple and banal, seesaws between the tonic and subdominant, sounding like a cross between a TV-commercial jingle, a tune from the *Barney* TV show, and supermarket Muzak. Yet the people sing it with, yes, at least a modicum of enthusiasm, waving their hands above them—in some cases one hand, in some cases both. This is charismatic worship, or a tepid and *pro forma* version thereof. When the song ends, the band and the congregation proceed straight into another one, and then another and another. Musically and lyrically, the songs are interchangeable; there is no variation whatsoever in theme or musical style. I am shocked when the band moves into a fifth song: How can the congregation bear it? But this is only the beginning. The song count continues to rise—ten songs, fifteen, twenty:

> *Lord I lift your name on high*
> *Lord I love to sing your praises*
> *I'm so glad you're in my life*
> *I'm so glad you came to save us*

The music continues for a full forty minutes. Plainly the point of this long stretch of music is to whip the people up into a frenzy and to drive home three basic themes: God's power, Christ's sacrifice, the Spirit's presence. And, of course, the obligation to praise. The emotional temperature in the room doesn't quite rise to the level of frenzy, but most of the people do seem to be getting into the intended spirit— or at least pretending to. When the music is finally over, the pastor says a prayer, which concludes, ". . . and God's people agreed when they said—"

The congregation yells back, "Amen!"

Time for the sermon. Again the people haul out their Bibles. The text is the epistle to Titus, whom Paul left in charge of the church in Crete. Though traditionally attributed to Paul, the letter is now thought by biblical scholars to have been written after Paul's time. Titus is one of the Bible's shortest books, only two or three pages long in most editions, but is frequently quoted in legalistic circles because it is jam-packed with strict directives on how to run a church. To be sure, Titus contains not only some of the more legalistic moments of the books attributed to Paul but also some of the more loving ones. The letter tells Titus, for example, to remind the Christians in Crete "to slander no one, to avoid quarrels, and always to show forbearance and a gentle disposition to all." On the other hand, it orders Titus to remind church members "to be submissive to the government and the authorities and to obey them" and enjoins him to "rebuke . . . sharply" those members who are "undisciplined"; it forbids him to appoint as an elder anyone whose children are not believers; and it slurs Cretans as "liars, vicious brutes, and lazy gluttons."

Nineteenth-century Southern Baptists found in Titus a scriptural warrant for their peculiar institution: "Slaves are to respect their masters' authority in everything and to give them satisfaction; they are not to answer back, nor to pilfer, but are to show themselves absolutely trustworthy. In all this they will add lustre to the doctrine of God our Saviour."

The epistle also sets forth a method by which members can be expelled from the church community. "If someone is contentious, he should be allowed a second warning; after that, have nothing more to do with him, recognizing that anyone like that has a distorted mind and stands self-condemned in his sin." This verse (Titus 3:10–11) is a favorite in legalistic churches today, in which it is often dragged out to justify expulsion—"disfellowship"—from congregations of people who have asked too many questions, violated sexual taboos, shown insufficient subservience, or professed the wrong doctrine. As it happens, this particular church in Georgia belongs to a chain of churches (it doesn't call itself a denomination) that is said to expel members who don't believe in the Rapture or who affirm the Calvinist doctrine of "once saved, always saved" rather than the Arminian view that one can fall from grace. (This chain of churches is, incidentally, one of the distinctive phenomena of today's legalistic Protestantism: The idea of a large church body in which power is centered, as in a privately held corporation, in a single entrepreneurial leader rather than in bishops or clergy or lay members seems characteristically American.)

Like the epistle to Titus, the pastor's sermon proves to be a mixture of Church of Love and Church of Law. He begins by mentioning the TV show *Rescue 911*. It's exciting, he says, to see real-life rescues. And sometimes it's especially exciting because people who are rescued can then rescue someone else. I'm a bit surprised at the obviousness of where he's going with this: Plainly this is the beginning of an evangelism sermon. Sure enough, he goes on to say that evangelism can be very much like *Rescue 911*. Some of us are rescued for Christ, and others aren't: "There's not an in-between place." But there *is* a category of the rescued who don't use their lives properly afterward to rescue others. "They are divisive, they are actually hinderers. . . . Some of them think that they are saved but in fact they are not." He says that the chief question facing Christians is, "How can God use me to contribute to the process of rescuing other people?" This is what it's all about: not *Rescue 911* but "Rescue one-on-one." God, the pastor tells us, "died in Christ for *you*. Put your name there. God died in Christ for *Nancy*." He points to a woman seated near the front. "He died in Christ for *Joe*." He points to a man a few seats away. The pastor continues to repeat the line over and over, each time inserting the name of a different member of the congregation whom he looks at and points to.

This grammar-school spelling-drill approach is anything but unique in the world of legalistic Protestantism. In a novel titled *Piercing the Darkness* by the popular fundamentalist writer Frank E. Peretti, a Christian woman named Bernice Krueger evangelizes a troubled atheist who identifies herself as Betty. First Bernice outlines the atonement:

"Jesus satisfied divine justice on that Cross. He bore the punishment in full, and God never had to bend the rules. That's why we call Jesus our Savior." Betty doesn't inquire into the logic of this divine transaction; she doesn't ask what would have been so awful about God bending the rules, or even what the rules were, exactly. What she does ask is, "Did . . . Did Jesus die for *me?*" Bernice replies: "Yes, He died for you." Betty presses her: "For me, for . . . For Betty Smith?" Bernice replies: "He died for Betty Smith just like he died for Bernice Krueger." Like the pastor in Georgia, Peretti is telling his readers: Jesus died for *you,* too. Getting that idea firmly fixed in people's heads and keeping it there is perhaps the most important part of a legalistic pastor's job.

After quoting the passage from Titus about submission to government, the pastor explains that this means "Christians are to be exemplary citizens." He provides some historical background: "Rome had gotten so pagan and so blinded by Satan" that its leaders couldn't see that the Christians were their best citizens. *Gotten* so pagan? He makes it sound as if the Romans had been something *other* than pagan. As for the part about Christians being exemplary citizens, the pastor has, I note, failed to tell the full story: Once the Christians took over the Roman Empire, they became extremely intolerant citizens, carrying out, as the theologian Hans Küng has described it, "a persecution of heretics unique in the history of religion." Does anyone in the congregation know this? Guess not.

"It's time," the pastor goes on to say, "for us to take another look at the way the church views the world around us. *The world,*" he states emphatically, "*needs your influence.*" His is the New Evangelical message of involvement in the world, not the strict fundamentalist principle of separation from it. "The world," the pastor declares, "can be very cruel in the way it treats Christians." But we mustn't, he insists, be cruel in return. Paraphrasing the letter to Titus, he tells his congregation, "Don't slander and hurl insults. Don't stir quarrels and conflicts. . . . Take a stand in a godly way, mature, faithful. Don't be offensive. . . . We've had enough offense on the part of Christians."

Am I imagining a slight restiveness around me at the sound of this Church of Love rhetoric? Are some members of the congregation actually resisting what their pastor is saying? But no matter: The

moment passes. The pastor stops lecturing about the need for inoffen-
siveness and returns to his emphasis on confronting the world. "Let's
take a stand against Satan!" he suggests. "There's a better country than
the one we're in and that's Heaven." The exact relationship of this last
comment to the preceding is unclear, but the congregation doesn't
seem to notice. "Amen!" they shout lustily, pleased to hear what is
plainly a familiar formula. (At the Christian Coalition convention in
Washington in September 1996, the Reverend Daniel de Leon proclaimed, "We are all aliens in this world." And William Bennett told
the audience, "Don't worry, this is not your city. Your city is the one
that lasts forever!")

The pastor then proceeds to leave the Church of Love talk in the
dust. In Paul's time, as in our own, he pronounces darkly, there have
been people who "followed false guides." These guides were awash in
"hedonism . . . malice . . . envy"; they were "foolish" and "disobedi-
ent"; they were, in short, "unsaved." He reads a few sentences from
Titus as the people follow along in their Bibles, many of them running their fingers along the page. "When we're dealing with the
unsaved," he tells them, we need to exhibit "patience, forbearance."
Saved and unsaved, saved and unsaved: The sermon has now come to
rest on this all-important black-and-white dichotomy. The alternation
is as simple and relentless as that between the tonic and subdominant
in the praise songs. Looking around, I feel that a calm has settled over
the church. This is the only message these people have come here for,
the only one they want to hear—that they are destined for heaven and
others are destined for hell.

Out of the blue, the pastor mentions Christ's atoning sacrifice, and
says, "It is what?"

The people shout back, "A gift!" Plainly this is a routine in which
they have been drilled.

When you accept Christ as your savior, the pastor proclaims, you
"kill the old thing and replace it with something new!"

The fortyish man behind me says softly, "Amen."

None of this, of course, has any particular relevance to the sermon
text; what the pastor is doing, I realize, is carrying out a weekly attempt
to keep the basic tenets of legalistic Christianity set firmly in these
people's minds. His method: sheer numbing repetition. I remember the

grammar-school teacher who made us write every new vocabulary word a hundred times. And the college German instructor who began every class by drawing on the blackboard the same chart showing the declension of the definite article. *Der, des, den, dem. Die, der, die, den.*

The drill continues. "When a person's been saved," the pastor says, "he is what?"

The people shout back, "A new creation!"

"If you're out of Christ," says the pastor, "you're condemned. If you're in Christ, you're justified. . . . Christ is the hope of eternal life." Pausing, he looks out over his flock. "What would you do," he asks the congregation, "if I walked up to you after the service and told you I'd been in touch with a lawyer, and this lawyer had told me that you have an elderly relative that you've never heard of who lives in a faraway place, and that that relative is a millionaire, and that as soon as that relative died, you'd get it all? Would you be interested in the state of health of that relative?"

There is scattered laughter.

"Sure you would! Well, I'm here to tell you that we already have that relative and he's already died for you and left you a treasure that's much, much greater than millions of dollars—and do you know who that relative is?"

"Jesus," murmurs the man behind me.

"Jesus!" other people shout.

"That's right," the pastor proclaims. "That relative is Jesus Christ!"

"Amen!"

The theology is chilling. As if the idea of substitutionary atonement weren't brutal enough, the pastor has managed to make the whole business even more monstrous by comparing Jesus to a rich stranger whose death we look forward to with glee because he has left us money. It is a conception of Jesus from which love has been entirely excluded and in which naked self-interest is everything. I look around for any indication that someone is disturbed or offended by the pastor's analogy. Nope.

The pastor closes his sermon by asking his flock if they are "among those who have already been rescued" by Christ. "If so," he says, "you have every reason to be filled with zeal" to rescue others. If not, "I don't care how comfortable you are. . . . If you are not inside Jesus

Christ, you are outside Jesus Christ. . . . You need to be rescued, because you are standing on the precipice of an eternal hell" when instead "you could be standing as an inheritor of glory."

So ends the sermon. The lights go down. The people take Communion. There is another bad song. The pastor ends the service by saying, "May the love of Christ fill you through this week. That's provided we have a week! He may be back before we get to the parking lot. I wouldn't be sorry, would you?"

"No!" the people shout back.

After the service, a stout fiftyish man walks up to me in the aisle, shakes my hand firmly, and barks out his name. I identify myself, and he suddenly drops what, by all indications, was going to be an effort at proselytizing. What was it that changed his mind? My non-southern accent? A certain resistance that he read in my voice? Or was one spoken word enough for him to tell that I'm gay?

Outside the air is a bit nippy, but the sun warms my face. Walking to my car, I reflect on the service. Though the pastor connected Christianity and love more than once, his emphasis in addressing his congregation was on the fact that God loves *them* and on their need to love one another; absent from his remarks was the idea that they should love people outside the congregation too. One rescues others for Jesus not out of love for them but in order to confirm one's own salvation.

On the surface, I muse, the church service I've just witnessed might seem pretty harmless, especially to someone unaccustomed to any other form of worship. But the whole tone of the proceedings was so strikingly different from what Christian worship can and should be. A successful church service—which may range from the austere to the magisterial—gives worshippers the feeling of having come closer to God, to one another, and to all creation; of having shed at least some degree of self-concern and anxiety about death; and of having been filled, at least to some extent, with gratitude, love for all humankind, and a desire to serve. This service I've just attended has done almost exactly the opposite: It's sought to appeal to the congregation's most selfish instincts, likening heaven to a killing in the lottery.

To say this is not to criticize the people in the congregation. These are people brought up on TV and country music, not on books and complex ideas. The descendants of no-nonsense pioneers, they were not raised with a vocabulary for the spiritual or a habit of reflecting on ultimate meanings. That they attend a church like this is an indictment less of them than of the culture in which they have spent their lives—one in which it is possible to be rich in material goods but to starve culturally, intellectually, and spiritually without even realizing it. Many of them have doubtless been driven here by difficult circumstances, by empty lives that they need to believe have value and meaning. The theology of resentment works on them as effectively as does the politics of resentment. Certainly none of them are sufficiently well educated to recognize how *un*-traditional their "traditional Christianity" is, or to know how much their pastor and their favorite televangelists distort everything from biblical scholarship to the views of the founding fathers. These are, in short, people who have been hurt; the problem is that churches like this one make it their business not to heal their pain but to exploit it, to turn it into a potentially lethal weapon against others, outsiders, the "unsaved."

By the time I get to my car, members of the congregation are already starting their engines around me, pulling out of the lot, turning toward home. It's an ordinary Sunday in Georgia; no Rapture this morning.

"The God that holds you over a pit of hell, much as one holds a spider or some loathsome insect over the fire, abhors you, and is dreadfully provoked: His wrath toward you burns like fire; He looks upon you as worthy of nothing else but to be cast into the fire; He is of purer eyes than to bear to have you in His sight; you are ten thousand times more abominable in His eyes than the most hateful venomous serpent is in ours. You have offended Him infinitely more than ever a stubborn rebel did his prince; and yet it is nothing but His hand that holds you from falling into the fire every moment. . . . O sinner! Consider the fearful danger you are in."

On July 8, 1741, Jonathan Edwards spoke these words from a pulpit in Enfield, Connecticut. Many years ago, when I first read "Sinners in the Hands of an Angry God" in a school textbook, I was glad that I lived in late-twentieth-century America, when such beliefs and preaching were a thing of the past. What I didn't realize was that many ministers in my own time, while less gifted than Edwards at conjuring up vivid images of eternal punishment, subscribed to a very similar theology. "Those of you who are hung up on love stories," the Pentecostal evangelist Stephen Hill roared in a 1997 sermon at his Pensacola megachurch, sounding very much like a latter-day Edwards, "need to hear the wrath of God! Don't live on Twinkies."

Few legalistic pastors today, however, specialize in this kind of sermon, notwithstanding the occasional one-line reminder of the sort offered up by the pastor in Georgia ("You need to be rescued, because you are standing on the precipice of an eternal hell"). Edwards preached hellfire because his congregation contained people who had not declared themselves saved by Jesus and who, he believed, needed to be urged to "fly from the wrath to come" and sin no more. Edwards believed this so passionately, in fact, that he went too far for most of his flock: When, in a 1750 sermon, he named as "backsliders" the close relatives of some of his more powerful Northampton parishioners, he was voted out of his pulpit by a 10–1 majority.

The situation in today's legalistic churches is very different. Most legalistic Protestants consider themselves saved. If an Edwards showed up and preached a sermon like "Sinners in the Hands of an Angry God," they would be baffled. "But we don't need to hear this," they would say. "Our salvation is assured. It's those *others* who are going to hell." Yes, legalistic pastors do preach on sin. But when they do, they almost invariably focus on sexual acts, especially those committed by *other* people, such as homosexuals. "Hell is other people," wrote Sartre; one might observe that in the view of legalistic Protestants today, hell is *for* other people.

There is plenty of talk in many legalistic churches about God's love, but it is a love that is not often truly experienced as love. The Georgia pastor's comparison of Jesus to a millionaire whose death one eagerly awaits is typical of the way in which many legalists think about the God whom they claim to love and whom they describe as loving them. In a two-page "Statement of Faith" issued by First Baptist Church of Atlanta—which is one of the nation's most important legalistic churches and whose pastor, Charles Stanley, is a leading Southern Baptist—several doctrines are cataloged, including "Atonement for Sin," "Salvation," and "The Great Commission." There is no mention of the Great Commandment; nor does the word *love* appear anywhere in the document. The word *lust* does make an appearance, though, under the heading of "The Christian Walk": "We are called with a holy calling, to walk not after the flesh, but after the Spirit, and so to live in the power of the indwelling Spirit that we will not fulfill the lust of the flesh." Though Jesus excoriated wealth, violence, and inhumanity while going out of his way to affirm his fellowship with prostitutes and adulterers, "the lust of the flesh" is the only sin cited by name in First Baptist's "Statement of Faith." Churches like First Baptist would do well to heed the words of the distinguished theologian E. P. Sanders: "Jesus was not given to censure but to encouragement; he was not judgemental but compassionate and lenient; he was not puritanical but joyous and celebratory."

"How these Christians love one another!" exclaimed observers of the early followers of Jesus. Nowadays many self-styled Christians are more notable for whom they hate. For many, the doctrine of eternal punishment for unbelievers is not a stumbling block to faith but one of its attractions. What, after all, is the good of being saved unless others are damned? Why go to church and put money in the plate unless you're guaranteed a payoff that others are denied? A line from the second letter to the Corinthians—"Be ye not unequally yoked together with unbelievers: for what fellowship hath righteousness with unrighteousness? and what communion hath light with darkness?"—represents one of Saint Paul's uglier moments, and is a favorite of legalistic Protestants, quoted frequently in both churches and homes. Legalists are taught to view strangers not as fellow children of God but as possible agents of Satan. As an ex-fundamentalist told the writer Stefan Ulstein in an interview for his book *Growing Up Fundamentalist,* "When you go to school you're 'behind enemy lines.' Your teachers, your classmates, are all potential enemies, and you have to be on guard all the time."

Indeed, to be a committed legalistic Protestant is to have a powerful, black-and-white sense of the conflict of good and evil. A former fundamentalist described the mind-set to me as follows: "There's *no more gray.* You're separated from this world and at the same time inhabiting an unseen world, in which you're fighting an unseen battle against the unseen Enemy. That's what fundamentalism is about: the Enemy."

For legalistic Protestants, Satan is a constant, overwhelming presence, the same yesterday, today, and forever. "It's a whole different mentality," the ex-fundamentalist explained. "You not only think about God all the time, you think about the Devil all the time. Everywhere you go, in every encounter with other people, you ask yourself whether this is of the Devil. He's under every bush." One thing the charismatic revival brought to fundamentalists and evangelicals, she added, was a heightened sense that they were able to detect such demonic activity. "We believed we had entered into this spiritual realm that other people just aren't tuned in to."

This aspect of the legalistic sensibility is vividly illuminated by two novels entitled *This Present Darkness* (1986) and *Piercing the Darkness* (1989). Written by Frank E. Peretti, these books, as the theologian Mark A. Noll has written, "set the tone for evangelical assessment of cause-and-effect connection in the world." In addition to enjoying a huge readership among legalistic Christians—the cover of the paperback edition of *This Present Darkness* boasts that over two million copies of it are currently in print—they have served as the models for a whole genre of legalistic fiction.

As both novels are extremely similar in story and theme, I will focus here only on the earlier novel, *This Present Darkness*. It is set in Ashton, a small town that "for generations . . . had taken pride in its grassroots warmth and dignity and had striven to be a good place for its children to grow up." But things have changed. Now Ashton is beset by "inner turmoils, anxieties, fears, as if some kind of cancer was eating away at the town and invisibly destroying it." What with crime and a loss of neighborliness, "life here was gradually losing its joy and simplicity, and no one seemed to know why or how." Summed up neatly here is the way legalistic Christians of every generation feel about the changes they're living through. Their modest knowledge of history enables them to believe that the past was simple, virtuous, and changeless; their undereducation makes it easy for them to be confused and daunted by what they see happening around them.

Peretti's story centers on a David-and-Goliath face-off between good and evil. The story's David is a slight young man named Hank

Busche, the newly hired fundamentalist pastor of the town's "little dinky" house of worship, Ashton Community Church. As the story begins, Hank has just disfellowshipped a member, Lou, for committing adultery. As he tells his wife, Mary, "We did just what the Bible says: I went to Lou, then John and I went to Lou, and then we brought it before the rest of the church, and then we, well, we removed him from fellowship." Yet some members of the church, led by police chief Alf Brummel, are angry: "They started giving me all this stuff about judging not lest I be judged." Replies Mary (who, in good legalistic fashion, is consistently meek and supportive of her husband): "Well, what on earth is wrong with Alf Brummel? Has he got something against the Bible or the truth or what?" Thus does Peretti make it clear at the outset that, from a legalistic point of view, Hank and Mary are the good guys, obeying Saint Paul's strict, legalistic guidelines for church leadership and dismissing out of hand Jesus' injunction to "judge not, lest ye be judged."

Hank and Mary face formidable odds. First there's the local college, which Peretti depicts as a hotbed of pretentious elitism and dangerous anti-Christian ideas. Early in the novel, Marshall Hogan, the editor of Ashton's newspaper, drops by the campus and hears part of a lecture as he passes a classroom. "Yeah," he reflects, "here was more of that college stuff, that funny conglomeration of sixty-four-dollar words which impress people with your academic prowess but can't get you a paying job." When he enters his daughter Sandy's class and sees her professor, a woman named Juleen Langstrat, Marshall senses something powerful and negative in the air; he later learns that Langstrat has all kinds of ideas about "the Source, the Universal Mind," that she has derived "from the Eastern religions, the old mystic cults and writings." All these terms are designed to set off legalistic Christians' alarm bells: paganism!

Another danger zone is the town's major house of worship, Ashton United Christian Church, which is directly across the street from Hank's little church. Peretti describes it at some length: "one of the large, stately-looking edifices around town, constructed in the traditional style with heavy stone, stained glass, towering lines, majestic steeple. . . . It was a respected establishment, Young was a respected minister, the people who attended the church were respected members of the community." The average legalistic Protestant reader will immediately get the point: Peretti is depicting the typical mainline church, the kind that such readers regard as apostate. Legalistic Protestant readers will also know what to think of Pastor Young. When Marshall, a member of his parish, comes to discuss Sandy, who has left home and hasn't called, Young replies as follows:

> *Marshall, it sounds like she's just exploring, just trying to find out about the world, about the universe she lives in. . . . I'm sure she would feel much more free to call if she could find understanding hearts at home. It's not for us to determine what another person must do with himself, or think about his place in the cosmos. Each person must find his own way, his own truth. If we're ever going to get along like any kind of civilized family on this earth, we're going to have to learn to respect the other man's right to have his own views. . . . All the questions you're struggling with, the matters of right and wrong, or what truth is, or our different views of these issues . . . so many of these things are unknowable, save in the heart. We all feel the truth, like a common heartbeat in each of us. Every human has the natural capacity for good, for love, for expecting and striving for the best interests of himself and his neighbor. . . . Your God is where you find Him, and to find Him, we need only to open our eyes and realize that He is truly within all of us. We've never been without Him at all, Marshall; it's just that we've been blinded by our ignorance, and that has kept us from the love, security, and meaning that we all desire.*

People like Peretti have taught legalistic Protestants how to react when they hear speeches of this sort from people claiming to speak for God—they should pull back reflexively, for such pap is the work of Satan, who is trying to sucker them in. In the real world, of course, many nonlegalistic Christians do speak in such terms to legalists (even Ralph Reed talks like this when he's trying to make his movement seem mainstream) and don't realize that their words are falling on deaf ears because these people have been trained how to process them. Indeed, the scene between Young and Marshall is very effectively designed to reflect legalistic notions of family and church relationships out of control. In the legalistic view, the husband should be the unquestioned leader of his home, and the pastor the unquestioned leader of his flock. From a legalistic perspective, the truth of Sandy's situation is clear-cut: She is a rebellious daughter whom Marshall should have been more careful to protect from her professors' anti-Christian lies and to whom he should now lay down the law in no uncertain terms; Young, as his pastor, should be commanding him to do so. Instead Young serves up rhetoric about the need to tolerate and understand, to find one's "own way" and "own truth," and to view other people as family—all of which is precisely the sort of stuff that legalists have been taught to dismiss as modernist claptrap. Even Marshall is coming to feel this way. "Kate," he asks his wife, "don't you ever get the feeling that God's got to be, you know, a little . . . bigger? Tougher? The God we get at that church, I feel like He isn't even a real person, and if He is, He's dumber than we are."

Peretti's God turns out to be tough indeed—but then so does his Devil. In this novel angels and demons are ever-present, often in great numbers, but usually invisible. The angels travel with Hank, Mary, and other good people, watching over them protectively, while the demons hover around the bad people and seek out occasions to turn the good people toward sin. As far as one can tell, all the humans in this book are white, as is the most prominent angel, who is tall, blond, Nordic, and handsome; the demons, however, are invariably described as black and hideously ugly. (Peretti mentions their blackness repeatedly.) They have names like Complacency and Deception, the latter of whom brags to a fellow demon that "his weapon . . . was always a compelling, persuasive argument with lies ever so subtly woven in." There is, Peretti makes clear, one guaranteed way for a human to overcome a demon's attempt to influence his thoughts: to say (as Hank and Mary do at various points), "I rebuke you in Jesus' name!" This makes the demons scatter. Jesus' name, then, serves as a magic word, an abracadabra; in *This Present Darkness,* it is repeated in this manner so often that, like a mantra, it is eventually robbed of all meaning.

The plot of *This Present Darkness* is the stuff of paranoiac fantasy. After picking up various hints and following up a few leads, Marshall establishes that Brummel, Langstrat, and Young, along with several people who have lately moved to Ashton from other places, are part of an evil conspiracy involving a satanic entity called the Universal Consciousness Society; this organization (which seeks to take over not only the souls of Ashton's townsfolk but also their real estate) later holds a dinner in New York "for its many cohorts and members in the United Nations." This cluster of details is designed to push several buttons at once: For legalistic Protestants, New York is (to quote one of Peretti's demons) "Babylon the Great," "The Great Harlot"; the United Nations is a tool designed to subordinate God's Country to the power of non-Christian foreign countries; and terms like "Universal Consciousness" suggest pagan forms of spirituality that, again, are of the Devil. As one of Peretti's demons puts it, "Universal Consciousness" is "the world religion, the doctrine of demons spreading among all the nations. Babylon revived right before the end of the age."

Tensions mount in Ashton, and soon Hank, his saints, and God's angels are hard at work combating the evil conspirators and demons. Figuring in this struggle is Sandy's college friend Shawn, who sounds like Pastor Young when he tells her that "God is big enough for everybody and *in* everybody. Nobody can put Him in a jar and keep Him all to themselves, according to their own whims and ideas." This is also, of course, satanic thinking. Telling the story of the blind men who touch different parts of an elephant and thus come away with different images of what an elephant is, Shawn uses it to explain how different religions, which offer different understandings of the same God, can all be true at once. Shooting down this analogy is so routine among legalistic Christians that Peretti doesn't even bother to have anyone in the novel counter it: He knows that his legalistic readers have been taught to recognize the analogy on sight as a satanic lie. (The legalistic answer, by the way, is that all religions *aren't* different parts of one animal; since their truth claims, if understood in an absolute, literal sense, contradict one another, one has to be true and the others false.) Yet Sandy hasn't been taught how to respond to this analogy; little does she know that while Shawn is speaking to her about how "everything is fitted together, interwoven, interlocked," the demon Deception is standing behind her, "stroking her red hair and speaking sweet words of comfort to her mind."

Such is the real world as seen through many legalistic Protestants' eyes. It cannot be stressed too strongly, indeed, that a book like *This Present Darkness* is intended not as a fantasy but as a picture of the way the world actually is. It's a world in which the immensely human Jesus who preached and lived a gospel of love is replaced entirely by a fantasy Jesus who stands at the head of an army of beings with names like Triskal and Krioni who seem to have dropped in from some Norse myth. And it's a world in which everything and everyone divides up neatly into two categories—black and white, satanic and godly. As Noll observes, it depicts a world "where the line between good and evil runs not, as Solzhenitsyn once wrote, through the heart of every individual, but between the secular forces of darkness on one side and the sanctified forces of light on the other."

One function of books like *This Present Darkness* is to establish and reinforce for legalistic Christian readers how those two categories divide up—to teach some and to remind others, that is, which kinds of thoughts and feelings and behaviors are of God, and which are of the Devil. Peretti makes it clear throughout who the enemies are—among them, churches that preach the oneness of humanity and universities that fill your children's heads with ideas that challenge the things you've taught them. Indeed, Peretti does a very fine job of exploiting his audience's resentments, fears, and prejudices—their sense of intimidation by higher education, their desire for a "tougher" God with black-and-white answers, and their wish to believe that evil is *out there* and that they are the saints of God. "To the extent that Peretti's book reflects evangelical perceptions more generally," writes Noll, "it shows an evangelical community unwilling to sift the wheat from the chaff in the wisdom of the world, unprepared to countenance the complexity of mixed motives in human action, and uninterested in focusing seriously on the natural forces that influence human behavior."

Peretti shares legalistic Protestants' notions about what churches are for—and the answer is decidedly *not* loving thy neighbor. More than once in this novel we are told that Hank, unlike other pastors in Ashton, "preaches the gospel"; this, in the novel's view, is plainly his primary role. Yet the one time we see him at the pulpit, he is preaching not on a Gospel lesson but on a passage from the fourth chapter of 2 Timothy that is a favorite of legalistic Protestants: "Reprove, rebuke, exhort, with great patience and instruction," Timothy is told. "For the time will come when they [the Christians in Timothy's care] will not endure sound doctrine, but wanting to have their ears tickled, they will accumulate for themselves teachers in accordance to their own desires; and will turn away their ears from the truth, and will turn aside to myths." After preaching on this passage, Hank mentions his absorption in "the gospel," as if 2 Timothy were a Gospel. This detail is in fact realistic—for legalistic Christians sometimes do act as if "the gospel" consisted of every part of the New Testament *but* the Gospels.

12

"A LIE STRAIGHT
FROM THE DEVIL"

In fundamentalism, notes Charles Strozier, "nonbelievers are rejected by God and thus in some inexplicable way are only tentatively human. As such, nonbelievers are dispensable. If they intrude in the believers' world, the psychological conditions exist to make it possible for believers to accommodate violence toward nonbelievers."

This is true not just of fundamentalism but of legalistic Protestantism generally. And the failure to focus on the Gospels that enables legalists to view other people as only "tentatively human" also makes it possible for them to hold chilling attitudes toward biblical morality. The Bible contains more than a few passages that pose grave ethical questions to anyone who reads it literally. For instance, the Book of Joshua records in horrific, repetitive detail how God "delivered" thirty-one Canaanite cities, one after the other, "into the hands of the Israelites," and how, at his direction, they "put every living thing" in these cities to the sword "and left no survivor there." "It was the Lord's purpose," we are told, that the Canaanite cities "should offer stubborn resistance to the Israelites, and thus be annihilated and utterly destroyed without mercy" (Jos. 8–11). In *God: A Biography,* Jack Miles quite properly describes this campaign as "genocidal slaughter." In a similar vein, the second book of Kings records an occasion when "some small boys" jeered at the prophet Elisha, saying to him, "Get along with you, bald head, get along." In a response that is clearly meant to be seen as admirable, Elisha "cursed them in the name of the Lord; and two she-bears came out of a wood and mauled forty-two of them" (2 Kings 2:23–24).

What to make of such passages? Nonlegalistic Christian readers, recognizing them as the artifacts of a culture with an understanding of God and morality that differs dramatically from our own, dismiss the idea that the God they worship could sanction the slaughter of children or the mauling of little boys by she-bears. Biblical inerrantists, however, put themselves in the position of having to defend such actions as the perfectly moral acts of a loving deity. To this end, Harold Lindsell, a former president of Fuller Theological Seminary, editor of *Christianity Today,* and author of *Battle for the Bible,* has made the scripturally unwarranted suggestion that the Canaanite children must all have been so evil that they deserved to die; as for Elisha's taunters, some inerrantists have contended (without, again, any scriptural justification) that the word used to describe them should be understood to mean not children but "teenage punks" (as if this made their slaughter so much less horrible).

In their desperation to maintain the doctrine of inerrancy, then, legalistic Christians compel themselves to be dishonest about the very words that are on the page before them and to defend the morality of patently horrible acts. The Southern Baptist writer and former seminarian Joe E. Barnhardt has not pulled any punches in writing about this. Pointing out bluntly that the picture of God presented in Joshua "is that of a marauding sociopathic killer," Barnhardt writes that "many of the same fundamentalists who take seriously the golden rule and practice deeply moving acts of kindness toward their own children and their neighbor's can at the same time weave intricate webs of nightmarish rationalizations to justify Joshua's atrocities." Inerrantists maintain that while an individual's reason and conscience are suspect, the Bible can always be relied on as a firm source of knowledge about the nature of virtue; they believe, as Barnhardt puts it, "that individuals cannot know what goodness is unless they go to the Bible to learn it." Yet any Christian who seriously turns to the above-cited passages about Joshua and Elisha to learn about the nature of goodness is a potential danger to civil society.

Of course, the willingness of legalistic Protestants to believe that a loving God would support genocide is of a piece with their violent, bloodthirsty End Times theology. After all, if they gladly worship a God who plans to subject most human beings to eternal torment, why not a God who would engineer the mass slaughter of children? Many legalistic Christians have claimed that the atrocities of the twentieth century teach us that we need to retreat from the secularism that is supposedly responsible for these happenings and return to religion—by which they mean, needless to say, their own brand of Christianity. Yet their religion is altogether too close for comfort to modern totalitarianism. The evils of two world wars, of the Stalinist gulags and Mao's Cultural Revolution, and of genocide in Nazi Europe, Armenia, Cambodia, and Rwanda—none of these is any more horrible than legalistic Protestantism's vision of the fate of nonbelievers. As James Sibley, head of the Southern Baptist Convention's mission to the Jews, said in a 1997 interview, "As terrible as the Holocaust was, it will fade into insignificance in comparison to God's future judgment. There will be the Holocaust of all people who don't accept Jesus."

Many people, including those without any religion whatsoever, insist that this is how all religion works: You believe you've got it right and are saved, and that other people have got it wrong and are damned. But this is *not* how all religion works. No faith that can equate love with genocide can be ethically defended. And no society that observes such moral depravity in millions of its members and pretends to see it as moral virtue because it calls itself by the name of religion can itself be regarded as moral—or honest.

✣

The Georgia congregation's presentation to their pastor of framed Washington and Jackson pictures was hardly surprising. Legalistic

Protestants in the United States tend to draw a strong connection between their identity as Americans and as Christians; like their Puritan forebears, and in violation of Jesus' preaching against national and tribal self-regard, they view America as the New Israel, God's Country. The phrase *New World Order* fills many legalists with dread not because it offends some carefully reasoned position on international relations but simply because they resist recognizing the United States as part of a large, diverse planet. Theoretically, legalists understand that some foreigners are Christians—and that a few of them even count as "true Christians" by legalistic standards—but for many legalists, those people's foreignness makes them very much the Other.

The Other. For many legalistic Protestants, Christianity is almost synonymous with "family values," which, to most of them, means caring for one's own family unit (and, by extension, one's own church family) and taking an indifferent or even adversarial posture toward outsiders, especially those who look different or live differently. "It always seemed to me," a former fundamentalist says in *Growing Up Fundamentalist,* "that 'family values' was code for looking out for ourselves in this ugly, scary world." In a similar spirit, a conservative Episcopalian once said to me, in all seriousness, "After all, Christianity is about looking out for one's own, isn't it?" When I explained to her that Christianity, in my view, was about exactly the opposite, she was genuinely incredulous.

Jimmy Allen, a former president of the Southern Baptist Convention, notes that many Baptist churches "don't minister to those in need because we cannot afford to offend and lose paying members or prospects for membership. . . . We have gotten caught up in a church growth movement that reflects what people are looking for—homogeneous, comfortable, and secure surroundings in which emotional needs and family needs are met." Allen records that "a pastor of one of the largest evangelical churches in the nation" told him that the members of his congregation "don't like wheelchairs in the sanctuary. It just makes them feel uncomfortable." So people in wheelchairs are excluded from services. A church that takes such a position simply doesn't understand what it means to be a church.

Such an emphasis on giving the people what they want—however much it violates the spirit of Christianity—has been increasingly apparent in legalistic Protestant churches. It is a standard complaint of legalistic Christians that mainline churches compromise too much with the world; yet in fact mainline churches, while attempting to adjust their doctrines to modern learning, have also sought to retain the essence of Jesus and to convey it poetically through liturgical forms that help people transcend their horizontal concerns and experience the vertical. Legalistic churches have, on a huge scale, done precisely the opposite: While retaining old doctrines that cannot be harmonized with contemporary scientific understanding of the universe, they junk traditional forms of worship and model their services on TV talk shows, rock or country-music concerts, and other horizontal entertainments. The pastors at such churches often say that they seek to eliminate traditional elements of worship—such as crosses, pews, and hymns—that make people "uncomfortable"; but the discomfort that people feel when encountering such elements is, in reality, a discomfort over encountering the vertical dimension. Not to experience that discomfort is to domesticate religion—to turn it into something that isn't really spiritual at all. It is to turn it into that ultimate American desideratum—a successful business.

Indeed, the idea of church as business has never been more prevalent than it is now among America's legalistic churches. "In many churches," complains Jimmy Allen, "the strategy of gathering new members has become a science. We have learned well the techniques of church growth. To thrive in the user-friendly, what's-good-for-me era of modern Christianity, churches are supposed to be homogeneous, well-cared-for, comfortable, and entertaining." Like the authors of *The Churching of America,* pastors around the country have learned to think of church as a commodity to be tailored to the marketplace. Believing that the bigger a church gets, the better, they have learned to admire and mimic uncritically the methods employed by their most successful colleagues. Citing statistics on the sizes of church congregations around the country, Pat Robertson has written that "Atlanta, Los Angeles, Houston, and Dallas/Fort Worth topped the list of most spiritually dynamic cities." One should expect, I suppose, that Robertson would consider spiritual dynamism to be so easily quantified a commodity. What is alarming is that tens of thousands of ministers think the same way.

For such ministers, the nation's premier ecclesiastical success story is that of Willow Creek Community Church in South Barrington, Illinois, forty miles northwest of Chicago. Founded in 1975 in a small rented theater, Willow Creek is the most famous of the new wave of monster churches in America that are known as megachurches and that serve as models for legalistic churches around the country. The key to Willow Creek's success is that its founder, Bill Hybels, did extensive research to find out what Chicago suburbanites wanted and didn't want in a church and, like any enterprising small businessman designing a product to fill a market niche, carefully tailored his church to those desires. What he ended up with was a church that was, as he put it, "culturally relevant" but "doctrinally pure." On the one hand, it cleaved to standard legalistic dogma ("we embrace historic Christian teaching on all doctrines, emphasizing Jesus Christ's atoning death; salvation through repentance and faith as a work of divine grace; and the authority of the unique, God-inspired Bible"); on the other hand, it threw out virtually every element of traditional liturgy. At Willow Creek there are no crosses, pews, processions; the church staff is called its management team and the whole church experience is called the product. Willow Creek's promotional materials note that the Wednesday- and Thursday-evening services for "believers," as well as the Saturday-evening and Sunday-morning services for "seekers," use "up-to-date language, music and drama to communicate God's Word for today's culture." An article in *USA Weekend* describes the church's "slick, show-biz service where drama and soft rock are served up on a stage washed in pink and blue spotlights." What people at such megachurches tend to get, then, is an atmosphere from which all those elements are eliminated that, in traditional churches, spell *difference,* removing the worshipper from ordinary space and time and creating holy space and time. A religious service at such a church seeks not to be a communal activity but a show with a passive audience—more of an entertainment than a spiritual excursion.

One legalistic church in Ohio that seeks to be "culturally relevant" complains on its Web site that "in the liberal church, even the doctrines of the Bible are allowed to change. But even then, they often continue to refuse change in structural and cultural areas. This is the worst-case scenario—changing the things we should never change, but holding fast to the things we should be willing to change." This is the cry of many a legalistic pastor, and it is 180 degrees off on both counts. Legalistic churches by definition cleave to doctrines that can't hold up, while discarding liturgies designed to create holy space and time. Hans Küng, in his 1996 book *Christianity: Essence, History, and Future,* traces how "the abiding substance of the faith"—the person of Jesus—has endured through the centuries despite radical changes in the doctrines, values, and laws that make up its context or "paradigm." What legalistic churches do routinely is confuse the form with the essence—which is understandable, because doctrines *look* like essence, while liturgies look like form. But Christianity isn't about doctrines; it's about an experience that is conveyed largely through liturgy. Doctrines, meanwhile, must continually be adjusted not only to harmonize with scientific knowledge but also to make spiritual truths vivid and comprehensible for people living in a certain time and place. It's not necessarily liturgies, then, but doctrines that must be changed from time to time. Certainly American popular culture today—dominated as it is by colorful, fast-paced entertainments that encourage in viewers a bland passivity—presents a challenge to those who seek to help people remove themselves from such shallow, horizontal distractions and to experience the vertical; but by modeling worship services on such entertainments, churches like Willow Creek fail even to take up the challenge and crush the possibility of fostering true spiritual experience.

To be sure, religion as popular entertainment is a long-standing American tradition. And in a sense legalistic Christianity *is* entertainment. Like entertainment, it simplifies. If nonlegalistic Christianity, like true art, recognizes that the world is complex, ambiguous, and full of gray areas, and seeks to engage the world as it is, legalistic Christianity, like entertainment, denies these complexities. Just as the crudest popular novels and movies divide the world into shallowly conceived and easily identified good guys and bad guys, legalistic Christianity divides the world into saints and sinners, the saved and the damned. One reason why legalistic Christianity, in the form of tent-meeting evangelism, succeeded in nineteenth-century America was that rural folk had pretty monotonous lives and were hard up for diversions. In many cases, evangelists were the only show that ever came to town. Today millions of Americans who have access to the Internet and to hundreds of TV channels still don't have much live entertainment available to them locally other than church services; and the habit of experiencing the world through TV may make such people all the more susceptible to the power of live performance (and of mob psychology) that is exploited to the hilt at places like Willow Creek.

If Willow Creek's services are designed to seem more like entertainments than like liturgies, the big white church building itself is designed to look less like a church than like a shopping mall. Today, Willow Creek is a nondescript 352,000-square-foot modern structure set on a 141-acre campus that looks like a suburban office park, with a fountain and a large pond; in addition to the main auditorium, which seats five thousand (a total of fifteen thousand people attend Willow Creek services every week), the building contains a large food court, a full gym, a bowling alley, and movie theaters. There are over fifty pastors on staff with a variety of specializations, over eleven hundred small Bible groups, and hundreds of different ministries, many of which sound more like shopping-mall specialty stores than like aspects of church mission. Indeed, Willow Creek's promotional materials tend to address "seekers" not as potential congregants but as consumers. Instead of striving to awaken such would-be members' desire to know and serve God, the materials stress the church's ability to serve their perceived needs. The word *needs,* in fact, is ubiquitous: "Our vision is to see churches better relating God's solutions to the needs of both seekers and believers. . . . Our services are designed to meet your spiritual needs. . . . If you are in need, we would like to help you. . . . [Willow Creek's] various programs and ministries can help them [members] fulfill their personal and relational needs." So popular has Willow Creek's formula been that it has led to the formation of the Willow Creek Association, through which Hybels and company market their methods to over a thousand other churches in over fifty denominations, helping them to relate "God's solutions to the needs of both seekers and believers." This is the language of the "church growth movement," which, as Jimmy Allen has written, centers on creating "homogeneous, comfortable, and secure surroundings in which emotional needs and family needs are met." (Such adjectives, of course, point to an atmosphere that is precisely the opposite of what Jesus cultivated: Being a follower of his was most decidedly *not* about being part of something homogeneous, comfortable, and secure.)

Though Willow Creek affirms the usual legalistic doctrines about the substitutionary atonement and biblical inerrancy (and is officially "pro-life"), it presents itself to outsiders as being nondenominational, inoffensive, and inclusionary so as not to turn them off. Accordingly it places less public emphasis on its creed than on a list of ten vague "Core Values" that "grew out of multiple discussions between Willow Creek Community Church and Association staff members." This litany, which seems to have been designed in such a way as to sound nonlegalistic and unthreatening to anyone, includes statements that "churches should be led by men and women with leadership gifts," that "anointed teaching is a catalyst for transformation in individuals' life and in the church," that "Christ-followers should manifest authenticity," that "a church should operate as a unified community of servants," and that "loving relationships should permeate every aspect of church life."

Far from bearing any resemblance to historic creedal statements, the ten Willow Creek "Core Values" represent an attempt to connect Jesus Christ with ideas about how to "transform" lives within the context of a church community made up largely of conventional middle-class families. Indeed, the culture of a place like Willow Creek suggests that the name of Jesus Christ has been attached to something that is less about the gospel than it is about people's desire to achieve for their families a controlled, safe environment—the ecclesiastical equivalent of a gated community. Observers have noted that Willow Creek members can spend a whole weekend at the church's campus, eating at the food court and enjoying various other services and diversions; members who need, say, an emergency car repair or tooth extraction can call day or night on fellow members who do those things for a living. Yes, Willow Creek does have outreach services to the homeless, the poor, and prisoners, but many large legalistic churches today do not; and even in those megachurches that do, the chief appeal is generally not that the place calls members to involvement in the world but that it allows them to live somewhat apart from the world among families very much like their own.

That religion in America has spawned such a phenomenon as megachurches should hardly be surprising. Americans have always been drawn to the outsized; we want to be part of something big, successful, "happening." As one man told a *New York Times* reporter, in explaining why he attends a large, fast-growing fundamentalist church in rural Ohio, "I like being around successful people on Sunday." We are a people in search of meaning and definition; but we also have developed in the Television Age a terrifying passivity, an insatiable desire to be entertained, and a discomfort with experiences that disturb the surfaces of our lives. Americans flock to megachurches to find a home, and to be less alone, and yet there seems nothing more lonely and less like a home—and nothing more dramatically removed from the earthly ministry of Jesus of Nazareth, who soiled his feet treading from village to village—than these immense, bland, antiseptic, impersonal structures that have nothing about them to suggest transcendence or immanence, but that speak only of efficiency, material security, and the insidious ability of modern popular culture to deflect our attentions incessantly from the things of God.

For legalistic Protestants, the only fully legitimate way of relating to nonbelievers is by evangelizing. Even when you are not explicitly evangelizing, you are "witnessing"—that is, providing an example of Christian righteousness and of the peace and joy that Christ brings to his people. This emphasis on witnessing encourages the tendency to put up a false front. For millions of legalistic families, the need to present the world with a phony facade is so deeply ingrained that the facade can come to seem more real than the reality. Whether because legalism forces people to develop their gifts for self-deception, or because it draws into its ranks people who are already masters of self-deception, legalists are notorious for their often crippling inability to confront, discuss, and deal honestly and productively with family problems. This is a running theme in Ulstein's book *Growing Up Fundamentalist;* one after another, his interviewees describe families that "stressed the *appearance* of perfection," that were "never interested in getting intimate and honest," that "lived in a world of denial and appearances," that "don't know how to ask for help" because "they have to appear like they're in charge." One women speaks of how her mother "can't consider the *possibility* that she made mistakes. It threatens her whole world." Another says: "Everything they do is for show, or, as they would say, a good witness. . . . No one asks for help, because it would blow their cover." One element of the psychology here is that God is believed to protect his "saved" children from problems; so if you want to be seen as saved, you pretend not to have problems.

For legalistic Christians, some of the dirtiest words are those that suggest generosity of spirit toward other people. One such word is *broad-minded;* another is *tolerant.* One legalistic ministry's home page contains the following jeremiad on broad-mindedness:

> *There is no room for broadmindedness in the chemical laboratory. Water is composed of two parts hydrogen and one part oxygen. The slightest deviation from the formula is forbidden.*

> *There is no room for broadmindedness in music. The skilled director will not permit his first violin to play even so much as one-half note off the written note, chord, and key.*

And so on: There is no room for broad-mindedness in mathematics, biology, athletics, car repair. "How then shall we expect that broad-mindedness shall rule in the realm of Christianity and morals? He that forsakes the truth of God, forsakes the God of truth." The home page for Charles Stanley's *In Touch* magazine strikes a similar note:

> *Are you a person who considers himself to be broad-minded, open to various points of view? If so, consider several examples of decision-making. . . . Suppose your doctor said: "You have a heart disease that requires bypass surgery." Would you say "Well, any doctor will do. Give me a pediatrician, maybe a general practitioner. Any physician is acceptable"? Of course not. You are very narrow-minded when it comes to your health. You want the finest cardiologist available.*

The same holds, we are told, when we are picking out a wife or a new suit. "In truth, none of us are as broad-minded as we think we are. We are broad-minded about some things, but we are very narrow-minded about some other things. The greater the importance or the more serious the consequences of our decisions, the more narrow-minded we become."

The ways in which legalistic narrow-mindedness works to stifle life, love, and honest communication were strikingly demonstrated by a series of messages posted on an Internet message board maintained by *Campus Life*, a magazine for evangelical youth. The author of the messages was a twenty-four-year-old man who did not identify himself. In the first of these messages, posted in June 1996, he asked, "Should Christian young people be dying of loneliness?" He explained that "legalism . . . sometimes makes it hard to meet people. In a church where everyplace is a sin (dance clubs, other churches' activities, even Christian concerts!) you sometimes end up scared out of knowing anyone. . . . I am scared to say this, but I myself am considering leaving my church for a different congregation. Where I attend, this is unequivocally considered backsliding. If we leave our congregation, it is said it's because we're worldly, or fleshly, and really don't care about the Lord." He said that he

> could call up the one or two young people from my church and ask them what they're doing, but I usually feel nervous when around them, like I'm under a microscope being examined for sinfulness. I don't feel I can talk to them about my weaknesses, struggles, or that I can even talk the way I normally do.
>
> Because of the isolation I've gone through for the last year, I actually got to where I attended a service at a big local church close to where I live. My church considers every member of this group deceived, worldly, ungodly, unreligious, and fake, and that none of them are going to heaven. . . .
>
> I now fear that God will be angry with me for what I did, and for writing this. But, I cannot go on in life being this lonely. I need to find someplace where there's a young singles group, not just so I can find a girlfriend, but so I can have a new set of friends who I can be around. Legalism makes freindship [sic] hard, and it makes us look at our brothers and sisters instead as "cops." It's like, we think when they're talking to us, they're looking for sins to catch us in. I still run and hide in malls or stores if I think I see someone who knows me from church, I don't know why, except that I'm afraid.

Of his loneliness, he wrote: "I pray that Jesus will change this swiftly, because it hurts. . . . Does anyone relate to any of this????" Writing again in July, the young man noted that "in a harsh, legalistic setting, the 'sinful worldly people' often seem more compassionate than many others." (This is a theme one encounters often in the memories of people who were raised in legalistic churches: their amazement at the generosity of spirit demonstrated by people whom their parents and pastors told them to view as evil.) In legalistic churches, "communication becomes fake, as the 'perfect Christian' masks go up. . . . I love these people, and I know God uses them to help me in my life. These people care deeply about the Lord and do a lot more for Him than I do. But, I feel like I just can't tell them what's going on in my life, due to legalism."

September brought another message:

> I guess what I'm talking about in legalism is a Christian person creating rules about things around them in the world that aren't found in the Word, then condemning others for not following these regulations. I'm referring to when brothers and sisters in God can't even get together at dinners or flea markets without talking about rules and regulations, and condemning one another, and can't seem to even have love and fellowship one with another, only fear of "getting caught."

> I'm referring to Christians being so hung up on rules like exact hair length and style for men and women, whether or not it's sinful to read the sports page, sinful and unsinful brands of blue jeans, sleeve lengths, what types of cars are humble and what aren't, being afraid of accidentally saying slang words like "dude," "man," or "what's up," and on and on. . . .

> When people focus more on these rules and how much they follow them, and how much everybody else doesn't, and how others need to follow them so they can be as right as me (notice—no mention of Jesus Christ, the cross, or forgiveness of sins) that sounds like something that makes it hard to have friends at church.

Two days after this message, the young man's series of self-disclosures concluded abruptly with the following note: "This is important. I want to say here that I have spoken some things which were wrong, because they concern a man of God and his ministry that is ordained of God. . . . To speak against a God ordained preacher is a terrible sin, and a big mistake. If anything I have written here in this whole folder (especially about dating) is wrong, I ask God to forgive me. I did not

do it being led by God, but by sin. I repent . . . . and I will not
post anything here ever again . . . . may God forgive me."

Many secular people have a lingering sense that being a Christian
means "being a good person," or at least trying or aspiring to be, and
assume that all Christians also think this way. Legalistic Protestantism
strongly rejects the notion, however, that an individual's goodness or
lack thereof has any ultimate value or significance. Indeed, according
to many legalists, the very idea that individual virtue plays a role in
determining whether one will go to heaven is an evil one, deliberately
planted in people's minds by Satan. In October 1996, on the day before
Halloween, I went into a "Christian" bookstore in a small Georgia
town and found on the counter, next to a case of Testamints ("Christian breath mints" with a Bible verse on every page), several stacks of
tiny booklets selling for twenty-five cents apiece.

"Most Christian bookstores," says an article on the Christian Broadcasting Network's Web site, "carry small pamphlets about the Lord—
designed especially for children on Halloween. These could be taped
to candy and dropped into each trick-or-treater's bag." Chick Publications, the California-based company that published the booklets on
sale at the Georgia store, appears to be the world's leading supplier of
such materials.

The covers of the booklets on sale at that Georgia bookstore were
pretty innocuous. Spelled out in white block letters on a black background were the words *Happy Halloween;* beside them, in orange and
white and black, was a cartoon of a witch placing a skull in a cauldron. Inside the booklet was a comic strip telling the story of a boy
named Tommy and his two friends, Bobby and Timmy. Scared on
Halloween by actors dressed up as demons and witches at a simu-
lated "haunted house," the boys run out into a street, where Timmy is
struck by a car and killed. He wakes up in hell, where the Devil tells
him he'll be there forever because he died in his sins. The next day,
Tommy tells his mother, Mrs. Baxter, that if he'd listened to her,
Timmy would still be alive. Bobby speaks up, offering the consolation
that at least Timmy is in heaven. No, Mrs. Baxter corrects him. Timmy
isn't in heaven. She affirms says that she loved Timmy, who was one of

her favorite students in her Sunday school class. But Timmy, she informs the boys darkly, made a mistake; he refused to repent. He refused to give himself over to Jesus. When Timmy quit Sunday school recently, she says, she cautioned him that salvation was possible only through Jesus; Timmy's response was to laugh at her and call her a fanatic. As a result of that decision, Mrs. Baxter tells Bobby and Tommy, their friend will spend eternity in hell.

"But that's *IMPOSSIBLE!*" Bobby said. "Timmy was a *good* kid."

Mrs. Baxter replies that it's wrong to think that good boys go to heaven and bad boys go to hell. "That's a *lie* straight from the devil," she insists. We're all sinners, she says, and thus all deserve eternal punishment; the only way any of us gets to heaven is through Jesus' sacrifice on the cross.

Having heard this, Bobby tells Mrs. Baxter that he doesn't want to reject Jesus' sacrifice. She instructs him therefore to turn away from his sins and to offer his life to Jesus. Immediately he falls to his knees, lowers his elbows to the floor, places his hands over his eyes, and prays to Jesus. In his prayer he declares his belief in Jesus' sacrifice, repents of his sins, and begs forgiveness. Finally, he asks Jesus to come into his heart and save him. Then he stands up and announces with a broad grin that he feels safe now—for he knows that when *he* dies, he'll go to heaven, unlike Timmy.

The comic strip concludes with a direct plea to the little boy or girl reader who has presumably found this booklet taped to candy in a trick-or-treat bag. "Make this *your* greatest Halloween," it says. How? First, you must "REPENT"—be genuinely penitent for your sins and be prepared to repudiate them. Second, you must "RECEIVE"—namely, receive "God's free love by inviting Jesus into your heart to save you." Then, above two pictures of Satan and Jesus: "Don't make the same mistake Tommy did. The choice is yours."

There are two important points to be made about these comic strips. The first is that legalistic Christians who have pilloried children's books like *Heather Has Two Mommies* as evil and antifamily—and have made such books the subjects of intense controversy—cheerfully purchase Halloween pamphlets like these, which use terror as a tool for evangelizing children, and drop them every year into countless trick-or-treaters' baskets. And this has *never* become the stuff of controversy.

The second point is that the comic strip about Tommy and his friends is not the product of some mind that has wandered off the beaten track: What it presents is standard legalistic Protestant theology. Let there be no misunderstanding of what the theology reflected in these pamphlets says about God and Satan. Satan strives to convince people that they need not embrace Jesus in order to be saved, but need only be good; thus Satan is, in effect, a force for virtue. To Jesus, by contrast, it is infinitely less important that people be good than that they accept him as their savior; Jesus is, then, effectively *not* a force for virtue. "We believe," says the "Statement of Faith" of Atlanta's First Baptist Church, "that Satan is a person, the author of sin and the reason for the fall of man, and is destined to the judgement of an eternal punishment in the lake of fire." Author of sin or not, however, the legalistic notion that salvation through goodness is a Satan-inspired doctrine means that the contest with God is, for legalists, not a clash between good and evil, or love and hate, or sinlessness and sin, but is, quite simply, a struggle for raw power between two transcendent entities in which people can choose up sides and take the consequences: end up with Satan in a lake of fire or with Christ at the right hand of God. Millions of legalistic American Protestants cheerfully embrace this theology that condemns "good kids" to everlasting torment because they didn't realize how important it was to accept Jesus as their savior.

Children. As I was reminded in that Georgia church, legalistic pastors often treat their parishioners like children. To be sure, Jesus said that "except ye . . . become as little children, ye shall not enter into the kingdom of heaven" (Matt. 18:3); but the next words out of his mouth—"Whosoever shall humble himself as this little child, the same is the greatest in the kingdom of heaven"—make it clear that he meant his followers should be like children in their humility, not in their understanding. "Brethren," wrote Paul, "be not children in understanding; howbeit in malice be ye children, but in understanding be men" (I Cor. 14:20). Too many legalists choose to be children in understanding, even as they remain all too "adult" in malice, greed, resentment, and cruelty. Indeed, if many nonlegalistic Christians feel that their religion obliges them to be constantly open to growth and discovery, legalistic Christianity can be genuinely infantilizing; at its worst, indeed, it can be nothing more or less than a formula for arrested development—intellectually, aesthetically, and spiritually. What better way to cut off growth, after all, than to lay down the law that any sign of growth is a thing of the Devil?

The flip side of the congregation's childlike role, of course, is the pastor's paternalism. Legalistic pastors insist that God demands obedience and has ordained a hierarchy that must be respected: pastor over flock, husband over wife. A favorite text is Ephesians 5:22–24, which is traditionally (but, most biblical scholars now say, erroneously) attributed to Saint Paul: "Wives, be subject to your husbands, as to the Lord. For the husband is the head of the wife as Christ is the head of the church, his body, and is himself its Saviour. As the church is subject to Christ, so let wives also be subject in everything to their husbands." Wives are told to look to their husbands for spiritual leadership and to obey them without question; husbands, in turn, are expected to submit with equal deference to the church pastor and elders. Though the nature and extent of pastoral authority varies from congregation to congregation, members of legalistic churches as a rule are remarkable for the degree to which they allow—and even invite—their pastors to interfere in their personal lives, ordering them how to handle everything from financial problems to troubles with their children. It doesn't take much for many legalistic pastors to establish themselves as authorities in the minds of their flock: An October 1996 *New York Times* article profiled an Ohio minister who supplements his Bible lessons "with an impressive knowledge of current events that comes from reading the *Wall Street Journal* daily, *Newsweek* and *U.S. News and World Report.*" For many legalistic parishioners, such reading habits qualify the pastor as a first-class intellectual.

Parishioners' obligation to obey is absolute. Church members are not to heed the promptings of their own minds, emotions, and consciences, because, they are told, those things can be manipulated by Satan; only by obeying one's God-given superior can one be sure that one is doing what God wishes. A former member of a legalistic church shared with me a nine-page document that she had been given by her pastor and that is typical of the kinds of materials that such men distribute to their female parishioners. Entitled "Seven Basic Needs of a Husband," it is a set of instructions designed to create wives who are perfectly subordinate in every way and to support the idea that such subordination is biblical. Under the heading "A HUSBAND NEEDS A WIFE WHO ACCEPTS HIM AS A LEADER AND BELIEVES IN HIS GOD-GIVEN RESPONSIBILITIES," it lists several points:

1. Husbands are commanded to govern their wives. (Gen. 3:16)
2. Wives are commanded to submit to their husbands. (Eph. 5:22; Col. 3:18; 1 Pet. 3:1)
3. A wife's submission qualifies her husband for church leadership. (1 Tim. 3:4,5)
4. The headship of the husband is illustrated in Christ and the church. (1 Cor. 11:3)

As these citations indicate, those who insist on the submissiveness of women have leaned heavily on the epistles traditionally attributed to Paul. Other directives are offered without biblical citation: "Wife should dress to please her husband." "KEEP THE HOME FREE OF CLUTTER." "PROVIDE GOOD MUSIC THROUGHOUT THE DAY." The list mandates how women should dress and style their hair; it tells them to allow their husbands time to be alone or with other men (so that the man may "sharpen his thinking" in conversation with them); and it insists that women should not have any expectations of their husbands: "Expectations destroy gratefulness . . . EXPECT NOTHING AND BE GENUINELY GRATEFUL FOR EACH LITTLE EVIDENCE OF YOUR HUSBAND'S LOVE." Millions of American men gladly embrace such rules as legitimate Christian theology, and millions of wives try their best to live by them, having been told that they are God's law. To a great extent, indeed, legalistic Christianity can be understood as a means by which many men, in the age of feminism, have succeeded in maintaining and justifying their authority over women.

This insistence on unquestioning submission by women—and by children, as well—results in an extraordinary degree of sexual, physical, and psychological abuse within legalistic Christian families, and of tacit acceptance of that abuse by its victims and by the church generally. To talk to former legalistic Christians is to hear an astonishing number of stories about abuse going unpunished and unacknowledged in order to preserve appearances and power structures. The high rate of abuse among legalistic Christians should not be surprising. This is, after all, a subculture of authoritarian control and unquestioning obedience; a subculture in which people are taught that sexual feelings are evil and consequently can't bring themselves to openly acknowledge, discuss, explore, and understand their own physical impulses; a subculture in which people are taught to put up a false front of virtue, are discouraged from being honest about their own emotional problems and from seeking counseling, and are taught not to peer beyond their fellow legalists' facades. An interviewee in *Growing Up Fundamentalist* tells of a Christian counselor who instructed a victim of spousal abuse "to kneel and assume the position of Christ in Gethsemane while her husband beat her. This was supposed to increase her knowledge of Christ and be a witness to her husband." Another interviewee recalled a pastor who "excommunicated a woman for not submitting" when her husband beat her. These are not extreme cases. (This is, after all, as the Halloween pamphlets demonstrate, a subculture in which adults are encouraged to terrify other people's children with the threat of hellfire.)

For all their coverage of controversies instigated by the Religious Right, such as those over NEA funding and gays in the military, the mainstream media rarely notice that behind the family-values rhetoric of legalistic Christians lies an extraordinary amount of unacknowledged family dysfunction and abuse. The history of Susan Smith—the South Carolina woman who, after murdering her two small sons, turned out to have been the victim of sexual abuse at the hands of her stepfather, a local Christian Coalition leader—is not a rare exception in the legalistic Christian subculture but instead reflects a widespread reality behind that subculture's Norman Rockwell images. In 1995, *New York Times* columnist Frank Rich noted Newt Gingrich's characterization of the murder as a by-product of the sixties counterculture. "The only way you get change," Gingrich said, "is to vote Republican." Yet after Gingrich's remarks, it came out that Smith's stepfather had begun molesting her when she was fifteen—"once," Rich pointed out, "after he'd returned from plastering the town with 'Pat Robertson for President' posters."

Legalistic Christians grow up with such hypocrisy. They live it, they breathe it, they take for granted the jarring difference between the reality of their lives and the way they represent those lives to themselves and others. Just as they are raised not to confront the contradictions within scripture, and between scripture and scientific truth, so they also learn to deny the contrasts between the deep, hidden problems in their own families and the wholesome faces they present to the world. This denial becomes an essential, automatic part of the way they view and interact with the world; so much a part, indeed, that it is fair to say that one of the things they deny is the very fact of their denial. It was this kind of denial that made possible, among much else, the abuse of Susan Smith—and, in turn, her murder of her two children.

The extent of such abuse should hardly be surprising, for such acts are simply one manifestation of an attraction to violence that is widespread among legalistic Christians and that is implicit in much legalistic theology. Strozier describes a fundamentalist of his acquaintance who, though "a gentle man," nonetheless "nourished in his mind a stirring cauldron of images of end time destruction" and was perfectly happy with the idea that God would "wipe out 2.5 billion people . . . because they are not saved." Strozier quotes another fundamentalist who enthusiastically imagined that when the End Times come, the sinners will (as foretold in 2 Kings 8:12) "fall by the sword . . . their little ones will be dashed to the ground, their pregnant women will be ripped open." Strozier observes that "this deferred violence and shift in agency from himself to God" allowed the man "to separate himself from responsibility for his intense loathing for sinners, especially gays and lesbians"; in the apocalyptic, he found "a vehicle for his own violence toward those whom he felt threatened his fragile self" as well as something that "protected him from having to own these feelings in any real emotional sense. Punishment was in the hands of God, who will carry it out with terrible vengeance after history ends."

This ardor for divine punishment of others is not confined to strict fundamentalists but can be found across the spectrum of legalistic belief. And its profound effect on legalists' attitudes toward good and evil should not be ignored. The tracts distributed by evangelical Christians routinely quote John 3:16: "For God so loved the world, that he gave his only begotten Son, that whosoever believeth in him should not perish, but have eternal life." "God loves you with an eternal love," declares the author of an August 1996 advice column in Charles Stanley's *In Touch* magazine. Yet Stanley and other legalistic Protestants have affirmed that this loving God will brutally condemn us to eternal hellfire if we fail to recognize him and acknowledge him in just the right way. He will do this, as that Halloween booklet pointed out, even to an extraordinarily good and loving child. It is impossible to believe in and worship this kind of God, and to call him a God of love, without having a profoundly distorted—and dangerous—understanding of the nature of good and evil.

Indeed, as Sally Lowe Whitehead recalls in her 1997 memoir, *The Truth Shall Set You Free,* a fundamentalist pastor once told her that "Satan must ask God's permission to touch any one of us. And when permission is granted, it is for the sake of discipline, which *is* God's mercy." Thus does Satan himself, in the theology of many legalists, become the tool of divine grace.

Bound up with the concept of the authority of God, pastor, and husband, of course, is the concept of the authority of scripture. Though some evangelical churches don't insist on the total inerrancy of the Bible, most of them nonetheless preach something that is very close to inerrancy and that in practice amounts to essentially the same thing. Certainly most of the people in the pews of conservative evangelical churches combine a sentimental devotion to the idea of the Bible as the "Word of God" with a very spotty knowledge of its contents, and thus look with suspicion (or worse) upon any suggestion that the Good Book contains inaccuracies and inconsistencies. One way in which the fundamentalists won control of the Southern Baptist Convention was by casting doubt on their opponents' devotion to the Bible. The lamentable truth is that many Americans today would rather read a Scofield Reference Bible and *know* what they are supposed to believe than pore through the texts, pro and con, concerning such matters as the "historical Jesus" controversy and figure out for themselves what they believe. In the late twentieth century, many Americans feel that there is already too much to think about, and unfortunately we live in a society whose educational system and popular culture don't help children to grow into adults who are comfortable with the idea of thinking critically.

For legalistic Protestants, it is important to believe not only that the Bible is true, but that in some sense it contains *all* that is true. Other potential sources of knowledge are looked upon with grave suspicion. Nothing that any book or teacher presents as true is to be accepted as such until it has been tested against the Bible—or, one should say, against the Bible as one's pastor interprets it.

In most legalistic Protestant churches, dogmatism extends far beyond the Bible itself. Many such churches have their own strict, narrow bodies of doctrine that are said to be based in scripture. Many of these directives have nothing to do with the Bible, but instead represent the codification of a pastor's own prejudices and predilections— and usually intersect pretty neatly with the social and political attitudes of the men in that pastor's congregation. As one ex-fundamentalist told Stefan Ulstein in *Growing Up Fundamentalist,* "It's not about following Christ. They take rules and cultural norms that a certain group of people have grown up with and try to sanctify those norms as though they came from God." Another Ulstein interviewee agrees: "Modern fundamentalism's lack of biblical and historical grounding makes it highly susceptible to fads. If it sounds good and draws a crowd, it gets added to fundamentalist dogma. Fundamentalism has changed more than most fundamentalists would like to admit. It's hardly the unchangeable, rock-hard doctrine that it's made out to be."

Curiously, many of those who defend legalistic Protestantism as "the old-time religion," unchanged and unchanging, nonetheless acknowledge and approve of many of the changes that have taken place in the legalistic concept of God. When he was asked by *New York Times* reporter Gustav Niebuhr, for example, about a book entitled *The Management Methods of Jesus*—in which a sports marketer named Bob Briner depicts Jesus as a model business manager—Luke Timothy Johnson, a conservative professor at the Candler School of Theology, replied, "I don't think there's anything problematic about finding in Jesus our own ideals." Christianity, however, demands not that we identify our own ideals with Jesus but that we question those ideals and test them against Jesus. A perennial problem has been the eagerness of Christians like Briner to remake Jesus in their own images, however selfish or brutal, and the willingness of Christians like Johnson to approve of those actions to the extent that they bring Jesus more closely into line with the kind of institutional establishment that Jesus taught His followers to question.

In many legalistic churches, the emphasis on law and doctrine represents, in large part, an explicit response to other churches' emphasis on love. "I think that we were actually taught not to love," one of Ulstein's ex-fundamentalist interviewees recalls. "The liberals were always talking about love and the social gospel, so it was probably a reaction. It was almost as if our fundamentalist elders were saying, 'We will preach the truth. To hell with love.'" Interestingly, the specific content of this "truth" is less important than the *idea* of truth. The more extensively one examines legalistic Christianity in America today, in fact, the more one recognizes the validity of William D. Dinges's observation, in an essay on traditionalist Catholicism, that "fundamentalism is not distinguished by the specific content of its orthodoxy . . . but by the priority of 'correct belief' itself." It doesn't matter much, in other words, what one claims to believe; what matters is that one maintains it unquestioningly and that one reject every kind of belief that deviates from it even slightly as false, evil, satanic. "Space scientists," says Southern Baptist fundamentalist Paige Patterson, "tell us that minute error in the mathematical calculations for a moon shot can result in a total failure of the rocket to hit the moon. A slightly altered doctrine of salvation can cause a person to miss Heaven also." Such conviction as to the importance of absolute doctrinal precision is commonplace among legalistic Protestants. To be sure, many legalistic Christians don't think much about specific theological propositions: For many, Jesus is savior, and that's about it; the complexities of theology are a matter of indifference to them. But they retain a strong, stubborn attachment to the *idea* of orthodoxy. They need to believe that one set of statements is right and that all others are wrong, and that *their* set—whatever it may consist of—is the right one. One would think that those people for whom it is vitally important to hold fast to the one single truth would be those most likely to examine all the options, all the faith statements of believers, Christian and otherwise, to see which ones seem to them most persuasive; but the exact opposite is usually the case. The most inquisitive people tend to be the least dogmatic and exclusivist; for the dogmatic, indeed, "faith" becomes an excuse for—even a synonym for—*not* examining respectfully the ideas and beliefs of others.

Dean M. Kelley, in *Why Conservative Churches Are Growing,* cites Herbert H. Stroup's observation, in a 1945 study of Jehovah's Witnesses, that "the will to believe is so great among Witnesses that the content of belief becomes incidental" and that "one gets the impression . . . that they could just as well manage all that they are doing for and receiving from the movement if some other absolutist theology were to be substituted." The implicit point here is relevant not just to Jehovah's Witnesses but to members of all legalistic Christian faiths: For such people, the substance of a church's doctrine is all but irrelevant; what matters is that it be harsh, exclusionary, preached with zeal, professed without a hint of doubt, and regarded as the key to all truth and to eternal salvation.

One can get angry at legalistic Christianity for its lovelessness—and then one can chide oneself for getting angry. For isn't such anger a self-contradiction? Isn't it wrong to take a judgmental stance toward judgmentalism?

Yet Jesus got angry, too. Or at least that's what we're told in the twenty-third chapter of Matthew, in which Jesus assails the scribes and Pharisees. Nowhere else in the Gospels do we see Jesus as angry as he is here. Indeed, his anger seems to jump off the page, as if this were not a third-person account composed decades after the fact but a letter by Jesus himself, composed in the white heat of rage. As it happens, biblical scholars say that this speech was in all likelihood put in Jesus' mouth by Matthew; if the anger seems fresh, it may be because what we are witnessing is Matthew's anger toward the scribes and Pharisees of his own day.

But let's be legalists for a minute, and accept the idea that every line of the Bible is inerrant, and that this is unquestionably Jesus talking. What does the twenty-third chapter of Matthew tell us, then, as legalists? It tells us this, quite plainly: that nothing got Jesus angrier than legalism. His speech is a barn burner. Addressing a crowd, he repeatedly says, "Alas for you, scribes and Pharisees, hypocrites!" Alas why? Alas for several reasons.

- Alas because of their fixation on *hierarchical power:* "The greatest among you," he says, "must be your servant. Whoever exalts himself will be humbled; and whoever humbles himself will be exalted."

- Alas because of their *judgmentalism:* "You shut the door of the kingdom of heaven in people's faces."

- Alas because of their fixation on *meaningless doctrinal distinctions:* "You say if someone swears by the sanctuary that is nothing, but if he swears by the gold in the sanctuary he is bound by oath."

- Alas because of their fixation on *trivial laws* at the expense of the more important and more charitable demands of God's law: "You pay tithes of mint and dill and cumin; but you overlook the weightier demands of the law—justice, mercy, and good faith."

- And alas because of their show of attachment to *tradition* even as they attack their contemporaries who will be part of the tradition for future generations. "You build up the tombs of the prophets," he charges, "and embellish the monuments of the saints, and you say 'If we had been living in the time of our forefathers, we should never have taken part with them in the murder of the prophets.' So you acknowledge that you are the sons of those who killed the prophets. Go on then, finish off what your fathers began."

What Jesus is railing against here is, in a word, legalism. For these are the very ways in which legalism manifests itself: in an attachment to hierarchy, power, heartless judgment, meaningless doctrine, trivial laws, and things of the past that are clung to out of habit, prejudice, and fear. "Snakes! Vipers' brood!" Jesus calls them. "How can you escape being condemned to hell?"

Hell: There's that word. This isn't familiar talk from Jesus. He doesn't speak of hell to the tax collectors and prostitutes he socializes with. But if we're going to be legalists about this, we've got to recognize that the one thing he gets so worked up about that he brings up hell is legalism.

Hypocrites, he calls them. Hypocrites. He uses the word over and over. Is there any place in the Gospels where Jesus repeats himself so much? But he can't help it. He's losing it. Jesus loses it! This isn't the Sermon on the Mount. This isn't the Beatitudes. This is a rant. Jesus is angry—angry not just because of what has happened in the past and in his own time, but because he knows that the same thing will happen again in the future. Other prophets will come, and the scribes and Pharisees will harass them viciously, mercilessly, brutally.

"O Jerusalem, Jerusalem," he cries, "city that murders the prophets and stones the messengers sent to her! How often have I longed to gather your children, as a hen gathers her brood under her wings, but you would not let me." What an amazing image: Jesus as a mother hen, kept from her children by those who claim to be God's anointed. This is the reason for his anger—this is the one thing that can move him to the point of emotional outburst.

This passage in Matthew is so strong, so stunning, that you might think that it would have made church people forever after think twice before setting themselves up as institutional dictators and merciless judges, before standing on the most trivial religious laws and hard-hearted doctrines, before invoking the names of past saints in order to extinguish the flames of present saints. And yet from generation to generation, the spiritual descendants of those scribes and Pharisees have done precisely that.

But those of us who are not legalistic Christians must remember one thing: We don't believe that every word of the Bible is literally true. We don't delight in dividing humanity into the saved and the unsaved. If Jesus did speak of hell, we're inclined to see it as an outburst of his all-too-human frustration and not as a revelation of his divine judgment. We don't want to see legalists burn in hell and we don't believe in a God who wants that, either. What those of us who are nonlegalistic Christians can have little trouble believing in, however, is a Savior who, in the fullness of his humanity, responded with a compassion as perfect as his Father's to those who sought to cut him off from the children he loved.

13

THE DOCTOR
AND THE COACH

IN THE TYPICAL legalistic church, it is not only one's own
pastor who is seen as a fount of truth. A few celebrated figures are widely revered as authorities—prophets, even—
whose word is nearly the equivalent of scripture. One such
figure is Hal Lindsey. Another is James Dobson, founder of
the Colorado Springs–based organization Focus on the
Family and author of several best-selling books on marriage
and child-rearing. Though he is a psychologist, not an
M.D., the lean, bespectacled, and distinguished-looking Dr.
Dobson (as he is universally known throughout the legalistic Christian community) is the very image of a family doctor out of a movie from the 1950s—kindly, all-knowing,
thoroughly unflappable, unfailingly dependable. He brings
to mind a time before health-insurance controversies and

malpractice suits, a time when a doctor was almost by definition a white male whose knowledge was seen as boundless and whose consummate expertise was beyond question.

Among legalistic Christians, Dobson has precisely that kind of aura. His books are read reverentially. If he tells his mostly female readership to do or not to do something—for example, to forbid their kids certain activities, or to discipline them in a particular way—millions comply. Indeed, while many Americans view the Christian Coalition as the public face of legalistic Christianity, most legalistic Christians feel more intimately allied to Dobson and Focus on the Family. Two generations of legalistic Protestant mothers have raised their children on Dobson's books, which bear such titles as *Dare to Discipline, The Strong-Willed Child, Love Must Be Tough, Parenting Isn't for Cowards,* and *Children at Risk: The Battle for the Hearts and Minds of Our Kids* (with Gary Bauer). For these women, Dobson is what Dr. Benjamin Spock was for mainstream mothers in the 1950s and '60s. Millions around the world listen to Dobson's daily radio program, purchase his videos, attend his "community impact seminars," subscribe to one or more of his dozen-odd magazines, and phone his Colorado Springs headquarters to ask members of the huge counseling staff questions about marriage and parenting.

The son of a Nazarene evangelist (the Nazarenes are a Holiness sect who believe that they are incapable of sin), Dobson is a child psychologist who, after earning a Ph.D. in psychology, taught pediatrics for many years at the University of Southern California School of Medicine and served on the attending staff at Children's Hospital of Los Angeles. In 1976, appalled by the "radical feminist agenda" of an international conference on women and families, he founded Focus on the Family. He has written that the organization's goal is "to help preserve the family and to spread the good news about Jesus Christ throughout the world. That's why we are here. . . . More than 1,300 dedicated staff members are working every day to defend the cause of righteousness and assist your family in surviving the pressures of the '90s."

In fact Dobson's real mission, and that of his huge staff, is to roll back the clock. In the letters he contributes to Focus on the Family's monthly newsletter, he offers up a 1950s-style vision of family life that makes *Father Knows Best* look like *Mommie Dearest*. Dobson's letters teem with sentimental anecdotes about happy weddings, about the joys of motherhood, and about high-school sweethearts marrying and living happily ever after. He also tells an occasional story that is intended to pull at the heartstrings. In one such story, a recently widowed, childless woman receives as her Christmas gift a puppy that her husband, before his death, had secretly arranged to be given to her. Dobson's comment: "Isn't that a touching story of love between a man and woman?" (If the couple were both men, Dobson wouldn't find it quite so touching.)

Dobson constantly harkens back to the 1950s and to his own youth during that decade. He is full of homespun personal anecdotes about such matters as "the day I nearly destroyed my dad's new Ford" and the wholesome fun he and his pals had at the beach a week before his high-school graduation. On various occasions Dobson has told readers how safe his neighborhood was when he was growing up, how good and loving his dad and mom were, and what a devoted lady he is married to. (Her high-school homecoming queen picture was featured alongside Dobson's monthly letter in his June 1994 newsletter.) Back in the 1950s, he remembers fondly, "Grandfatherly Dwight Eisenhower was president of the United States . . . and most of our congressmen, even those who professed no particular faith, understood and defended the Judeo-Christian system of values."

The emphasis here on image—"Grandfatherly" Ike, atheistic congressmen who made Christian noises—is typical of Dobson, whose anecdotes consistently conjure up a picture of the 1950s in which everyone is white and middle-class and without serious problems. He doesn't acknowledge the poverty and racial prejudice that existed then, and ridicules the "liberal historians" who paint a more nuanced picture of 1950s life than he does. "Let me offer an eyewitness account from a teenager who was there in 1954," he says in one letter. "It was a very good year." To be sure, he acknowledges that there were snakes in the garden: "Every now and then, a girl came up pregnant (it was called being 'in trouble'), and she was immediately packed off to some secret location. I never knew where she went." Far from criticizing this way of handling pregnancy—shaming a girl, ruining her life—Dobson implicitly signals his approval. Teen pregnancy doesn't belong in his

Norman Rockwell picture, and for him that's the important thing—
the integrity of the picture.

Indeed, one reason why Dobson appeals so strongly to legalistic
Christians is that he is as fixated as they are on projecting an image of
wholesome, happy family life. Deep down, they know that certain
things will always be with us—there will always be unmarried teenage
girls getting pregnant, and there will always be young men who discover that they are attracted to other young men—but legalistic Christians want these things out of the picture. Sweep pregnancy under the
rug; keep gays in the closet. Dobson is one psychologist who doesn't
ask legalistic Christians to face and deal with the reality of their lives
and other people's lives; he approves of their desire to embrace ideal
images and to pretend, not only to other people but to themselves as
well, that they're living in an Andy Hardy movie. What is remarkable
about his anecdotes and images of wholesome, happy family life is
how clichéd and generic they are. They evoke a life without texture
or individuality—a life not only free of problems but free of any sur-
prises whatsoever. Dads are always strong and hard-working, moms
always loving and deferential, boys always absorbed in cars and sports,
girls always sweet and quiet and on their way to becoming perfect
homemakers.

A more positive way of putting this is to say that ordinary women
who view their lives as empty, difficult, and meaningless can read Dobson and, however briefly, feel that their lives are in fact rich and full,
and that they are heroic in their devotion to the thankless task of rais-
ing children and putting food on the table. In his monthly newsletter,
Dobson frequently reminds these women that he's there for them: "To
every parent who feels alone in this day of high-tech wickedness and
gross immorality, we at Focus on the Family are pulling for you. . . .
Your stresses are of great concern to us. Your needs are our needs. . . .
We will do everything we can to support families. We are here because
we care." Indeed, one great reason for Dobson's popularity is that he
makes middle-class wives and mothers feel that he personally *does* care
about them.

In order to retain his appeal for these women, however, Dobson
must play a careful game: He must acknowledge their frustrations over
the ways in which their lives have fallen short of their dreams, yet at

the same time must feed their desire to believe that their lives are, in fact, crowded with joys and rewards. Even as he exalts 1950s America as a lost paradise of family values and condemns 1990s America as a moral cesspit, he affirms that "committed, loving, dedicated families are not disappearing from the face of earth." He concludes one of his wistful tributes to 1950s life by saying that "the scenario I have described, with all its nostalgia and warmth, is highly controversial in some circles within our culture. 'That's not the real world,' some would say. 'Sounds like Ozzie and Harriet to me.'" Dobson's whole point is that it *is* real, or can be. Yet if his idealized family images appeal to readers, it is precisely because those images *aren't* real; they reflect not the behind-the-scenes reality of those readers' lives, but an ideal of which they dream and a model for the facade they strive to construct.

If they haven't really achieved the ideal of a wholesome, happy family, Dobson constantly tells his readers, it's not through any fault of their own. It's through the fault of others. And he tells them who those others are, giving them enemies on whom they can blame the imperfections of their lives. Among these enemies are university professors who fill kids' heads with stuff like evolution and liberal politicians who favor government support for poor people. And at the top of the enemies list are feminists and homosexuals. If not for these people, Dobson suggests, American life would still be the heaven it was in the 1950s. In one newsletter, he describes these groups as "those influential people who hate families" and who are "out there working to undermine them." He strikes this paranoid note constantly: "Thousands of social engineers are out there today, many of them working for the government, who would like to get their hands on your home. Heaven forbid!" Among those "social engineers" are supporters of the Children's Rights Movement, which he despises. (For all his rhetoric about the need to protect middle-class American children from Hollywood values and humanistic education, Dobson expresses virtually no interest in the millions of Third World children who die every year of disease and starvation.)

At times Dobson implicitly identifies these enemies with Satan himself: "we must defend the family from the assault of hell. It must not be allowed to wither and die. On the shoulders of this divinely inspired institution rests the welfare of our entire civilization and the hopes of future generations." One reason why Dobson is so popular among legalistic Christians is that he affirms their black-and-white vision of morality: For him, as for them, the world comes down to a clear-cut battle between the evil, destructive gays, feminists, and other "social engineers" who march behind Satan's banner and the wholesome American families who comprise the army of God.

It's not just the 1950s that Dobson depicts as heaven in contrast with the hell of today. In a 1997 article in *Focus on the Family* magazine, he imagines at length a man from the 1870s cross-examining a man from our own time about contemporary pornography, violence, and such, and eventually accusing him of failing to take care of "your women and children." Dobson's 1990s man, predictably, fails to say anything in reply about nineteenth-century suffrage laws, lynchings, or child labor; the implication throughout the exchange is that the 1870s were a golden time when men took care of women: "We've read about your commitment [to family] in our history books," the 1990s man acknowledges.

"You've come a long way, baby!" Dobson comments ironically toward the end of the piece. The phrase (which he seems not to understand is no longer a potent feminist slogan ripe for sarcasm but a quaint twenty-something-year-old scrap of pop culture) crops up as an ironic refrain throughout Dobson's writings: He finds it ludicrous that any woman today could think she's better off than her counterparts were a century or more ago. To him, God, happiness, and family are all synonymous with perfect order, with "conforming to an eternal standard of behavior" and cleaving to "the divine plan" (of which strict male and female roles form an integral part), and all he can see in women's freedom today is rebellion, selfishness, and rejection of "absolute truth."

One of the elements of contemporary culture that Dobson has branded as an instrument of corruption is MTV, "with its fixation on sex and violence." In this context I might mention that not long ago, when I attended a high-school event in a small Southern town whose residents are overwhelmingly white legalistic Protestants, I was surprised at the students' easy acceptance of an openly gay classmate. One of the students told me that while most of the kids' parents were extremely racist and homophobic, the kids were the opposite. I asked why. His answer: "MTV." Dobson—and his readers—prefer not to rec- ognize that while legalistic churches in such communities have sup- ported prejudice for generations, it has—scandalously—taken such MTV programs as *The Real World* to expose younger people to a world in which race, gender, and sexual orientation are matters of indiffer- ence. For Dobson, the mainstream culture's emphasis on diversity serves only to pit group against group: "Now it's blacks against whites. It's haves against have-nots. It's men against women. It's the abused against abusers. It's liberals against 'right-wing extremists.' It's Jews against Muslims. It's homosexual activists against Christians. It's children against parents. It's Caucasian men against minorities. It's everybody against everybody." His is the voice of every middle- class white heterosexual male who feels that everything was just fine in the old days, when blacks didn't dare cry out against their oppression, gays huddled voicelessly in the closet, and women were meek, pliant housewives.

I have quoted Pat Robertson's and Ralph Reed's litanies of con- temporary problems; here is Dobson's: "The cultural revolution . . . was brought about by many influences working together, including the secularization of society, value-neutral schools, homosexual activism, easy-out divorce laws, pornography, crime and violence on television and in the movies, 'safe-sex' ideology, socialistic and humanistic col- leges and universities, governmental bureaucracies with destructive purposes, oppressive tax laws, radical feminism, abortion on demand, the drug culture, and overworked and exhausted parents." Few Amer- icans would disagree with Dobson about the lamentable effects of at least some of these developments; part of the reason for the strength of his movement, in fact, is that he has some valid things to say about the effect on children of the more sordid aspects of today's culture, and says them in a tone perfectly pitched to his audience. On paper at least, he comes off as far more pastoral than Robertson and as far less polit- ical than Reed; he often can seem more a disciple of a God of love than of a God of wrath.

Yet for all his occasional gentleness of rhetoric, Dobson's chief allies—and those he quotes most often in his newsletters—tend to be among the most mean-spirited political bullies of our time, such as Pat Buchanan, Cal Thomas, Bill Dannemeyer, and Bob Dornan. And when

Dobson starts discussing the family-negative elements of American life today, he almost invariably zeroes in on gays, and he does a far more vigorous—and vicious—job of this than the Christian Coalition ever has. While Reed appears to engage in the minimal amount of gay-bashing necessary to placate his constituency and even occasionally goes out on a limb to urge tolerance, Dobson exploits his readers' homophobia to the hilt. Though Dobson has never demonstrated any way in which homosexuality threatens families, he focuses much more energy on this putative threat than he does on any other. Children, he writes, must be shielded "from homosexual and lesbian propaganda and from wickedness and evil of every stripe."

There is a deep irony in this statement, because when it comes to wicked propaganda about homosexuality, Dobson takes a backseat to few. One of the things in which Focus on the Family specializes is personal narratives by people who claim to have been delivered out of homosexuality. These testimonies appear in Dobson's own publications and are syndicated to other legalistic periodicals. These narratives all have the same "happy ending": marriage and family. Usually there is a picture of the happy "ex-homosexual" with his or her spouse and children. Invariably the agent for conversion to heterosexuality is Jesus Christ: If you accept Jesus as your savior, he will help you change. One such account is entitled "The Transforming Power of God." The title perfectly illuminates the invaluable role that gay people play for legalistic Christians: Having been taught to connect evil with the Other and to identify themselves as good, legalists find in gay people—who seem to legalists to be as different from themselves as possible—the perfect Other, and thus the perfect embodiment of evil. For Dobson, it is a fixed and guiding idea that gay people (however decent and virtuous) are by definition creatures of the Devil, and members of "traditional families" (however odious) are holy.

Of course almost all psychologists and psychiatrists nowadays recognize that "therapy" designed to make gay people straight doesn't do any such thing. To be homosexual is not just to experience sexual attraction to another person of the same sex; it is to feel the same sense of comfort, rightness, and wholeness in a same-sex relationship that a straight person feels in an opposite-sex relationship. What "ex-gay therapy" does is to build up precisely those unhealthy elements of a gay person's psyche—his or her self-hatred and willingness to live a lie—that psychotherapy should seek to dissolve. To encourage such "transformation," and to celebrate such a person's marriage to a person of the opposite sex, is to embrace a lie about that person and to do something that is cruel to both parties in the marriage. It is not surprising that Dobson, with his fixation on ideal but phony family images, should so emphatically embrace such deceptions. In a 1993 Focus on the Family newsletter, Dobson writes about "the worth of the child, especially the handicapped and needy. . . . Each of them is precious." Yet his organization's propaganda about homosexuality shows that Dobson is more willing to sacrifice the lives of gay youth—who, devastated by hatred, commit suicide at an alarming rate—than to change the societal attitudes that cause them to take their lives. He needs gay people—including gay youth—as scapegoats, in the literal ancient sense of the word: people who are sacrificed to keep society together. We look back at other cultures, such as the Egyptians and Romans, and are appalled at the brutality that made possible, say, the sacrifices of virgins to the gods, the working of slaves to death to build the pyramids, and gladiators' deaths as a form of public entertainment. Yet the way in which legalistic Christians have been encouraged to victimize gay people is no less horrific. The only difference is that the worst abuse takes place behind closed doors, where parents, affirmed by the likes of Dobson in their antigay hatred, put their own children through unimaginable psychological torment that often leads to self-slaughter.

Dobson's antagonism toward gays is so powerful that it leads him into self-contradiction. In a question-and-answer section of *The New Dare to Discipline,* the question is posed: "Is AIDS God's plague sent to punish homosexuals, lesbians and other promiscuous people?" Dobson's answer begins: "I would think not, because little babies and others who bear no responsibility are suffering." Yet he finds the idea of AIDS as punishment too appealing to leave it at that, and goes on to affirm that when gay people get AIDS, it is indeed a consequence of moral violation. "Sickness and death," he writes, "befall those who play Russian roulette with God's moral law."

Dobson's antagonism toward homosexuals is plainly a symptom of his fixation on traditional sex roles. "When reduced to the basics," he wrote in 1995, "women need men to be romantic, caring and loving. Men need women to be respectful, supportive and loyal. These are not primarily cultural influences that are learned in childhood, as some would have us believe. They are deeply rooted forces in the human personality." (Presumably Dobson would insist that the desire of a homosexual to be with another person of the same sex is *not* "deeply rooted," but is rather a result of "cultural influences.") "The Creator," he continues, "observed Adam's loneliness in the Garden of Eden and said, 'It is not good for the man to be alone.'" So he gave Adam a wife, and thus "invented the family and gave it His blessing and ordination." Dobson's comment: "How redundant it would have been for the Creator to put Adam to sleep and then fashion another man from his rib! No, He brought forth a woman and gave her to Adam. He put greater toughness and aggressiveness in the man and more softness and nurturance in the woman—and suited them to one another's needs. And in their relationship, He symbolized the mystical bond between the believer and Christ, Himself. What an incredible concept!" From the Adam and Eve story—which Dobson (a critic of Darwin) adverts to frequently, always as if it were a literal historical account—Dobson derives what he calls "the biblical concept of masculinity and femininity." He insists that "boys and girls should be taught that the sexes are equal in worth, but very different from one another. Girls should know they are girls, and boys should know they are boys." Indeed, "self-awareness begins with an understanding of our sexual identity. It must not be blurred by those who have an avant-garde agenda of their own."

Dobson's antique attitudes about sex roles are on display throughout his work. In *Marriage and Sexuality: Dr. Dobson Answers Your Questions,* he writes: "It is a woman's prerogative not to have a baby. . . . However, there's something ambiguous about insisting on a 'right' which would mean the end of the human race if universally applied!" He quotes with approval the passage from Ephesians beginning "Wives, be subject to your husbands." And he affirms "that a family must have a leader whose decisions prevail in times of differing opinions. If I understand the Scriptures, that role has been assigned to the man of the house."

In Christ, wrote Saint Paul, "there is no such thing as Jew and

Greek, slave and free, male and female" (Gal. 3:28). This is the ultimate statement of what Jesus was really about—the eradication of alienating distinctions and a radical assertion of equal human worth. Yet Dobson is fixated on what he describes as "the countless physiological and emotional differences between the sexes," and tells readers it is their obligation as Christians to heed these differences and to assign roles and establish hierarchies on the basis of them. In arguing for these differences' supreme importance, Dobson bounces back and forth oddly between biology ("the sexes differ in their basal metabolism") and the Bible ("Eve, being suited to his particular needs, was given to Adam as a 'help-meet'"). In the guise of learned discourse, Dobson recycles tired stereotypes: Women need love, men don't; "flowers and candy and cards are more meaningful to her than to him"; the woman has greater "emotional instability—she laughs and cries more easily"; "female physiology is a finely tuned instrument, being more complex and vulnerable than the masculine counterpart." Much of his "advice" in this area is amazingly banal, and often outrageously sexist:

> Men need to understand that women tend to care more than they about the home and everything in it. Whether your wife or fiancée has a nest-building instinct or not, I don't know, but for years I have observed this feminine interest in the details of the family dwelling. Admittedly, not every woman keeps a neat house. I know some messy ladies whose mothers must have been frightened by garbage trucks when they were pregnant. But even in those cases, there is often a female concern for the house and what is in it.

Like Ralph Reed, Dobson claims to believe in pluralism. "Our vision," he has written, "is for a just and righteous society that protects religious liberties for people of all faiths. We believe in the concept of pluralism, which acknowledges the widely differing values and beliefs among our citizens." Yet Dobson is more convincing when, in the familiar tradition of American legalistic Christianity, he is using military imagery. The difference is that instead of seeming to glory (as Robertson and others do) in the *Sturm und Drang* of battle and in the destruction of the foe, Dobson concentrates on the valor and self-discipline of the warrior hero. "How long has it been," he writes,

since we've thought of ourselves as highly disciplined soldiers in the army of
the Lord? That was a familiar theme in years past. "Onward Christian
Soldiers" was one of the favorite songs of the church. Christians, it
proclaimed, were "marching as to war, with the cross of Jesus going on
before." We also sang, "Stand up! Stand up for Jesus, ye soldiers of the
cross." Then there was "Dare to be a Daniel, dare to stand alone. Dare to
have a purpose firm, dare to make it known." That was the way Christians
saw their responsibility in days past. Well, we've come a long way, baby.

Dobson may calculatedly not emphasize the idea of the foe (perhaps because he feels that violent language would turn off his female readership), but his attraction to war imagery is still offensive, for a foe is certainly implied. And we know who the foe is: anyone who violates the idealized image of the family that Dobson and his admirers cherish.

Every now and then, to be sure, a sentence or two in a Focus on the Family publication will surprise. A 1997 *Focus on the Family* article called "When HIV Hits Home" quoted an HIV-positive man who said that his church had "turned its back" on him after his diagnosis and that "the only ones who reached out were those in the gay community"; another HIV-positive man quoted in the article described the heartlessness of a pastor and a "Christian doctor" who had rejected him. The article concluded with one interviewee's hope that "fear and judgment" in churches would be replaced by compassion. One has the impression that in Focus on the Family there are at least some people who may, after Dobson's retirement or death, seek to turn it into an organization that helps families live with integrity in the real world of the present rather than feed them false images of the past and unrealistic dreams of the future.

For two decades, legalistic Christian women have had "Dr. Dobson" to turn to with their problems. Now legalistic men have "Coach McCartney." In 1990 Bill McCartney, who until 1994 was the head football coach at the University of Colorado, came up with the idea of establishing a men's Christian movement. With the help of his connections in the legalistic Christian community—including Dobson—

McCartney founded Promise Keepers and installed as its president a man named Randy Phillips, who, like the coach, was an ex-Catholic who had converted to a charismatic denomination called the Vineyard Fellowship. Together these men came up with the "Seven Promises of a Promise Keeper." The promises are these: to honor Jesus Christ; to pursue "vital relationships with a few other men" (because a man "needs brothers to help him keep his promises"); to maintain moral and physical purity; to build "strong marriages and families through love, protection and biblical values"; to support one's church and pastor; to reach "beyond any racial and denominational barriers to demonstrate the power of biblical unity"; and to live out the Great Commandment and the Great Commission. The movement's basic text, *Seven Promises of a Promise Keeper,* contains essays by Dobson, McCartney, Phillips, Campus Crusade for Christ founder Bill Bright, and others, and was published in 1994 by Focus on the Family Press.

In 1991, Promise Keepers held its first rally in the football stadium at the University of Colorado. Featuring addresses by several evangelists and closing with a pep talk by McCartney, it drew 4,200 men; similar events at the same site in 1992 and 1993 drew 22,000 and 53,000 men respectively. In 1994, Promise Keepers went national, holding seven rallies with a total attendance figure of 280,000. The next year, 750,000 men attended thirteen rallies; in 1996, over a million men packed twenty-two stadiums from Seattle to Jacksonville. Included in the 1996 total was a "conference" in Atlanta's Georgia Dome that drew 39,000 pastors and that probably represented the largest assemblage of clergy in world history.

The Promise Keepers movement has taken many observers by surprise. Why do so many men—mostly white, middle-aged, and middle-class—attend these rallies? "Many men come to Promise Keepers feeling despair about their lives—their inability to communicate with their wives and children, their suburban rootlessness, their emotional aridity, their professional immobility," notes Michael Joseph Gross, a journalist and former theology student. "Midway on life's journey (the average Promise Keeper is 38), they come to the stadiums searching for new ways to make their lives make sense." In a 1996 *Village Voice* article about Promise Keepers' first rally in New York City,

James Hannahan described the oratory of one speaker, the evangelist Luis Palau, as having been "designed to pierce straight guys in the Achilles heel—their relationship with their fathers." Indeed, the Promise Keepers Web site contains an essay entitled "Man to Man about Being a Son of God" that explains Christian faith as a father-son thing. The essay begins by noting that "a man's relationship with his father is basic," and that the first such relationship on earth was bungled when Adam "willingly joined his wife in doubting their Father's word and ignoring his instructions." As a consequence, Adam and Eve were "expelled from God's presence."

The essay goes on to describe Adam's post-Eden life in terms designed to make it meaningful to the average middle-American man. Adam "failed his wife. . . . [he] lost his job and was kicked off the family farm. He found some temporary jobs until he could get back with his Father. But this work was cursed from the start and resulted in pain and difficulty. His family relationships went from bad to worse. One of his sons even killed another!" From Adam, accordingly, "we have inherited a diseased spiritual DNA" that has brought sin and problems into our lives. In order to turn things around, we need "the bonds of communion with our Father that all of us are meant to have." How can these bonds be restored? Through Jesus, of course. "Pray this prayer to accept or reaffirm your acceptance of Christ: 'Father, I've come home. Please make me your son. I turn from my sin. . . . Let today be the beginning of my new journey as your son and a member of your family. You have always kept your promises. Help me to keep my promises, too. In Jesus' name. Amen.'" It is not difficult to imagine millions of middle-class American men—men with dead-end jobs, tired marriages, and no sense of what to do or where to go—responding emotionally to such charged rhetoric, which taps into their feelings about their own fathers and uses these feelings to win their commitment to Christ.

The mainstream media were slow to pick up on the importance of Promise Keepers. When they did, they focused almost exclusively on three sociopolitical aspects of the movement, one of which was seen as positive—its emphasis on overcoming racial divisions—and two as negative: the group's attitudes toward gays and women. As to the gay issue, McCartney (a prominent supporter of the 1992 antigay amendment to Colorado's constitution) has made antagonism toward homosexuality a hallmark of the movement and has allowed so-called "ex-gay ministries" to proselytize at his rallies; as to the issue of women, Promise Keepers, which doesn't allow women to attend its rallies, feeds men the standard legalistic Protestant line that God wants the husband to be the family boss. In *Seven Promises of a Promise Keeper,* Tony Evans writes that a husband who wishes "to be a spiritually pure man" should begin as follows. "Sit down with your wife and say something like this: 'Honey, I've made a terrible mistake. I've given you my role. I gave up leading this family, and I forced you to take my place. Now I must reclaim that role.'" Evans goes on, "Don't misunderstand what I'm saying here. I'm not suggesting that you ask for your role back. I'm urging you to *take it back.* If you simply ask for it, your wife is likely to say, 'Look, for the last ten years, I've had to raise these kids, look after the house, and pay the bills. I've had to get a job and still keep up my duties at home. I've had to do my job *and* yours. You think I'm just going to turn everything back over to you?'" Evans says, "Your wife's concerns may be justified. Unfortunately, however, there can be no compromise here. If you're going to lead, you must lead. Be sensitive. Listen. Treat the lady gently and lovingly. But *lead!*"

Like many megachurches, Promise Keepers presents itself as nondenominational, ecumenical, and unencumbered by exclusionary doctrines; in theory, it welcomes all Christian men—Catholics included—regardless of the official doctrines of the churches they belong to. Yet Promise Keepers is in fact a strongly legalistic movement. To decree that a "spiritually pure" man must assert his authority as head of his family, after all, is to insist on a legalistic Protestant conception of family structure that, like Dobson's teachings on the family, is radically at odds with mainline Protestant thinking as well as with Saint Paul's statement that in Christ there is no male or female. In Christ as reimagined by Focus on the Family and Promise Keepers, the difference between male and female is of primary importance. Promise Keepers also teaches biblical inerrancy; like Focus on the Family, it represents its understanding of marriage as being based, in part, on the experiences of Adam and Eve, which it purports to regard as historical.

Coach McCartney has often tried to soften the sound of Evans's directive about the husband's authority. "For the guy to be the leader," McCartney has said, "means he out-serves his wife." But this remark only draws attention to another problem with Promise Keepers: its appeal to male competitiveness. At a Promise Keepers rally in Portland, Oregon, according to one observer, a group of men began to chant, "We love Jesus, how 'bout you?" More men joined in, and soon men on the opposite side of the stadium were shouting back. Plainly, it had become a competition to see which side could shout the loudest. This sort of competitiveness would appear to be ubiquitous. "Promise Keepers," comments Michael Gross, "replaces a secular pathology of achievement with a spiritual one. Conversion is an achievement and devotion is competitive, in a faith uniquely suited to men who grew from Little League into Regional Sales. The very name—Promise Keeper—defines a man by what he does. There is no time for a man to be held by God, to rest in God, to imagine that God delights in him for anything that he is. There is, in short, no time for grace." Promise Keepers, adds Gross, "work furiously to prove themselves. From the day they are re-born, they are told they can do better."

Like Focus on the Family, Promise Keepers identifies Christianity with "the family" and right-wing politics. At the organization's rallies, men can find literature advocating, among much else, the teaching of creationism and the prohibition of nontraditional families. Liberals have raised concerns about the political motives of Promise Keepers' founders. Hannahan writes that "the goal of PK seems clear: By pandering to religious people of color, while maintaining a pretense of nonpartisanship, they're beginning the process of winning over the souls—and votes—of black folk, many of whom are culturally conservative but vote Democrat because they perceive Republicans as racist. Smart plan." Michael Gross points out that Wellington Boone, a black minister in the Promise Keepers leadership, "does not seriously challenge white people to notice, let alone rectify, the injustices they benefit from."

Promise Keepers also identifies Christianity with manliness. It is not the first movement to attempt to draw men to Christianity in this way. The Christian Socialist movement in mid-nineteenth-century England, a forerunner of Rauschenbusch's Social Gospel, was popularly known as Muscular Christianity; one of its founders, Thomas Hughes, wrote a book entitled *The Manliness of Christ*. Billy Sunday, the early-twentieth-century American evangelist, was a former baseball player who preached a gospel containing heavy doses of machismo and patriotism. "The manliest man," he exhorted, "is the man who will acknowledge Jesus Christ." It is true that many American men need to deepen their relationships with other men. But is such deepening really going on under the auspices of Promise Keepers? Like Focus on the Family, the movement identifies Christianity with prefeminist conceptions about the family and sex roles; as a rule, the men who are drawn to Promise Keepers bring those conceptions with them, and also bring notions of manliness gleaned from a lifetime of observing athletes. Instead of challenging those conceptions, Promise Keepers reinforces them; instead of helping men to grow beyond the macho concept of being a "real man," the organization sells T-shirts that read "Real men love Jesus." The leaders of Promise Keepers recognize that millions of men need to be reminded that in Christ there is no black and white; what they have failed to see is that most of those men must also learn that in Christ there is also no male and female. Instead of being taught to identify love with assertion of authority over women, those men must learn some humility and respect for women. And they must learn that the notion of God as male, on which the entire emotional structure of Promise Keepers is based, is only a metaphor—that God is neither man nor woman, and that all human beings, male and female, are equally precious to him.

Not surprisingly, given its endorsement of traditional concepts of masculinity, Promise Keepers is big on military rhetoric. Indeed, some of the organization's literature and speakers would seem to imply that it plans to develop into a paramilitary movement. Promise Keepers issues "calls to arms"; McCartney has preached about "spiritual warfare"; at the Atlanta rally, he announced that "the fiercest fighting is just ahead. . . . Let's proceed. It's wartime!" Kenneth Clatterbaugh, a professor of philosophy at the University of Wisconsin, observes that Promise Keepers shares with other groups spawned by the men's movement the idea "that men are best able to help men become men and that warrior men are what we need." An article in *The Nation* noted that McCartney "has referred to the clergy as 'the commissioned officers' of his movement" and that "the Atlanta clergy conference

included a special meeting to organize military chaplains." Another
Promise Keepers director, James Ryle, describes the organization as an
"army of God" that, according to the *Nation* reporters, he regards "as
the fulfillment of the Bible's prophecy of a great force that will destroy
sinners and infidels in the period preceding Armageddon." "Never have
300,000 men come together throughout human history," says Ryle,
"except for the purposes of war.'"

Yet just as many Baptists find the SBC insufficiently fundamentalist, so many legalistic Christians are alarmed by Promise Keepers
because it's not legalistic enough. On a fundamentalist Web site, a
writer complains about a Promise Keepers book called *The Masculine
Journey* in which one Robert Hicks writes that when he met "Christians who were homosexuals and Marxists," he "listened, tried to
understand, debated back and forth, but was left with the conviction
that they were sincere about both their faith in Christ and their views
on sexuality and politics, though those views differed from mine."
Hicks adds that he learned a great deal from a Catholic priest who told
him that

> *The way to look at God or the world is not necessarily through the lens or
> categories I currently believe are the correct ones. The labels don't matter all
> that much. . . . I think I now see the world and people differently because I
> try to look beyond the labels to the person, his unique situation, station,
> and needs. I fail often and get hooked back into my old warrior responses,
> but now I consciously recognize that pattern for what it is, I believe this is
> the way Jesus related to people, and His modeling provides me with a much
> richer and broader perspective on ministry.*

In a 1995 open letter to McCartney, a pastor named Bill Randles
complains that Promise Keepers is insufficiently devoted to "truth"—
a legalistic way of saying that it's not doctrinally stringent enough. "If
a Mormon keeps all seven of your promises," writes Randles, "that
could well make him a moral person, but that moral Mormon will go
right to Hell." Why? "Because he doesn't believe the testimony God
gave of His Son." Promise Keepers, Randles complains, is too inclusive. "Catholics, Mormons and even homosexuals are encouraged to
be 'included and welcomed in all our events.'" Randles's comment:

"When the true God-ordained organization, the Church, upholds the Word of God, it divides people either onto the broad way that leads to destruction or the narrow way that leads to life." That's legalistic Protestantism in a nutshell. For legalists, any proposed approach to salvation is suspect precisely to the degree that it is inclusive, and the door to heaven is precious in exact proportion to its narrowness.

14

"THESE SECULAR TIMES"

UNTIL VERY RECENTLY, the mainstream media have paid insufficient attention to the phenomenal growth of legalistic Protestantism in America. Secular Americans are more likely to dismiss Pat Robertson as vulgar and perhaps weirdly amusing than to find him and his movement truly dangerous. When things do happen—as in Waco and Rancho Santa Fe—that underscore the dangers inherent in legalism, the media back off from drawing connections between the beliefs and practices of so-called cults and those of legalistic Protestantism in general. Yet those cults, which are routinely characterized as extremist aberrations, are in fact absolutely at one with the rest of legalistic America in their apocalyptic obsessions, their violent End Times scenarios, and their implicit view of the unsaved as being less

than completely human. Far from violating the letter and spirit of contemporary legalistic Protestantism, the cults, militias, survivalists, and
so-called Christian Identity groups have taken standard legalistic beliefs
to their natural conclusion. (Remarkably, as I write this—on March 11,
1997—an anchor on MSNBC is announcing a breaking news story
from Detroit, where "a man reciting the Lord's Prayer" walked into a
bank and started shooting.) As long as millions of American children
continue to be brought up to view the world through legalistic eyes,
no one should be surprised at the proliferation of communities that do
not know the difference between religion and terrorism.

Or, for that matter, between salvation and self-slaughter. In the wake
of the astonishing mass suicide of the Heaven's Gate cult in March
1997, observers sought ways to distinguish the beliefs of Marshall
Applewhite and his followers from those of "mainstream" religion—
meaning not just mainline churches but such widely professed faiths as
Mormonism and Adventism. Some argued, for example, that "mainstream" religions have ancient roots while Heaven's Gate was the brain-
child of one disturbed individual; yet the Mormon and Adventist
churches, among many others, were themselves cults only a century
ago, and their founders were routinely dismissed by their contemporaries as cranks. Commentators have ridiculed Heaven's Gate because
its theology included space-age elements that seemingly owed less to
the Bible than to *Star Trek;* David Gelerntner sneered in the *New York
Times* that "their souls needed religion but their minds were stocked
only with Hollywood junk." Yet Hal Lindsey's vision of the End
Times, to which millions subscribe, also owes a great deal to modern
American pop culture, just as the theologies of Mormonism, Adventism, Christian Science, and other nineteenth-century cults that are
now "mainstream" reflect many of the popular preoccupations of the
times and places in which they were founded.

In point of fact, it's impossible to draw a clear line between Heaven's
Gate and legalistic Protestantism. The parallels, indeed, are striking. A
conviction that the world is corrupt beyond redemption; a commitment to live apart from the world under the tight control of a leader
who sets strict rules that enforce conformity; a belief that a few (those
who do and believe the right things) will be saved and most will not;
a detailed vision of impending apocalypse, preceding which the few

will be raised up from earth to safety; an assertion of absolute certitude about life, death, and the universe—all these attributes are common to both dispensationalism and Heaven's Gate.

Both theologies draw heavily on the Book of Revelation. The two "witnesses" in the Book of Revelation, who figure importantly in dispensationalist dogma, were identified by the cult with Applewhite and his late co-leader. The assurance, expressed by one member in the cult's valedictory videotape, that the cult was in possession of "the real facts, the real truth" mirrors fundamentalists' fixation on "real truth" and their insistence that they, and no one else, possess that truth.

Finally, and importantly, both Protestant fundamentalism and Heaven's Gate involve a powerful loathing of sex and a denial of sexual identity. In his young manhood Applewhite, son of an evangelical Presbyterian minister, had homosexual relationships and sought a "cure" for his homosexuality. Well, he finally found a cure: suicide. And he took over three dozen people with him. Would the Heaven's Gate cult, with its enforced suppression of sexuality—to the point, in some cases, of castration—ever have existed but for the self-loathing that a conservative evangelical upbringing brought about in the young Applewhite? I doubt it.

Yes, there are differences between contemporary Protestant fundamentalism and Heaven's Gate. Most of those differences, however, cut in the cult's favor: By all reports, the cultists were kind and gentle; they didn't seek political power in order to deny the rights of others; and they didn't hurt anyone but themselves.

If anything should amaze us, it is not that events like the mass suicide at Rancho Santa Fe take place, but that more legalistic Christians have not chosen to act out in conspicuous and sensational ways the loathing of this world, the disgust with the human body, and the capacity for violence at the heart of their faith. On this score, Americans have been luckier than people in some other countries. During the same period that has seen the rise of legalistic Christianity in America, growing numbers of societies in the Moslem world—which, not long ago, had seemed to many Western observers to be irreversibly set on a track of social and cultural modernization—have fallen under the sway of militant Islamic fundamentalism. The rise to power of Islamic fundamentalists in Iran was followed by similar takeovers in Sudan,

Algeria, and elsewhere. In Egypt, the struggle to protect democracy against the growing threat of Islamic fundamentalism has become the major preoccupation of that country's government. In Turkey, the 1996 election victory of a conservative Islamic party was followed by apparent government efforts to desecularize the nation, which since the 1920s had been an officially religion-neutral state. And the takeover of Afghanistan in late September 1996 by fundamentalist militiamen plunged that nation's capital into what the *New York Times* called a "medieval labyrinth"; in the four days after the fall of Kabul, the nation's new rulers—members of a movement that originated in religious schools—closed movie theaters, shut down the country's sole television station, and forbade all music. Male government employees were told to grow beards and leave Western-style suits at home; women were ordered to wear traditional garb in public. Though no one would deny the huge differences between American and Afghan society, the takeover provided a terrifying illustration of what can happen when legalistic religion moves from theory to practice. (To be sure, Islamic fundamentalism does not seem fated beyond question to triumph: In a May 1997 election, Iranians surprised the world by rejecting the fundamentalist candidate for president in favor of a "moderate"; a month later Turkey's military forced the resignation of that country's pro-Islamic premier.)

Elsewhere around the world, other fundamentalists have also raised threats to democratic pluralism. Consider the results of 1996 elections in various countries. In Israel, the number of Knesset seats held by strongly anti-Arab Orthodox Jewish parties rose from 16 to 24 out of a total of 120. In Russia, the nationalists, who appeal not only to Russian pride and patriotism but to anti-Semitism and to many people's historic identification with the Russian Orthodox Church, almost managed to bring down Boris Yeltsin's democratic government. And in India, a Hindu nationalist party which in 1984 had held only 2 seats in the Parliament won 186 seats, more than any other party, largely on the strength of its anti-Moslem rhetoric. Like all fundamentalisms, the ones in these foreign countries are defined largely by whom and what they are against.

Just as respected right-wing American intellectuals have defended legalistic Protestantism, moreover, so they have also—incredibly—

stood up for fundamentalist Moslems and against "moral relativism." In a 1995 item about the UN Conference on Women in Beijing, *American Enterprise* condemned "a group of Western lesbian feminists" who protested at that conference as "forces of cultural decadence" while claiming to find it "heartening" that fundamentalist Moslems were uniting with legalistic Christians to stand up for "wholesomeness and sanity." Among the manifestations of "wholesomeness and sanity" for which Islamic fundamentalists have been responsible in recent years are the execution of adulterers and homosexuals, the total subjugation of women, and the crushing of democratic institutions, religious freedom, and civil rights generally. That respected institutions of the American Right can describe this as "wholesomeness and sanity" only underscores the need for the rest of us to know the real truth about legalistic religion both at home and abroad (for *American Enterprise* and its ideological bedfellows have done a splendid job of whitewashing both) and to oppose potentially totalitarian phenomena wherever they may be found and however they may represent themselves.

During a relatively brief period in the 1970s, gay rights made huge strides in American society. Then the organized Religious Right established itself as a force of resistance against the nascent movement, and nothing has been the same since. In the years that followed, Americans grew accustomed to the spectacle of legalistic Christians railing against homosexuality. Because those legalists did such an effective job of misrepresenting the nature of sexual orientation, many Americans who might have come to understand and accept homosexuality instead came to fear and hate it. As a result, homosexuality became a controversial issue, and the whole nation argued—and continues to argue—about whether homosexuality is a danger to society. The mainstream media have covered this debate, giving all points of view full coverage, thereby lending credence to the idea that antigay animus has intellectual legitimacy.

Yet in all these years the mainstream media, which legalistic Christians routinely smear as liberal and anti-Christian, have almost entirely refused to treat legalistic Christianity in the same way they do homosexuality—as an issue with two sides. In recent years, legalistic Christians have argued fiercely against allowing gay couples to raise children. It would be interesting to see a study comparing the children of gay couples with the children of legalistic Christians, showing which are more well-adjusted socially and more successful academically or professionally. Independent investigations of these two groups suggest what the results of such a comparative study might be: Children raised by gay parents have been shown to suffer no ill effects therefrom and to do at least as well in all respects as other children; meanwhile, sociological studies and voluminous anecdotal evidence suggest that children raised in legalistic Christian families tend to suffer to an unusual degree from severe alienation, emotional and sexual abuse, drug problems, and compulsive sexual behavior. Yet this has never been treated as an issue in the mainstream media.

While people in the media routinely soft-pedal criticism of legalistic Christianity, however, former legalistic Christians are less hesitant to call a spade a spade. An interviewee in *Growing Up Fundamentalist* describes legalism as "fake Christianity . . . a distortion of the gospel." Secular defenders of legalistic Protestantism—prominent among whom are many neoconservative Jewish intellectuals—admire it because they believe that it helps preserve social stability and civilized values. On the contrary, legalistic Protestantism encourages a host of socially negative traits: selfishness, self-righteousness, ignorance, bigotry, intolerance, and antagonism to education and social concern and high culture.

Why haven't the mainstream media, then, viewed all of this as a legitimate issue? Probably because they don't dare to do anything that makes them look as though they're attacking religion. Legalistic Protestants know this and have shamelessly used Jesus as a front man for their prejudices. If these people assailed in their own names the individuals and groups whom they despise, fear, and resent, and the ideas and social developments that they find strange and threatening, they would not receive much of a hearing—and would be laying themselves open to full-scale criticism. But to make attacks in the name of Jesus changes the equation entirely. The simple word *religion* lends dignity to prejudice, muffles opposition, and obliges the media to tread carefully. Not only politicians but journalists, too, are less likely to criticize frankly the attitudes of individuals or groups when they identify themselves as Christian and attribute their attitudes to their faith.

This is not to deny that the media cover major Religious Right figures when they do and say things that cause offense. When the televangelist Oral Roberts told his viewers that God had revealed plans to bring him home to heaven by a certain date if they didn't contribute a certain amount of money to his ministry, the media gave the story ample coverage. When SBC president Bailey Smith declared that God does not hear the prayers of Jews, he made headlines around the country. Yet the newspapers, newsmagazines, and network news divisions generally didn't follow up on the implications of these events. Such stories tend to be treated as isolated embarrassments, not as symptoms of sensibilities and theologies that merit closer inspection. In recent years, with the Christian Coalition's rise to power, the media have paid increasing attention to legalistic Christianity. But they focus almost exclusively on the movement's political manifestations rather than on its underlying mind-set. The few prominent exceptions to this rule—the names of television commentator Bill Moyers and *New York Times* columnist Frank Rich come most readily to mind—stand out all the more for their efforts to shed light on the reality of legalistic Christianity.

Indeed, despite such admirable exceptions, and despite claims by Robertson, Reed, and others of media bias against them, the mainstream media have almost invariably handled legalistic Christians with kid gloves. The questions that reporters ask people like Cardinal O'Connor and Pat Robertson are rarely as tough as those they ask of politicians; yet these men are not only religious leaders but political leaders who head up organizations with explicit political agendas. Reporters and commentators are disinclined to address the outrageous contradictions between traditional Christian precepts and the words and actions of people like O'Connor and Robertson. Some media people don't want to offend the religious members of their audience; others just don't take either religion or legalistic Christians seriously enough to subject a man like Robertson to the sustained analytical attention that they would bring to a report on any politically active tycoon—and that is necessary to make the public at large sit up and take notice.

In a demonstration of frankness about legalistic Christianity that is rare in the 1990s, a *New York Times* article quoted a British Christian lecturer as saying that "the assumptions of fundamentalism are so preposterous, alike in theory and practice, I am not altogether surprised when I call to mind my experiences in America twenty-five years ago. It was pitifully manifest then that both the science and theology of many of those who posed as authorities were half a century behind the times. But one would have hoped the intervening years would have opened their eyes." That article, and that quotation, appeared in the *Times* on July 11, 1925, in an article headlined "Europe Is Amazed by the Scopes Trial." The difference between 1925 and the late 1990s is that New York newspaper editors and reporters in those days were mostly modernist Christians who felt no qualms about publishing honest critical commentary on fundamentalism; as Christians, they took their faith seriously and recognized fundamentalism as a threat to its essentials. Today the powers that be at publications like the *Times* tend to be secular people who, fearful that they might be branded as anti-Christian, hesitate to criticize anything that goes by the name of religion in anything but muted terms.

When Michael Lind published an exposé of Pat Robertson's anti-Semitism in a 1995 issue of the *New York Review of Books,* the only remarkable thing was that no one had done it earlier. Lind's article created a sensation in the political and intellectual community and throughout the mainstream media. What had Lind done? Simply this: He had read Robertson's books. They had been best-sellers, had been read (or at least purchased) by plenty of ordinary Americans on the Religious Right—but apparently no major media or political or intellectual figure had bothered to read them. None of these people, apparently, was sufficiently interested in seeing what was on the mind of the paramount leader of the most powerful single constituency in American politics today.

In the same way, programs like *60 Minutes, PrimeTime Live,* and *Dateline NBC* investigate all kinds of corporate scams and small-scale con artists, but a phenomenon as widespread, as politically influential, and as socially destructive as legalistic Christianity goes scandalously unexamined. Consider the *60 Minutes* episode broadcast on Easter Sunday 1996, which featured a segment on the Mormons. Given the series' history of vigorous investigative reporting and exposés, and given the fact that the Mormon Church had recently been engaged in strenuous efforts to kill gay-straight high-school student clubs in Utah and same-sex marriage in Hawaii, one might have expected the segment to touch on these stories. Certainly one assumed that some reference would be made to the church's notoriously brutal intolerance for non-conformity and dissent, its long-standing policy of suppressing the truth about its own dubious origins, and perhaps even the fact that of all major American religious institutions, the Mormon Church is the single most difficult one to grow up in if you're gay. Yet none of these things was mentioned. The segment was a total puff piece, celebrating the wealth, vibrancy, and expansion of the Mormon Church, now the seventh-largest religious body in the United States and one of the fastest-growing churches in the world.

To be sure, some attention was paid to peculiar Mormon traditions such as the wearing of "sacred undergarments," which supposedly protect one from harm. And Mike Wallace did (respectfully) ask Gordon Hinckley, the head of the church, about the fact that blacks had only recently been allowed to become priests. "That's behind us," Hinckley replied affably. "Don't look at these little fits of history." Wallace seemed happy to oblige. Throughout the segment, the two men's interaction was utterly congenial. The story concluded with an exchange about life after death: In a ringing tone of assurance, Hinckley mentioned his "hope of heaven"; Wallace replied haltingly that "I haven't been able to persuade myself" as to heaven's reality; Hinckley rejoined amiably, "Then you haven't thought about it long enough." Both men laughed, as did the several others (all men) who were present. Such is the mainstream media's view of the religious state of the nation: Either you're a secular overclass atheist, like Wallace, or you believe in sacred undergarments. It was dismaying that *60 Minutes,* which week after week intrepidly discloses the petty crimes of small-town merchants, was unwilling to do anything short of a stunningly laudatory profile of the huge, powerful Mormon Church—which, in my view, merits far more serious attention from national TV journalists than does some neighborhood realtor or muffler shop.

Behind the scenes, of course, many people in the media will acknowledge that they recognize what a danger legalistic Christianity represents. But on-screen and on the printed page, they pretend to believe that religion, except when it takes the form of David Koresh–type cults, is an unqualifiedly positive force in American life. They

refuse to acknowledge the extent to which the so-called Christian values touted by Religious Right leaders are not Christian at all, and to
which the agendas of such groups as the Christian Coalition are based
not on the gospel but on their members' own prejudices and antago-
nisms. To be sure, there is often a tone of condescension in the media
toward legalistic Christians; but at the same time there is a tacit implication that, good or bad, this is authentic religion and that nonlegalistic faiths and believers are just watered-down versions of the real thing.
In taking such positions, the media have performed a criminal disser-
vice to America—and to real Christianity.

One evening in the fall of 1996 I was at a friend's book party at a New
York bookstore when I ran into a longtime acquaintance, a brilliant
critic who told me about the biography she had recently finished writing. She wanted to know what I thought about the fact that her editor, a devout Roman Catholic, had cut from her manuscript a reference
to "these secular times." "These aren't secular times," he had told her
bluntly. She had been surprised. What, she asked, did I think?

I told her that I agreed with her editor. The great majority of Americans, I said, believe in God. Most go to church. In fact the percentage of churchgoing Americans was probably higher now than ever. She
nodded; this information was hardly new to her and she didn't dispute
it. Yet she, a secular Jew who lived in New York City, still seemed puzzled. She knew all these things were true, and yet somehow she
couldn't accept that these were *not* secular times.

It was not difficult to understand why. We were having this conversation in a high-toned Madison Avenue bookstore. We were surrounded by shelves full of novels, histories, literary biographies, music
criticism, and expensive coffee-table books full of travel photographs
and art reproductions. If there was a single Bible there, or any other
religious book, I didn't see it. Indeed, few places could have felt more
removed from the world of legalistic Christianity—and more representative of the intensely secular corner of the world in which both
the critic and I live.

It is, indeed, the same intensely secular corner of the world in which
most of the nation's public intellectuals and influential media figures

live. Few of these people are religious. Few are even close to people
who are religious. Yes, they know that most middle Americans are
churchgoers—but in some sense, they can't quite think of those middle Americans as being real, and can't take those people's religious
beliefs seriously. Most of these intellectuals and media figures have had
years of education at the best schools; most have social and professional
lives that include some of the smartest people of our time; most enjoy
a steady diet of the *New York Times,* the *Wall Street Journal,* and sundry
intellectual journals. Yet few have ever attended a service at a legalistic Protestant church or spoken for five minutes with a fundamentalist; few have ever glanced at a book by Dobson or Robertson. As a
result, these people's picture of America is a highly distorted one.

Confront these educated urbanites with the fact of this distortion,
moreover, and most of them will not be pleased. Truth to tell, they
find comfort in the notion that these are "secular times." It makes them
uneasy to think that millions of their fellow citizens believe that the
Bible is inerrant and that Satan is a living being; they may also feel
unsettled, frankly, by the very idea of the "dimension of depth."

I've mentioned the play *Inherit the Wind,* and its role in establishing
misapprehensions about legalistic Christianity. I might add that the play
has been understood by many secular readers as implying that religion
in general is a thing of the past. Even some of us who grew up in
mainstream Protestant churches got accustomed early on to hearing
teachers and other authority figures speak matter-of-factly about the
contemporary era as "postreligious" or "post-Christian." Why do so
many people speak this way? Either they genuinely don't know that
most Americans nowadays are churchgoers, or they somehow simply
can't take churchgoers seriously, can't think of them as people who
really matter. In March 1995, I was invited by a humanities foundation
to participate in a private roundtable discussion in New York City
about the future of American culture. Most of the other participants
were upper-middle-class Ivy League graduates. During the meeting, a
professor of medieval literature mentioned that the church remains an
important social institution. A young stockbroker shook his head.
"Who goes to church?" he asked. "Nobody. Maybe one percent of the
population." Did he really mean one percent of the population? Or
only one percent of the sort of people he knows and socializes with—

the people that "matter"? In any case, the reactions of the others at the meeting made it clear that they shared the stockbroker's view. Such is the level of knowledge about religion in America today on the part of many powerfully placed secular Americans.

This attitude toward religion is routinely reflected in the writings of the secular liberal intellectuals who shape public debate on social and cultural issues. Consider Andrew Delbanco's 1995 book *The Death of Satan: How Americans Have Lost the Sense of Evil.* The title itself is remarkable, given that millions of Americans think of themselves as literally being accompanied by angels and stalked by demons. "When American culture began," writes Delbanco, a humanities professor at Columbia University, "this devil was an incandescent presence in most people's lives. . . . But by 1700 he was already losing his grip on the imagination—a process that has continued ever since and that has left us, in the words of the psychologist Henry Murray, with a Satan who is 'no more than a vestigial image.'" Later in his book Delbanco reiterates the point: "Few people still believe in what the British writer Ian McEwan has recently called 'a malign principle, a force in human affairs that periodically advances to dominate and destroy the lives of individuals or nations, then retreats to await the next occasion.'"

On the contrary, as we have seen, tens of millions of Americans do indeed believe in such a force. They are haunted by it. They call it Satan. In America today, Satan is constantly on the minds of more people than in any place at any time in history. When Delbanco describes contemporary Americans as being reluctant to speak of evil or to label people as evil, he could not be more mistaken. If he presented his book as a study of secular America, or of the small intellectual class to which he belongs, his observations would be correct and, in fact, highly perceptive. But he doesn't present the book in this way; his subtitle refers to "Americans," not American elites or the secular American overclass. It is as if America's tens of millions of legalistic Christians simply didn't exist. Delbanco quotes from scores of contemporary academic and literary works in an attempt to convey how today's writers treat the subject of evil, but he doesn't mention Hal Lindsey or Pat Robertson or Frank Peretti, each of whom has influenced popular conceptions of evil far more than all the writers Delbanco cites put together.

I do not mean to single out Delbanco, an exceedingly intelligent and gifted writer, for criticism; on the contrary, I offer him as an example of how liberal intellectuals of the first rank routinely leave legalistic Christians out of their picture of America, quite without realizing that they are doing so. Another example of this habit of mind is provided by the *New York Times* writer Richard Bernstein, who notes in his book *Fragile Glory* that "Like most children of the 1960s, I had read Camus and Gide, Sartre and Malraux, not to mention Hemingway and Fitzgerald." Of course, most American "children of the 1960s" never heard of most of these writers. Bernstein would doubtless explain that he was referring to the young people he grew up with, who attended Ivy League schools and went on to careers in government, media, higher education, or corporate boardrooms. This habit of mind has caused both the academy and the mainstream media, during the last generation, to offer an increasingly skewed picture of America, one in which there is no place for legalistic Christians except perhaps as a question mark somewhere near the edge.

Owing to this ingrained blindness to legalistic America, nonlegalistic Christians and secular liberals at the highest levels of our serious mainstream culture are *always* being shocked—not only by the rise of the Moral Majority and then the Christian Coalition, but also by the popularity of Ronald Reagan (whose chances to win the presidency many secular and nonlegalistic Americans saw as nil) and by the sudden meteoric rise of Promise Keepers.

If many liberal intellectuals have routinely omitted legalistic Christians from their picture of American life, their right-wing counterparts have in recent years been engaged in a bizarre strategic alliance with those same Christians. Among the things that make it bizarre is that many of the most prominent right-wing intellectuals are urban secular Jewish neoconservatives with strong backgrounds in the arts and culture, while legalistic Christians tend to be anti-intellectual, anti-Semitic philistines who live in suburbs or rural areas and whose End Times theology happily looks forward to the conversion of some Jews and the eternal torture of the others. In spite of all these differences, Jewish neocons have supported legalistic Christianity for pragmatic reasons: They feel that political rights and social entitlements are expanding beyond reason, that culture (both high and popular) is being marred by liberal politicization, and that legalistic Christians are a necessary ally in resisting these trends.

In order to keep this alliance harmonious, Jewish neocons have even gone so far as to echo legalistic Christians' rhetoric to the effect that America is a "Christian nation" and their calls for laws and Constitutional amendments that would secure that identity. In a 1995 *Wall Street Journal* article defending "the Christian conservative movement," for instance, Irving Kristol, editor of *The Public Interest* and publisher of *The National Interest,* recalled how his son, the conservative-movement leader William Kristol, attended a Calvinist private school that had compulsory chapel. "The fairly large numbers of Jewish students simply went through the motions," wrote the elder Kristol, "understanding that a certain courtesy was owed the Christian majority of this country." Kristol implied that compulsory prayer in public schools would not be so bad, either. But no thoughtful person who takes religion seriously would want to be on either side of the kind of situation Kristol describes. What conscientious Jewish student would say prayers he didn't believe in? What Christian who took his or her prayers seriously would want to be surrounded at a prayer service by nonbelievers who were only pretending? This is a scenario designed to appeal to legalistic Christian sensibilities—for it's all about appearances, not about genuine religious belief and spiritual experience. It is a shared fondness for such appearances—those that reflect order, discipline, and "traditional values"—that has bound legalistic Christians and Jewish neocons in unholy alliance.

In late 1996, to be sure, there were some signs of serious rupture in this *entente.* When the magazine *First Things,* edited by the traditionalist Roman Catholic priest Richard John Neuhaus, published a symposium whose legalistic Protestant and Catholic participants suggested that the U.S. government had forfeited its legitimacy by supporting "un-Christian" policies, some neocons reacted with alarm. The historian Gertrude Himmelfarb, who is married to Irving Kristol, warned that such rhetoric on the part of conservatives would make them look "extremist"; the polemicist Midge Decter cautioned against the danger of "strengthening the devil's hand" through "reckless" rhetoric. These and other neocons seemed not to understand anything about the people they were dealing with. Himmelfarb is a historian, but if she knew more about the history of legalistic Christianity in America, she would know that these people's views *are* extremist; as for Decter, she seems unaware that for most legalistic Christians, she—as a secular Jew—is herself very much of the Devil. In her writing, a reference to the Devil may be a rhetorical flourish, but in the views of many of her legalistic Christian associates, the Devil is a living creature whose deputies are everywhere this side of heaven and who seeks to deprive Christians of salvation. This controversy illuminates something that many people with connections to neoconservatism have warned about for years: the fact that the neocons, while vigorously defending legalistic Christians, have never taken religion very seriously (except as a social and moral force) and have thus not taken their allies' theologies very seriously. Indeed, on some level those neocons seem to have failed to recognize that their allies do indeed actually believe certain things and live by them. What they have further failed to realize is that people who believe and live by legalistic Christian theology are by definition extremists who feel that the state should be run according to God's law as they perceive it.

The *First Things* controversy came along shortly after the publication of a book entitled *Dumbing Down: Essays on the Strip-Mining of American Culture,* in which political and cultural conservatives took on various liberal targets. The book opened with several pages of excerpts from the popular press designed to show that "the national intelligence is plummeting" and that "*something particularly bad is happening in this country right now*" (italics in original). Among the excerpts was one from a *New York Times* article about a Lutheran pastor who, after observing a long line of people waiting to see the movie *Batman* at a shopping mall and deciding that "entertainment is really the medium of the day," began offering electric bands and dramatic skits at his church, which as a result grew into a megachurch with weekly attendance in the four figures. The editors' reason for including this excerpt is obvious: The megachurches (which are overwhelmingly legalistic in their orientation) exemplify the vulgarization, the "dumbing down," of American religion.

One turns to the book's essay on religion, which is entitled "Kitsch Religion" and was written by a Jewish intellectual named David Kling-

hoffer, expecting to see this argument made at length. Instead Klinghoffer takes precisely the opposite line. In his view, the success of legalistic Protestant churches, as exemplified by the burgeoning
megachurches, is a good thing and reflects those churches' seriousness
about religion; meanwhile the empty pews of many "liberal" churches
reflect the fact that, "from a strict marketing perspective," their lack of
seriousness (as he describes it) just doesn't pay off. For Klinghoffer,
who was raised as a liberal Jew, seriousness about religion comes down
to one thing: doctrinal orthodoxy. "Liberal religion upholds general
principles of kindness and sympathy," he writes, "but particular
demands of the type familiar to previous generations have largely been
booted out the temple, or church, door." He rails against liberal Christians' acceptance of homosexuals, maintaining that if one reads the
Bible, "there can be no . . . quibbling about God's views on gay sex."
He plainly doesn't understand how Christians read the Bible.

Klinghoffer's essay centers on a distinction borrowed from the art
critic Clement Greenberg. Citing the contrast drawn by Greenberg
between real art, which can be challenging but "offers an enormous
payoff, in the form of an aesthetic experience," and kitsch, which
"makes things easy for us" by providing "a simulation of aesthetic
experience right off the bat," Klinghoffer dismisses nonlegalistic religion as "synthetic religion, kitsch religion." In explaining this judgment, he displays the same confusion about what is and isn't essential
and traditional about Christian belief that one observes in many other
non-Christian commentators:

> *In a religious system centered on an orthodoxy, the system asks the believer*
> *to subscribe to a set of faith principles, deriving what it asserts as the Truth*
> *about God and the universe, from which also follow definite standards of*
> *conduct. After the believer has accepted these principles and sought to order*
> *his life by them, he gets the payoff: the experience of God and His*
> *transcendence.*

This vulgar description of spiritual experience as a "payoff" will be
familiar to many legalistic Christian readers, who have been taught to
think of salvation not as an act of love but as a transaction. What is
even more striking here than the vulgarity, however, is Klinghoffer's

peculiar understanding of religious experience as involving a kind of dogmatic alchemy: Only if you give yourself over heart and mind and soul to a rigorous set of prefabricated precepts do you get to experience "God and His transcendence." To Klinghoffer, in other words, spiritual experience is something that emerges *only* in a context where an individual has agreed to submit entirely to an orthodox set of theological statements and to the dictates of someone else who claims absolute authority. By this standard, of course, Jesus had no real spiritual experience, and neither did Saint Francis. Plainly, Klinghoffer's understanding of the relation of spirituality to orthodoxy and hierarchy is quite in line with the Church of Law's understanding of how religion works—and utterly at odds with the core message of Jesus.

Klinghoffer speaks up for all the key ingredients of the Church of Law: law, dogma, institutional authority. Real religion, he says, centers on truth that is found in scripture, and in order to discern that truth, "an institution is needed." He explains that in real religion, rabbis and priests base their biblical interpretations "on the authority of ancient traditions" such as the papacy. Yet things have changed, he complains: "Now, say the liberal denominations, let the people decide! In place of these hallowed traditions, kitsch religion substitutes the prevailing opinions of the secular world. . . . The Protestant mainline churches increasingly reject the authority of their own traditions, allowing men and women to believe what they wish about virtue, sin, and salvation." Klinghoffer seems utterly unaware that Protestantism was founded on a belief in the supremacy of individual conscience and a repudiation of the intermediary role of religious institutions; he seems not to know about Anglicans' and Baptists' historic emphasis on individual conscience. He has, in fact, got his American religious history exactly backward: If he is looking for the supreme contemporary example of betrayal of religious tradition, he should look not to the "liberal" mainline churches but to the legalists in the Southern Baptist Convention who have renounced the traditional Baptist doctrine of the priesthood of the believer and replaced it with an increasingly rigorous—and un-Protestant—doctrinal orthodoxy. If there is one thing that left- and right-wing intellectuals have in common, it would appear to be an uncanny ability to get American religion wrong.

15

DID
LUCY CONVERT?

AT BOTH ENDS of the ideological spectrum, then, American intellectual discourse has offered up highly distorted images of the nation's religious life. While liberal intellectuals have accustomed upscale Americans to the bogus idea that we live in "secular times," conservative intellectuals have fostered the equally false notion that legalistic Christianity is, in some sense, the "real thing" and that nonlegalistic Christianity is a secularized, watered-down version of it.

As intellectual culture has given a warped picture of American religion, so, in its own way, has popular culture. Over the course of the twentieth century, the entertainment media came to define mainstream American culture far more than religion did, and these media, by largely omitting religion from the picture they painted of American life, encouraged the notion, at whatever level of the popular consciousness, that faith was not a proper subject for public discourse. It was almost as if sex and religion had switched places: Sex, which had earlier gone virtually unmentioned in public or in print, became a routine subject of magazine articles and TV talk-show discussions; religion, which had been a much-discussed topic as well as a universally recognized foundation of American culture, disappeared behind closed doors. In the 1920s the *New York Times* covered the sermons delivered in the city's major churches as fully and responsibly as it covered major-league baseball games; by the second half of the century, the *Times*'s religious coverage (which was still far better than that in most American newspapers) had been essentially reduced to a brief weekly column in the back pages of the Saturday paper. In the 1920s, developments in the fundamentalist-modernist controversy routinely made front-page headlines; in the decades after World War II, few religion stories were seen as meriting more than a small item on the inside pages.

From the beginning of the century until the advent of television, movies were the quintessence of American popular culture and the chief means by which foreigners came to shape their understanding of the United States. The era of American talkies began in 1927 with *The Jazz Singer,* a movie about a young Jewish man (Al Jolson) who alienates his father, a cantor, by rejecting the older man's profession to become a jazz singer. (One could view the film today as an allegory about how entertainment, in the early decades of the century, essentially replaced religion at the heart of mainstream American culture.) This age of talkies has coincided almost exactly with the period of secular hegemony over the nation's culture; to examine how American film has dealt with religion during this period is to be reminded how aggressively secular the mainstream American culture became in this century and how removed it continues to be, for the most part, from the realm of the spiritual.

Religion, of course, is scarcely the only topic that Hollywood has treated with slickness, crudity, and lack of depth. Yet no subject matter has more dramatically underscored the superficiality of American popular film—and, by extension, the shallow, horizontal nature of mainstream American culture in the twentieth century. In Hollywood movies, characters are rarely shown to be regular churchgoers, except when the intention is to telegraph their wholesomeness, primitiveness, or hypocrisy; houses of worship tend to appear only in the context of weddings or funerals. On the infrequent occasion when a church service is depicted, the order of service and vestments are almost invariably wrong, suggesting either that nobody involved knew better or that they assumed no one in the audience would be able to tell the difference. To be sure, movies made by American whites about blacks, such as *The Color Purple* (1985), often include church scenes, perhaps because for many white filmmakers religion is part of what makes black life exotic. (When, in the 1994 movie *Forrest Gump,* the white hero enters a church to pray, it's a black church.) *Friendly Persuasion* (1956) and *Witness* (1985) feature main characters with faith-centered lives, but in these films their Quaker and Amish ways of life, respectively, function principally as atmosphere and as plot devices accounting for their isolation from mainstream society and its concerns. In general, religion is seen as something that may be a part of some people's lives in a conventional, ceremonial sense but that attains significance for them only in times of crisis, as in *Mrs. Miniver* (1942), which, set in the early days of World War II, closes in a bombed-out Anglican church with a stirring sermon by a vicar who does not otherwise figure significantly in the film.

One problem here is that Hollywood has always had its unwritten dictates about human behavior, and they aren't highly consistent with the precepts that some Christians, at least, believe they are supposed to live by. If a man is bullied, Jesus says he should turn the other cheek; Hollywood says he's a sissy if he doesn't eventually beat the bully up. More broadly, Hollywood rules instruct that men—when they're movie heroes, anyway—have to be *men,* according to the prevailing standards of certain middle-class American communities. And while Americans are far more likely to be churchgoers and to consider themselves religious than people in other developed countries, many are also likely to have narrow, un-Christlike convictions about gender-appropriate behavior that leave them uncertain how to think about clergymen. (Forget about clergywomen: I, for one, still haven't seen any in American movies.) So it was that while the 1940s saw some earnest (if dullish) stories about creditable, and more or less credible, clerical careers—Fredric March as a small-town minister in *One Foot in Heaven* (1941), Gregory Peck as a Scots missionary priest in nineteenth-century China in *The Keys of the Kingdom* (1944)—the decade also saw several conspicuous attempts to show clerics as Regular Guys, a process that got firmly under way with Bing Crosby as Father O'Malley in *Going My Way* (1944) and *The Bells of Saint Mary's* (1945). Much the same sort of thinking was plainly behind the casting of Frank Sinatra as a priest in *The Miracle of the Bells* (1948). Though men of God, these priests knew their way around the block; they could talk sports as well as theology, and were at least as familiar with the Hit Parade as with their hymnody. Enabling audience members to feel comfortable with these collared characters, moreover, was their knowledge that the actors themselves were, in real life, far from priestly. This approach to clerical protagonists—underlying which would seem to be a combination of reflexive respect for the ministerial vocation and a profound discomfort with the spiritual aspects of their lives—may have reached its apotheosis in 1968 with *The Shoes of the Fisherman,* in which the central figure, a Russian pope, was played by Anthony Quinn, who as Zorba the Greek four years earlier had etched himself forever in moviegoers' minds as an exuberant lover of wine, women, and song: the quintessential Regular Guy.

Though 1940s movie priests were Regular Guys, 1940s movie nuns were hardly Regular Gals. If they spent considerable time trying to raise money—Ingrid Bergman to endow a church in *The Bells of Saint Mary's,* Loretta Young to build a hospital in *Come to the Stable* (1949)—it was because the filmmakers, by showing them clumsily (yet charmingly) engaged in such endeavors, were able to underline how sweetly naive they were about the secular, materialistic "real world" of twentieth-century America. During the 1950s, furthermore, such varied films as *The African Queen* (1951), *Guys and Dolls* (1953), and *Heaven Knows, Mr. Allison* (1957) demonstrated filmmakers' fondness for romantic pairings of ingenuous women of God—whether Catholic nuns or Protestant evangelists or missionaries—with worldly (if not downright earthy) men. In later years, both *The Singing Nun* (1966) and *Sister Act* (1992) showed that a nun's career was generally thought interesting by Hollywood only if she went into show business. *The Nun's Story* (1959), a sensitive and intelligent portrait, proved a rare exception to this rule.

Among the weirder documents in the history of American popular culture's deracination of Christianity is *The Next Voice You Hear* (1950), in which a stolid middle-class couple (the wife played by the future Nancy Reagan) listen with bland respectfulness to messages from God on the radio. Most religious movies in the decade or so after the Second World War, however, looked to the example of such silent-era Cecil B. DeMille spectacles as *The Ten Commandments* (1923, remade 1956) and *King of Kings* (1927, remade 1961). In that period of advances in wide-screen technology, popular novels about early Christians became splashy celluloid epics. *Quo Vadis* (1951), *The Robe* (1953), and *Ben-Hur* (1959) were uniformly marked by outrageously anachronistic music, costumes, and decor (all of which tended to erase the vast cultural differences between first-century Palestine and 1950s America) as well as by garish pageantry, solemn performances, and statuelike posture (all of which created a huge, artificial distance between 1950s moviegoers and the spiritual experience of early Christians). The end of the decade saw a remarkable exception to this trend in the form of Richard Brooks's 1960 adaptation of Sinclair Lewis's 1927 novel *Elmer Gantry*, a frank examination of a revivalist con man and of the combination of slick hucksterism and genuine spiritual hunger that frequently characterize big-scale evangelical movements.

It should not be forgotten that the most popular American movie since *Gone with the Wind* was the story of a novice nun. Of course had Maria, in *The Sound of Music* (1965), stayed in the convent, there would never have been a movie. But Maria doesn't fit in with the other sisters. Why? Not because she's insufficiently holy, but because she enjoys life and nature and music too much—the implicit message being that a high-spirited life is incompatible with a life of the spirit. When Maria is undecided as to whether to marry Captain von Trapp, the reverend mother sings "Climb Ev'ry Mountain," whose lyric is hardly Christian: "follow every rainbow till you find your dream." *Every* rainbow? In *The Culture of Disbelief*, Stephen L. Carter notes how in real life, at this point in the story, Maria requested the reverend mother's permission to wed Captain von Trapp, and the nun prayed over the matter, after which she told Maria that it was the Holy Spirit's will that she marry. "Climb Ev'ry Mountain," with its bland affirmation of perseverance, optimism, and the power of positive thinking, is the closest that secular American show business can easily come to such blatantly religious happenings.

The Sound of Music spawned other movies about nuns, including *The Trouble with Angels* (1966), a lightweight teen comedy set at a convent school that did a better job than most American pictures of portraying nuns as human and of taking their calling seriously. The even lighter sequel, *Where Angels Go, Trouble Follows* (1968), shows how much American society had changed in two years: While giving a nod to older nuns' wisdom, it affirmed the "relevant" if shallow political involvements of a young sister. The Aquarian-age urge toward hipness also eventuated in *Godspell* and *Jesus Christ, Superstar* (both 1973), which for all their indelicacy at least sought to engage in some way the nature of the relationship between the human and the divine; meanwhile, *Rosemary's Baby* (1968) and such subsequent thrillers as *The Exorcist* (1973) and *The Omen* (1976) exploited Christian motifs—and, in particular, the legalistic Christian belief in the personal reality of Satan—with increasing coarseness and cynicism.

The last two decades of American movies have seen precious little in the way of serious religious content. While an Australian director (Bruce Beresford) and Canadian writer (Brian Moore) have given us an account of seventeenth-century Jesuit missionaries (*Black Robe,* 1991), and Italy has given us a Tolstoy-inspired tale of a young priest's sexual and spiritual conflicts (*Black Sun,* 1990), and Britain has given us biographies of Gandhi (1981) and C. S. Lewis (*Shadowlands,* 1993) as well as a story of eighteenth-century Jesuits in South America (*The Mission,* 1986), the American movie industry has presented us with a generally shallow, glossy, and monolithic vision of the world, a vision that is nominally Judeo-Christian but effectively secular, materialistic, and bicoastal. The handful of movies centering on nuns and preachers and the like, such as *Wise Blood* (1979) and *Agnes of God* (1985), have been adapted from other media; perhaps the only noted American director to engage religious ideas on a regular basis is Woody Allen, a secular Jew who does so humorously and in passing, and who for all his wit has never grown beyond a solipsistic preoccupation with his own mortality. The single most remarkable thing in Whit Stillman's 1994 comedy *Barcelona* is that one of the Yuppie protagonists actually reads the Bible and considers himself a Christian. With few exceptions, the closest that post-Vietnam American movies have come to examining religious experience is in portraying encounters with extraterrestrials. In *Close Encounters of the Third Kind* (1977) and *E. T.* (1982), salvation, meaning, and transcendence come down from the heavens in a spaceship; in Allen's Ingmar Bergman–inspired *Stardust Memories* (1980), metaphysical inquiries take the form of a question-and-answer session with imaginary aliens. The obsession of the Richard Dreyfuss character in *Close Encounters* with meeting creatures from outer space, and his eagerness to return with them to their home planet, comes across—intentionally or not—as a sad, rather puerile transference of the deep spiritual longing and confusion that are rampant in America today and that are satisfied neither by our multitudinous temporal pleasures nor by the insipid legalism that passes for Christianity in our time. Given what American film is, alas, perhaps it can't come much closer than this to a serious treatment of spiritual reality.

When film did come closer, in the remarkable *Little Buddha* (1994), it took an Italian director, Bernardo Bertolucci, whose achievement American critics failed to appreciate. Reading the notices, which dismissed Bertolucci's film as corny, sentimental, and inchoate, one could not help thinking that reviewers accustomed to a steady diet of secular-humanist Hollywood fare couldn't make anything out of a work that reflected an entirely different sensibility. *Little Buddha* shuttled between two stories. One story, set in contemporary Seattle and Bhutan, was about a young American boy a group of Tibetan monks think may be the reincarnation of their deceased leader. Several of those monks travel to Seattle and teach the boy about the Buddha. Thenceforth the story of the boy alternates with the story he is being told about how a rich young prince, Gautama, became the Enlightened One.

The film can be seen on one level as narrowly sectarian, supporting a Buddhist worldview, including a belief in reincarnation. But it can also be experienced, as it was by this viewer, as a beautifully spiritual vision of life that transcends a narrow sectarianism and that, in fact, resonates with Christian allusions. The many parallels between Jesus and Buddha are everywhere apparent if nowhere explicitly insisted upon. The film does not reject any particular spiritual tradition but is

rather an affirmation of the reality of spiritual experience, the importance of a spiritual life, and the validity of different means of articu-
lating, establishing, and celebrating one's connection with spiritual
reality. The Seattle boy and his parents are a typical 1990s Hollywood
movie family. They're well off, thoroughly secular, discombobulated
not by the monks' foreignness but by the fact that their lives are centered in spiritual and not material reality. Perhaps many American
reviewers saw themselves too clearly reflected in that portrait, and were
discomfited by what they saw, and by what it said about them. Yet the
wide distribution of movies like *Little Buddha*—and of more recent
American films like *Michael* (in which John Travolta plays an angel) and
The Preacher's Wife, both released on Christmas Day, 1996—is itself a
reflection of the fact that as we approach a new millennium, we find
ourselves in a time of rising spiritual consciousness on the part of many
Americans, who in increasing numbers are recognizing the ultimate
emptiness of contemporary American secular culture—and whose
newfound spiritual interests may lead either to a revitalized Church of
Love or an even stronger Church of Law.

If Hollywood movies tell us a good deal about the secular mainstream
culture's perspective on religion, the reaction of legalistic Christians to
some of those movies—in particular, to those rare movies that *do* seek
honestly to deal with the reality of spiritual experience—reflects some
important truths about legalistic Christianity.

It seems exceedingly odd, for one thing, that while legalistic Christians have assailed the lack of "family values" in popular culture, many
of those same Christians have, over the decades, embraced as wholesome fare fantasies that evince outrageously unchristian metaphysics.
One thinks of the ghosts in *Topper* (1937), *The Ghost and Mrs. Muir*
(1947), *The Bishop's Wife* (1948, remade in 1996 as *The Preacher's Wife*),
Carousel (1956), *Ghostbusters* (1984), and *Ghost* (1990); of the witches
in *I Married a Witch* (1942) and *Bell, Book, and Candle* (1958); of the
visions of afterlife proffered in *Here Comes Mr. Jordan* (1943), *A Guy
Named Joe* (1944), *Heaven Can Wait* (1978), and *Defending Your Life*
(1991); of the devil in *Damn Yankees* (1956); and of the angels in *Angels
in the Outfield* (1951, 1994) and, in particular, *It's a Wonderful Life* (1946),

which has become the quintessential American Christmas movie, despite the picture it paints of a world in which angels earn their wings by leading would-be suicides on tours of alternate universes. One might add to this roster the other perennial yuletide favorite, *Miracle on 34th Street* (1947), which, like Christmas-oriented American popular culture generally, effectively replaces Jesus with Santa Claus.

Perhaps the ultimate irony is that while the Religious Right hasn't loudly protested any of the above entertainments, it denounced as profane Martin Scorsese's *The Last Temptation of Christ* (1988), which (despite its dull pacing, Method-style overacting, and inane pop-psych dialogue) represented a serious attempt by a brilliant director to grapple with the relation between the human and the divine as embodied in the person of Jesus. Pat Robertson, while praising such vapid biblical spectacles as *The Ten Commandments* and *Ben-Hur*, condemned *The Last Temptation of Christ* as "scurrilous and thoroughly artless" and said that the film "set out to prove the corruption and hypocrisy of Christianity and the Church." On the contrary, Scorsese's film plainly springs from a profound interest in the humanity of Jesus. It reflects not a "hatred of religion," as Robertson claimed, but an unwillingness to be shackled to safe, trite, deadening formulas—whether those of Hollywood or of religion. If spiritually inert spectacles like *Ben-Hur* appeal to popular religiosity, a movie like *The Last Temptation of Christ* offends those who don't want to think about what it really means to say that God became man, and who conceive of religion as essentially a matter of clinging to sentimental images and familiar catch phrases.

That legalistic Christians can enthuse over movies like *Ben-Hur* and picket a movie like *The Last Temptation of Christ* reflects more than a devotion to banal, greeting-card notions of God, angels, and the afterlife. It reflects, for one thing, a profound discomfort with the idea of Jesus' humanity—and in particular his physicality and sexuality. It reflects a discomfort with the idea of truly engaging the spiritual dimension of life; in fact it reflects an inability to recognize such engagement as genuine religious experience. So accustomed are many legalistic Christians to a thoroughly horizontal religion, indeed, that when they are exposed to an authentic artistic attempt to engage the vertical, their tendency is to think they are looking at something heretical. During his ministry on earth, Jesus was not about affirming the familiar, but about upsetting expectations, issuing challenges, and forcing people to see things anew; yet the rare American filmmaker who seeks to remind us of this fact—and who seeks in his work to emulate Christ's example—is likely to offend and outrage legalistic Christians.

A more recent film occasioned much the same kind of furor that greeted *The Last Temptation of Christ. Priest*—which was made by a British filmmaker and released in the United States through Miramax, a subsidiary of the Disney Company—concerns Father Greg, a conservative young Roman Catholic priest who has been assigned to a church in a working-class neighborhood of Liverpool. There he assists the respected Father Matthew, a liberal older priest who, it turns out, has a long-standing sexual relationship with his housekeeper, Maria. The apparently straitlaced Greg upbraids him for this; but we discover the complexity of Greg's situation when we see him remove his collar, go out to a gay bar, and leave the bar with a young man named Graham. Greg's double life eventually leads to arrest and scandal; when the parishioners discover his secret, they harden their hearts, and Father Matthew, in a passionate sermon, tells them that "God doesn't give a damn what you do in bed!" and that Jesus is not about prudishness and judgmentalism but about love, forgiveness, and understanding.

Priest was not meant to titillate or to tear down the church, as some critics insisted, but to inquire into the tensions within the soul of the young priest, who is tortured by guilt over his homosexuality and who has been taught by his traditional Catholic mentors to view sexual activity, especially homosexual activity, as sinful. On a larger scale, the film strikingly dramatizes the conflict between the Church of Love and the Church of Law—between, on the one hand, the human need for kindness, affection, and reconciliation and, on the other, the human capacity for abusiveness, hypocrisy, betrayal, and unthinking devotion to institutional authority. Directed by Antonia Bird and written by Jimmy McGovern, the film sensitively explores the difficult position of someone who, though identified in other people's minds with God and with inflexible institutional doctrine and authority, is nonetheless as confused and as needful of human intimacy as the next person. The film also perceptively examines the desire, common among many legalistic churchgoers, to embrace the illusion that their clergyman enjoys a moral perfection and a pipeline to God that they don't—and the unforgiving rage that erupts when that illusion is broken. In the end, *Priest* amounts to a stirring affirmation of the Church of Love that one cannot imagine being made under the auspices of a major American studio.

Roger Ebert, in his review of the film, offered an illuminating example of the mainstream media's perspective on religion. "The question of whether priests should be celibate is the subject of much debate right now," Ebert wrote. "What is not in doubt is that, to be ordained, they have to *promise* to be celibate. Nobody has forced them to become priests, and rules are rules." For one thing, to say that "nobody has forced them to be priests" is to dismiss the idea of a calling and to see priesthood as just another job; for another thing, there is the question, Who sets the rules? Many Catholics today have challenged the moral and spiritual need for celibacy requirements. To answer such challenges by saying that the church can set whatever rules it wishes is to fail to accept the church as being what it represents itself as being, namely the Body of Christ, whose members are all theoretically equal in God's sight, and all of whom thus have an equal right to raise passionate objections to its rules—and even, if they feel compelled to perform acts of prophetic obedience, an equal right (indeed, an obligation) to break them. The typical member of the mainstream media doesn't understand such considerations.

"Take away the occupations of the two central characters," writes Ebert of *Priest,* "and the rest of the film's events would be laid bare as tiresome sexual politics." But the whole point is that for these two men, priesthood is *not* simply an occupation; it is a vocation. Ebert goes on to question whether audiences would get as worked up over the story if Greg were a doctor or a lawyer; what he doesn't seem to understand is that Greg's status as a priest reflects the fact that the film is about ultimate meanings, about the significance of his actions *sub specie aeternitatis,* under the aspect of eternity. In the end, Ebert scores the filmmakers for their "prejudices," by which he presumably means prejudices against the church; but to take the church seriously enough to mount an eloquent critique of its current leadership's approach to sexual morality is hardly to be prejudiced. What Ebert does not understand is that the people *are* the church—and they can hardly be prejudiced against themselves.

Ebert was not alone in denouncing *Priest* as antichurch; legalistic

Protestants did so as well. In a 1996 resolution, the Southern Baptist Convention criticized the Disney Company in very strong terms for, among other things, "producing . . . the film *Priest* which disparages Christian values and depicts Christian leaders as morally defective." (This is a surprising complaint, given that the theology of the fundamentalists who control the Southern Baptist Convention doesn't regard Roman Catholic priests as saved Christians.) To suggest, as the Southern Baptist resolution did, that the lightweight movies Disney used to make (such as *Herbie the Love Bug* and *The Absent-Minded Professor*) embody "Christian values" and to see *Priest,* by contrast, as anti-Christian is to be very misguided about what the word *Christian* really means, or is supposed to mean. And to deny that all Christian leaders are not, in some way, "morally defective" is to set them up as immaculate in the same bizarre way the Roman Catholic Church has done with the Virgin Mary.

In the mid-twentieth century, television entered the American home and soon became the center of family life and of the common culture. Yet the newly introduced medium almost never reflected the fact that the United States was the most churchgoing nation on earth. James Dobson and other champions of "family values" fondly invoke the 1950s as a time of domestic stability and harmony, yet even during that decade television almost entirely omitted religion from its picture of American life. Such television series as *Father Knows Best* and *Leave It to Beaver,* which are nowadays lauded by some (and mocked by others) for their idealized depictions of white suburban households, almost never showed their characters attending church or talking about it. The same goes for the most popular series of that decade. Was Lucy McGillicuddy, who married the presumably Catholic Ricky Ricardo, raised Protestant or Catholic? If the former, did she convert? Did he? Was little Ricky ever baptized? If so, into what faith? None of these questions was ever answered on *I Love Lucy.* Already Americans were so accustomed to the idea of the entertainment media as a religion-free zone that few even noticed these omissions.

In later decades, religious themes did figure from time to time on some TV series. The families on such programs as *The Waltons* and *Lit-*

tle House on the Prairie attended church regularly—yet on both these shows, set during the Great Depression and the frontier era respectively, churchgoing functioned principally as an emblem of the innocence and uprightness of America's "good old days." On situation comedies, a favorite plot device was that of the handsome would-be inamorato who turns out to be a Catholic priest. (Television writers hardly seemed to know what else they might do with a character in a collar.) When a regular on *The Mary Tyler Moore Show* considered becoming a nun, it was, predictably, not out of a sense of vocation, but out of frustration over her love life. (Though Mary Richards identified herself as a Presbyterian in the first episode of that series, viewers never learned, during the next seven years, if she ever actually attended church.) One of the more controversial aspects of Norman Lear's situation comedies of the 1970s, among them *All in the Family* and *Maude,* was that the characters actually talked—and even argued—about God and faith; Edith Bunker even went to church on Sunday mornings, and Archie, irked by his son-in-law's atheism, sneaked his baby grandson off to church and baptized him. A more recent exception to the rule is the series *Touched by an Angel,* in which three heavenly messengers involve themselves in the lives of people in need. (The God that these angels serve, incidentally, is very much a God of love: In one episode, angel Della Reese tells a gay man dying of AIDS that God loves him just as he is.) Yet American television's overall approach to religion is pretty much reflected in the fact that the only series most Americans can recall that centered on a man or woman with a religious vocation was *The Flying Nun.*

The growth of television has been a crucial factor in the rise of legalistic Christianity. In a sense, legalistic Christianity started out as a branch of the nation's folk culture and has, in the latter half of the twentieth century, become a branch of its pop culture. Jerry Falwell's *Old-Time Gospel Hour* (the title of which recalls Charles E. Fuller's mid-century radio show *The Old Fashioned Revival Hour*) made Falwell a national figure and enabled him to launch the Moral Majority; *The 700 Club* and other programs on Pat Robertson's Christian Broadcasting Network did the same for him and his Christian Coalition. Certainly the nature of television is far better suited to the purposes of legalistic Christianity than to those of nonlegalistic Christianity. The spiritual experience at the heart of the Church of Love is not something easily communicated through the medium of television; for one thing, that experience, as attained in worship, necessarily involves interaction in community rather than mere spectatorship. At best, worship services, whether simple and austere or liturgically and musically rich, succeed in creating vertical experiences in the hearts, minds, and souls of congregants. Whole shelves of books have been written about how to design liturgies to create sacred time and space that are demarcated from the nine-to-five grind, from quotidian domestic drudgery, and from, yes, television. To participate in such worship services involves seeking, in communion with one's fellow human beings, to disengage oneself from the horizontal context of daily life and to touch the vertical. The Church of Law, by contrast, embraces the horizontal and encourages worshippers to play a passive role, listening obediently as the preacher tells them what the Bible says and what they are expected to believe, to do, and to condemn. It does not seem entirely a coincidence that the advent of television has coincided with the rise of legalistic Christianity—for television has made America a nation of passive viewers, and passive people are much more likely fodder for legalistic than for nonlegalistic systems of belief.

Another way to put this is to say that television has created a nation of people many of whom, consciously or not, now think of themselves as audiences and think of politics and education—and even, yes, religion—as forms of entertainment. Accordingly, many legalistic ministers have designed their worship services—whether at small fundamentalist chapels, at large megachurches, or on televangelist programs—to make them more like TV talk or variety shows. This is not difficult to do, as the legalistic message is essentially a matter of black-and-white doctrines and not of nebulous, numinous experience. At such services, there is little sense of strangeness, of spiritual depth, of mystery; everything is made familiar, comfortable, unchallenging, *horizontal*. Such services are less about being actively involved than about watching, less about being an integral part of something than about being an audience member, less about being transformed than about being diverted. In practice, then, though legalistic Christian churches today tend to present themselves as being in conflict with mainstream culture, many of them conform to that culture in style and tone far more than most nonlegalistic churches do. Indeed, it could be said that the principal achievement of men like Jerry Falwell and Pat Robertson has been to repackage legalistic Christianity—which in my childhood was, on television anyway, a very clunky-looking commodity—into a very slick one.

How can one discuss Christian television without mentioning Tammy Faye and Jim Bakker, whose *PTL Club* represented both television and religion at their most vapid? To mainstream Americans, the Bakkers—who began their joint TV career with Robertson's Christian Broadcasting Network and who saw it ended by a financial scandal—were veritable cartoon characters. Neither Tammy Faye, with her grotesquely painted face and her frequent on-air sobbing, nor Jim, with his perpetual preacher-on-the-make grin, ever evinced any spiritual depth, or for that matter any gravity, humility, or awe in the presence of the divine. There was, indeed, nothing in *The PTL Club* (the initials stood for both "Praise the Lord" and "People that Love") that any member of any religion in human history would recognize as spiritual; with its mix of bland chitchat, insipid music, and homespun advice, it differed little from other daytime talk shows of the era, its wall-to-wall babble almost seeming designed to drown out the intrusion of any still, small voice. It is, indeed, a measure of legalistic Protestantism's essential lack of spiritual depth and intellectual seriousness that these two buffoonish figures not only won millions of fans (the word *fans* seems more appropriate here than *followers*) but were treated as esteemed colleagues by Billy Graham, Robert Schuller, and other figures whose public images differed dramatically from their own.

If the Bakkers and their followers were "people that love," what they seemed to love more than anything else was money, fame, and worldly amusements, and the Jesus they worshipped was one who rewarded his followers with these things. It can be said in their favor that the Bakkers, unlike most of their legalistic colleagues, engaged in relatively little hate rhetoric; this seems, however, to have been a function not of principle but of a total aversion to anything remotely conceptual. If the program didn't represent legalistic Christianity at its most legally and doctrinally obsessed, it was certainly an extreme example of legalistic Christianity's retreat from the vertical dimension and its utter capitulation to such horizontal phenomena as rampant materialism, showbiz glitz, and the cult of celebrity. Far from holding fast to any tradition, *The PTL Club* was a classic case of legalistic Christianity embracing all the most trite, shallow aspects of contemporary culture—and affixing the name of Jesus to the whole shebang.

It is illuminating to examine in a legalistic Christian context the more recent daytime TV talk shows hosted by such people as Ricki Lake and Sally Jesse Raphael. These programs cater to middle Americans by setting before them people like themselves who are willing to bare their lives on camera. These shows have been said to derive from *Donahue,* and in fact many elements of the format do owe something to Phil Donahue's program. But the substance doesn't. Donahue started out many years ago by focusing on serious issues of the day; his format was geared to secular and nonlegalistic Christian viewers. The newer talk shows, by contrast, emphasize personal confession. The guests are everyday Americans who candidly discuss their private problems, family conflicts, and marital crises, and audience members offer blunt comments and suggestions. These spectacles plainly derive from the legalistic Christian tradition of offering "testimony" to one's fellow churchgoers about how one erred before finding one's way to Christ. Mainstream media commentators, because they tend to be ignorant of that tradition, have entirely missed this connection, which helps to explain the extraordinary appeal of such shows in middle America.

Over the course of the twentieth century, Americans—the vast majority of whom identify themselves as Christians—have grown used to a secular mainstream culture in which religion has little or no place. This marginalization of religion has greatly redounded to the benefit of the Church of Law—for a culture in which religion is not a regular subject of serious, free public meditation and discussion is one in which constricting, unreflective legalistic faith has a much more powerful sway over people's minds than it would otherwise have. When religion *does* enter into today's secular culture, moreover, it is almost invariably treated with kid gloves—and a culture in which questioning of irrational and morally offensive metaphysical propositions is discouraged is, again, one in which legalistic faith will enjoy an unnatural advantage.

Indeed, all the elements of secular mainstream culture in America today—high and low, left and right—have come together to reinforce in the public mind the view that anything calling itself Christianity thereby places itself above criticism, or at the very least establishes itself as something that must be handled with particular delicacy. As a result religion has, in this century, rarely been examined in the public square in the kind of open, honest way that would almost certainly have made Americans more well-informed and contemplative than they are in matters of religion—and that would accordingly have kept millions of Americans from considering legalistic Christianity (to the extent that they consider it at all) as the serious, traditional, and moral entity that it represents itself as being.

16

ABIDING MESSAGES, TRANSIENT SETTINGS

IF THE CHRISTIAN right has won millions of allies who don't share Pat Robertson's bizarre theology or extreme politics, but who respond to his message of alienation from the current cultural and political mainstream, one factor in this development is that in the second half of the twentieth century, secularism became so dominant in certain sectors of society that many of us who were brought up during the baby-boom years were raised in settings utterly devoid of spirituality, settings that didn't acknowledge anything that might go by the name of religion. Our parents were "Depression Children"; we were "Prosperity Children." Many of us were middle-class kids whose parents had been members of the working class or the lower middle class. Many of our fathers had served in World War II or Korea and attended college on the G.I. Bill; many were the first members of their families to attend college. Many of them prospered, married, reproduced, moved from the cities to the suburbs, and proceeded to supply their children—us—with *things.* Not to use the word pejoratively, they were materialists—at least on our behalf. Many felt uncomfortable buying expensive things for themselves, or taking expensive vacations or retiring early. But they were devoted to their children. They bought us plenty of toys. They planned for us to attend college. They wanted us to have things they hadn't had, things they would feel uncomfortable having themselves. They brought us up to be materialists.

And, whether they meant to or not, they brought us up as secularists. Chances are they'd been taken to church as kids, but many of us weren't. Yet every Christmas we had a tree, and the floor under it was crowded with presents. We grew up accustomed to the idea that we lived in the most powerful, affluent nation in human history. Thanks largely to our own comfort, and to the wealth and power and security of the nation we lived in, we didn't feel drawn, as earlier generations might have been, to spiritual pursuits. Religion seemed something that might have served a purpose in other times and places, but that we couldn't see as having any purpose in our own lives. Death? Most of us had grandparents, even great-grandparents, who were living longer than earlier generations had done. When they grew ill or senile or came to require constant care, they went into hospitals or nursing homes instead of being nursed at home. Illness and old age and death were kept out of view to an unprecedented degree.

Given this sheltered upbringing, the Vietnam War came for many of us as a great shock, an introduction to the frightening reality of death, chaos, and pointless destruction that existed beyond our highly controlled, materially affluent daily lives. Though the war had much more of a reality for middle-American legalistic Christians, who sent their sons to war, the antiwar movement was a secular phenomenon, because secular culture as opposed to legalistic Christian culture recognized citizens' right—indeed, their obligation—to challenge their government on the morality of its conduct of a war. The hippie phenomenon represented something more than antiwar protest—namely a reaction by kids belonging to the older half of the baby boom, kids who recognized that something was missing in the worldview that they'd been brought up on.

Most, to be sure, didn't quite get what was missing and didn't know how to go about supplying it in their lives. They'd been spoiled, brought up to think of themselves as the center of the universe. That itself was a big part of what was wrong. But they didn't realize it. While changing their lives in often very dramatic ways, they continued to put themselves at the center. Their new ways of thinking were as selfish and solipsistic as the ways they'd been brought up on. They made a show of rejecting consumerism, capitalism, and democracy, and of embracing communalism, Communism, and various Eastern religions. Yet in most cases their dedication to these things was shallow and narcissistic. What else, however, could one expect? They had been shielded so efficiently from serious awareness of any higher or deeper reality that when they began to get glimmers of such a reality, they didn't explore it humbly, patiently, and selflessly, but rather believed that they had discovered it, maybe even invented it, and behaved accordingly.

Most of them didn't discover it in the religions on which they had (at least nominally) been brought up. To them, those religions were part of the phony materialistic world that they were rejecting. Many, of course, while dismissing the institutional church, were drawn to the figure of Jesus, the radical teacher whose preaching against war and avarice they recognized as having been brutally distorted by the church.

As the seventies wore on into the eighties, some baby boomers continued to live as social rebels, as "aging hippies." Some pursued New Age spirituality. But most turned their backs on youthful rebellion and embraced their parents' material values, and then some. They were yuppies, the very personification of materialism. And they lived, increasingly, in a culture of irony—a culture marked by a chic postmodern suspicion of the reality of objective truth and a deep cynicism about the possibility of such things as honor, integrity, and ultimate meaning.

Yet as they entered the 1990s, many yuppies found themselves in or approaching middle age; many had children nearing adulthood. Many had achieved, early on, the material goals they'd set for themselves. Unlike their parents, they had no qualms about buying things for themselves and taking expensive vacations and even, in some cases, retiring early and enjoying the fruits of their labors. As they did these things, however, they came to realize that these material pursuits didn't fulfill them as they had expected. The older they got, the emptier mere material success seemed to be; the older they got, the more they found themselves thinking of death and God, those subjects they'd been brought up not to think about at all. Their grandparents died, and perhaps their parents as well; and their own children reached an age at which they, a generation earlier, had perhaps been confirmed or bar mitzvahed. Something important, something vital, seemed missing in their lives. So it is that in the 1990s, many baby boomers found themselves attending worship services for the first time in decades—and, alas, in most cases, swelling the ranks of the heavily evangelizing Church of Law, which promised not mystery but unambiguous answers, not a radical vision of common humanity but individual salvation and a material heaven.

In these times when the Church of Law dominates the picture of organized Christianity in the United States, we can do worse than to look to Harry Emerson Fosdick for some pointers toward shaping a vibrant and appealing Church of Love. In *The Modern Use of the Bible,* published in 1925 at the height of the fundamentalist-modernist controversy, Fosdick made some observations that are as true now as they were then. Seeking to explain to ministers how, at a time when "the new knowledge" had altered many people's understanding of biblical truth, they could continue to "preach Biblically," Fosdick wrote that "the first essential of intelligent Biblical preaching in our day" was this: "a man must be able to recognize the abiding messages of the Book, and sometimes he must recognize them in a transient setting." Modern Christians should not feel obliged to take literally the biblical descriptions of hell and angels, which are grounded in the worldview of another time and place and culture; angels, for example, should be understood not as actual beings but as tokens of the presence of God. In any event, belief in the reality of angels or in hell as an actual place is not central to the Christian faith, and should not be central to Christian preaching—which, Fosdick maintained, "primarily consists in the presentation of the personality, the spirit, purpose, principles, life, faith, and saviorhood of Jesus." For Jesus, he wrote, "has given the world its most significant idea of God."

Fosdick knew that behind the fundamentalists' strident assertions of certitude was, in most cases, a grievous spiritual emptiness; that stridency, he recognized, often masked a desperate fear and insecurity. If the church as a whole "looks very God-conscious," he wrote, its individual members "often are not God-conscious at all. . . . One by one they too often lack vital personal religion." Why? Largely because they think that in order to remain "believers," they must cling to doctrines that they recognize on some psychological level as untrue and must do everything they can to resist the voice of reason in their heads that tells them so. They call this act of clinging to resistance "faith," and they identify that voice of reason with the Devil. Such dogged adherence to traditional doctrines is not a strength but a handicap to true, vital Christianity. For Christians, Fosdick said, the whole point of opening one's mind up to the new thinking about the Bible and about "the obvious changes in mental categories between Biblical times and our own" is to

> liberate our minds from handicaps and summon our souls the more clearly to the spiritual adventures for which the Scriptures stand! Being a "Bible Christian" in this sense is a great matter. Too often it is made a small matter. To be a Bible Christian must we think, as some seem to suppose, that a fish swallowed a man, or that sun and moon stood still at Joshua's command, or that God sent she-bears to eat up children who were rude to a prophet, or that saints long dead arose and appeared in Jerusalem when our Lord was crucified? Is that what it means to be a Bible Christian?
>
> Rather, to be a Bible Christian is a more significant affair than such bald literalism suggests. To believe in "the God and Father of the Lord Jesus," creator, character, comforter, consummator,—that is to be a Bible Christian. To know moral need which our wit and will could not meet, and inward salvation from it through the power of the Spirit, and to live now in undying gratitude that overflows in service,—that is to be a Bible Christian. To have found in Christ, revealer of God and ideal of man, one who calls out our admiration, captivates our love, centralizes our ambition, and crowns our hopes,—that is to be a Bible Christian.

Fosdick emphasized that doctrinal formulations are only ways of trying to convey divine and mystical truths in ultimately inadequate human and earthly terms. For Jesus' disciples, "the divinity of Jesus was

not primarily a doctrine; it was an experience. The disciples felt in him
something not of this world. They were sure about his manhood, but
it was manhood suffused and irradiated. It subdued them, awed them,
fascinated, and mastered them. The glory of their lives came to be that
they had known him, loved him, believed in him. They did not start
by believing in opinions about him, doctrines concerning him; they
started by believing in him. The objective of their faith was not a theory; it was his personality, his life." Jesus opened up for them a truth
about the universe, revealed to them "a universal force everywhere
available and belonging to the substance of creation." Those followers
of Jesus "were not primarily philosophers, metaphysicians, theologians"
but "men of profound religious life endeavoring to get their vital experiences conveyed to others in such terms as were at hand." For us today,
similarly, the important thing is to "take Jesus in earnest"—a task that
Fosdick described as "the most searching ethical enterprise ever under-
taken on earth" and as one that involves recognizing that the Bible's
heart lies not in its theological formulations but in "its reproducible
experiences." This, he stressed, must be the primary element in defining what it means to be a Bible Christian. "Whatever else loyalty to
the Book may mean, one element must be put first: the spirit and quality of Jesus were meant to be reproduced in his followers. Nothing is
Christian which leaves that out or makes that secondary." Jesus, after
all, "did not think first of usages, institutions, traditions; primarily he
thought about people who were missing an abundant life."

Fosdick contrasted Jesus' teachings to the religious orthodoxy of
Jesus' day, a time when many of those around him were preoccupied
with such questions as "whether Gerizim or Jerusalem was the proper
place to worship" or "how ceremonially one should cleanse the pots
and pans." From such concerns, Fosdick wrote, "one turns to Jesus. It
is another world. He never taught anything in religion except the great
matters that make for a richer life." Fosdick cited several theological
traditions—among them those of Luther, Calvin, Anglicanism, and
the Baptist movement—and asked what Jesus would say about the
differences among them. "Surely, it is not hard to guess: *Nothing matters in all this except the things that lead men into more abundant life.*" And
what, Fosdick asked, does it mean to be led to a more abundant life?
His answer:

There are just a few things in religion that lead to a more abundant life. To have your sins forgiven, to have the burden of your guilt roll from you as from Bunyan's Pilgrim at the Cross—that does it. To know God in your heart, and as you draw from the physical world the sustenance by which you live so to draw from the eternal Spirit the power by which you live indeed— that does it. To know Christ, the revelation of the Eternal and the ideal of man, and in a deepening discipleship with him to behold as in a mirror the glory of the Lord and to be transformed into the same image from glory to glory—that does it. To be led up by him into the expanded life of service and the dignity of helpfulness to man, to share his hopes of God's triumph on this earth and the assurance of the everlasting privilege of going on hereafter—that does it. What horizons lift, what deeps unfold, what heights allure through such a faith! These are the things that make life rich and full.

Toward the beginning of the twentieth century, Harry Emerson Fosdick set a goal for modern Christianity which, near the end of the century, it has hardly begun to try to meet. Fosdick wrote *The Modern Use of the Bible* over seventy years ago, and nonlegalistic Christianity has since then taken only random stabs at building up the "new orthodoxy" he called for. Indeed, it is only very recently that some nonlegalistic Christians have begun to suggest that legalists should not speak as if they have an exclusive right to the name of "Bible-believing Christian." Few nonlegalistic Christian ministers, moreover, have set forth the faith as forthrightly and articulately as Fosdick did. In his 1995 book *Heretics,* the German theologian Gerd Lüdemann writes of the modern "splitting apart of piety and scholarship which amounts to schizophrenia"; what Lüdemann means is that nonlegalistic clergy whose understanding of Christianity is essentially the same as Fosdick's nonetheless maintain a discreet silence about such matters as biblical literalism when speaking to their congregations. At Christmas they preach sentimental sermons about the birth of the Christ child at Bethlehem, even though they know that Jesus was almost certainly born in Nazareth; at other times they preach earnestly on, say, the Epistles to Titus and Timothy, speaking as if they were written by Paul even though they really believe otherwise. Why do they do this? Presumably because they're reluctant to rock the boat and fear the consequences of preaching on the Bible with total candor. They may legitimately worry, Will I lose my job? Will people in the pews lose their faith? Too often, such clergy choose to placate the most insecure and literal-minded in their congregations rather than to edify the most inquisitive and spiritually fervent.

Though they may occasionally sermonize, moreover, about the excesses of fundamentalism, such ministers and members of their flocks have almost invariably failed to connect their moral and social concerns explicitly and publicly with their faith. Ralph Reed himself has pointed out this failure. "The reason religious conservatives have risen as an effective political movement in recent years," he writes, "is that the left dropped its use of religious and moral language in the late 1960s and the early 1970s. The religious left lost its soul, and we stepped into the vacuum." There is a great deal of truth here—not only about the Left but about the center. Liberalism once looked for inspiration and leadership to religious figures like Rauschenbusch and Fosdick (and, more recently, Martin Luther King); today, liberal Christians are usually made to feel that if they spoke openly of their faith in political contexts, it might give offense to non-Christians or invite mockery. Though many active liberals today are Christians whose activism is motivated by their faith, such people do not usually bring their faith openly into the public square.

This has, to be sure, begun to change. Recently a group of mainstream Christian and Jewish leaders calling themselves the Interfaith Alliance have begun to speak up against the Christian Coalition agenda. Founded in 1984 as a grassroots movement, the Interfaith Alliance has sought to challenge the Christian Coalition by, among other things, mailing out its own voter guides, which feature candidates' positions on such issues as health care and tobacco subsidies. In a mid-1995 press conference taking exception to the "Contract with the American Family," many of the religious figures associated with the Interfaith Alliance—among them Episcopal, Presbyterian, Methodist, and Unitarian clergy, as well as Reform Jews—spoke eloquently about the obligation of religious institutions to the helpless, suffering, and oppressed. Yet the press conference had little clout: It was televised after midnight on C-SPAN, was not covered widely in the papers (with the notable exception of an approving Frank Rich column in the *New York Times*), and received no attention on the network news programs.

What's more, the conspicuous presence of representatives of nonreligious liberal groups like the People for the American Way blunted the focus on faith as the basis for a dissenting response to the Religious Right; in the end, the conference came off less as a faith-motivated statement by religious people than as a parade of liberals mouthing political clichés.

The same unfortunate strategy was still being pursued in March 1997, when the Interfaith Alliance sent out a fund-raising letter signed by Walter Cronkite and attacking the Christian Coalition as a "radical movement." The selection for this purpose of Cronkite—a television journalist who has never been known for his religious beliefs, if any, and who for many conservatives, indeed, is the very personification of the secular liberal media—only reinforced the impression that the Interfaith Alliance was pursuing familiar secular-liberal approaches rather than trying to stir the spirits of people of faith.

Another grassroots organization, Call to Renewal, was founded in 1995 by the liberal evangelical minister Jim Wallis, editor of *Sojourners.* Like Interfaith Alliance, Call to Renewal brings Christian clergy together with leaders of other religions and with secular liberals in support of a liberal social and economic agenda. So far it is not clear how effective a counterweight Call to Renewal will prove to be. One problem is that its familiar Great Society rhetoric about racism and poverty fails to answer conservative arguments that some entitlement programs do more harm than good; another problem is that Call to Renewal pragmatically refuses to speak up emphatically for that group of Americans—namely gays—that has been most consistently reviled by the Religious Right. It is to be hoped that Interfaith Alliance or Call to Renewal will develop into an effective movement to promote a genuine Church of Love, but, given the secular influence in both groups, the tiredness of much of their political rhetoric, and their reluctance to address homophobia head-on, it is hard to see how either group, without serious changes in tone and emphasis, can reasonably be expected to inspire a broad cross-section of nonlegalistic Christians to weigh in publicly against the Religious Right and for the Church of Love.

Love. In early 1996, in preparation for an article about the then-pending heresy trial of Episcopal Bishop Walter Righter, who had been charged with ordaining a sexually active homosexual, I placed calls to a couple of the "presenters," the bishops who had brought the charges against Righter. They were downright hostile. I don't know whether they knew I was gay, but perhaps that didn't matter: They knew I was writing for the *New York Times,* and that may have been bad enough. When one of them quoted scripture to me in defense of the heresy charge, I asked if he believed that every word in the Bible was literally true. He shot back, perplexingly, "Is every word in the *New York Times* true?"

These bishops' rancor, their fierce determination to cling to manifest untruths about the nature of sexual orientation, and their enthusiasm for law, dogma, and institutional order, made clear their allegiance to the Church of Law. When the time came for me to travel to Wilmington, Delaware, for the pretrial hearing I didn't look forward to it. Talking on the phone with these mean-spirited bishops was unpleasant enough. What would it be like to sit in a cathedral meeting hall surrounded by dozens of them, and be obliged as a journalist to keep my feelings to myself?

On the morning of the hearing I took the elevator down to the lobby of my hotel and asked for a cab. Another hotel guest, a distinguished-looking man of about sixty-five, was also heading for the cathedral. So when a cab came, we shared it. As we drove off, we introduced ourselves. I recognized his name. He was a theology professor who had written an essay that I'd read in which he declared that homosexual orientation was a sign of the Fall. In other words, something that is intrinsic to my identity and to the way I experience love is, in his view, not a reflection of God's love but the very opposite of that. We made polite small talk.

At the cathedral I took my seat in the press section of the large meeting hall. In front of me two men were sitting together, one with a clerical collar and the other with a briefcase on his lap. It turned out to be full of propaganda against the accused, which he shoved at reporters enthusiastically. Across the aisle, a couple of the presenters sat surrounded by their allies. I looked at them, trying to find something in their faces that would help me understand their devotion to their cause.

During the breaks we mingled. It was not a situation that I had looked forward to. And yet I felt weirdly exhilarated. At the end of the day, when the head of the court asked us to stand and pray, I did so. I stood and bowed my head and closed my eyes and prayed in the midst of these people who considered my life, my identity, an abomination. And I prayed *for them*. And it was then, as I stood there praying, that I realized why I felt so joyful: It was because I knew that what these people thought about me ultimately didn't matter. What they did, ultimately didn't matter. I knew, not only in an abstract intellectual sense, but with all my heart and soul and strength, that however hard they tried, they *could not separate me from the love of God*.

"Neither death, nor life, nor angels, nor rulers, nor things present, nor things to come, nor powers, nor height, nor depth, nor anything else in all creation, will be able to separate us from the love of God in Christ Jesus our Lord." Saint Paul, whose pronouncements are not always perfectly consistent with the spirit of the gospel, was never closer to its core than when he wrote these words to a group of outcasts who worshipped together in catacombs in the capital of the known world. And yet the history of Christianity since then has been, to an appalling extent, a history of one group of self-identified Christians after another bringing charges, condemning, and doing their damnedest to separate other people from the love of God. Many of the early church fathers declared one another heretics, because they disagreed over abstruse doctrinal points that today can seem entirely semantic. In the Middle Ages, Crusaders slaughtered countless Moslems because they didn't accept Christ as their savior. The Inquisition did the same thing to the Jews. In later centuries, Protestants did it to Catholics, and Catholics to Protestants. Today, millions of legalistic Christians claim that if you don't read the Bible the way they do, you aren't a true Christian at all. Over the centuries, those who have preached and dreamed and served and longed for a true Church of Love have found themselves challenged, disfellowshipped, tried, stoned, crucified by those whose highest loyalty is to the Church of Law.

When you examine the historical record, in fact, it's miraculous that the real message of Jesus wasn't washed away centuries ago in the rivers of blood shed in his name. It's miraculous that when Francis of Assisi came along and lived his life in a truly Christlike way, people around

Italy, even at the Vatican, actually recognized him as a saint—eventually. They even recognized that one of the saintly things he did was to walk into that mosque in Egypt, to pray there with a Moslem, and to say to him, "God is everywhere." For Francis, God's love was a palpable fact and a source of joy. So full was he of that joy, and so eager to share it with the world, that he preached the good news of God's love to everyone who would listen, even birds and animals. But for some Christians—many of whom, curiously enough, think of themselves as evangelicals—God's love just isn't any fun unless you can find somebody else to deny it to.

Of course Paul's Epistles contain other lines, too, including passages routinely cited in support of slavery, female submission, and the claim that being gay is "unnatural." All too often Saul the Pharisee, the upholder of law and the reviler of all things carnal, gets in the way of Paul the Apostle, who knew that love was higher than the law, and the spirit not hostile to the flesh. Ultimately, which of these men you choose to listen to—Saul or Paul—depends on which of them reflects your sense of what Jesus is about. Is Jesus about enforcing rules that deny equality, freedom, and personal integrity to a considerable proportion of the creatures God made in his image? Or is he about love?

"Love the Lord your God with all your heart and with all your soul and with all your mind," Jesus said. "And love your neighbor as yourself. On these two commandments hang all the law and the prophets." The thrust here is not that love liberates us from law—it's that Christian loving can be far more difficult than obeying the law, and can sometimes compel us to set the law aside. To abide in the love of Christ is a calling that challenges us in a profound and mysterious way that the black-and-white regulations of Leviticus do not. And it's a calling that tells us in our hearts that *nothing* is more unchristian than saying to someone else, or believing of someone else, that we're loved and they're not.

Why, after all, do—should—we become Christians? Because we think God is going to love us more than he loves non-Christians, and will give us a ticket to eternity that he denies to them? Because we think he'll give us everything we want and solve our problems exactly the way we want him to? No. We become Christians because we can't help becoming Christians—because we've fallen helplessly in love with what Jesus is about. We become Christians knowing that God loves non-Christians every bit as much as he loves us and knowing that in our baptismal covenant we promise to seek and serve Christ in *all* persons and to respect the dignity of *every* human being. We become Christians knowing that some of the most Christlike people in our society are atheists and that some people who do call themselves Christians have made the term a synonym for horrible things. We become Christians knowing what a lie it is to suggest that any of us is a model of Christian love. We become Christians knowing that even if we're sinful, God will love us and forgive us—but precisely because we do know that, we struggle *not* to be sinful. And we struggle, and struggle, and struggle.

And, like Paul, we evangelize—we spread the good news of God's love. We don't do this by buttonholing people with pamphlets warning of hellfire. We don't do it by becoming Bible-thumping missionaries. We do it by loving. *Loving.* When on May 15, 1996, the Episcopal Church's Court for the Trial of a Bishop dismissed the charges against Bishop Righter and proclaimed that no "core doctrine" of the church forbids ordaining people in committed same-sex relationships, it marked a small step toward an American church that is truly about love and not power, a church that does not reject the commandments of God in favor of the traditions of men, a church in which there is no Jew or Greek, slave or free, male or female, gay or straight. But the struggle continues. On the day before the charges were dismissed, I received a phone call from a newly out friend of mine, a young man of seventeen who lives in a tiny Indiana town. He told me that his mother, who was raised in a conservative Lutheran family, had ordered him out of the house that morning, saying that his homosexuality was against her religion. Falling to the floor and clinging to her ankles, he begged her not to throw him out. He cried, "You have to love me." She replied, "Unless you change, you're going to hell." Eventually, in order to be allowed to stay at home for another year and finish high school, he had to promise to drop his gay friends and never again speak of being gay. His mother gave him one last brief phone call to me. This was it.

"What does her religion say about love?" I asked him.

"I don't know," he replied flatly and defeatedly, "and I don't care."

I wanted to say more to him about God. I wanted to tell him that it was for people like him that Jesus had conducted his ministry and gone to the cross. "I give you a new commandment: Love one another," Jesus said. "As I have loved you, so you are to love one another." Jesus came to tell his disciples "you are loved," not "you are going to hell." But in the home of that boy's parents, God is a trump card for bigotry. How do you talk about God to somebody who thinks his only hope lies in getting far away from people who talk about God, and who has to get off the phone in five minutes? All you can do is give him love. All you can do is assure him that you care about him and are there for him, and pray that the Holy Spirit will help him to discern, to accept, and to return that higher, all-subsuming love that no one can take away from him. That, in this world, is our job as Christians.

Legalistic churches do have one lesson to teach nonlegalistic churches: a lesson about evil. The fact is that most churches that seek to be Churches of Love need to acknowledge evil more often and more emphatically than they do. One appeal of the legalistic church for people who have difficult lives is that it offers a clear answer to the question of why such difficulty exists: It's because of the Devil, and because of certain groups of people (such as homosexuals, foreigners, and university professors) who are of the Devil. Some mainline Protestant ministers who preach a God of love, by contrast, fail in their preaching not only to account for the existence of evil but also sometimes even to acknowledge its power, its horror, its scope. Unless one is a privileged person who has had a very fortunate life, one will eventually find such preaching inadequate to one's situation. Though one can scarcely expect the mainline churches to pull out of a hat a thoroughly satisfying answer to the age-old problem of evil, there is certainly room for more recognition of its reality.

What mainline Protestants need not do, in their attempts to make the church of tomorrow less a Church of Law and more a Church of Love, is to feel that they must dismiss theological traditions entirely and pluck new doctrinal formulations out of thin air. On the contrary, both the Anglican and the Baptist heritages, to name two, offer strong foundations for a twenty-first-century Church of Love that honors reason, conscience, and experience. In a sense these two very different traditions—one of which originated in a rebellion against the other—are perfectly complementary: While the liturgical majesty, theological sophistication, and homiletical polish of the finest Anglican churches come together to convey a powerful sense of God's transcendence and grandeur, Baptist churches, at their best, achieve in their services a simplicity, urgency, and intimacy of worship that communicate with zeal and conviction the immanence of God and the equality of all human beings before their Maker. The two traditions may be understood as encapsulating the two halves of the Great Commandment: Love God and love your neighbor. Both traditions place great importance on conscience. Too often in the mainline churches, one runs across the unfortunate attitude that because God loves us no matter what we do, it doesn't matter what we do. The answer to that problem is not more legalism, more institutional control over individual thought and action, but more emphasis on individual conscience—and I mean conscience understood not as a civil right but as a sacred responsibility.

There is also a need for greater emphasis on spirituality. Contemporary American experience seems almost to have been consciously designed in such a way as to shut the spiritual out of our lives. Many of us keep a television on constantly to avoid the silence—to drown out the still, small voice. We are used to having things handed to us neatly—food processed, illness and death sanitized, all uncomfortable aspects of reality removed from our sight so that we don't have to think about them. We exaggerate the value of material possessions grotesquely, and in the name of prosperity and convenience rob ourselves of beauty by dotting the landscape with mile after mile of strip malls and fast-food outlets. It is no wonder that traditional liturgical churches make many Americans uncomfortable: Such churches make them realize, on some level, how far removed their lives really are from the truly spiritual. Naturally millions of Americans respond more enthusiastically to mall churches and to *The 700 Club*—for they present religion as another consumer item, and sell faith like a can of spray-on hair. And their theology appeals to the American sense of competitiveness, the need to have a bigger house or a nicer car than one's neighbor: *Ha, you're going to spend eternity in a lake of fire and I'll be at the right hand of God!*

The materialism of American life, and the closing off of American lives to a large extent from the realities of death and illness, make it difficult for many Americans to relate to the idea of the kingdom of heaven in a mystical sense, or for that matter to experience their lives in a mystical way; we are so overwhelmed by possessions, by the daily news headlines, by E-mail and phone messages and our scores of TV stations, that to distance ourselves from all this horizontal experience and connect with the vertical plane—and then to live out the truths of our vertical experience in our daily lives—can be an immense challenge. So it is that for many Americans who call themselves Christians, religion is not at all a matter of spiritual experience, of seeking to live out God's radical love, but rather of adhering to certain laws and pledging assent to certain doctrines. In this business-centered culture, religion is widely seen as a matter of quid pro quo dealmaking: We give God ourselves, and he gives us salvation.

Yet beneath the spirituality-killing surface of contemporary American culture lies a deep, unfulfilled hunger for genuine spiritual experience. Too often, alas, Americans who jettison traditional religion fill its place with shallow means of seeking connection to the Ultimate— astrology, est, Scientology, the palm reader down the block, the Psychic Friends Network. When it comes down to it, most of these things are, like legalistic Christianity, about the first-person singular: What's *my* fortune? What's best for *me*? Where will *I* go after death? One test of true spiritual experience is that it lifts one above petty solipsism and enhances one's sense of connection to, affection for, and responsibility toward others. Yet as much of the history of the Church of Love has shown, it is not enough to focus a church's mission on selfless rhetoric and socially responsible outreach programs; at the core of the church's communal life must be a genuine spiritual vitality—a sense of one's connection to the God of the universe and to the entirety of humankind that is so powerful that one experiences God's love for oneself even as one transcends self-concern.

While the Church of Love has much to learn, indeed, from the examples of Jefferson, Rauschenbusch, and Fosdick, what is sometimes insufficiently apparent in the examples of all of these men is an emphasis on spiritual experience. From the teachings of Jesus, Jefferson distilled a personal ethic for himself and other men of privilege; Rauschenbusch distilled a social program by which to help the poor;

and Fosdick distilled a life philosophy for college-educated men of the middle class. It is plain that Rauschenbusch and Fosdick—if not Jefferson—were deeply spiritual men, but all too often they failed to emphasize sufficiently the spiritual foundation of their messages of love and service. Sometimes, to people desperately in search of the vertical, these men could seem too horizontal, too indifferent to life's mystical dimension. The same may be said of such immensely popular twentieth-century ministers as Norman Vincent Peale and Robert Schuller, who, while preaching (usually) a God of love and not of law, focused less on spiritual growth than on materialistic success, and on a distinctively American—and horizontal—"prosperity gospel" that too often appealed not to people's altruism but to their selfishness. At its worst, this prosperity gospel devolved into Jim and Tammy Faye Bakker's wholesale endorsement of gross materialism. One of the lessons of such ministerial careers is that in order to motivate people to act selflessly on the horizontal plane, churches need to do the best job they can to bring those people into meaningful contact with the vertical plane, and not simply feed them messages that God wants them to be rich.

Example after example demonstrates that if the Church of Love is to bloom in the new millennium, it will do so through a renewed emphasis on spiritual experience as the necessary heart of Christian community life. In *The Empty Church,* his legalistic jeremiad against the "liberal" mainline church, Thomas C. Reeves grudgingly acknowledges that All Saints Episcopal Church in Pasadena, despite its extremely "liberal" and gay-friendly stance, draws huge numbers of people because it takes seriously its obligation to provide spiritually meaningful worship services. The equally nonlegalistic Episcopal Cathedral in Seattle is said to attract upward of fifteen hundred people, most of them reportedly between eighteen and twenty-five and with little or no formal religious background, to its traditional Compline services. It is the failure of many nonlegalistic churches to respond seriously to people's hunger for such worship that has caused many Americans to reject those churches' politicized atmospheres in favor of legalistic churches that at least purport to concern themselves with things transcendent.

More and more nonlegalistic churches do appear to be recognizing the need for them to focus more seriously on the spiritual dimension. In a December 1996 *New York Times* article, Gustav Niebuhr noted that even the Unitarians—members of that ultrarationalistic, noncreedal fellowship that Thomas Jefferson saw as the future of American religion, and which now has about 200,000 members in the United States—have changed their tune. The Unitarian-Universalist Association has not dropped its social conscience, its inclusiveness, its respect for the individual and the intellect; but what it has done is to turn sharply away from its often unspiritual—and sometimes even antispiritual—past. Unitarian congregations, wrote Niebuhr, "are increasingly exploring ritual, forms of prayer and meditation, candle-lighting and music, drawn from Western, East Asian, American Indian and other religious sources."

In George Orwell's 1949 novel *1984,* set in a dark totalitarian future, the protagonist's ultimate capitulation to the political authorities is illustrated by his willingness to assent to the statement that two plus two equals five. If one thinks of mathematics as a metaphor for religion, this is what the mathematics of legalistic Christianity amounts to—the simple Orwellian arithmetic of two plus two equals five. To be a legalist, in other words, is to embrace as true a proposition or set of propositions that plainly and directly contradict the facts of observable reality, even though one does not admit the contradiction to others and tries not to admit it even to oneself. By contrast, the mathematics of, say, mainstream Anglican belief can be said to involve the theological equivalent of imaginary numbers. Imaginary numbers, which represent something that is absolutely real but that cannot be explained in terms of the world of three spatial dimensions and one temporal dimension in which we live, become necessary when one seeks to find the square root of a number below zero. The square root of -4, for example, is $2i$, with the letter i indicating that this is not the "real" number 2 but the "imaginary" number 2. "Imaginary" does not mean that the number exists only in the imagination; it means that the number designates something that cannot be described or understood in the terms of this material world and the nature of which the human mind must strive imaginatively to apprehend. Imaginary numbers are very real indeed in the sense that they "work" mathematically: One can carry out a mathematical operation that takes one through steps involving imaginary numbers and find one's way back to a "real" solution, the correctness of which can be verified by practical experience. Such, too, is the realm of the spiritual.

In the 1920s, when Fosdick was fighting the fundamentalist wars, making Christianity and science cohere seemed to many (Einstein notwithstanding) to mean being obliged to make religion conform to the strictures of Newton's rational, mechanistic, determinate universe. Today, however, quantum physics and chaos theory are helping us to see that while a mechanistic, determinate view of the universe may seem consistent with most phenomena at the level of human experience, the reality of activity at the subatomic and cosmic levels is something else again. We have learned things that at first blush appear to make no sense—that something can be at once a wave and a particle; that some infinities are greater than others; that neither space nor time is as straightforward and objective a phenomenon as people used to think; and that the closed four-dimensional system that we call the universe may well be only an infinitesimal part of a vast creation of many dimensions and universes, each of them "splitting" at every moment into an infinitude of parallel universes in which are represented every possible outcome of every subatomic event of the previous moment. Einstein taught us that matter can be converted into energy; now we know that time can turn into space, space into time. To contemplate such facts is to contemplate spiritual mystery; it is, as the title of a book by the Australian physicist Paul Davies suggests, to seek to grasp the mind of God.

Many legalistic Christians—to the extent that they are aware at all of the theories and discoveries of modern physics—view them, along with evolution, as threats to established belief. Some nonlegalistic Christians, too, see modern science as a threat: Though they accept its discoveries, they regard the gradual expansion of the sphere of scientific knowledge as diminishing, bit by bit, the sphere of mystery over which religion presides, and as placing religion thereby in a defensive position, forced continually to reformulate its postulates in order to conform with established truth. Yet science should properly be seen not as something to be adjusted to defensively but as an aid, an ally, a means of inquiry that can help us to discern the whole truth of God. Indeed, there is something about many of the new scientific insights that makes them feel quite consistent with the notion of spiritual experience. A universe more complicated than one can imagine fits with a God who is greater than we can imagine. It might even be said that science's new insights make room for the miraculous—not for virgin births and weeping Madonna paintings, to be sure, but for certain genuine instances of déjà vu and other violations of time's apparent one-way street, as well as for sundry apparent experiences of the numinous. If many contemporary works of theology—especially legalistic theology—can make the whole idea of God feel like a quaint, anachronistic self-delusion, many works of modern physics seem almost to be pointing to and insisting upon the reality of God and of what we call spiritual experience, even if they never employ words like *God* and *spirit*. Such works, indeed, can at times recall the works of Christian mystics, who in their struggle to characterize the nature of mystical experience and of the realm beyond the immediate and tangible often speak a language that has its affinities to the language of modern physics.

In a June 1996 *New Yorker* piece about a memorial service for former *Time* magazine editor Richard M. Clurman, the writer Christopher Buckley quotes a comment made at the service by his father, the conservative columnist William F. Buckley. "It came to me last Thursday," said the elder Buckley, "when the news [of Clurman's death] reached me just after midnight, that I have always subconsciously looked out for the total Christian, and when I found him he turned out to be a nonpracticing Jew." This comment was especially striking since it was made by a staunchly traditionalist Roman Catholic whose writings make clear his devotion to some of his church's most rigorous, exclusionary dogmas. Implicit in the elder Buckley's remarks about Clurman is a deep insight to which one wishes Buckley would devote some serious reflection. What Buckley perceived in reflecting on the life of his friend, presumably, was that being a Christian, in the deepest sense, is a matter not of theology but of love.

Indeed, the church needs desperately to grapple with the fact that when we insist on faith statements as the core of the faith, we assault not only truth but virtue. Decades ago, Reinhold Niebuhr wrote that "no Christian church has a right to preach to a so-called secular age without a contrite recognition of the shortcomings of historic Christianity which tempted the modern age to disavow its Christian faith." While secularism, Niebuhr noted, can be "the expression of man's sinful self-sufficiency," it can also be "a reaction to profanity"—to the profanity, that is, of some Christian faith statements. For some people "are atheists because of a higher implicit theism than that professed by believers. They reject God because His name has been taken in vain, and they are unable to distinguish between His holiness and its profanation." In other words, they rebel, both intellectually and morally, against what legalistic faiths have made of God, "both in the realm of truth and in the realm of the good, in both culture and ethics."

Paul Tillich pointed in the proper direction when he wrote that "if we want to speak in truth without foolish, wishful thinking, we should speak about the eternal that is neither timelessness [n]or endless time. The mystery of the future is answered in the eternal of which we may speak in images taken from time. But if we forget that the images are images, we fall into absurdities and self-deceptions. There is not time *after* time, but there is eternity *above* time." Religion, Tillich insisted in his contribution to a 1950 *Partisan Review* symposium on "Religion and the Intellectuals,"

> is not *a collection of theoretical statements of a questionable or absurd or superstitious character. Such a religion could not be accepted by any intellectual who is not willing to sacrifice his intellectual honesty. Some of them make this sacrifice and surrender their intellectual autonomy to Ecclesiastical or Biblical authorities. But their turn to religion is still an expression of their despair, not a victory over it. Others are waiting for a religious answer which does not destroy reason but points to the depth of reason; which does not teach the supernatural, but points to the mystery in the ground of the natural, which denies that God is a being and speaks of Him as the ground and depth of being and meaning, which knows about the significance of symbols in myth and cult, but resists the distortion of symbols into statements of knowledge which necessarily conflict with scientific knowledge.*

Such an understanding of faith statements remains beyond the grasp of too many Americans today. A typical contemporary comment appeared in a 1996 *Newsweek* article that claimed that if the theologians of the controversial Jesus Seminar were correct in denying the historical veracity of the virgin birth and other biblical events, then every tenet of traditional Christianity would go "out the window," including the Resurrection. Such a statement could be made only by someone with a legalistic understanding of the nature of Christian belief—someone who doesn't recognize that *every* religious statement is a metaphor, a stab in the dark, an attempt to express in human words something that lies beyond human understanding or expression. To choose a religion is to choose a set of metaphors that comport best with the promptings of one's own instincts and conscience and that seems to point most truly, virtuously, and beautifully to the "depth of reason."

The point that Christianity is essentially about the person of Jesus and not about doctrine has been made forcefully by Hans Küng, perhaps the most distinguished theologian of our time, in his recent book *Christianity: Essence, History, and Future*. This work of theological history distinguishes between the "abiding substance" of Christianity, which Küng locates in the person of Jesus, and its "shifting paradigm," which he identifies with religious institutions, dogma, and law, which change from age to age. "The distinctive Christian feature," writes Küng, "is christological. It is not a doctrine of Christ to be speculated on, not a dogma of Christ which one 'must believe,' but . . . Jesus Christ whom one must follow." What, he asks, "is the decisive factor for Christian action, for Christian ethics? What is the criterion of the Christian, the distinguishing mark of the Christian in practice . . . ? The answer is: Jesus as the normative concrete person."

Küng's point about the absolute importance of Jesus and the relative unimportance of doctrine has been made forcefully over the generations. As George M. Marsden has noted, Augustus H. Strong, a president of Rochester Seminary in Rauschenbusch's time, believed that "truth was not doctrinal or propositional, but rather 'the truth is a personal Being, and that Christ Himself is the Truth.'" Strong complained of the church in his time that its view of truth "was too abstract and literal"; yet he also expressed legitimate concern about "the liberal drift away from supernaturalism in Christianity," the tendency to turn Christ into "a merely ethical teacher." Fosdick's fundamentalist critics accused him of doing precisely this, complaining that he encouraged young people to approach Christianity as an intellectual construct and not as a matter of spirit and grace. On the contrary, Fosdick's whole point was to encourage young people to look beyond the outmoded intellectual formulations of earlier generations to the enduring and spiritually enlivening truths inherent in the person of Jesus Christ, and to seek modern terms in which to convey their profound experience of those truths. That is an experience, he emphasized, that no mere doctrine should be permitted to hinder.

Indeed, one may safely make the following observations about religious doctrine: The more elaborate a set of doctrines, the more likely it is to be wrong to some degree; the more elaborate a set of doctrines, the greater the number of people who will find it impossible to believe; the more elaborate a set of doctrines, the more likely it is to be an esoteric academic exercise and not an expression of living belief. What is religious doctrine, after all, but a set of metaphorical statements? What does it mean to say that Jesus was the Son of God, a part of the Trinity along with God the Father and the Holy Spirit? What does it mean to say that these are three Persons but one God? Certainly Jesus was not the son of God in any biological sense; and when we speak of God as three persons we do not mean *Homo sapiens*. To discuss God in such terms is to apply metaphorically to the deity words that are ordinarily used to describe human natures and relationships. The idea is to find some way of imagining the unimaginable by characterizing it in human terms. That Jesus is the son of God and that God has three persons are among the faith statements to which many Christian communions require their members to subscribe. Yet for a Christian to use some other set of metaphorical formulations to speak of God is not necessarily to deny Christianity.

And what of the statement that Jesus was at once wholly human and wholly God? This paradoxical claim, by which Christians have always felt challenged, was first formulated in an attempt to express the powerful sense of early Christians that Jesus, though wholly human, had been related to God in a unique way. Was it a matter of his being more intimate with God than other human beings, or of his being, in some astonishing way, actually identical with God? The church pronounced that it would be heretical to believe the former and orthodox to believe the latter: Jesus had, in short, been God. But what does it mean to say this? Jesus never claimed to be anything but human. In his preaching and on the cross he addressed God as Father, intimate yet still Other, and never spelled out the precise nature of his relationship to that Father. Early on, when some people sought to understand Jesus as being rather like the Greek and Roman deities who, in various myths, had been said to take on the guise of a human being for one reason or another, the bulk of Christians forcefully rejected the idea. They realized that it was vital to retain the understanding of Jesus as human. To view Jesus as a "God in disguise" was to diminish what he was, what he accomplished, and what he suffered. Yet many legalistic Christians today are extremely uncomfortable with the implications of Jesus' humanity—with, among much else, the notion that he experienced such emotions as fear, vulnerability, and sexual attraction. Legalists tend to prefer the totally transcendent Christ who, according to the theological visions of Darby, Scofield, Lindsey, and Robertson, will return to Earth in power, will judge, and will destroy.

The real Jesus—the Jesus who was incontrovertibly human, even as he was connected to God in a remarkable way that utterly transformed the lives of the people who knew him—was not about asserting power, judging, or destroying; he was about love. To many legalistic Christians today, this sounds trivial, simplistic, and irrelevant to their perceived religious needs and desires. People whose lives contain an insufficiency of love may indeed find it difficult to believe that love—mere love— is really what it's all about. They are likely to be more impressed by power, hate, vengeance, and destructiveness than they are by love. In the world as they know it, love may seem a fragile commodity and may be more often connected with weakness than with power. But Jesus came precisely to speak to people like them and to tell them otherwise—to reveal to them the ultimate supremacy of love. Lose Jesus as a human being and you lose that: You lose Jesus as a model of how to lead a human life; you lose the possibility of love as a guiding principle of human relations; you lose Christianity—or, at least, you lose any Christianity worth the name.

And that's what legalistic Christianity in America today is about. If you wanted to destroy the idea of a Church of Love once and for all, you would target the real Jesus and attach his name instead to a vengeful, bloodthirsty monster. This is what legalistic Christianity does at its most extreme. Even some of the less-extreme legalistic churches, while invoking the idea of love, try to redefine the word in a way that would not have been recognizable to Jesus' original followers. "Love the sinner, hate the sin," legalists say, as an excuse for despising people who either refuse or are unable to change themselves in such a way as to eliminate those aspects of themselves that legalists consider sinful. Jesus would never have made such a distinction.

In Mark Twain's *Adventures of Huckleberry Finn,* the white boy Huck, who has helped the slave Jim to escape from his owner, Miss Watson, feels "the plain hand of Providence slapping me in the face and letting me know my wickedness was being watched all the time from up there in heaven, whilst I was stealing a poor old woman's nigger that hadn't ever done me no harm." He decides that in order to get right with God and avoid "everlasting fire," he's got to "do the right thing and the clean thing, and go and write to that nigger's owner and tell where he was." He does so, and then feels "good and all washed clean of sin for the first time I had ever felt so in my life."

But before posting the letter, Huck thinks of Jim. "And got to thinking over our trip down the river; and I see Jim before me, all the time, in the day, and in the night-time, sometimes moonlight, sometimes storms, and we a floating along, talking, and singing, and laughing. But somehow I couldn't seem to strike no places to harden me against him, but only the other kind." He thinks about how sweet and good and gentle Jim always is with him, and what a good friend he is. Then Huck looks around and sees the letter he's written to Miss Watson.

> I took it up, and held it in my hand. I was a trembling, because I'd got to
> decide, forever, betwixt two things, and I knowed it. I studied a minute,
> sort of holding my breath, and then says to myself,
> "All right, then, I'll go to hell"—and tore it up.

Though his society and its churches, which have set God up as a supporter of slavery, tell him he's wrong to help Jim escape and will go to hell for it, Huck's love and his conscience compel him to help Jim anyway. In the end, by acting in accordance with his love and conscience,

Huck does the truly Christian thing. The story offers a useful lesson in the failings of the institutional church, and in the nature of real Christian thought and action. The true disciple of Jesus, Twain tells us here, is not someone who follows Church dogma out of fear of hell; it is someone who, in defiance of everything, up to and including the threat of hellfire, does the right thing out of love.

It should not be surprising that many people are not only willing but eager to believe in the kind of God who supports slavery or who has a Great Tribulation in store for all but a few of his children. Growing up in a culture fixated on material possessions and on the price tags attached to them can make it easy to believe in a God for whom the afterlife is a matter of cold-blooded dealmaking: *Believe in me and I'll give you heaven; refuse and you go to hell.* Given how much evil and pain there is in the world, one can hardly fault some people for believing in a wrathful God. But *worshipping* such a God? Rather than do so, I would suggest that we shake our heads firmly, affirming our allegiance to Jesus, and say with Huckleberry Finn, "All right, then, I'll *go* to hell."

Such is the kingdom of heaven.

BIBLIOGRAPHY

Here follows a highly selective list of resources that are suitable for a general readership and available in at least some bookstores or libraries or online.

THE ANGLICAN TRADITION:
The Study of Anglicanism, ed. Stephen Sykes and John Booty (SPCK/Fortress Press, 1988), provides an excellent introduction. *The Spirit of Anglicanism,* ed. William J. Wolf (Morehouse-Barlow, 1979), contains essays on theologians who shaped Anglican spirituality; *To Believe Is to Pray* (Cowley, 1997) is a collection of Michael Ramsey's writings on Anglican belief. An unofficial Episcopal Church home page at http://www.ai.mit.edu/people/mib/anglican/anglican.html has links to the official home pages of other mainline denominations and to such organizations as the World Council of Churches.

THE BAPTIST TRADITION:
E. Y. Mullins's *Baptist Beliefs* (1912, still in print from Judson Press) and Walter Shurden's *The Baptist Identity* (Smyth & Helwys, 1993) summarize historic Baptist principles; *The Struggle for the Soul of the SBC* (Mercer, 1993), edited by Shurden, recounts the moderate-fundamentalist conflict. Ex-SBC president Jimmy Allen's memoir *Burden of a Secret* (Moorings, 1995) describes some of his friction with SBC fundamentalists. The home page for Charles Stanley's First Baptist Church of Atlanta is at http://www.worship.com/fbca; Stanley's In Touch Ministries Web site is at http://www.intouch.org. Available at http://www.utm.edu/martinarea/fbc/bfm.html are a copy of the Baptist Faith and Message and links to other SBC sites.

BIBLE:
L. William Countryman's *Biblical Authority or Biblical Tyranny?* (1982, available in a revised 1994 edition from Trinity Press International and Cowley) examines the nature of scriptural authority; Uta Ranke-Heinemann's *Putting Away Childish Things* (HarperCollins, 1994) separates biblical truth from "fairy tales"; John Shelby Spong's *Rescuing the Bible from Fundamentalism* (HarperCollins, 1991) assails literal interpretations; Peter Gomes's *The Good Book* (Morrow, 1996) shows how the Bible has been used to justify bigotry.

CHARISMATIC CHRISTIANITY:
The standard account of the movement, *They Speak with Other Tongues,* by Robert Sherrill (Revell, 1964), is available in a 1993 Spire paperback.

CHRISTIAN BROADCASTING NETWORK AND CHRISTIAN
COALITION:
The Internet sites are at http://www.cbn.org and http://cc.org respectively.
Key works include *The Autobiography of Pat Robertson* (Bridge, 1972); *The Col-
lected Works of Pat Robertson* (Inspirational Press, 1994), which contains *The
New Millennium, The New World Order,* and *The Secret Kingdom;* Ralph Reed's
Active Faith (Free Press, 1996); and *Contract with the American Family* (Moorings,
1995).

CHURCH GROWTH:
Dean Kelley's *Why Conservative Churches Are Growing* (Harper & Row, 1972, 1977,
1986) and Roger Finke and Rodney Stark's *The Churching of America 1776–
1990* (Rutgers, 1992) offer convincing analyses and unsettling priorities; Thomas
C. Reeves's *The Empty Church* (Free Press, 1996) is a legalistic Episcopalian's
diatribe.

CULTURE WARS:
James Davison Hunter's *Culture Wars* (Basic, 1991) has a prolegalistic slant.

DISPENSATIONALISM:
The Scofield Reference Bible (Oxford, 1909) and the New Scofield Reference
Bible (Oxford, 1967) are both in print; E. Schuyler English's *Companion to the New
Scofield Reference Bible* (Oxford, 1972) and Charles C. Ryrie's *Dispensationalism*
(Moody, 1995) provide partisan overviews.

DOCTRINE:
Jaroslav Pelikan's five-volume *The Christian Tradition: A History of the Development
of Doctrine* (Chicago, 1971–1989) is definitive; Hans Küng's *Christianity: Essence,
History, and Future* (Continuum, 1996) brilliantly reviews the evolution of Christian belief, showing how its faces have changed while its essence has not. Gerd
Lüdemann's *Heretics* (Westminster-John Knox, 1995) argues that the more authentic Christians lost early church battles over heresy.

EVANGELICALISM:
George M. Marsden's *Understanding Fundamentalism and Evangelicalism* (Eerdmans,
1991) surveys both movements; his *Reforming Fundamentalism: Fuller Seminary and
the New Evangelicalism* (Eerdmans, 1987) traces the New Evangelicalism's rise by
focusing on its flagship seminary's history. Mark A. Noll's *The Scandal of the Evangelical Mind* (Eerdmans, 1994) indicts the movement's anti-intellectualism. Contents
of current and back issues of *Christianity Today, Campus Life,* and other magazines
can be found at http://www.christianity.net and on AOL (keyword: "Christianity
Today"), as can message boards aplenty in which legalistic Christians of every stripe
dispute theological particulars.

FICTION:
Frank Peretti's *This Present Darkness* (1986) and *Piercing the Darkness* (1989) are both
in paper from Crossway. Pat Robertson's name adorns an End Times novel, *The
End of the Age* (Word, 1996).

FOCUS ON THE FAMILY:

James Dobson's best-selling *Dare to Discipline* (Tyndale, 1977) has been succeeded by *The New Dare to Discipline* (Tyndale, 1996). Tyndale's *Dr. Dobson Answers Your Questions* series contains volumes on marriage, child-rearing, and other topics. Excerpts from *Focus on the Family* magazine and other FOF magazines—two focusing on politics and media, and others directed variously at children, teenagers, single parents, doctors, teachers, and pastors' families—are available at FOF's America Online site (keyword: "Focus on the Family"). Dobson's longtime radio cohost, Gil Alexander Moegerle, has written an exposé, *James Dobson's War on America* (1997, Prometheus).

FUNDAMENTALISM:

The Fundamentals (1920) is in print from Garland in a costly 1988 edition edited by George M. Marsden, whose *Fundamentalism and American Culture* (Oxford, 1980) superbly recounts American fundamentalism's genesis. James Barr's *Fundamentalism* (Westminster, 1978) and Nancy Tatom Ammerman's *Bible Believers* (Rutgers, 1987) anatomize the movement; Carl Henry's *The Uneasy Conscience of Modern Fundamentalism* (Eerdmans, 1947) is a mid-century critique by a leading New Evangelical; Harold Bloom's *The American Religion* (Simon & Schuster, 1992) offers an idiosyncratic treatment of the Mormons, the SBC, and other legalistic groups; the five-volume *Fundamentalism Project,* edited by Martin E. Marty and R. Scott Appleby (Chicago, 1991–95), comprehensively examines fundamentalisms worldwide. Charles B. Strozier's *Apocalypse: On the Psychology of Fundamentalism in America* (Beacon, 1994) scrutinizes the fundamentalist sensibility as exemplified by members of a contemporary New York church; Stefan Ulstein's *Growing Up Fundamentalist* (Inter-Varsity, 1995) offers riveting testimonies; Sally Lowe Whitehead's *The Truth Shall Set You Free* (HarperCollins, 1997) recounts her family's journey through fundamentalism.

GENERAL:

The Yahoo search engine has a magnificent directory of resources at http://www.yahoo.com/Society_and_Culture/Religion/Christianity.

GOD:

Karen Armstrong's *A History of God* (Knopf, 1993) limns the changing perceptions of God in Judaism, Christianity, and Islam; Jack Miles's *God: A Biography* (Knopf, 1995) traces the changing view of God as reflected in the Hebrew Bible; Marcus J. Borg's *The God We Never Knew* (HarperSanFrancisco, 1997) seeks to move beyond legalistic images of God.

GOSPELS:

The Jefferson Bible is in print from Beacon (1989). *The Five Gospels* (Macmillan, 1993) presents the Jesus Seminar's conclusions as to what Jesus did and didn't say. Stephen Mitchell's *The Gospel According to Jesus* (HarperCollins, 1991) distills the Gospels into a single narrative. Spong's *Resurrection: Myth or Reality* (HarperCollins, 1994) reinterprets that event.

THE HISTORICAL JESUS:

John Dominic Crossan's *The Historical Jesus* (HarperCollins, 1991) and *Jesus: A Revolutionary Biography* (HarperCollins, 1994), Marcus Borg's *Meeting Jesus Again for the First Time* (HarperCollins, 1994), and E. P. Sanders's *The Historical Figure of Jesus* (Allen Lane, 1993) offer revisionist views; in *The Real Jesus: The Misguided Quest for the Historical Jesus and the Truth of the Traditional Gospels* (HarperCollins, 1996), Luke Timothy Johnson assails the revisionists; Russell Shorto's *Gospel Truth* (Riverhead, 1997) provides an overview of the controversy. Huston Smith's *The World's Religions* (HarperCollins, 1991) is wonderful on Jesus.

HISTORY:

Sydney Ahlstrom's *Religious History of the American People* (Yale, 1974) and Mark A. Noll's *History of Christianity in the United States and Canada* (Eerdmans, 1992) provide comprehensive accounts; Martin E. Marty's *Pilgrims in Their Own Land* (Little, Brown, 1984) shapes American religious history into an engaging narrative. Jonathan Edwards's "Sinners in the Hands of an Angry God" is available in many standard anthologies of American literature as well as in *The Puritans: A Sourcebook of Their Writings* (Harper, revised 1963), a useful two-volume compendium edited by Perry Miller and Thomas H. Johnson. Christine Leigh Heyrman's *Southern Cross* (Knopf, 1997) surveys primary sources to show how different early Baptists and Methodists were from today's "traditional" members of those faiths.

INERRANCY:

Inerrantist manifestos include W. A. Criswell's *Why I Preach That the Bible Is Literally True* (Broadman and Holman, 1995) and Harold Lindsell's *The Battle for the Bible* (Zondervan, 1978). Critiques include Gordon James's *Inerrancy and the Southern Baptist Convention* (Southern Baptist Heritage Press, 1986).

INTELLECTUALS:

Examples of intellectuals' views of American religion are Andrew Delbanco's *The Death of Satan: How Americans Have Lost the Sense of Evil* (1995), Richard Hofstadter's *Anti-Intellectualism in American Life* (Knopf, 1962), and David Klinghoffer's essay in *Dumbing Down: Essays on the Strip-Mining of American Culture,* edited by Katharine Washburn and John F. Thornton (Norton, 1996).

MEGACHURCHES:

Charles Trueheart's "Welcome to the Next Church" in *Atlantic Monthly* (August 1996) is a fine overview; also see Willow Creek Community Church's site at http://www.willowcreek.org.

MODERN THEOLOGY:

Hans Küng's *On Being a Christian* (Image, 1976) is a capacious meditation from a nonlegalistic perspective; his *Credo* (Doubleday, 1993) elegantly rereads the Nicene Creed. *Love and Justice* (Westminster/John Knox, 1992) collects some of Reinhold Niebuhr's shorter works. Though the 1988 Collier reprint of *The Essential Tillich,* which introduces Paul Tillich's work, is out of print, his *The Courage to Be* (Yale, 1952) is available.

PROMISE KEEPERS:

Seven Promises of a Promise Keeper, edited by Al Janssen (Focus on the Family, 1994), is the official introduction; the official Web site is at http://www.promisekeepers.org.

PROPHECY:

Hal Lindsey's books include *The Late Great Planet Earth* (Zondervan, 1970) and *Planet Earth—2000 A.D* (Western Front, 1994, 1996).

RELIGIOUS RIGHT:

William Martin's *With God on Our Side: The Rise of the Religious Right in America* (Broadway, 1996), the accessible companion volume to the PBS series of the same name, avoids taking sides; Clyde Wilcox's *Onward Christian Soldiers* (Westview, 1996) is more academic but also more forthright.

SEXUAL MORALITY:

John Boswell's *Christianity, Social Tolerance, and Homosexuality* (Chicago, 1980) is definitive; *Our Selves, Our Souls and Bodies: Sexuality and the Household of God* (Cowley, 1996), edited by Charles Hefling, Jr., contains superb essays on sex and Christianity; L. William Countryman's *Dirt, Greed and Sex* (Fortress, 1988) examines the contemporary implications of New Testament sexual ethics.

THE SOCIAL GOSPEL AND AFTER:

Walter Rauschenbusch's *Christianity and the Social Crisis* (1907) is in paperback from Westminster/John Knox Press; Paul Minus's biography of Rauschenbusch (Macmillan, 1988) is out of print. None of Harry Emerson Fosdick's works is in print; libraries may own *The Modern Use of the Bible* (West Richard, 1925) or *As I See Religion* (Greenwood reprint, 1975). *Christian Century* is the leading journal of "liberal Christianity." Jim Wallis has written *The Soul of Politics* (New Press, 1994) and edits *Sojourners.* The Interfaith Alliance has a Web site at http://www.intr.-net/tialliance.

INDEX

Abortion, 17, 159, 175, 190, 195, 196, 198, 253
Absolutism, 11, 122, 134
Abusive relationships, 238–39, 272
Active Faith: How Christians Are Changing the Soul of American Politics (Reed), 68, 74, 171, 173, 177–78, 179, 188–89, 192, 195, 196–97, 198
Acts of the Apostles, 56, 74, 88–89, 98, 132
Adam and Eve, 84, 256, 257, 260, 261
Adams, John, 67, 68, 69–70, 71, 72, 73
African Americans, 29–31, 109, 120, 133, 143–44, 194, 196, 253, 262, 275, 287
Ahlstrom, Sydney E., 84, 110, 155
Allen, Jimmy, 37, 224, 225, 228
American Revolution, 66–67, 68, 72
Anger: of God, 211–12, 328; of Jesus, 244–46; of legalistic Christians, 11–12
Anglican Church, 51, 62–65, 308, 320–21; and Church of Love, 316–17; as established church in Virginia, 71; and individualism, 157, 283; Jefferson's views about, 71, 72; as liberal, 173; and Methodists, 79; Reed, 173
Anti-intellectualism, 8, 9, 61, 141, 146, 279
Anti-Semitism, 57, 270, 274, 279
Armstrong, Karen, 10, 65
Ascension, 89, 99–100, 106
Asimov, Isaac, 24–25
Assemblies of God, 8, 79, 133
Atheism, 7, 72, 183, 323
Atonement, 6, 40, 42, 48, 88, 92, 93, 111, 116, 209, 212, 229
Augustine of Hippo, 40, 58
Authority: of Bible, 7, 41, 58, 241–42; Catholic Church as, 60; of clergy, 133, 236–38; and early Christianity, 55; and founding fathers, 70; of God, 234–36, 240–41; government as, 55–56, 205; of husbands, 237–39, 256, 261–62; individual as, 47; institutional, 283; Jesus' resistance to, 56; Klinghoffer on, 283; and legalistic Christians, 5, 11, 205, 247, 262; love as, 62; "Nature" as, 73; and nonlegalistic Christians, 47; papal, 62; paternal, 81; philosophy as, 121–22; for Puritanism, 64; for teachings of Jesus, 47; of tradition, 283

Bakker, Tammy Faye and Jim, 299–300, 319
Baptism: Anabaptists on, 64; of Bawer, 2, 16, 18, 26; and dispensationalism, 99; of Holy Spirit, 133; Jefferson on, 72; by Jesus, 46; and legalistic Christians, 202; in Matthew, 57; Rauschenbusch on, 95
Baptists, 9, 22–23, 79–82, 88, 132–33, 137, 156–59, 174, 283, 308, 316–17. *See also* Northern Baptist Convention; Southern Baptist Convention
Baylor University, 158
Bertolucci, Bernardo, 291
Bible: and anger of Jesus, 244–46; authority of, 7, 41, 58, 241–42; Congressional, 74–75, 98;

contradictions in, 85, 88–89, 98, 99, 112, 161; and culture wars, 164–65; and dispensationalism, 85; and evangelicalism, 241; and evolution, 84; and fundamentalism, 24, 41, 88; as history, 7, 84–85, 117; and homosexuality, 282; and individualism, 9, 164; and inerrancy, 111–12, 116, 140–41, 142, 158–59, 161–63, 222–23; as inspiration, 114; and intellectuals, 277; and legalistic Christians, 7, 9, 89, 203, 205–6, 208, 221–22, 229, 242, 246; and literalism, 9, 24, 84, 85, 87–88, 89, 90, 92, 96–97, 105–6, 117, 122, 127, 133, 147, 161–62, 164, 309–10; and modernism, 87–88, 178; and morality, 222–23; and nonlegalistic Christians, 7, 309–10; as poetry or prose, 115, 116, 117; and Promise Keepers, 261; prophecy in, 147; and science, 179–80; and Scopes trial, 124–28; and secularism, 277; selective interpretation of, 165; and Social Gospel, 95; and takeover by Southern Baptist Convention, 161–63; as truth, 7, 184–85. *See also* Gospels; New Testament; Old Testament; Prophecy; Scofield Reference Bible; *specific book of Bible, person, or denomination*
Bloom, Allan, 175
Brotherhood of the Kingdom, 93–94, 95
Bryan, William Jennings, 124, 125, 126–27, 180, 191
Buckley, Christopher, 322
Buckley, William F., 322
Buddha, 291–92
Buddhism, 112, 183

Call to Renewal, 9, 311
Calvin, John, 21, 62, 308
Calvinism, 206. *See also* Puritanism
Capitalism, 168, 180–81, 305
Carter, Jimmy, 144, 170, 190, 191
Catholics/Catholic Church, 3–5, 8, 9, 17–19, 23, 37–38, 58–62, 133–37, 164; ecumenism of, 174; in movies, 294–96; and New Evangelicalism, 140; and Promise Keepers, 264; and Southern Baptist Convention, 162, 296
Celibacy, 295–96
Chalcedon, Council of, 47
Charismatic religion, 7, 8–9, 132, 133, 162, 168, 169, 204, 214, 259
Children: abuse of, 238–39, 272; Dobson's views about, 248, 251, 253, 255; and gay parents, 272; and good and evil battle, 241; Halloween publication for, 234–36, 241; and legalistic Christians, 272; love of, 6; parishioners treated like, 236–38; submissiveness of, 238. *See also* Baby boom generation
Christian Broadcasting Network (CBN), 68, 169, 170, 177, 181, 234, 297, 299
Christian Coalition: agenda and rhetoric of, 196–98; and categorization of Christians, 9; and civility, 196; and family issues, 182–83; founding/rise of,

26, 163, 170, 273; and homosexuality, 195, 196, 254; ignorance about, 172–73, 198; image of, 173, 182; and intellectuals, 279; and Interfaith Alliance, 310, 311; and liberalism, 279; mainstreaming of, 198; and media, 9, 273, 297; and military metaphors, 196–98; and morality, 196; and politics, 157–58, 171, 188–99; prejudice in, 276; as public face of legalistic Christians, 248; Reed's departure from, 199; "Samaritan Project" of, 198–99; and secularism, 279; and separation of church and state, 185; and social programs, 178, 182, 192–93, 198–99; "stealth tactics" of, 191; and tolerance, 182; and U.S. as Christian nation, 67. *See also* Reed, Ralph; Robertson, Pat
Christian Right. *See* Conservatives; Legalistic Christians; Religious Right; *specific person or organization*
Christian Science, 21, 23, 87, 174, 268
Christianity: as Church of Law, 90; Jesus as center of, 324; legalistic Christians as speakers for, 14; main business of, 113; as revolutionary, 93; as state religion, 57
Christians: connotation of, 13, 14–15, 57; definitions/categorization of, 1–10, 56, 57; founding fathers as, 73–75; Reed's views about, 189; who are, 3–10, 115–18, 184–85, 314–16, 322–28. *See also type of Christian, e.g.* Legalistic Christians
Church: as body of Christ, 63; burning of black, 194; in conflict with mainstream culture, 298–99; emergence of institutionalized, 57–58; as entertainment, 225–30; established U.S., 71; purpose/need of, 96, 219; stigma imposed by, 135–36; strong versus weak, 134–35. *See also* Megachurches; Membership; Separation of church and state; *specific church, denomination, or sect*
Church of Jesus Christ of Latter-day Saints. *See* Mormons
Church of Law, 13, 54, 90, 169, 298, 300–1, 306, 312; need to challenge, 13–15; and Paul, 54–56; and premillennialism, 87; Protestantism's movement toward, 83–90; and salvation, 306. *See also* Fundamentalism; Legalistic Christians
Church of Love, 13, 316–18; and early Christianity, 54–55; and founding fathers, 73; in new millennium, 316–22; *Priest* as affirmation of, 295; Protestantism's movement away from, 83–90; and television, 298. *See also* Love; Nonlegalistic Christians
The Churching of America 1776–1990 (Finke and Stark), 134–39, 161–62, 225
Civil War, 27, 78
Clergy: authority of, 133, 236–38; celibacy of, 295–96; education of, 137; functions of, 118; hierarchy of, 58, 79; as intellectuals, 137, 237; Jefferson on, 72; and legalistic Christians, 214–20, 236–38, 294–95; in movies, 287–88, 294–96; paternalism of, 237; and Promise Keepers, 259, 263–64; speaking against, 233–34. *See also specific denomination or sect*
Clurman, Richard M., 322
Collected Works (Robertson), 171–77
Communism, 96, 152, 177, 181, 223, 305
A Companion to the Scofield Reference Bible (English), 99–103

Confucianism, 112, 183
Congregational Church, 78–79, 110, 137
Congressional Bible, 74–75, 98
Conscience, 7, 79, 80, 283, 317
Constitution, U.S., 66–67, 69–70, 195, 196, 280
"Contract with the American Family," 195, 198, 310
Conversion experience, 2–3, 22, 65, 160, 168–69, 179, 279
Corinthians I and II, 54–55, 88–89, 213, 236, 238
Craig, Samuel, 118–19
Creationism, 159, 262. *See also* Evolution
Criswell, W.A., 159
Criswell College, 158
Crucifixion, 6, 40, 43, 44, 48, 88, 99–100
Cults, 267–69, 275
"Culture wars," 8, 11, 65, 110, 163–65, 183
Current events: Dobson's views about, 253; and prophecy, 147–48, 152–53, 172

Damnation/Hell, 9, 31–32, 65, 211–12, 245, 328. *See also* Eternal life; Other; "Saved"
Darby, John Nelson, 83–86, 103; on history, 98–99; influence of, 86, 87, 91, 148, 150; on Jesus, 326; and kingdom theology, 93; as lawyer, 167; on prophecy, 171; "science" of, 85, 115, 152; as unknown, 103. *See also* Dispensationalism
Darrow, Clarence, 124–27
Darwin, Charles, 27, 84, 85, 86, 87–88, 179–80, 256
Davies, Paul, 321
Death, 58, 99, 304. *See also* Eternal Life
The Death of Satan: How Americans Have Lost the Sense of Evil (Delbanco), 278–79
Declaration of Independence, 67, 69–70
Decter, Midge, 280–81
Deism, 66, 69, 73
Delbanco, Andrew, 278–79
Democratic Party, 157–58, 182, 190, 262
Deuteronomy, 34, 35, 80
Disney Company, 160–61, 195, 294, 296
Dispensationalism, 22, 83–90, 95, 97–104, 132, 269; Fosdick on, 115; and Heaven's Gate, 269; Parker on, 192. *See also* Great Tribulation; Rapture
Dobson, James, 14, 27, 28, 247–58, 259, 277, 296
Doctrine, 5, 33–35, 57–59, 63, 122, 133, 136, 225, 227, 242–44, 282–83, 324–28; Fosdick on, 307–8, 325; and fundamentalism, 242; Jesus' lack of, 41–42, 46–47; and legalistic Christians, 11, 227, 242, 243–44; and liturgy, 227; and love, 51, 58, 113; of mainstream religion, 225; and Promise Keepers, 261; and Protestant Reformation, 62; and spirituality, 318. *See also specific doctrine or denomination*
Dogma, 242, 243–44, 283, 324, 328
"Dumbing down" of American culture, 281–82

Early Christianity, 53–59; and heresy, 313; and Jesus as human and God, 47, 325; movies about, 289, 293; and prophecy, 7; and "saved," 208; spirituality of, 48. *See also specific person*
Ebert, Roger, 295–96
Ecumenism, 71, 174, 261
Eddy, Mary Baker, 21, 87
Education: of clergy, 137; and critical thinking, 241–42; and evolution, 191; and faith, 137; and

Education: of clergy (*cont.*)
  globalism, 184; and legalistic Christians, 211, 272;
  and liberalism, 143; Lindsey on, 145; and New
  Evangelicalism, 142–43; Robertson on, 177,
  178–79, 184; and secularism, 143, 279. *See also*
  Intellectualism
Edwards, Jonathan, 211–12
Elect, 6, 21, 58, 64, 65. *See also* "Saved"
Elections, political, 170, 182, 191, 196, 197
Elisha, 222, 223
Ellen, 160
Elmer Gantry (Lewis), 25–26, 133, 289
The Empty Church (Reeves), 106, 316
"End Times" theology, 22, 99–104, 145, 151–52;
  and legalistic Christians, 267; Lindsey's views
  about, 145, 148; and morality, 223; and pop
  culture, 268; and prophecy, 145; and Robertson,
  168, 177; and Southern Baptist Convention, 81;
  and violence, 240
English, E. Schuyler, 99–104
Entertainment, 225–30, 281, 286, 296, 298–300. *See
  also* Movies; Television
Ephesians, 237, 238, 256
Episcopal Cathedral (Seattle, Washington), 316
Episcopal Church, 3, 78–79, 157; and
  homosexuality, 311–13, 315; and love, 64, 79,
  316; membership in, 137; and modernist-
  fundamentalist controversy, 123, 124; and New
  Evangelicalism, 143. *See also* Anglican Church
Episcopal Theological Seminary, 123
Epistles, 74, 238. *See also specific epistle*
Eternal life: and categorization of Christians, 6; and
  conservatives, 5, 8; English on, 100; and good
  Samaritan parable, 33–34, 35–37, 38, 39; Jesus'
  words about, 41, 94; and legalistic Christians, 209;
  and *Lumen Gentium,* 34–35; and Mormons, 275;
  as quid pro quo, 328; and Resurrection, 48; and
  Sadducees, 50; Tillich on, 323. *See also*
  Damnation; Heaven; Other; "Saved"
Evangelicalism, 3, 4, 7–9, 133, 214; and Bible, 241;
  and culture wars, 164; and good and evil battle,
  219, 240–41; growth of, 143; and Moral Majority,
  163; in 19th-century America, 77–78; and
  politics, 170, 198; pre-Revolutionary Southern,
  81–82; and race issues, 144, 193–94; Reed's views
  about, 190, 193–95. *See also* New Evangelicalism;
  Robertson, Pat; *specific denomination*
Evangelism: and African Americans, 29–31; and
  baby boom generation, 306; as Church of Law,
  306; and conservatives, 5; and Jehovah's
  Witnesses, 22; by Jesus, 46–47; and legalistic
  Christians, 15, 136, 206–7, 230; and love, 315; in
  New Testament, 175; of Paul, 315; and Promise
  Keepers, 259–60; Reed on, 194; tent-meeting,
  133–34, 227
Evil, 10, 65, 254, 278–79, 316. *See also* Good and
  evil battle
Evolution, 24, 27, 82, 84, 85, 86, 87, 105, 121, 159,
  191, 251. *See also* Scopes (John T.) trial

Faith: Anglican views about, 63; confessions of, 57;
  doctrine about, 58; and educational level, 137;
  Fosdick on, 307, 309; healing by, 79, 132;
  justification by, 89; leap of, 47, 49; and legalistic

Christians, 162; and nonlegalistic Christians, 310;
  and orthodoxy, 164; Tillich on, 323; and truth,
  162; and world view, 59
"Faith of our fathers" argument, 119–21
False fronts, 230–31, 232–34, 239–40
Falwell, Jerry, 27, 163, 297, 299
Family issues: and abuse, 238–39, 272; and Christian
  Coalition, 182–83; and Gospels, 182; and
  homosexuality, 160; and Jesus, 182, 183; and
  Jews, 183; and legalistic Christians, 14, 224,
  238–39; and love, 183; and Promise Keepers, 261,
  263; Reed on, 177–78; and Religious Right, 183;
  and Republican Party, 182; Robertson on, 177,
  178, 182–83; and Southern Baptist Convention,
  160; and television, 296. *See also* Dobson, James;
  Focus on the Family; *specific denomination*
Feminism, 190, 248, 252, 253, 271
Finke, Roger, 78, 134–39, 161–62, 225
First Baptist Church (Atlanta, Georgia), 212–13,
  236
First Presbyterian Church (New York City), 110,
  111, 123, 124
Flexner, James Thomas, 70, 72, 73
Focus on the Family, 183, 247, 248, 250, 254, 255,
  258; and Promise Keepers, 259, 261, 262, 263. *See
  also* Dobson, James
Fosdick, Harry Emerson, 92, 98, 110–24, 128, 129,
  136, 189, 197, 306–10, 318–19, 321, 324–25
Founding fathers, 10, 66–75, 161, 174, 185. *See also
  specific person*
Francis of Assisi, 60–62, 146, 174, 283, 313–14
Franklin, Benjamin, 67, 69–73
Fuller, Charles E., 132, 134, 140, 141, 142, 297
Fuller, Daniel, 142
Fuller Theological Seminary, 140–41
Fundamentalism, 4–5, 7–9; Anglicanism compared
  with, 63; assumptions of, 273–74; and Catholics,
  140; decline/death of, 24–26, 129; emergence of
  term, 107; growth of, 143; internal dissension in,
  140–43; Islamic/Moslem, 152–53, 269–70, 271;
  lack of knowledge about, 24; as modern
  phenomenon, 26–27; modernism versus, 107,
  110–28, 197, 286; and Southern Baptist
  Convention, 157–63. *See also* Conservatives;
  Legalistic Christians; *specific person, denomination, or
  church*
The Fundamentals: A Testimony to the Truth (Stewart
  brothers), 104–6, 107, 118, 121, 178

Galatians, 55, 256–57
Garden of Eden, 64, 65, 99, 256. *See also* Adam and
  Eve
Good Samaritan parable, 33–39, 46, 139, 184, 185
Good works, 5, 37–38, 47–48, 102
Gospels: and anger of Jesus, 244–46; and Baptists,
  80; and Congressional Bible, 98; and family issues,
  182; Fosdick and 117; and legalistic Christians,
  220, 221, 244–46; prophecy in, 146; and Social
  Gospel, 193; synoptic, 39–42, 56, 74–75, 88. *See
  also specific gospel*
Government: authority of, 55–56, 205; dispensation
  of human, 99
Grace, 58, 99, 197, 262
Graham, Billy, 43, 140, 162, 299

Grant, Percy Stickney, 124
Gray, James M., 115, 116–18, 119, 120
Great Commandment, 5, 50–51, 103, 160, 213, 259, 317
Great Commission, 5, 160, 212, 259
Great Tribulation, 22, 83–84, 100, 101, 148, 149, 151, 192, 328
Greenberg, Clement, 282
Gross, Michael Joseph, 259, 262
Growing Up Fundamentalist (Ulstein), 213, 230, 239, 242, 243, 272

Halloween publication, 234–36, 241
Hannahan, James, 260, 262
Hardin Simmons College, 158
Heathenism, 61–62, 105
Heaton, Lee W., 123
Heaven, 39–40, 41, 58–59, 81, 102, 328. *See also* Kingdom theology
Heaven's Gate cult, 268–69
Hellfire. *See* Damnation/Hell; Eternal life; Other; "Saved"
Heresy, 57, 80, 123, 311–16, 325–36
Heyrman, Christine Leigh, 81–82
Higher Criticism; 84–85, 86, 87, 92, 104–6, 110, 121, 146
Hill, Stephen, 212
Himmelfarb, Gertrude, 280, 281
Hinckley, Gordon, 275
Hinduism, 174, 190
"Historical Jesus" scholarship, 118–19, 241
History: Bible as, 7, 84–85, 117; Darby's views about, 83, 98–99; as dispensations, 83, 98–99; Dobson on, 249; Robertson's distortion of, 172, 173; teaching of, 19–21, 23–24
Holiness churches, 132–33
Holy Spirit, 79, 132, 133, 156, 289, 316. *See also* Trinity
Homosexuality, 2, 253–55, 269, 271–72, 311–16; and Bible, 282; and Call to Renewal, 311; and Christian Coalition, 195, 196, 254; and civility, 196; and conservatives, 198; Dobson on, 249–58; and Episcopal Church, 311–13, 315; and family issues, 160; and Heaven's Gate, 269; and "Holiness Code," 51; and Islam, 271; and legalistic Christians, 212, 240, 252–53, 254, 255, 271; and liberalism, 282; and media, 271–72, 274–75; and Mormons, 274–75; in movies, 294–96; and Promise Keepers, 260–61, 264; Reed on, 189, 190, 194–95, 254; and Religious Right, 271; Robertson on, 175; as sin, 30–31, 195; and Southern Baptist Convention, 160; suppression of, 253
Hooker, Richard, 63
Hughes, Thomas, 262–63
Hunter, James Davison, 163–65
Husbands, authority of, 237–39, 256, 261–62
Hybels, Bill, 226, 228

In Touch magazine, 105, 231, 241
Incarnation, 40, 99
Inherit the Wind (film and play), 24, 26, 126–27, 277
Interfaith Alliance, 9, 310–11
Islam/Moslems, 152–53, 174, 269–70, 271, 313
Israel, 179, 194, 270

Jackson, Andrew, 203, 223
The Jazz Singer (film), 286
Jefferson, Thomas, 69–75, 77, 96, 98, 131, 198, 318–20. *See also* Founding fathers
Jehovah's Witnesses, 8, 21–22, 87, 174, 244
Jerusalem, 83, 101–3, 148, 246
Jesus, 58, 99, 103–4, 107, 209, 212, 217, 227, 242–43, 308; anger of, 244–46; authority for teachings of, 47; baptism by, 46; Buddha compared with, 291–92; as business manager, 242; as center of Christianity, 324; chief purpose of, 6; as crazy/liar, 105, 106; divinity of, 72, 77, 79, 88, 92; and doctrinal system, 41–42, 46–47; and eternal life, 41, 94; evangelism by, 46–47; father-son relationship, 260; genealogy of, 89; as God, 47, 325–26; God's relationship to, 325–36; and good Samaritan parable, 33–39, 46, 139, 184; historical, 118–19, 241; as human, 47, 325–26; and legalistic Christians, 326–27; and love, 6, 49, 53–54, 79, 184, 213, 294, 311–16, 326–27; ministry of, 6, 39–42, 88, 183, 230; names for, 92; and nonlegalistic Christians, 47, 118–19; as radical teacher, 305; resistance to authority by, 56; similes and parables of, 33–42; spirituality of, 283; in temple, 42, 50, 88, 182; transfiguration of, 99–100. *See also* Crucifixion; Gospels; Incarnation; Resurrection; Trinity; Virgin birth; *specific person, denomination, sect, gospel, or topic*
Jews, 4, 16–18, 23; Christians' killing of, 57; conversion of, 160, 179, 279; and "End Times" theology, 101, 279; and family issues, 183; and good Samaritan parable, 35–37; and Holocaust, 223; and legalistic Christians, 223, 272, 279–83; Lindsey's views about, 147, 148; Reed on about, 194; Robertson on, 179; and Southern Baptist Convention, 82, 159, 160, 273. *See also specific person*
John, Gospel of, 39, 40, 46, 56, 88–89, 103, 116, 183, 240–41. *See also* Gospels
John Paul II, 34–35, 60
Johnson, Luke Timothy, 242–43
Jones, Philip L., 80–81
Joseph, 42, 43, 89
Joshua, 88, 127, 221–23
Judgment, by God, 22, 58, 84, 100–101, 102, 103
Judgmentalism, 215, 244–46
Justification, 58, 89

Kelley, Dean M., 134, 135, 139, 244
Kierkegaard, Søren, 47
King, Martin Luther, 91, 193, 310
Kingdom theology, 81, 93–94, 95, 96, 99, 101, 318. *See also* "End Times" theology; Premillennialism; Second Coming
2 Kings, 222, 240
Klinghoffer, David, 281–83
Kristol, William, 280
Küng, Hans, 57–61, 207, 227, 324

The Last Temptation of Christ (film), 293–94
The Late Great Planet Earth (Lindsey), 41, 144–52, 153
Law, 5, 11, 33, 51, 80, 99, 314. *See also* Church of Law; Legalistic Christians

Lawrence, Jerome, 24, 26
Leap of faith, 47, 49
Lee, Robert E., 24, 26
Leviticus, 34, 35, 51, 80, 165, 175–77, 314
Lewis, Sinclair, 25–26, 133, 226, 289
The Life and Morals of Jesus of Nazareth (Jefferson), 74
Lind, Michael, 179, 190, 274
Lindsell, Harold, 158–59, 222
Lindsey, Hal, 41, 144–51, 171–72, 173, 247, 268, 278, 326
Little Buddha (film), 291–92
Luke, Gospel of, 5, 41, 42, 44, 88–89, 182–83. *See also* Good Samaritan parable; Gospels
Lumen Gentium, 34–35
Luther, Martin, 20, 62, 308
Lutheran Church, 3, 315–16

Macartney, Clarence Edward, 114
McCartney, Bill, 258–65
McPherson, Aimee Semple, 25, 133
Madison, James, 67, 69–71
Malone, Dudley Field, 125–26
Manliness, 81, 262–63, 287
Mark, Gospel of, 43, 50. *See also* Gospels
Marriage: Dobson's views about, 248, 256–57; interracial, 164; and Promise Keepers, 261; same-sex, 69, 160, 255, 274–75
Marsden, George M., 9, 85, 89, 90, 128, 140, 141, 142–43, 144–45, 324
Mary, 42–43, 58, 164, 182, 183, 296. *See also* Virgin birth
Materialism, 9, 33, 299–300, 304, 305–6, 317–18, 319, 328
Matthew, Gospel of, 5, 42, 43, 44, 57, 88–89, 168, 236, 244, 246. *See also* Gospels
Media: and Christian Coalition, 9, 273; and fundamentalism, 273–74; and fundamentalism-modernism controversy, 286; handling of religion by, 272, 285–86; and homosexuality, 271–72, 274–75; and Interfaith Alliance, 310–11; and legalistic Christians, 11, 12–13, 14, 239–40, 260, 267, 271–76; and nonlegalistic Christians, 9, 12, 14; and politics, 273; and Reed, 187, 197, 273; and religion, 295; and Scopes trial, 127; and secularism, 12, 279; and sex, 286; and values, 14. *See also specific media*
Megachurches, 225–30, 261, 281, 282
Melick, Richard R., Jr., 158
Mercer University, 158
Messori, Vittorio, 34–35
Metaphors: doctrine as, 325–26; and God's gender, 263; martial, 119, 136, 177, 196–98, 213–14, 257–58, 263–64; mathematical, 320–31; religious statements as, 324 sports, 197
Methodist Church, 3, 8, 19, 79, 81–82, 110, 132–33, 137, 138, 157
Mellennium, 100, 101, 111, 193. *See also* Premillennialism
Miller, Calvin, 118–19
The Modern Use of the Bible (Fosdick), 119, 306–9
Moody Bible Institute, 90, 115, 143
Moral Majority, 26, 163, 279, 297
Morality, 221–23, 310; and Christian Coalition, 196; and culture wars, 163–6; Dobson on, 252;

Fosdick on, 307; and intellectuals, 271; Parker on, 192; Reed on, views about, 190, 193; relativistic, 164, 165; and Robertson, 179
Mormons, 8, 87, 164, 264, 268, 274–75
Moslems/Islam, 152–53, 174, 269–70, 271, 313
Movies, 15, 21, 253, 286–95
MTV, 252–53
Murray, Henry, 278
Muscular Christianity, 262–63
Mystery, love as, 48, 51
Mysticism, 7, 41, 318, 322

National Bible Institute, 123
Nationalism, 223–24
Nazism, 96, 177, 223
Neoconservative Jews, 272, 279–83
Neuhaus, Richard John, 280
New Evangelicalism, 140–43, 159, 169–70, 207
"New learning," 87–88, 110, 128
The New Millennium (Robertson), 66–67, 171–77, 184–85
New Testament, 57, 80, 89, 132, 175, 220. *See also* Gospels; *specific book*
New World Order, 171–77, 224
The New World Order (Robertson), 171–77
The New York Times, 12–13, 180, 195, 229–30, 237, 239, 270, 273–74, 281–82, 286, 312; and modernist-fundamentalist controversy, 110–11, 114, 122–28. *See also* Bernstein, Richard; Niebuhr, Gustav; Rich, Frank
Niagara Bible Conferences, 88, 89–90
Niebuhr, Gustav, 12–13, 242, 320
Niebuhr, Reinhold, 322–23
1984 (Orwell), 161, 320
Noll, Mark A., 214, 219
Nonlegalistic Christians, 6–15. *See also specific person, denomination, sect, or topic*
Northern Baptist Convention, 107, 138

Ockenga, Harold, 140–42.
O'Connor, John Cardinal, 36, 273
The Old Fashioned Revival Hour (radio program), 132, 297
Old Testament, 10, 74, 80, 82, 89, 95, 146, 147, 175
Ordination, 83, 311–13, 315
Original Church of God, 23
Orthodoxy, 57, 163–65, 243, 282–83, 308, 309
Orwell, George, 161, 320

Parham, Charles F., 132
Park Avenue Baptist Church (New York City), 110, 124
Parker, Theodore, 192–93
Patterson, Paige, 157, 161, 243
Paul, 54–56, 75, 83, 119, 213, 313; and adults as children, 236; and birth of Jesus, 89; and church leadership, 215; epistles of, 11, 205, 314; on equality, 256–57, 261; evangelism of, 315; and justification by faith, 89; as lawyer, 167; legalistic; Christians and 116; and love, 103; and women's submissiveness, 237, 238. *See also specific epistle*
Peale, Norman Vincent, 16, 319
Pelikan, Jaroslav, 75, 98
Pentateuch, 11, 36

Pentecostalism, 8, 79, 132–33, 143. *See also*
  Robertson, Pat; *specific church*
People for the American Way, 185, 311
Peretti, Frank E., 206–7, 214–20, 278
Peter I and II, 116, 238
Pharisees, 50, 103, 244, 246, 314
Philadelphia, Pennsylvania, Presbyteria of, 114
Phillips, Randy, 258–65
Piercing the Darkness (Peretti), 206–7, 214
Planet Earth—2000 A.D. (Lindsey), 152–53
Plymouth Brethren, 83, 84
Predestination, 21, 58, 65
Premillennialism, 83–86, 87, 90, 97, 104–7, 152. *See
  also* Dispensationalism
Presbyterian Church, 3, 21, 78–79, 88, 111, 114,
  122, 124, 143, 157
This Present Darkness (Peretti), 214–20
Pressler, Paul, 157, 161
Priest (film), 160, 294–96
Priesthood of the believer, 5, 156, 159, 283
Princeton Theological Seminary, 89
Progressivism, 112, 163–65
Promise Keepers, 183, 258–65, 279
Prophecy, 7, 21, 79, 92, 132, 144–53, 171–72, 175,
  264
Prophetic obedience (Saint Francis), 62, 146
Protestant Reformation, 20–21, 62
Protestantism, 4, 78–79. *See also* Prostestant
  Reformation; *specific denomination or topic*
Puritanism, 9, 19–20, 64–65, 78, 224

Quakers, 9, 21, 23, 287

Race issues, 143–44, 193–94; and Baptists, 157; and
  culture wars, 164; and equality, 82; and legalistic
  Christians, 136, 164; and Promise Keepers, 260;
  and Republican Party, 262; and Southern Baptist
  Convention, 157, 160, 205. *See also* African
  Americans; Segregation
Rapture, 22, 83–84, 86, 100, 148–50, 151, 206
Rauschenbusch, Walter, 91–97, 110, 181, 189, 193,
  310, 318, 319. *See also* Social Gospel
Redemption, 88, 197
Reed, Ralph, 14, 27–28, 74, 127, 144, 163, 171–74,
  182, 185, 187–99, 216, 253, 254, 273, 310. *See
  also* Christian Coalition
Reeve, J. J., 104–7, 118, 121
Reeves, Thomas C., 106, 316
Religious diversity. *See* Religion, fragmentation of
Religious Rights, 11, 71, 189; and African
  Americans, 143–44; and Congressional Bible, 75;
  and culture wars, 164; and definitions of
  Christians, 4; and family issues, 183;
  formation/rise of, 27, 143, 153; and
  homosexuality, 271; image of, 182, 195; and
  Interfaith Alliance, 311; and Islam, 271;
  mainstream acceptance of, 13; and media, 273;
  and movies, 293; and politics, 192; and racism,
  143–44; as Robertson's audience, 172; and social
  programs, 181; and values, 276. *See also*
  Conservatives; *specific person, denomination, or
  organization*
Republican Party, 26, 157–58, 182, 189–90,
  195–96, 262

Resurrection, 43–45, 48, 50, 74, 88–89, 99–100,
  324
Revelation, 8–9, 58, 59, 164. *See also* Revelation,
  Book of
Revelation, book of, 11, 21, 31, 41, 65, 74, 83, 100,
  102, 269
Revivals, 133–34, 227
Rich, Frank, 239, 273, 310
Ridout, George Whitfield, 119, 120, 121, 122
Righter, Walter, 311–13, 315
Riverside Church (New York City), 110, 128–29
Roberts, Oral, 134, 273
Robertson, Pat, 9, 14, 27, 28, 47, 66–75, 78, 105,
  133, 167–85, 188, 196–98, 225, 239, 253, 267,
  273, 274, 277, 278, 293, 299, 303, 326. *See also*
  Christian Broadcasting Network; Christian
  Coalition; *The 700 Club*
Rockefeller, John D., 128–29
Romans, 42, 54, 55–56, 89
Roosevelt, Franklin Delano, 68, 189
Russian Orthodox Church, 270

Salvation, 5, 22, 45, 115, 117, 210, 212, 268, 282,
  306; by grace, 20–21; and legalistic Christians, 5,
  63, 83, 86, 99, 212, 236, 244, 281; Lindsey on,
  149, 150; and modernists, 88; Rauschenbusch on,
  94; as transaction, 282, 318; by works, 20–21. *See
  also* Atonement
Salvation Army, 23, 79
"Samaritan Project," 198–99
Satan, 80, 117, 123, 197, 307, 316; Delbanco on,
  278–79; Dobson on, 251–52; and "End Times"
  theology, 101, 102; and legalistic Christians, 207,
  208, 213–14, 234, 281, 316; Lindsey on, 173; and
  Puritanism, 65; Reed on, 197; Robertson on,
  168–69, 178; and secularism, 278–79; strangers as,
  213; and tolerance, 173. *See also* Evil; Good and
  evil battle
Schools: Bible reading in, 81; Dobson on, 253;
  integregation/segregation of, 143, 185; prayer in,
  68, 81, 144, 159, 185, 196, 198, 280; Robertson
  on, 185; role of religion in, 15–16, 23. *See also*
  Education
Schuller, Robert, 299, 319
Science, 66, 85, 104–6, 110, 113, 115–16, 146, 152,
  179–80, 321–22. *See also* Evolution
Scofield, C. I., 85, 97–99, 102, 103, 145, 147, 150,
  151, 152, 171, 326. *See also* Scofield Reference
  Bible
Scofield Reference Bible, 22, 85, 97–99, 102, 145,
  241; English's companion to, 99–103
Scopes (John T.) trial, 24, 124–28, 131, 274
Scorsese, Martin, 293
Second Coming, 98, 99, 100, 101–2, 111, 112, 116.
  See also Kingdom theology
The Secret Kingdom (Robertson), 171–77
Secular humanism, 8, 14, 110, 127
Segregation, 136, 143–44, 157, 194. *See also* Race
  issues
Seminaries, 88, 90, 143. *See also specific denomination
  or sect*
Separation of church and state, 14, 23, 70–71, 156,
  158, 159, 185, 195
Seventh-day Adventists, 8, 9, 87, 111, 268

The 700 Club (TV program), 68, 69, 134, 168,
   170–71, 172, 181, 297, 317
Sex/sexuality: Dobson's views about, 252, 253; and
   false fronts, 239; and Heaven's Gate, 269; and
   legalistic Christians, 9, 212, 213, 239, 272; and
   media, 286; and Pentecostalism, 133; and Promise
   Keepers, 263; Robertson's views about, 177–78;
   and Southern Baptist Convention, 213. *See also*
   Homosexuality
"Shall the Fundamentalists Win?" (Fosdick),
   111–18, 122–23
Shurden, Walter, 155, 156
Sibley, James, 223
Sin, 6, 58, 99, 184, 195, 212, 213, 232–34
"Sinners in the Hands of an Angry God" (Edwards),
   211–12
60 Minutes (TV program), 274–75
Slavery, 55, 82, 157, 164, 205, 314, 327, 328
Smith, Bailey, 159, 273
Smith, Huston, 46–48, 49, 51
Smith, Page, 71, 72, 73
Smith, Susan, 239, 240
Social Gospel, 93, 94–96, 97, 104–6, 139, 182, 192,
   193
Society of Friends. *See* Quakers
Soul, 11, 58, 60, 80, 156
The Sound of Music (film), 289–90
Southern Baptist Convention, 8, 79–82, 88, 138,
   155–63, 213, 241, 296; "Baptist Faith and
   Message" of, 157; beliefs/doctrine of, 80, 81, 82,
   140, 157, 212–13, 283; and Bible, 80, 105,
   158–59, 161–63, 241; and Catholics, 162, 296;
   clergy of, 82, 137, 159, 162; and Disney, 195; and
   "End Times" theology, 81; intolerance of, 138;
   and Jews, 82, 159, 160, 273; and Landmarkian
   movement, 138; membership growth in, 136,
   158, 161; and modernism, 110; and priesthood of
   the believer, 283; and race issues, 82, 157, 160,
   205; and Scopes trial, 128; and sex, 213; and sin,
   213; and women, 159, 162
"Speaking in tongues," 7, 79, 132, 133
Spirituality, 5, 7, 33, 48, 282–83, 305, 317–20,
   321–22, 325
Spong, John Shelby, 1–2
Stanley, Charles, 212, 231, 241
Stark, Rodney, 78, 134–39, 161–62, 225
"Statement of Faith" (First Baptist Church of
   Atlanta), 212–13, 236
Stendhal, 172
Stewart, A. J., 125
Stewart, Lyman and Milton, 104, 107
Straton, John Roach, 114
Strauss, David Friedrich, 84–85
Strong, Augustus H., 324
Strozier, Charles, 102, 221, 240
Sunday, Billy, 25, 133, 263
Supreme Court, U.S., 68, 143, 144, 185, 195
Synoptic Gospels, 39–42, 56, 74–75, 88

Television, 15, 228, 230, 253, 296–300, 317
Tent-meeting revivals, 133–34, 227

"Testimony," offering, 3, 300
Theology, 49–50, 54, 59–60, 61, 86–87, 243, 322.
   See also Doctrine; *specific doctrine or theologian*
Tillich, Paul, 32–33, 45–46, 79, 92, 323
Timothy I and II, 116, 119, 219–20, 238, 309
Titus, 55, 205–6, 207, 309
Totalitarianism, 47, 125, 161, 223, 271
Traditional Christians, 4–5, 11, 26, 110, 152
Trinity, 54, 72, 92, 325 .
Triumph the Church and Kingdom of God in
   Christ, 23
Twain, Mark, 21, 327–28

Ulstein, Stefan, 213, 230, 239, 242, 243, 272
Unitarian Church, 9, 66, 72, 77, 79, 131, 320
United Church of Christ, 3, 8
United Methodist Church, 3, 8
United Nations, 179, 181, 218, 271
United States, 66–74, 78; as Garden of Eden, 64, 65
University of Colorado, 258, 259

Values, 7, 14, 65–66, 276. *See also* Morality
Vanderbreggen, Cornelius, 168
Van Dyke, Henry, 123
Vassady, Béla, 141
Vertical world view, 32–39, 46, 60. *See also specific
   topic or denomination*
Victory in Spite of All Terror (videotape), 68
Violence, 83, 240, 252, 253, 269. *See also* Genocide
Virgin birth, 42–43, 88, 89, 99, 111–12, 116, 117,
   123, 324
Voltaire, 172

Wallace, Mike, 275
War: Jesus' views about, 165, 305; metaphors about,
   119, 136, 177, 196–98, 213–14, 263–64. *See also*
   "Culture wars"; Genocide
Washington, George, 67, 68, 69–70, 72, 73, 203,
   223
Wesley, John, 21, 79
Why Conservative Churches Are Changing/Growing
   (Kelley), 244, 134, 135, 139
Willow Creek Community Church (South
   Barrington, Illinois), 226–29
Women, 164, 256; abuse of, 238–39; and culture
   wars, 164; Dobson on, 250–51, 252, 256, 257;
   and early Christianity, 55; equality for, 81, 159,
   162, 256–57, 261, 263; Islamic/Moslem, 270,
   271; and legalistic Christians, 237–38; in movies,
   288–90; and Promise Keepers, 260–61, 263; and
   Southern Baptist Convention, 159, 162;
   submission of, 237–38, 253, 256, 271, 314
Wright, Esmond, 71–73

Young Men's Christian Association (YMCA), 104,
   113
Young Women's Christian Association (YWCA),
   104

Zoroastrianism, 112, 183
Zwingli, Ulrich, 62, 64